THE THRESHOLD OF EXILE

THE THRESHOLD OF EXILE

Examining New Testament Prophecy and Eternal Destiny

-Second Edition-

MARC PALADINO

THE THRESHOLD OF EXILE

Examining New Testament Prophecy and Eternal Destiny

-Second Edition-

Marc Paladino

Published By CrossLight Publications
46075 Sterritt St., Utica, MI 48317
https://crosslights.net
Copyright © 2024 by CrossLight Publications, LLC

ISBN-13: 979-8-218-49980-8
E-Book ISBN-13: 979-8-218-50314-7

ACKNOWLEDGEMENTS

To Judy, my wife and fellow heir in Christ: Her patience and ever-present, loving support were a personal source of strength and motivation. Also, as always, her editing skills were a vital source of clarity in the manuscript's content.

To my long-time friend, pastor, and mentor, Mike (Oz) Osminski: A theologically well-versed Christian leader, he provided challenging, thorough, and often candid reviews of the manuscript, respecting even those perspectives with which he was not personally in full agreement. His encouragement regarding the relevance of this work helped immensely in moving it forward to completion.

To Tony, my brother according to the flesh and also in Christ: He offered thoughtful and insightful observations and timely, often-needed encouragement during our visits together at his home.

To Allyson Elliott: She substantially lightened my workload with her diligent efforts to obtain permissions from cited sources. Ally's service was invaluable and so clearly done *as unto the Lord*.

DEDICATION

To the incredible family with whom God has so richly blessed Judy and me:

The commitment of our sons and daughters to the Lord Jesus is steadfast. Their love and support for their parents is heartwarming. In addition, they have given us six beautiful grandchildren. Thank you, Dave and your wife Jen, Leah and your husband Paul, and Emily and your husband Steve. You all continue to bless us beyond words.

TO OUR GRANDCHILDREN
Noah, Ethan, Aiden, Daniel, Olivia, and James

. . . *I bow my knees before the Father, from whom every family in heaven and on earth derives its name, that He would grant you, according to the riches of His glory, to be strengthened with power through His Spirit in the inner man, so that Christ may dwell in your hearts through faith; and that you, being rooted and grounded in love, may be able to comprehend with all the saints what is the breadth and length and height and depth, and to know the love of Christ which surpasses knowledge, that you may be filled up to all the fullness of God (Ephesians 3:14-19).*

Love, Papa

TABLE OF CONTENTS

PREFACE

OBJECTIVE & PLAN OF THE BOOK

A very little key will open a very heavy door
-Charles Dickens

The prospect of writing this book challenged me for some time, and rightly so. It was undeniable that it would call into question long-standing beliefs concerning Christian eschatology. To be specific, the pages that follow will critically examine our mainstream Christian views about 1) the return of Jesus and 2) fallen humanity's presumed immortality, especially as it pertains to their alleged final destiny in hell. I intend to show how awareness and effective use of the New Testament's historical context can lead to a radically different understanding of these beliefs.

Eschatology is the branch of theology concerned with themes such as the return of Jesus, death, resurrection, judgment, the afterlife, and the final state of the creation. These are often referred to as the *last things* described in the Bible. Research has led me, as it has others, to conclude that some of our traditional understandings in this field of study appear to be established on questionable biblical foundations. Despite this, certain views (with varying perspectives) are widely accepted in both contemporary and historical Christian thought.

Recognizing the dominance of long-standing conservative interpretations, I nonetheless invite the reader to consider how a fundamental omission, if properly accounted for in the interpretive process, could cause many of us to reevaluate our popular eschatological perspectives. That omission is as follows:

> At the time of Jesus, Israel's place in the redemptive story was that of a nation on the very threshold of exile by the Roman Empire. Their historical situation was just as it had been centuries before, on the brink of the Assyrian invasion of 722 BC and, subsequently, the Babylonian invasion of 605–586 BC. This first-century historical context dramatically affects how we are to interpret the New Testament's eschatological language.

The historical setting of the New Testament should come as no surprise to any serious student or teacher of the Bible. The issue is not *whether* the historical context exists. It is the *extent* to which it is brought to bear on biblical prophecy in the teachings of Jesus and the apostles that matters. Our understanding of the New Testament's eschatological language must *first* be seen as inseparably linked to Israel's historical situation at the time of Jesus. Then, *second*, given that historical setting, it is necessary to understand how it affected the message of the Lord Jesus, his apostles, and the New Testament writings. They repeatedly called attention to similar Old Testament prophetic language, circumstances, and warnings and presented them as relevant to their own generation. This is an essential way in which the Old and New Testaments interact. The neglect of these interactions leads to potentially questionable conclusions about last things.

> *This is how assertions about allegedly future crises believed to be coming upon the entire world mistakenly displace prophetic warnings that were intended for first-century Israel.*

To avoid such errors, we must recognize how, in their writings, the New Testament heralds connected their own times with their history and then allow that to guide us in interpreting eschatological matters. Both Jesus and the apostles referred to historical conditions in the Old Testament that were similar to their own and wove them into their various teachings and narratives. These Old Testament references, their linguistic style, and their imagery were adopted to call the attention of the nation of Israel to their history. That history provided a vivid example of the tragic fate that awaited them in their unbelief.

Old Testament Historical Contexts

An enormous amount of Old Testament prophetic literature was written against the backdrop of historical crises facing the nation of Israel. Their international alliances, conflicts, and cultural intermingling with countries such as Egypt, Assyria, Babylon, and Greece played an important role in the messages of the great prophets of old. The Bible informs us that predictions of *the sufferings of Christ and the glories to follow* (1 Pet. 1:11ff) were central to their prophecies, but they also gave relevant, inspired messages for their own generations. We must consider those historical crises if we are to understand much of their written work. The ability to comprehend the descriptive nature of the language of those prophecies is critical because it affects our ability to see how that same language was used to describe the approaching events and their consequences looming in the background of the New Testament. The desolation of the cities of Israel, the destruction of Jerusalem and the temple, and the horrible fate of the Jews were fast approaching in the first century AD. These events, described in the same linguistic style as the prophets, must be considered a crucial element in our efforts to interpret final things.

Author's Approach

This book was not written for academics, although anyone who reads it will hopefully find it to be a worthwhile effort. In presenting the material in a manner suitable for the non-scholar, I will occasionally explain something that a theologically minded individual is most likely aware of but that a casual reader is not. However, this is not to suggest that the book's content has been "dumbed down." The casual reader may simply not be intimately familiar with certain concepts or terminology.

The reader must also consider that eschatological texts cannot be interpreted using a *free-wheeling, anything-goes* approach. Like all other texts, they are subject to fundamental interpretive principles. No part of the Bible should be read in a contextual vacuum, that is, without taking into account literary style, historical setting, and the writer's audience. The interpretation of symbolism must be consistent with the Bible's own internal application of symbols and metaphors in other texts.

As we explore and consider these elements, we are drawn into the world of the text. New perceptions often come to light that we never knew were there. Ideas we could never have believed may become surprisingly reasonable. These considerations do not take away from learning personal lessons for ourselves, for we know that "all Scripture is profitable," as we are informed by 2 Timothy 3:16. However, these background elements allow us to see the true story and learn more accurate lessons. Casual readers often seek first to obtain an immediate personal application from the text. This commonly stems from our impatient lust for instantaneous knowledge, a word to enlighten us, or the need for a *proof text* to support our theological precommitments. Thus, we neglect a more patient and contemplative approach to God's Word and unwittingly make the same mistake Eve did, reaching for the fruit that will give immediate gratification. Expectations and beliefs may be supported merely by a handful of weak and misunderstood texts lifted entirely out of their literary and historical context. It is comparable to reading American history in the 21st century and believing that *the British are coming.* The words, although true, are entirely out of their historical setting and applied to the contemporary reader. As odd as it may seem, this is how many of us interpret Bible prophecy when we interpret words detached from their history and audience. Furthermore, this is often compounded by the unhealthy assumption that *we, an alleged end-time audience,* are the only generation prophetically in view of Jesus and the Bible's writers.

In *hermeneutics,* which is the science or art of interpretation, the consignment of a writer's historical situation and audience to a place of irrelevance is referred to as *reader response.* This interpretive method assumes that the *reader* is the ultimate arbiter of the meaning of a text, regardless of the *author's* literary and historical context, intended meaning, and audience. In Bible interpretation, it unfortunately neglects a key principle that we will frequently see emphasized:

> *Scripture must interpret Scripture, and it is the final and absolute authority on how its words should be understood. God is his own best interpreter, and he has provided other texts to shed light on the context and meaning of any Scripture we seek to understand.*

The neglect of a proper approach to Scripture can occur knowingly or unknowingly, but in either case, it is an entirely self-centered way to interpret God's Word. None of us is exempt from these tendencies. An appropriate method of Bible interpretation requires that the author's context, intent, and the perspective provided by other passages be given priority in establishing the meaning of a text. From there, we can seek to determine what is relevant and what is not for our own personal or historical situation.

The Plan of the Book

Having elected to include most Bible texts in full, I encourage the reader to examine them carefully, as we often gloss over texts with which we are familiar. In doing so, we shut ourselves out from new possibilities that text may hold (this is called *familiarity blindness*). The reader may also observe that some cited texts are not in paragraph (narrative) form but in a line-by-line style. This is because the text cited is actually in the poetic genre, which is quite prominent in the Bible's prophetic and wisdom literature. I have sought to heighten the reader's awareness of how biblical imagery is often presented in poetic form. It is not always captured in some English versions of the Bible.

Part I (Chapters 1–4) offers important elements of the story behind the book and a general overview of its subject matter. Chapter 3 looks at Israel's history as a vital key to understanding New Testament eschatology.

Part II (Chapters 5–12) examines the Olivet Discourse (Matthew 23–25 and parallels). I hope to establish that the return of Jesus, as presented through the literary context, historical data, and use of prophetic language, must be understood as Christ's presence in judgment upon first-century Israel. This occurred during the Jewish-Roman War of 66–70 AD. I suggest that no part of Jesus' discourse includes anything relating to the end of the world. However, this should not be construed as a comprehensive theological statement concerning my views about *the end*. It is strictly an interpretation of the content of *that* discourse.

Part III (Chapters 13–16) addresses the issues of immortality and the destiny of the lost, offering contextual challenges for commonly cited texts that are *alleged* to prove eternal conscious torment. We will examine why no human being is inherently immortal and that *living forever* can only be bestowed by God through the agency of the Holy Spirit. This is referred to as *conditional immortality*, and it opposes the common belief in the intrinsic immortality of the soul.

These chapters *do not endorse universal salvation* but affirm final and permanent death (extinction) as the biblical alternative to eternal conscious torment (abbr. ECT). The reader will learn how the warnings and outcomes of the approaching Jewish-Roman War of 66–70 AD affect the interpretation of expressions such as *unquenchable fire*, which are wrongly associated with fallen humanity's believed immortal state of torment in hell.

Part IV (Chapters 17–22) examines material in the Book of Revelation that relates to all the preceding observations. However, our journey through the book will not be a full-scale commentary. We'll look chapter by chapter at relevant texts that point to Revelation's demonstrably historical context and its declarations emphasizing the approaching fulfillment in John's day. It will not endorse popular futuristic interpretations.

Appeal to the Reader

To the best of my ability, the perspectives being proposed in this book are not based on a collection of statements taken out of their literary and historical contexts merely to disprove other interpretations. They are rooted in allowing the context of the Scriptures and their inter-biblical (intertextual) references to provide their own meanings. We'll examine how a sound hermeneutical strategy can lead to significantly different interpretations of the Bible's eschatological outlook.

The astute reader may quickly realize that this work is far from exhaustive. *It does not attempt to answer every question or present a comprehensive eschatological system.* Its focus is to present the mid-first century AD as the threshold of Israel's approaching exile. That exile occurred in 70 AD, in the generation that witnessed the Lord's death and resurrection. The language that Jesus and the apostles employed to warn of this catastrophic reality affects not only how we understand the events surrounding his return but also immortality and the fate of the lost. The reader will see how Israel's first-century historical context affects our understanding of these subjects and how they rest upon the descriptive language of *judgment* and *exile* employed in both the Old and New Testaments. It is a hermeneutical key that I believe unlocks these aspects of eschatology and hopefully creates a foundation for further discussion among capable Christian pastors, teachers, and other leaders.

Finally, *The Threshold of Exile* examines, among other things, biblical statements regarding God's historical judgments that fell upon the nation of Israel because of their unfaithfulness to his covenant. It is important to understand that those episodes in the Bible's redemptive history have nothing to do with God's attitude toward Jews or any ethnic group today. The calamities, which are a focal point of this book, are just that–a New Testament perspective on the people and circumstances of that time–concerning Jews, Romans, and other ethnicities. They are seen through the lens of the first-century emergence of the Christian Church as a result of the life and ministry of our Lord Jesus Christ. Therefore, nothing in this book should be construed as promoting an antisemitic opinion of the Jewish people, either past or present.

PART I

INTRODUCTION
BACK STORY & OVERVIEW

CHAPTER I

THIS CAN'T BE TRUE!

"It is true! It's really true!" *She cried suddenly and in utter amazement. "Week after week, I've been sitting here listening to you and saying to myself, 'This can't be true! This can't possibly be true!'"*

The class came to a screeching halt. I stood momentarily speechless, having been interrupted mid-sentence by the outburst from the back of the room. It was the voice of a tearful young woman who, along with her husband, were the group's leaders. I remained silent while patiently allowing her to calm down and compose herself. Then, to my surprise, one by one, her students began nodding their heads and voicing their agreement with her. They were sharing the sense of utter liberation they experienced as their eyes began to open to what I had been speaking about during our recent weeks together.

Like most teachers of the Bible, I live for such moments, watching as long-standing fears melt away from the hearts of God's precious saints. For most of their young lives, they lived under the popular belief that they were on the brink of the end times. They all believed the antichrist would soon appear and ignite a global crisis that would be followed by the end of the world. In view of these approaching events, they were held captive by fear and confusion about the course their lives should take. Some even expressed their anxiety over the prospect that if they veered off the path ever so slightly, they might miss the *rapture* and be left here on earth to face the unthinkable, *the dreaded great tribulation.* Would that failure—*could that failure*—mean for them an eternity in hell?

Their previous Bible instruction, although well-intentioned, had left them unable to envision a future for themselves, even in the Lord. Their valid but tightly held questions had never been satisfactorily addressed:

> *If the apocalypse was near, should they skip college and stop thinking about a career, marriage, or even ministry?*

> *Should they just go to a mountaintop and wait?*

Frankly, if the end was indeed near, wouldn't these be legitimate questions? The apostle Paul thought so. Two thousand years ago, he addressed those very questions in his epistles. In his First Letter to the Corinthians, Paul warned the church of the crisis that was awaiting the Mediterranean world in their own day. His instructions to the church don't sound at all like he was attempting to write *A New Testament Guide to Marital Bliss*:

> I think then that this is good *given the present distress,* that it is good for a man to remain as he is. Are you bound to a wife? Do not seek to be released. Are you released from a wife? Do not seek a wife. But if

you marry, you have not sinned; and if a virgin marries, she has not sinned. Yet such will have trouble in this life, and I am trying to spare you. But this I say, brethren, *the time has been shortened, so that from now on* those who have wives should be as though they had none; and those who weep, as though they did not weep; and those who rejoice, as though they did not rejoice; and those who buy, as though they did not possess; and those who use the world, as though they did not make full use of it; *for the form of this world is passing away* (1 Cor. 7:26-31).

If his radical remarks are going to make any sense to us, it requires that we consider the setting in which the apostle offers such unusual directives. The letter was most likely written in *koine (common)* Greek, which is the principal language of our New Testament manuscripts. In verse 26, he uses the phrase, *this present distress.* Apparently, it was common among the Jews in their spoken dialect, which was Aramaic. The phrase referred to times of great affliction or adversity. The text expresses how these churches were facing calamities that would affect every aspect of their lives (see J. Gill[1] and M.R. Vincent[2] comments on 1 Cor. 7:26–31). Other commentators also note this. That present time of distress was the basis for Paul's concern that families would have trouble in the flesh. He was not warning about marital squabbles that couples might face in normal day-to-day circumstances.

The New Testament indicates that an end to the world as they knew it was fast approaching at that very time. With this in view, the churches had to be prepared for troubled times, even rethinking major life choices. The apostle was not misguided in warning them about *the shortening of the time* and the *soon passing of the form of the world.* If he was wrong, we would certainly regard him as a false prophet. Paul wasn't the only one. Warnings abound in the New Testament of something terrible yet glorious—both an end and a new beginning that were on the horizon. The inspired writers echoed that this was the very coming of the Lord, and it was approaching in their day:

Do this, knowing the time, that it is already the hour for you to awaken from sleep; for *now salvation is nearer to us than when we believed. The night is almost gone, and the day is near* (Paul: Rom. 13:11-12).

You too be patient; strengthen your hearts, for *the coming of the Lord is near . . . behold, the Judge is standing right at the door.* (James: Jas. 5:8-9; cf. Matt. 24:33; Mark 13:29).

The end of all things is near, therefore, be of sound judgment and sober spirit for the purpose of prayer (Peter: 1 Pet. 4:7).

Children, *it is the last hour*, and just as you heard that antichrist is coming, even now *many antichrists have appeared; from this we know that it is the last hour* (John: 1 John 2:18).

These inspired apostles were acutely aware that they were living in the waning hours of an age. The era of the Old Covenant was about to give way to a new era of grace. However, it would not arrive without great tribulation that would come about as an empire-wide sociopolitical upheaval and a great overthrow of spiritual dominions. If this expected end was a mere mistake in judgment, it would have been the greatest blunder and mass delusion the world has ever known. Entire churches throughout the Mediterranean world would have been entirely fooled by a misguided band of so-called gospel messengers.

Some would argue that these and similar New Testament statements are relevant for the entire church age and that Jesus' return is *always* imminent. It would seem to me that such an interpretation defies the very meaning of language. Statements in the Holy Spirit-inspired apostolic writings regarding the nearness of Christ's coming give a clear impression that they were intended to prepare their audiences for things pertaining to their own time, as we observed: *the coming of the Lord is near; the Judge is at the door; the end of all things is near; and, it is the last hour.*

Similarly, we might justify the idea that the Lord's "coming" is always near at any time in history, and for a variety of reasons. This, in the general sense, may be true concerning his divine interventions in history. However, the statements of the apostles regarding "the end of all things" and the affirmation that it was (in their time) "the last hour" support the fact that something extraordinary was about to take place. There can be little doubt concerning the overwhelming significance of the historical events about to occur in 66-70 AD. Given their implications, I would submit that:

- Jesus' promised return was about to take place

- the first century world was coming to an end

- a new world was dawning

- these were Christ's legitimate messengers, whose expectations were not misguided, but divinely inspired

Was Paul, the inspired apostle who wrote half of the books in the New Testament, which make up a quarter of its content, completely wrong about the times? Consider how he wrote to his young disciple, Timothy, to keep the faith, not until *death* but until he would experience the appearing of Jesus:

> . . . keep the commandment without stain or reproach *until the appearing of our Lord Jesus Christ* (1 Tim. 6:14).

Did the writer of Hebrews misinform Jewish believers in the first century AD when exhorting them that they would see *the day* (the day of the Lord and the dawning of the new age) drawing near?

> Not forsaking our own assembling together, as is the habit of some, but encouraging one another; and all the more as you see the day drawing near (Heb. 10:25).

Were the apostle John's following instructions to his first-century readers ill-advised when he affirmed that it was, at that time, the last hour of the age and that antichrist was already present?

Children, it is the last hour; and just as you heard that antichrist is coming, even now many antichrists have appeared; from this we know that it is the last hour (1 John 2:18).

The Setting

Returning to the aforementioned group of young Bible students, I was teaching the Book of Revelation. A dear pastor and long-time friend invited me to teach this great book to a collection of students who were teens and young adults. My friend was intrigued by my views, and after further discussion, we agreed to go forward with the class.

The apostle John's recorded visions are closely connected to various gospel accounts of Jesus' prophecies concerning what the Lord called the end of the age (not the end of the world). The most notable is the Olivet Discourse, found in Matthew 24, Mark 13, and Luke 21. He also made very important remarks in Luke 17, but in a different setting. As for the Olivet Discourse, there on the Mount of Olives, shortly before his arrest and crucifixion, Jesus informed his disciples of things about to come. This discourse, sometimes referred to as the *Little Apocalypse*, has long been a popular starting point among Bible instructors when teaching about the end times, so I began our class there.

Week after week, we gathered to unpack relevant details of the historical setting of the New Testament and how the destruction of Jerusalem occurred in 70 AD, forty years after Jesus gave this great discourse. Great persecutions, convulsions in nature, false prophets, famines, and military conflicts among the nations characterized the years leading up to Jerusalem's fall. These were the very conditions that Jesus told his disciples would occur before the passing of their generation. Even non-Christian historians of that era unwittingly preserved many of these things in their works.

I described how much of our flawed futuristic interpretation of his message comes from a failure to consider the style of language Jesus used when he spoke of the *stars falling from heaven* and the *darkening of the sun and the moon*. These cosmic events were described in the same highly poetic and symbolic style as their ancient Jewish prophets. The group learned that great prophetic descriptions of world-collapsing disasters never actually described the end of the material universe. These were prophetic descriptions of governments and economies falling from their places as *God came down* to bring judgment upon nations through war or internal civil unrest. The images often described a powerful nation being toppled and a new nation taking its place in the ancient world. The existing order, especially the political arrangements relating to Jerusalem and the Jews, was shown as ending and being replaced, and it was to be known that God was arriving on the scene to take care of business, *not at the end, but within* a strategic period of human and redemptive history.

For example, Isaiah 13 describes the fall of the Babylonian Empire to the Medo-Persian Empire in 539 BC. The prophet's language may appear to some as describing a great, world-ending judgment. However, the 17th and following verses provide the historical meaning (even verse one informs us how this oracle concerns Babylon):

> The oracle concerning Babylon . . .
> Behold, the Day of the Lord is coming,
> Cruel, with fury and burning anger,
> To make the land a desolation;
> And He will exterminate its sinners from it.
> For the stars of heaven and their constellations
> Will not flash forth their light;
> The sun will be dark when it rises
> And the moon will not shed its light.
> Thus I will punish the world for its evil
> And the wicked for their iniquity.
>
> (17 ff) I am going to stir up the Medes against them . . .
> And Babylon, the beauty of kingdoms . . .
> Will be as when God overthrew Sodom and Gomorrah.
> (Isa. 13:1, 9-11, 17, 19).

The dramatic description of the world ending and the stars falling reflects the highly charged, poetic style of speech of the ancient prophets. The "world" of Babylonian supremacy and the exile of the Jews from their land would see its end. King Cyrus of Persia was going to conquer Babylon and release God's people to return to the promised land to rebuild their city and temple:

> "*It is I* who says of Cyrus,
> *He is* My shepherd!
> And he will perform all My desire.'
> And he declares of Jerusalem,
> 'She will be built,'
> And of the temple,
> 'Your foundation will be laid.'"
> (Isa. 44:28; cf. Jer. 20:10; 2 Chr. 36:22-23; Ezra 1:1-4)

We carefully connected these ideas to both the Olivet Discourse and the Book of Revelation. We saw in more literal Bible translations how, in the Olivet Discourse and his parables, Jesus did not speak about *our* future at the supposed end of the world but the near-term future of his disciples and the end of *their* age. The age about to end was that of the Law of Moses. Key aspects of that age-ending Roman invasion of Jerusalem (66–70 AD) are also symbolically depicted in Revelation's visions. The outcome was the destruction of ancient Jerusalem in Revelation 17–19, where the city is described as the great harlot, *Babylon*. This became clear to the students when they saw that the true earthly theaters of Revelation's conflicts were not global.

The term *earth* is frequently and legitimately translated from the original Greek word *ge*, as land. This suggested that many of the judgments fell upon *the land of Israel*, not our entire planet. It is equally significant that the Greek term *oikoumene* frequently refers to the empire in the New Testament. Often assumed to mean the entire world, it more precisely refers to *the Mediterranean world of the Roman Empire of the first century AD*.

All of this is vividly summarized in Revelation 3:

"Because you have kept the word of My perseverance, I also will keep you from the hour of testing, that *hour* which is about to come upon the whole world [*empire*], to test those who dwell on the earth [*land*]. 'I am coming quickly; hold fast what you have, so that no one will take your crown'" (Rev. 3:10-11).

Note how this letter, written to Philadelphia, *a first-century congregation* in Asia Minor:

- warned that a time of great trial was *about to* commence

- included that it would affect the *entire Roman Empire*

- warned of a trial of those dwelling *on the land* (of Israel)

- promised that it was *Christ's coming*—and very soon

- told the church (first-century Philadelphia) *to hold fast*

Consider the all-inclusiveness of this text. It specifies the recipients, the time, the events about to begin, who would be affected, and the promise of Christ's coming amid the crisis.

Remarkably, this first-century church is told to hold fast because he was coming. How absurd that exhortation would be if Jesus' return was yet 2000 years or more removed from their time. It would have no relevant meaning for them.

The whole prophecy of Revelation was time-stamped using the terms *about to, near, at hand, soon,* and *quickly,* indicating that the events were about to occur very soon. Note also the command of the angel in the last chapter of Revelation that John should not seal his vision because the time was *near:*

And he said to me, "*Do not seal up the words* of the prophecy of this book, for the time is near" (Rev. 22:10)

In contrast, centuries earlier, the prophet Daniel was told to seal his visions because the time of their fulfillment was well beyond his own time:

> "But you, Daniel, roll up and seal the words of the scroll until the time of the end . . ." So I asked, "My lord, what will the outcome of all this be?" He replied, "Go your way, Daniel, because the words are rolled up and sealed until the time of the end" (Dan. 12:4, 8-9 NIV).

Daniel's visions were centuries away from their fulfillment, at the time of the end, not the end of time. This denotes the end of the Old Covenant world of Jewish national privilege. In the New Testament, it is referred to as the last days, or the end of the age. In contrast to Daniel's order, the Lord commanded John not to seal—but to send his book to the churches. Its message was urgent because the time was near.

The Question of When

As a matter of major importance, I presented to the students how the so-called late date theory (95–96 AD) of the writing of Revelation that is commonly taught is not necessarily fact. It is also not without problems and inconsistencies. We examined external evidence, which consists of historical, non-biblical sources, along with the internal evidence within Revelation itself. Both sources provided sound evidence of an earlier date of writing, sometime before the critical date of 70 AD. Kenneth Gentry's excellent book, *Before Jerusalem Fell*, is a must-read for anyone wishing to research the subject (see Gentry 2016).[3] This means that it is highly plausible that Revelation has *the theologically significant Roman invasion of 66–70 AD* (the Jewish–Roman War) prophetically in view. I also showed how the earlier dating of Revelation not only has convincing support from many current scholars but was also a widely held scholarly opinion until the middle of the19th century.

The more popular late-date theory proposes that John saw his Revelation in 95–96 AD, during Emperor Domitian's *supposed* reign of terror against Christians. One of the many fragments of evidence that I have found to be of particular interest seems to clearly conflict with Domitian's alleged banishment and execution of many Christians in the empire. It is an interesting piece of history composed by Pliny the Younger, a well-known Roman political figure (c. 62–115 AD). It raises serious doubts about the validity of those claims.

It is a letter to Emperor Trajan, dated c. 112 AD. Trajan had succeeded Nerva, who ruled briefly after Domitian's death. Trajan then ruled Rome from 98 to 117 AD. The following excerpt of this letter from Pliny is enlightening, given that he served as a senator and a governor and had *held a position in Domitian's court*:

> It is my practice, my lord, to refer to you all matters concerning which I am in doubt. For who can better give guidance to my hesitation or inform my ignorance? *I have never participated in trials of Christians. I therefore do not know what offenses it is the practice to punish or investigate, and to what extent.*[4]

Pliny, who had served in Domitian's court during the emperor's *alleged* bloodbath of persecution, writes less than a decade later that he had never witnessed a Christian trial. This strongly suggests that there was no widespread persecution of Christians during Domitian's reign. Pliny would have undoubtedly been an eyewitness to such atrocities. Domitian is known to have banished some *political* enemies and was not a particularly benevolent ruler, but neither was he the ferocious murderer of multitudes of God's people, as often suggested. In *The Emperor Domitian*, Brian Jones also points out that there is no conclusive evidence that Domitian was a persecutor of Christians.[5]

The season of great persecution in the first century was not during the reign of Domitian, but three decades earlier in the latter years of Nero's rule (64–68 AD). This would have been just a few years before the fall of Jerusalem in 70 AD. If John's visions took place during Nero's persecution, then his references such *as near, soon, and quickly* were especially important. Of equal significance were the references to his own exile and his audience's experience of tribulation expressed in Revelation 1:9:

> I, John, your brother and fellow partaker in the tribulation and kingdom and perseverance which are in Jesus, was on the island called Patmos because of the word of God and the testimony of Jesus (Rev. 1:9).

John's visions would have had the great trials, persecution, and war of that period in view. There is more for us to consider concerning the time of Nero. We will do so in our study in Part IV. As we journeyed through these realities, my students were awakened to entirely new and liberating perspectives on redemptive history and the new possibilities for their own lives.

> *As the reader will see, the great tribulation they feared was not waiting up ahead for us but is, in fact, behind us. When the apostles declared the nearness of the end, they were not mistaken, and perhaps it is we–not they–who are getting it wrong.*

How incredible it was to realize that when the New Testament writers used *nearness* terminology, they meant exactly that. It was near in their time. The physical universe was not collapsing. The first saints understood his *coming in the clouds* from the prophetic warnings given to their ancestors. It was a way of describing the presence of the Lord in judgment throughout their Old Testament writings:

> The Lord is riding on a swift cloud and is about to come to Egypt;
> The idols of Egypt will tremble at His presence
> (Isa. 19:1).

> *He bowed the heavens also, and came down*
> With thick darkness under His feet.
> He rode upon a cherub and flew;

And He sped upon the wings of the wind.
He made darkness His hiding place,
His canopy around Him,
Darkness of waters, thick clouds of the skies
(Psa. 18:9-11).

Similarly, in the Book of Revelation, John echoed the linguistic style of the prophets. His anticipation that Jesus was about to fulfill his promise to come in their generation in clouds of glory is evident:

Behold, *he is coming with the clouds*, and every eye will see Him, even those who pierced Him; and all the tribes of the earth [tribes of the *land*] will mourn over Him. So it is to be. Amen (Rev. 1:7).

Recognizing the historical setting into which New Testament prophecies were spoken serves as a critical key to clarifying their meaning. There is no need to twist, torture, or dance around the words of Jesus and the apostles in order to construct meanings for things assumed to be far off into the future. There is no reason to redefine, explain away, or create theological schemes in an attempt to justify futuristic ideas about the prophecies. How encouraging it was for these students to realize that when God said *soon*, that is precisely what he meant. When he said, *at hand* or *near*, grammatical gymnastics or theological explanations such as how *a thousand years equal one day to the Lord* (2 Peter 3:8) are not needed to interpret his words. Peter was merely affirming the patience of our God, who is not time-bound. However, when God time-stamps a message in the Scriptures, there is typically reasonable evidence of its audience and timing, as explained by James Stuart Russell:

. . . the promise which falls due in a day . . . and the promise which falls due in a thousand years will be performed with equal punctuality. . . . the apostle does not say that when the Lord promises a thing for to-day He may not fulfil His promise for a thousand years: . . . He does not say that because God is infinite and everlasting, . . . He reckons with a different arithmetic from ours . . .[6]

All Scripture provides lessons, examples, and hope for us. Similar historical conditions may often occur throughout time, and we are given these texts to learn from the experiences of those who have gone before. However, there are specific events prophesied in the Bible that are now history. It would have been confusing and paralyzing if these first churches had to decode ambiguities suggesting that:

- near might not mean near, but possibly far off
- at hand doesn't really mean within our immediate grasp
- soon, near, and at hand really mean partial fulfillment
- about to occur means 2000 years or more removed

Although stated in a different context, the apostle Paul had something to say in that regard:

If the bugle produces an indistinct sound, who will prepare himself for battle? (1 Cor. 14:8).

The apostles fully expected the churches to understand the times in which they were living. We see this in Paul's Letter to the Romans:

And this, knowing the time, that for us, the hour already *is* to be aroused out of sleep, for now nearer *is* our salvation than when we did believe (Rom. 13:11 YLT)

Henry Cowles (1871) writes concerning the importance of the Book of Revelation to those who first received it:

The writer meant to be understood; . . . If the seven churches of Asia to whom John wrote . . . could not understand the main and vital things it contains, then it was to them a dead letter . . . a "revelation" that revealed nothing. The notion that the great body of this prophetic book was unintelligible to its first readers and must be interpreted today to mean things which they could never have imagined must be, for every reason rejected.[7]

Philip Mauro offers this insight concerning the eschatological outlook of the Olivet Discourse:

> Our vision of things to come is greatly obscured and confused by the transference to the future of predicted events which, in fact, have already happened, and whereof complete records have been preserved . . . The Lord's own predictions and warnings concerning that event, [the fall of Jerusalem] which was then close at hand, were most explicit . . . "all these things shall come upon this generation."[8]

The prophetic warnings of the New Testament writers were addressed to and for the generation to which they were given. God did not overlook these precious, often persecuted saints in favor of far-off generations who would reap the benefits of their sufferings.

Ominous Clouds on the Horizon

Both history and the New Testament tell us that the first-century churches were living in a time when Rome, the instrument of divine judgment, was about to destroy everything the Jews had held sacred for over 1400 years since their deliverance from Egypt under Moses. However, the Roman conflicts and persecutions had little to do with religion. Rome was extremely tolerant of various religious beliefs within the empire, under the condition that Caesar was acknowledged as supreme. Loyalty to Rome was paramount. But tensions escalated between local Roman leaders and the Jews because of increasingly oppressive policies and unethical governance. Jewish resistance swelled as Rome's taxation policies became a detriment to the well-being of especially lower-class Jews. Eisenberg has observed how this created increasing economic hardship for the populace. Small farmers had to secure loans from the Sadducees, who were among Jerusalem's wealthiest elite. Eventually, many of these farmers lost their property.[9] Tensions heightened further as the gospel spread throughout the empire. Christians declared, *Jesus is Lord!* – which was a direct offense to the Roman decree that *Caesar is Lord!* The ever-increasing Jewish resistance, the Christian proclamation of Christ's lordship, and the Roman demand for absolute allegiance to the empire were on a three-way collision course. The clash was not only inevitable but also rapidly approaching. However, this was no mere conflict of worldviews or rebellion against socio-political oppression. The consequences of this upheaval were of immense redemptive significance, which we will examine in our study of the Olivet Discourse and the Book of Revelation.

The initial persecution of the church that began in Judea was followed by a period of growth and expansion during the reign of Claudius (41–54 AD). However, during Nero's reign of terror after his burning of Rome in 64 AD, hated Christians became the scapegoats and were subject to the most hideous tortures imaginable, which were on full display for Nero's garden party guests. Even *they* felt pity for Nero's victims. Tacitus, a recognized ancient Roman historian, writes:

> Those who confessed were the first to be caught, then those who were accused by informers. Those sentenced to death were also mocked: they were torn to pieces by dogs, after being disguised as wild beasts, or they were crucified and set on fire at the end of the day, as torches to illumine the night . . . Nero kept his gardens for this spectacle, hiding among the crowd, dressed as a charioteer . . . Thus, a feeling of pity for the victims was born, for it was obvious that they had not been sacrificed for the public good but due to an individual's cruelty.[10]

Considering the inconceivable circumstances and threats under which they lived, what benefit would these precious saints gain from prophecies concerning far-future nuclear bombs, armed helicopters, and swarms of strange, flying, or horse-mounted creatures supposedly found in the Book of Revelation? What hope would they derive from a prophetic letter promising that, while in their own time they were suffering such horrors, God was more concerned about revealing events to occur centuries beyond their generation that could only be understood by a future, technologically advanced civilization? What comfort would there be in the notion that after two millennia had passed, their future Christian brothers and sisters, many of us who are comfortably middle-class, would fly away in a so-called *rapture* before any troubling world events would occur? To the contrary, they needed meaningful words of hope and comfort in *their current circumstances*, not messages about mysterious visions that were well beyond their ability to grasp. John wrote to the seven historical churches in Asia for *their* benefit. It was to be read, understood, and obeyed.

> Blessed is he who reads and those who hear the words of the prophecy, and heed the things which are written in it; for the time is near. John to the seven churches that are in Asia: Grace to you and peace, from Him who is and who was and who is to come
> (Rev. 1:3-4).

No faithful Jewish believer would understand such language to merely apply to the physical function of the ears and eyes. To the Jew, *the call to read and to hear meant to understand and obey.* John's introduction to the churches echoes the *sh'ma* in Deuteronomy 6:4-5:

> "Hear, O Israel! The Lord is our God, the Lord is one! You shall love the Lord your God with all your heart and with all your soul and with all your might."

This was Yahweh's declaration that Israel was to harken to the words of God and obey with all of their human faculties—inner, physical, and even financial strength. It was echoed by Jesus in Mark 12:29-30 as the greatest commandment and remains foundational to our Christian faith. What blessing, therefore, could be derived from those words if John's primary audience was yet centuries beyond the time of his contemporaries? These churches—irrespective of the current trials, persecutions, want, and suffering they were experiencing—were to hold fast to their one and only loyalty: Jesus.

But What About Us?

As we will see, at the very least, the majority of the specific events of Revelation are not future but past. Those first kingdom saints were being assured that the God of heaven and earth was very much in control of history. They would soon enjoy his ultimate victory. However, upon hearing these things, a common response by those who are unfamiliar with them is, "What's left for us to look forward to?" Presently, I will refrain from commenting on what I perceive to be a somewhat self-centered inquiry. Suffice it to say, this is an odd response from my Christian brothers and sisters, who celebrate their victory in Christ every Sunday in worship and fellowship.

Despite the historical aspects of the prophecy, I'm not suggesting that Revelation is strictly a symbolic chronicle of times past. It remains an enduring model for all Christians everywhere, as the lessons from its visions resonate throughout the church's history. The call to read, hear, and obey its contents remains central to our faith in the same way as every other biblical book. Revelation reminds us that in the face of the most difficult assaults by forces seen and unseen against the people of God, Christ rules all things from his central sanctuary. This means that we, too, can be assured of ultimate victory as we remain faithful to his call to overcome. Our final chapters on Revelation will also offer answers to the question, "What's left for us?"

Back Once More to the Classroom

It was there, years ago, in that classroom, that I became utterly convinced that ideas have consequences. I realized this is not just optional theology. Our understanding of these things affects our perception of life, the world, and the God of the Bible. As we ponder the effects of popular, dramatized end-time propaganda, we must ask ourselves, "Does this theological construct allow our young saints to navigate through life in a healthy manner?" Or, "Does it unnecessarily instill fear and paralysis in them about their future?"

It was there that I began to realize that telling our children to prepare as though Jesus was coming today but plan as though it is a thousand years away is a feeble cliché that is wholly inadequate to prepare them for a life of Christian devotion and service.

Ill-informed prophetic viewpoints would have had lasting effects on the lives of these and many other young students. Some would undoubtedly abandon the faith because their indoctrination did not square with the facts on the ground. Repeated predictions about Russia, China, Israel, the European Union, implanted microchips, and their alleged relationship to Bible prophecy would fail to provide them with a solid foundation for true biblical discipleship. They would grow weary as each new tyrant arriving at the center of the world's stage was suspected of being the antichrist, assaulting the sensibilities of even newborn and inexperienced believers.

This is not to suggest that all who believe or teach a future tribulation and the appearance of an antichrist figure condone such drama. However, books, movies, and other propaganda continue to be marketed by influential Christians. How long would these tender young saints want to continue in such a charade, follow such a faith, and believe in such a God?

In contrast, the approach that we are examining is rooted in history and is sensible. It rejects the speculative and the sensational. Most importantly, it recognizes the central and universal impact of the cross and the resurrection of Jesus Christ, from whom a new, inclusive, and enduring biblical economy emerged. That economy consists of a new humanity born out of his redemptive work. It abolishes the privileged status of any ethnicity or culture and opens the door of faith to all, whether Jew or Gentile.

Since that first presentation, the response from subsequent audiences has been that, for many, the material is liberating. They have enthusiastically admitted that it totally altered their understanding of God and the Bible.

In the Olivet Discourse, Jesus declared that although he did not know the day or the hour, he knew the generation and the nature of his return. His disciples would witness his parousia (par-oo-**see**-ah, meaning presence or arrival) in their generation. He would come in clouds of judgment upon Jerusalem.

"Truly I say to you, this generation will not pass away until all these things take place" (Matt. 24:34; Mark 13:30; Luke 21:32).

Jesus (who is God!) came in a cloud-presence, that is, in judgment. This was entirely consistent with his "appearance" in prior divine judgment events in biblical history. Such events are described by the prophets as Yahweh (the LORD) came in judgment upon a nation or nations. Why should the New Testament suddenly change the nature of such an event?

As this reality gains more acceptance in the churches, and I believe it will, hopefully we will see more young Bible students being liberated from fear of the future and hear them (along with their adult contemporaries) exclaiming the words I will never forget:

"It's true! It's really true!"

CHAPTER 2

CAUTION: SHARP TURN AHEAD

Over the course of time, new questions arose regarding common beliefs about the end. Recognizing Israel's historical setting—their standing at the threshold of national destruction and exile—brought the realization that other eschatological texts might need to be re-evaluated against that background. It became apparent that the language of the New Testament concerning the destiny of the lost, such as *unquenchable fire* and the poorly translated word *hell*, also had connections to the first-century fall of Jerusalem. This prompted a whole new set of inquiries.

As my research continued, it became evident that the descriptions of the fiery end of the wicked were not at all what I had been taught to believe. It became more and more clear that such texts have nothing to do with the afterlife state of unredeemed people in never-ending conscious torment in hell. Many of the biblical contexts in which these descriptions of torment are found contain remarkably distinct allusions to the unfortunate fate of the Jews in 70 AD. The very language of the texts can be seen in earlier warnings by the prophets concerning great calamity, especially but not exclusively relating to 586 BC and the prior destruction of Jerusalem by the Babylonians. In addition, it became apparent that references to eternal fire consistently seemed to characterize God's fire as *consuming* rather than perpetually tormenting the wicked. (For an in-depth study of God's consuming fire, I recommend Edward Fudge's definitive work, *The Fire That Consumes*.)[11]

Pertinent Background

Like the conditions in the sixth century BC, the Jews had arrived once again at a threshold at the time of Jesus. The Lord himself, followed by the apostles, warned the nation in the same manner that the prophets of old warned their contemporaries. The warnings echoed throughout the ancient prophetic writings of the eighth through sixth centuries before Christ. They warned of approaching catastrophic events that were about to come upon Israel because of their disobedience. Jesus' audience, like their ancestors, would be subjected to a judgment resulting in a fiery end *called gehenna, which is not hell*:

> "So you testify against yourselves, that you are sons of those who murdered the prophets. Fill up, then, the measure *of the guilt* of your fathers. You serpents, you brood of vipers, how will you escape the sentence of hell [*Greek: gehenna*]? Therefore, behold, I am sending you prophets and wise men and scribes; some of them you will kill and

crucify, and some of them you will scourge in your synagogues, and persecute from city to city, so that upon you may fall the guilt of all the righteous blood shed on earth [land], from the blood of righteous Abel to the blood of Zechariah, the son of Berechiah, whom you murdered between the temple and the altar. Truly I say to you, all these things will come upon this generation" (Matt. 23:31-36).

This text (one of many) informs us that the Jewish nation would not escape the same judgments that their ancestors experienced. As we will examine in Part III, the warnings Jesus gave in his own generation concerning gehenna, fire, judgment, shame, and disgrace contain the same language and imagery used by his ancient prophets *concerning national destruction and exile.* He was not speaking of anyone's perpetual torment in what is commonly understood as hell.

The Critical Dependency

My growing insights into the alleged fate of the lost brought with them the realization that the doctrine of *eternal conscious torment* depends entirely on a popular yet dubious premise. Theologically, the traditional doctrine of torment requires that we embrace the widely held belief that every human possesses an immortal soul. This is called *inherent (or innate) immortality,* and it is necessarily foundational for eternal torment because if everyone is immortal, the lost must spend eternity somewhere. Many will find it surprising to discover that neither inherent immortality nor eternal torment represent the teaching of Scripture. For example, Jesus said:

[God is] "able to destroy both the *body and the soul* in hell [gehenna]" (Matt. 10:28).

We will examine this in more detail, but the obvious questions are: If the human soul is inherently immortal, why would Jesus say it can be destroyed? And just what is gehenna? Gehenna's meaning will be forthcoming, but as for the destruction that is mentioned in our text of

Matthew 10:28, the Greek word is *apollumi, to destroy.* Some proponents of eternal conscious torment point out that the term's legitimate semantic range allows for meanings such as *ruin, loss,* or some other term less final than complete annihilation. This interpretation might appear convincing until we examine other biblical references *in their contexts.* We will later examine those contexts that call into question this alleged state of perpetual ruin.

This commonly held view of punishment in hell is that, at judgment, God unites the so-called immortal soul of the unredeemed with their resurrected body. This occurs for the singular purpose of torturing (*continuously ruining or destroying*) them for eternity. The alleged assignment of the unredeemed to a continuous state of ruin means:

> . . . *the existence of the individual will never be completely terminated. Their eternal life is one of unimaginable torture, pain, and agony.*

This view also rests heavily on the entirely out-of-context use of Isaiah 66:24 and Mark 9:43-48, which we will examine in Part III. The uniting of the immortal soul with the resurrected body for torment is essentially the traditional version of eternal conscious torment and is a common understanding held by many (if not the majority) of Christian organizations.

Origins of the Immortality of the Soul

It is widely recognized that the doctrine of the immortality of the soul finds its earliest expression in the beliefs of ancient pagan cultures. The belief was promoted in the works of prominent Greek philosophers, first by Socrates (470–399 BC), then Plato (428–348 BC). This and other principles arising from Greek philosophy eventually affected the translation and interpretation of the term *soul* in the

Septuagint (LXX), which is the Greek version of the Hebrew Bible. The LXX was translated for the benefit of Greek-speaking Jews during the second and third centuries, BC. We will consider this further, but despite the translation's many benefits, there were unfortunate consequences. It also affected other key Hebrew terms, *resulting in the transportation of Hellenistic ideas into the Hebrew Bible.* The Greek translation influenced both Jewish and Christian readings of Scripture by inadvertently creating a syncretistic relationship (a blending of pagan and biblical concepts) between the Word of God and ideas that arose out of Greek philosophy, myth, and culture. In other words, certain key Greek expressions used in translation did not have the same meaning as their corresponding Hebrew terms. Thus, the Greek meanings contributed to both Jewish Second Temple beliefs and the church's doctrine. In later centuries, the influence of Greek would inevitably affect our English translations.

The doctrine of the soul's immortality was a regrettable development as it was integrated into Christian theology by early church fathers, most of whom, prior to their conversion to Christianity, were deeply rooted in Greek philosophy. Like most of us, they carried pre-Christian, cultural, and philosophical norms into their faith lives. Being human ourselves, we ought not to judge these great saints too harshly. However, the unfortunate result of their pre-Christian "baggage" was that Plato's conceptual influence, which had already affected the thinking in Hellenized Second Temple Judaism, would also find its way into the theology of the early church. This has been observed by notable scholars:

James Orr (*International Standard Bible Encyclopedia*):

We are influenced always more or less by the Greek, Platonic idea that the body dies, yet the soul is immortal. Such an idea is utterly contrary to the Israelite consciousness and is nowhere found in the Old Testament.[12]

Koffman Kohler (*The Jewish Encyclopedia*):

The belief in the immortality of the soul came to the Jews from contact with Greek thought and chiefly through the philosophy of Plato . . . who was led to it through Orphic and Eleusinian mysteries [ancient Greek cults] in which Babylonian and Egyptian views were strangely blended.[13]

F.F. Bruce (Foreword to *Death and the Soul After Life*):

In biblical usage immortality belongs inherently to God alone; otherwise, it belongs only to those to whom God gives it. Again, where human beings are concerned, immortality in the Bible is predicated of the body, not of the soul. In our western culture, thought and language about immortality have been largely determined by Plato's doctrine of the immortality of the soul. But any attempt to combine Plato's doctrine with the teaching of the Bible can lead only to confusion. For Plato did not mean by immortality what the biblical writers mean by it, and what Plato meant by the soul is not what the biblical writers mean by the soul. For the Christian, the hope of immortality is bound up with the resurrection of Christ.[14]

Historically, some who support the doctrine of torment suggest that inherent immortality, although not specifically stated, is self-evident and everywhere assumed in the biblical texts (see Berkhof 1938).[15] However, the question needs to be raised as to what extent is Greek philosophy the lens through which such "biblical" self-evidence is perceived? The Bible appears to speak in clear, didactic (instructive, non-symbolic) language that *the wages of sin is death* (Rom. 6:23). Fallen humanity's destiny is to return to dust (Gen. 3:19). This is seen consistently throughout the Word of God. Living eternally entirely depends on the indwelling of the Holy Spirit, as the apostle Paul affirms in Romans 8:11:

But if the Spirit of Him who raised Jesus from the dead dwells in you, He who raised Christ Jesus from the dead will also give life to your mortal bodies through His Spirit who dwells in you.

Paul exhorts the Roman believers that not only will their bodies be raised from the dead, but the Holy Spirit is also causing new life in Christ to work in this present life. However, this indestructible, immortal life is at work only in those who are in Christ:

> However, you are not in the flesh but in the Spirit, if indeed the Spirit of God dwells in you. But if anyone does not have the Spirit of Christ, he does not belong to Him . . . *for if you are living according to the flesh, you must die*; but if by the Spirit you are putting to death the deeds of the body, you will live (Rom. 8:9-13).

A permanent state of agony in hell requires immortality for both the unredeemed and Christians. According to Romans 8:19, a Christian's immortality is solely attributable to the indwelling Holy Spirit. The lost do not possess the Holy Spirit; therefore, only death awaits them. If not, by what means are they permanently kept alive? If the dead continue to live, then not only do Jesus and those belonging to him possess the power of an indestructible life, *but the lost also possess it*:

> [Jesus] has become [our High Priest] not on the basis of a law of physical requirement, but according to *the power of an indestructible life* (Heb. 7:16).

The proposition that we are inherently immortal gets harder to defend when considering biblical texts such as the preceding ones. The doctrine of the immortality of the soul does not align with the issues of life and death as they are presented in God's Word.

Election and Free Will

This concern is intensified when considering the *doctrine of election*, specifically the view called *double predestination*. It is the belief that, before the foundation of the world, God predetermined who would be saved and who would be damned in hell forever. Without question, Scripture clearly supports aspects of divine predestination, and I concur with the proposition that the cross was not God's "emergency response" to man's fall. It was the predetermined plan and purpose of God to reveal Christ to the world (Eph. 1:3-10). However, the idea that God created and destined some for heavenly bliss, but created the largest part of humanity merely to inflict torture on them for all eternity is a horribly chilling image of the God of the Bible. This is intensified when we consider that these outcomes would have been his decision *long before he created anything*, and with full knowledge that Adam and Eve would choose wrongly and bring corruption, sin, and death into the world.

Other confessions seek to soften the implications of election by assigning human choice to one aspect of the eternal destinies but not the other. They offer the somewhat puzzling doctrinal proposition that God only predestines the *saved*. However, the lost are damned by their own choice. Of course, we are encouraged not to question this because it cannot be understood. Therefore, it is conveniently stamped as a "mystery" and neatly tucked away. Still others leave these outcomes entirely to human choice (foreknown by God), which I also believe to be an unconvincing position. In any case, the outcomes are the same. According to these theological disciplines, the saved enter everlasting bliss, but the lost suffer never-ending torture in the fires of hell.

The horror of such a predetermined or at least foreknown outcomes (by the *omniscient* God) is further exaggerated because those outside of the faith appear to be the largest segment of humanity. Jesus makes the following charge to us in his closing remarks in the Sermon on the Mount:

> "Enter through the narrow gate; for the gate is wide and the way is broad that leads to destruction, and there are many who enter through it. For the gate is small and the way is narrow that leads to life, and *there are few who find it*" (Matt. 7:13-14).

Context . . . Please!!!

Part of the problem is that certain texts pertaining to predestination for judgment and wrath can be mistakenly thought to indicate eternal torment. This will be given more attention in Part III. However, let us, for example, weigh Paul's statements in Romans regarding this very issue. This is cited by some as referring to the issues of heaven and hell, but that is not the case. The apostle merely affirms that God may impose mercy or judgment based on his own sovereign discretion:

> So then He has mercy on whom He desires, and He hardens whom He desires (Rom. 9:18).

The context in which Paul makes this arresting statement does not suggest that anyone was created for eternal conscious torment. Note how the apostle quotes from the prophet Isaiah (Isa. 1:9) to convey that his point concerns Israel:

> And just as Isaiah foretold, unless the Lord of Sabaoth had left to us a posterity, we would have become like Sodom, and would have resembled Gomorrah (Rom. 9:29).

The apostle's central argument is that unless God preserved an elect remnant from among them, there would have been a total national annihilation of Israel that was like the all-consuming fires of Sodom and Gomorrah. The quoted text speaks of the near-complete destruction of a people who had abandoned their God and polluted their inheritance. It neither explicitly nor implicitly says anything about post-mortem torment in hell.

The election, God's foreknowledge, and his omniscience are all fearful and wonderful aspects of his nature and purpose. However, if we are to truly understand them, they must be wrenched from their association with the doctrine of hell. The prospect of multitudes standing before God's judgment seat and hearing the words "*Sorry, but before the foundation of the world I decided not to pick you, so off you go to unending, conscious torment*" results in an unacceptable and gross distortion of God's character and is, I believe, inconsistent with biblical truth.

> *Regardless of the theological perspective—election, choice, or a proposed middle ground—the ultimate outcomes of God's judgment have always been life or death, not life or torture.*

Subjectivity or Truth?

The most biblically sound explanation of the final judgment of the lost is extinction (often called *annihilation*). This refers to their final, permanent, and irreversible termination of existence. As we have seen, *conditionalism* is defined as the biblical proposition that only those in Christ receive the gift of living forever. Permanent (eternal) life can only be obtained as a gift from God through faith in Christ. Although there are differences in details among godly teachers, all conditionalists agree on this central fact.

It is common to assume that arguments against eternal conscious torment rest predominantly in the subjective realm, which is the realm of feelings. In plain language, eternal torment gives us the *creeps*, so it must be rejected. Admittedly, there are some who fall into that category. Given that, the reader should understand that most credible and theologically oriented concerns about the validity of eternal conscious torment are not driven by an emotional distaste for it.

As many Christians are discovering, the need for rethinking the destiny of the lost is driven by theological and objective reasons, meaning that eternal conscious torment does not have adequate support in the Scriptures. Despite its long history of acceptance in the church, the foundations of the doctrine are suspect. A careful examination of the texts used to support it reveals that they are all laden with often-ignored interpretive problems and assumptions. The texts are often read in a vacuum, neglecting references to pertinent biblical imagery, prophecy, and history. Proof texts are presented, assuming to endorse eternal torment by imposing ideas onto texts that say no such thing, neglecting the context in which they are presented or the type of literature in which they are expressed.

With due respect for Bible translations, I might also suggest (with deep regret) that there may be an occasional lapse in objectivity resulting in the translation of certain original texts being driven by theology rather than theology being driven by translation.

Hell is an unfortunate example. *It is not a biblical term*, which is not in and of itself a theological problem. The word *trinity* is not a biblical term, yet I am a trinitarian believer. The difference is that the word trinity is how we describe the Godhead outside of the Bible. Contrarily, hell is a *translation* of the Greek term gehenna in the Bible and is based on an *interpretation*. Gehenna is one among other Hebrew and Greek terms wrongly associated with hell. However, since it is alleged that Jesus frequently spoke of hell, we will focus initially on his words.

The word gehenna, as it appears in our Greek manuscripts, is derived from the Hebrew *ge-(ben) Hinnom, or Valley of (the sons of) Hinnom*. It is the proper name of a locality just outside Jerusalem. Why shouldn't it be left untranslated and uninterpreted, just like other Hebrew localities in the New Testament, such as Bethel, Nazareth, or Bethlehem? Some seek to legitimize the translation of gehenna as hell because it had a similar meaning to Jews who were in Jesus' immediate audiences (although they did not use the term hell). There is, of course, indisputable evidence available to us in non-canonical Second Temple Jewish literature concerning their belief in afterlife torment in gehenna, however:

Scripture must always be given priority as the authoritative interpreter of other Scripture, regardless of the prevailing beliefs of the time. This is especially true when a term such as gehenna has highly relevant Old Testament meaning. The contexts in which gehenna is used in the New Testament have unmistakable references to prophetic biblical literature. As we shall see, that literature had nothing to do with afterlife torment.

Even if eternal conscious torment in gehenna were true, it is my humble opinion that translators would translate or transliterate the original languages without imposing either Christian or any other theological or philosophical assumptions onto the text. Unarguably, the original texts must be made intelligible in the target language. In deference to those who translate, this is no simple task. However, their meaning should never be engraved in stone by a team of translators, as skilled as they may be in their profession. If the result is that the church must wrestle with the meaning of a text, so be it. This is clearly evidenced by the considerable variation in how other texts are translated in our Bibles and the variants that exist in ancient manuscripts. Unfortunately, however, such uncertainty is often not acceptable. We treasure certainty but abhor ambiguity, especially when it involves our most valued systematic Christian theologies.

Unquenchable Fire

A second example (we will examine these further) is the phrase *unquenchable fire.* It is commonly assumed to mean the fire of hell that burns unsaved people continuously and forever, or something similar. However, our recognized principle of interpretation, that *Scripture interprets Scripture,* disallows us from engaging in such an arbitrary interpretation. We are compelled to examine other texts to determine the biblical meaning of the expression.

For example, in Jeremiah 17:27, a warning of the advancing judgment upon Jerusalem that will be accomplished in 586 BC by the Babylonians reads:

> "But if you do not listen to Me to keep the sabbath day holy by not carrying a load and coming in through the gates of Jerusalem on the sabbath day, then I will kindle a fire in its gates and it will devour the palaces of Jerusalem and not be quenched."

Notice that the locality where the fire is kindled is Jerusalem. The unquenchable fire is not described as one that burns people forever. Babylon was employed to ignite it in 586 BC. However, neither they nor the Jews could quench it. It burned until its purpose was accomplished, which was to devour Jerusalem and her dead. That fire, though described as unquenchable, has long since burned out, having completed God's judgment. The same unquenchable fire was ignited again to consume the city and its inhabitants in the first century, as declared by John the Baptist:

> "His winnowing fork is in His hand, and He will thoroughly clear His threshing floor; and He will gather His wheat into the barn, but He will burn up the chaff with unquenchable fire" (Matt. 3:12).

In addition to his allusion to Jeremiah's unquenchable fire, John the Baptist's use of *threshing floor* imagery is especially significant. This is because the temple in Jerusalem was built on the threshing floor of Ornan, the Jebusite. King David purchased it from him, and it became the site of Solomon's Temple (2 Chr. 3:1). After his judgment encounter with the angel of the LORD, David declared the site to be "the house of the LORD God" (1 Chr. 22:1). John alludes to the fact that the impending burning of the temple, Jerusalem, and her inhabitants would result in a great separation (the wheat from the chaff) in God's household. When we properly apply the context, worldview, and biblical sources of the prophetic outlook of Jesus and the apostles, we avoid interpreting in a historical and contextual void. Their lives and work took place in a concrete historical situation, and their eschatological outlook arose out of their nation's historical and prophetic traditions.

Understanding this and applying it to the interpretive process will help us grasp how the issues of the return of Jesus, eternal destiny, and conditional immortality coalesce. These are not independent propositions derived from isolated proof texts. They are interdependent realities that emerge from the impact of the ministry of Jesus in the context of Israel's historical circumstances.

CHAPTER 3

ISRAEL'S HISTORY
AN INTERPRETIVE KEY

The Scriptures teach us that in the eighth through seventh centuries before Christ, the divided nation of Israel–both the tribes of Israel in the north and Judah in the south–repeatedly rejected the warnings of their prophets concerning their sins. Consequently, in 722 BC, Assyria invaded the land of Israel, conquering and scattering the ten northern tribes and destroying their capital, Samaria. A century later, King Nebuchadnezzar of Babylon defeated Assyria in c. 612 BC and emerged as the sovereign king of the world of the ancient Near East. Despite God's instructions to the contrary, Judah, who had barely survived the Assyrian invasion, continually resisted Babylon's sovereignty. This could not be tolerated and ultimately brought about their destruction as well.

We are informed that God ordained these tragic outcomes because of Israel's idolatry, neglect of God's Law, and continuing rejection of the warnings of their prophets. During the two decades following their first invasion in 606/5 BC (dates are approximate), Babylonian attacks resulted in the deportation of Judeans from their land and the destruction of Jerusalem and the temple in 586 BC. These histories are found in Second Kings 23–25 and Second Chronicles 36. Judah would remain exiled from land until 536 BC, when they were allowed to return under Cyrus, King of Persia (Ezra 1:1-3). He conquered Babylon in 538/9 BC, then permitted the Jews to return to their land and rebuild their city and their temple. This was completed two decades later.

These events and the advance warnings of the prophets as expressed in their writings are not merely interesting Bible stories. They are defining episodes in Israel's history and the basis for the New Testament's descriptions of last things.

Old Testament history and prophecy formed a reservoir. That reservoir served as the source from which Jesus, the apostles, and the New Testament writers obtained warnings and promises. Their use of the Old Testament far exceeds our familiar understanding of how Jesus' life and ministry fulfilled various messianic prophecies, as important as that is. These first New Testament heralds of the gospel extracted the very language of the Old Testament prophetic judgments and presented them anew to their own Jewish audiences. The texts drawn from those ancient prophets served as a warning of what was about to come upon them in their own generation.

Can Any Good Thing Come Out of Habakkuk?

For example, let us look at the prophecy of Habakkuk. In Habakkuk, Chapter 1, the prophet of the late seventh century BC contemplates the rise and aggressive expansion of the Chaldean Empire (Babylon).

His ministry takes place near the time of Nebuchadnezzar's assault on Jerusalem. He was given the message that God had raised up this godless nation to execute his judgments upon his own disobedient people. We have observed that the offensive began in c. 606/5 BC and ended twenty years later with the destruction of Jerusalem and the temple. Accordingly, the prophet Habakkuk warns the people of God in advance:

> "Look among the nations! Observe!
> Be astonished! Wonder!
> Because I am doing something in your days –
> You would not believe if you were told.
> For behold, I am raising up the Chaldeans,
> That fierce and impetuous people
> Who march throughout the earth."
> You, O LORD, have appointed them to judge;
> And You, O Rock, have established them to correct.
> (Hab. 1:5-12)

Centuries later, in the New Testament, we encounter a warning of the impending devastation by the Romans that was to occur in 70 AD. At the time of the events recorded in Acts 13, this (notably, as in Habakkuk) was also two decades away. During his first missionary journey, the apostle Paul arrives in Pisidian Antioch and visits the local synagogue of the Jews (c. 48 AD). Being invited to speak, he offers a brief recounting of Israel's history, including the events surrounding the life and ministry of Jesus. After introducing his Jewish audience to the power of the gospel, he warns that their unbelief would result in an approaching calamity like that of the Babylonian invasion, employing the exact language of Habakkuk:

> Take heed, so that the thing spoken of in the Prophets may not come upon you: "BEHOLD, YOU SCOFFERS, AND MARVEL, AND PERISH; FOR I AM ACCOMPLISHING A WORK IN YOUR DAYS, A WORK WHICH YOU WILL NEVER BELIEVE, THOUGH SOMEONE SHOULD DESCRIBE IT TO YOU" (Acts 13:14-41).

This was not to be interpreted as a "this fulfills that" prophecy. Paul cited Habakkuk as a warning to the Jews of his day to give attention to their history. What was about to be accomplished in their days was precisely what happened in 586 BC. It was destined to happen again.

Implications for Interpretation

It is essential that we recognize this as central to the apostolic understanding of their times. As I became aware of this, it became necessary, where appropriate, to employ that aspect of their historical context as a critical interpretive tool. It became evident that we often neglect to apply the language of the prophets properly where it is used in the New Testament regarding Jerusalem's judgment. Therefore, this results in regrettable misinterpretations of key teachings of Christ and his apostles regarding last things. Once we begin to integrate the crucial element of this broader historical context as an interpretive grid, it is not an overstatement to suggest that it can rewire much of our interaction with God's Word. Furthermore, it is well known among expositors that the likelihood of greater accuracy is achieved when we examine the broader context of a particular text or narrative.

Historical and Theological Consequences

Without question, the most noteworthy events of the New Testament's focus were the cross, the resurrection, and the ascension of Christ, resulting in the glorious arrival of the Holy Spirit. Through these events, the Lord Jesus accomplished redemption and assumed authority over all things in heaven and earth. The Spirit guided the New Testament writers to unpack the implications of those things in their writings.

However, once that series of events took place, there were historical and theological consequences of Christ's work that came into play in the New Testament narratives. They were the outcomes that Jesus himself emphasized throughout his ministry and are very apparent in the letters and preaching of the apostles who followed. These outcomes were central, not peripheral, and pertained to God's historical people, the Jews. What would become of the status of their land, city, temple, priesthood, and even the Law? How would the life and work of the Son of God affect those ancient pillars of the historical community of faith?

This was no small matter. Since the days of Moses, those prominent symbols collectively stood for fourteen centuries as the centerpiece of civilization, the testimony of Israel's God to the world. Would they maintain their standing and be integrated as essential elements of Christian worship? Would they simply remain landmarks of great historical events and people? The New Testament informs us that they would not. A major historical consequence of the cross of Jesus would be the utter desolation of those things. According to Jesus' own words, it was going to occur in that generation, within forty years after his life and ministry were completed. The temple system was now an outright impediment to the growth and expansion of a new era of biblical faith based on the centrality of Jesus Christ. The true purpose of those great, ancient apparatuses of historic Jewish faith became apparent. They had functioned as the husk, a protective casing for the wheat, until the fullness of time, when God would send his Son. Now the wheat of the gospel had matured, and the time of harvest had arrived. The chaff in Matthew 3:12, John the Baptist's message, was all that pertained to the old Jewish system. It had served its purpose and was no longer necessary. It was time to be separated and burned. To put it another way, God was not about to patch an old garment or put new wine into old wineskins (Matt. 9:16-17).

As affirmed in the Preface, nothing in this book or in my heart should be interpreted as a condemnation of the Jewish people. We must tread lightly here, considering Paul's selfless yearnings for their salvation and his warnings in Romans 9:15 and 11:18 about Christian arrogance. That being said, the fact remains that their wholesale rejection of both Christ and the apostles who were sent to them meant that their season of national privilege, along with its accoutrements, was coming to a destined end in that generation.

The inevitable fate of the previous economy of God was that it was fulfilled, giving way to the anticipated and universally inclusive New Covenant that was planned before the foundation of the world.

> . . . just as He chose us in Him before the foundation of the world. . . according to His kind intention which He purposed in Him with a view to an administration suitable to the fullness of the times, that is, the summing up of all things in Christ, things in the heavens and things on the earth. In Him (Eph. 1:3-10).

The Hope of Israel–the Promised One–had arrived, and it was incumbent upon them to bow to his lordship. God's ancient people were now being held accountable for their unbelief, yet, at the same time, they were being offered hope through the gospel. However, his arrival also meant that everything standing as representative of the Old Covenant was about to come to a devastating, age-ending conclusion:

- *The Kingdom:* "the kingdom of God will be taken away from you and given to a people, producing the fruit" (Matt. 21:43).

- *Their City:* "the king became enraged and sent his armies [the multinational Roman forces] and destroyed their city" (Matt. 22:7).

- *Their Civic Order:* "your house [their economy and national privilege] is being left to you desolate" (Matt. 23:38).

- *Their Temple:* "not one stone [of the temple] here will be left upon another" (Matt. 24:2).

These and other references (in their contexts) inform us concerning what was destined to take place in first-century Israel. In fact, they provide the entire historical context in which the New Testament narratives, letters, and prophecies take place. Something was coming that had happened previously to the Jewish nation, and it was imminent for the generation of those who lived at the time of Jesus. A new expression of the divine community of faith, made up of Jews and Gentiles alike, was emerging out of the resurrection of Jesus and the descent of the Holy Spirit. The people of God were being reconstituted. His long-awaited Spirit was the agent of the new and inclusive social order and mode of worship:

> ". . . the time is coming when neither in this mountain [Samaria] nor in Jerusalem will you worship . . . God is [S]spirit, and those who worship him must worship in spirit and truth" (Jesus: John 4:21-24).

It would be irresponsible to suggest that our great interpreters have been entirely unaware of what was on the horizon in the apostolic era. The tragic events of the revolt against Rome in 66–70 AD are well known in recorded history. However, I am perplexed by the lack of integration of these anticipated events into the interpretation of key eschatological texts by many who are intimately acquainted with them. Even some interpreters who have sought to integrate the events often devalue their meaning by suggesting that they are only types, shadows, or partial fulfillments of future events.

References to signs, his *coming in the clouds of glory*, and the *fiery end of the wicked* in hell (gehenna) are all too often lifted from their historical, cultural, and biblical context and employed to suggest meanings never intended by the New Testament writers. Jesus and his inspired heralds saw looming events of enormous theological significance that were historically relevant to their own immediate audiences. The calamities they foresaw, which were specific to their own historical Mediterranean context, have been sensationalized by some and erroneously projected into *our* future. Moreover, they are often misconstrued as catastrophic, world-ending developments alleged to conclude with an unimaginable, eternal, and conscious torment for those outside the faith. Texts isolated from their literary and historical context result in mistaken assumptions. Thus, the Bible is interpreted to infer all kinds of questionable things, both about the biblical story and about its central figure, the biblical God. The results are both dubious doctrine and a distorted perception of God himself.

The Theological Significance of 70 AD

Much of the New Testament content relating to eschatology was drawn directly from statements made by the Old Testament prophets. These were warnings originally issued in anticipation of the demolition and burning of Jerusalem by the armies of Nebuchadnezzar, King of Babylon, in the sixth century BC. The relevant texts are quoted and alluded to in the New Testament with the intent of calling the attention of the Jewish nation to their history. They were meant to serve as warnings of the similarity of those historical situations to their own generation. This means that at the time of Jesus, the nation of Israel stood at the threshold of exile from its land, capital city, and temple, much in the same way it had centuries before.

These New Testament references and allusions to the fall of Jerusalem in 586 BC are among the most powerful keys that unlock a true understanding of biblical eschatology, both in terms of the "return" of Jesus and the "fiery" end awaiting those outside of the Christian faith.

The powerful Roman Empire was about to burn and destroy the Jewish temple and city. An *imminent* end that paralleled the events of 586 BC was in view and was certain to take place within a few decades.

Jesus announced it, and his apostles understood and echoed it. Although it permeates the entire New Testament, it appears to be all too often marginalized in the interpretive process. However, it is central to gaining a whole new perspective on the often-misinterpreted expectations of the authors of the New Testament Scriptures. It means that:

> *The great tribulation and the anticipated return of Jesus were coming in their near-term future, not ours. Furthermore, the so-called fiery end of the wicked had more to do with Jerusalem's burning and the complete and final annihilation of the wicked than a so-called eternal torture chamber called hell.*

I must emphasize again that one major conclusion resulting from both my experience and my research is that *eschatology matters*. To consign it to "peripheral" status in theology does injustice to God's Word and his church. What we believe and teach has consequences in the lives of God's people, our children, and our witness to the world, and it reflects our understanding of the truth and character of God. At the same time, the opposite of indifference to eschatological matters (the "it doesn't matter" approach) are those who are entrenched in hardened theological positions, unwilling to consider other possibilities. It may be too expensive due to vested interests such as professional and denominational status, long-standing theological commitments, and highly publicized, income-producing books and media. Others who are mainly "lay" Christians may have an unfortunate lack of knowledge of the Old Testament and its use as the basis for New Testament prophecy and theology. Whatever the case, we must open our hearts to new possibilities and allow God to take us to new places if he so desires. I believe it is a sign of spiritual health to examine ourselves and our theological comfort zones and be willing to change if the truth requires it.

Excursus:
"ISMs": A Necessary Overview

As relating to Israel's history, it is necessary at this interval to briefly explain some terms for those who may not be familiar with various approaches to eschatology. This is not a comprehensive overview, but a brief description of a few perspectives relevant to this book. It was only after much personal deliberation that I elected to include the following information, mainly because it is laden with baggage and is the source of unseemly conflicts between Christians of differing opinions.

Part of the difficulty is that in our time, popular Christianity holds an eschatological view of an impending *end of the world* that includes the rise of an antichrist figure and a great tribulation. It is alleged that this will be a world-ending season of unparalleled apocalyptic events, possibly occurring in our time but most certainly in the future. This is called the *futurist* view, or simply *futurism*. This theological construct has proponents who are sensible and reserved, as well as those who promote speculative and sensationalized drama about the end in books and other media.

Due to its dominance in modern Christian thought, an alternative view that many or all the signs and events attributed to the end pointed to something completely different, something that occurred in our past, may seem untenable. Yet much of that historical perspective is based on sound biblical exegesis and should not be ignored or, especially, *condemned*.

Preterism:
It's Not a Four-Letter Word

The alternative perspective that most, if not all biblical prophecy (including the Book of Revelation) has been fulfilled in the past is called preterism. I must acknowledge that I care little for the term, mainly because the mere mention of it sends up red flags and activates the defense mechanisms of many evangelicals who are familiar with it. All that aside, I ask the reader to set those reactions out of the way and to be charitably open to many important and reasonable approaches to Scripture that are within this theological perspective.

Preterite is a term derived from Latin meaning *pertaining to the past*. The preterist perspective, often referred to as *fulfilled eschatology*, has, in some measure, always been a part of orthodox Christianity. Practically speaking, all Christians are preterists to some extent. We all hold that at least *some* biblical prophecy has been entirely fulfilled in the past. So, the question remains: how much of the Bible is now fulfilled history?

In answer to that, within preterism, there are two primary schools of thought, the first of which is *partial* preterism. This is the orthodox or classical perspective on preterist eschatology. It recognizes the historical fulfillment of many eschatological events, particularly that the Roman invasion resulting in the fall of Jerusalem in 70 AD was a significant fulfillment of New Testament prophecy. It holds that the cloud-presence of Christ in judgment, like the divine visitations described in the Old Testament, occurred in the Jewish-Roman War of 66–70 AD. This great conflict had theological consequences of incredible import. Primarily, the fall of Jerusalem and the Jewish temple resulted in the conclusion of the Old Covenant age, which Jesus referred to as *the end of the age*. This is understood as the primary focus of the Olivet Discourse in Matthew 24, Mark 13, Luke 21, as well as portions of Luke 17 and much of Revelation.

However, partial preterists still expect the future return of Jesus at the end of the world. Some hold to a partial fulfillment, double fulfillment, or even a typological method of interpretation of the Olivet prophecy. This suggests that even though many events were fulfilled in the past, they are types that foreshadow events yet to occur in the future. Most partial preterists view Matthew 24 as pertaining to the fall of Jerusalem, but see Matthew 25 (a continuation of the discourse) as a transition to a future return of Jesus. The designation *partial* preterism specifies that the prophecies of Jesus' return have only been partially fulfilled.

A second school of thought is *full* preterism, or *consistent* preterism, which asserts that *all* prophecies in both the Old and New Testaments have been *completely* fulfilled. Their contention is that all biblical prophecy ended with the one and only promised return of Jesus in that same Jewish-Roman War. They hold essentially the same view as the partial preterists concerning the ushering in of the promised age to come. However, they point out that, since that age has arrived, there is no *future* return of Jesus or end of the world promised in the Bible, which is to say, there is only one "second coming," and it occurred in 66–70 AD.

As for Matthew 24–25, full preterists see this as one continuous flow concerning the outcome of first-century events. The stated prophecies have only one fulfillment, which is now in the past. As support, some observe that *"there will be no end to the increase of his* [Christ's] *government or of peace"* (Isa. 9:7), and regarding Jerusalem's fall: *". . . these are days of vengeance, so that all things which are written will be fulfilled* (Luke 21:22). Such texts are taken to mean that the church age will continue indefinitely and that *all* prophecy is fulfilled.

Many orthodox churches believe that full preterism (sometimes called *radical* or *hyper*-preterism) is heresy, departing from historic orthodox Christian faith. I make no such assertion, as there are potential heresies in any system of theology or in extremist views arising from those systems. Our generalizations rarely lead to healthy perspectives on what constitutes heresy. The question of Christian orthodoxy is one that is highly complex. We can all point at someone else's theological perspective and cry, error! heresy! However, by which creed or church authority is that determined? What denomination has the final authority on infant and adult baptism, predestination, free will, and foreknowledge? What about the gifts of the Spirit, or the apostolic and prophetic offices of the church? Is the communion table transactional or symbolic? What statement of faith cannot be challenged by a different point of view? The list goes on.

Although this book presents a preteristic view on eschatology, there are open questions that cause me not to fully identify with either of these schools of thought. It is important that the reader understand that there is often a broad range of opinion even *within* theological systems, which is self-evident. We find branches within various denominations who do not fully agree on certain things. Evangelical Lutheran Churches ordain women; the Missouri Synod does not. Some charismatic believers are very partial to Reformed theology, others are not. Given these things, we can be appreciative and, at the same time, cautious about the details and the theological implications that arise from various approaches. Given that, our study will seek to understand each biblical text or account on its own merits without fully identifying with any specific theological system.

No expositor of the Scriptures can lay claim to an ironclad theology. Although we all heartily agree that no one has complete and indisputable knowledge, we often act just the opposite. We need to be reminded that intellectual humility must overtake our often-arrogant theological strongholds. That being considered, nonetheless, I am strongly convinced that a preterist approach *in some form* is a necessary starting point for the church's conversation about the interpretation of prophecy and, by extension, eternal destiny. This, I would suggest, is because it is rooted in history rather than popular speculations about the future that often depend on wooden, literalistic interpretations of highly symbolic biblical imagery, such as that found in the prophets and the Book of Revelation.

Other Perspectives

There are additional views of Christian eschatology as it relates to the Book of Revelation and the return of Jesus, such as historicism, idealism, and dispensationalism (the popular form of futurism). They are briefly described as follows:

Historicism was the popular eschatological view during the Reformation, promoting a continuous historical perspective suggested in books such as Daniel and Revelation. They were believed to describe the entire course of the history of the church. The pope was commonly believed to be the antichrist (as some still believe). This view also proposes that the seven churches to which John wrote can be viewed as church eras and encompass significant events in world history.

Idealism interprets eschatology as representing existential biblical truths that are not necessarily confined to any specific historical events, whether past or future. Idealists emphasize that prophetic language and symbols are always relevant to the church's confrontations with powers and portray Christ's interventions in history. This does not suggest that all idealists entirely disregard the historical content of prophecy. Importantly, idealists remind us not to look at eschatological events through purely historical or futuristic lenses but as having relevant lessons for all Christians everywhere at all times.

Dispensationalism arose in the mid-nineteenth century and is the popular *futurist* view among most evangelicals at the time of this writing. It divides the entire Bible into seven distinct periods, called dispensations. Each period, including the church age and the millennium, ends in human failure. This view holds that prior to the end, the world will witness the restoration of Israel, the rapture of the church, the rise of the antichrist as a world leader, a seven-year period of tribulation, and a literal one-thousand-year reign of Christ on earth. It should be noted that all futurists are not necessarily dispensationalists but simply hold to a future return of Jesus, a future tribulation period, and, in some cases, a literal one-thousand-year reign of Christ referred to as the millennium.

Despite these many approaches to eschatology and their various subsets, I am personally convinced that one thing remains very clear. The first-century churches were not wrong in their expectations regarding the coming of Jesus in their own generation. His presence in judgment (66–70 AD) was a historical event of enormous redemptive significance. According to his promise, he came with the clouds of judgment, a judgment evidenced in the utter decimation of all that represented historical Jewish privilege. He came "in the clouds" not to end the physical universe but to judge Jerusalem and bring the satanic beastly powers concentrated behind the Roman Empire to an end. With that, and with specific regard to the Jews, God was not condemning any ethnicity but affirming that the door was open for all Jews and Gentiles alike to embrace the reign of Christ and together enter God's New Covenant kingdom as one new redeemed humanity.

> For He Himself is our peace, who made both groups into one . . . so that in Himself He might make the two into one new man, thus establishing peace, and might reconcile them both in one body to God through the cross . . . (Eph. 2:14-16).

The End

Despite my indebtedness to many brilliant Christian expositors, I do not yet feel that any Christian school of thought adequately answers the questions regarding the end of the world. There are currently far too many unanswered questions in the theological options presently available to us. This is especially apparent in our understanding of Revelation 20–22, which is subject to a wide variety of interpretations. In Part IV, I will offer my thoughts with the understanding that, for me, the end remains an open question.

And Then There's Hell

Conditionalism offers a reasonable alternative to the traditional doctrine of eternal conscious torment. First, the age-ending, fiery destruction of the wicked, seen in its various biblical contexts, makes more sense as a description of the calamities attending the historical burning of Jerusalem (visibly and materially). *Second*, it is also seen as God's consuming fire that annihilates the post-mortem lost (invisibly and supernaturally). Eternal conscious torment proof-texts, in their contexts, can be demonstrated to say something quite different from what is commonly assumed. Despite this, the doctrine remains the majority scholarly opinion.

Aside from conditionalism and traditionalism (eternal conscious torment), the third option is *universalism*. It holds that the cross brought universal salvation, so that in the end, *all* will be saved. Universalist views are diverse, with some believing that for many, salvation occurs through a post-mortem process of purgation from sin. I do not support this view, if for no other reason than my understanding that the Scriptures teach that we all enter a final and irreversible fate at our demise. Biblically, that fate is either life or death.

To briefly conclude, some may feel that the preceding hasn't done justice to these various views. *Mea culpa.* It was not intended to be a comprehensive analysis, but to introduce the reader to ideas with which they may not be familiar. Our focus now remains on how both preterist and conditionalist theologies coalesce when seen through the lens of Israel's historical location in the New Testament as being on the threshold of exile.

CHAPTER 4

THE NEW TESTAMENT
HISTORY MEETS THEOLOGY

We will now expand our historical and theological sketch of the centuries prior to and including the life and ministry of the Lord Jesus and the first-century church. This will especially benefit those who may not be familiar with the exceedingly significant background of the New Testament. Please note that this is, by design, a bird's-eye view. It includes only sufficient detail to acquaint us with the larger contemporary setting in which Jesus and the apostles lived. It also contains critical reference points in biblical history to which the New Testament refers.

The Bible is high-context literature. It possesses a distinctly Jewish flavor, and therefore the New Testament assumes the reader must have or have acquired a measure of cultural and religious understanding of Old Testament history. It is the historical and theological background out of which the New Testament emerged. The Jewish Christians in the first century AD would have understood the words of Jesus that referenced Old Testament stories and events. They could also explain them to their Gentile fellow Christians. However, many of *us* who have no such knowledge often fail to comprehend important concepts drawn from the Old Testament that were recorded by the authors of the New Testament.

Beside the direct quotes from the Old Testament, there are allusions known as *metalepsis* (see Hays).[16] This is an important type of reference that directs the hearer or reader to a specific historical (Old Testament) narrative that parallels what is being spoken about in their own story. We observed this in Chapter 3 regarding Paul's use of Habakkuk in Acts 13. The speaker or writer alludes to or cites a text to bring an older text's entire story line to bear on their own current message.

It is an observable interaction between older and newer texts that, as I have mentioned, goes beyond the common idea that *this* event fulfilled *that* Old Testament prophecy. In this intertextual relationship, the older text shapes and provides historical and theological context for the newer text. In other words, it is as if Jesus or a New Testament writer is telling us to go back to the Old Testament story and the setting being referred to. Examining that in its context will help us understand what's being talked about in the new historical situation.

For example, in Matthew 10:34-35, Jesus alludes to Micah 7:5-6, where the prophet described eighth-century BC conditions in Israel. At that time, the Assyrian invasion was an imminent threat to the nation.

The Micah reference is not recorded in Mark, Luke, or John. It is recorded only in Matthew's gospel, which was written for a primarily Jewish audience uniquely familiar with the historical context. First, Micah writes:

> Do not trust in a neighbor;
> Do not have confidence in a friend.
> From her who lies in your bosom
> Guard your lips.
> For son treats father contemptuously,
> Daughter rises up against her mother,
> Daughter-in-law against her mother-in-law;
> A man's enemies are the men of his own household
> (Mic. 7:5-6).

In the following dialogue, Jesus invites his disciples to reflect on the conditions surrounding Micah's statement:

> "Do not think that I came to bring peace on the earth [lit. *cast peace on the land*]; I did not come to bring peace, but a sword. FOR I CAME TO SET A MAN AGAINST HIS FATHER, AND A DAUGHTER AGAINST HER MOTHER, AND A DAUGHTER-IN-LAW AGAINST HER MOTHER-IN-LAW; AND A MAN'S ENEMIES WILL BE THE MEMBERS OF HIS HOUSEHOLD" (Matt. 10:34-36).

Jesus' preface to this quote from Micah has nothing to do with peace in the world or on earth, or the lack of it. According to Luke 2:14, God's peace is reserved for those with whom he is well pleased. However, in Matthew 10:34-36, the key element is *the sword about to be wielded upon the land of Israel*. Jesus is warning his disciples that the Jewish rejection of the gospel would have consequences. He alerted them to the harsh reality that the outcome of his ministry would not be their anticipated messianic era of peace in the homeland. Instead, his sword of judgment was about to be employed through the agency of Rome. He drew from the Micah text to forewarn them of the coming invasion by the empire.

Again, Jesus had to recalibrate the disciples' understanding of the outcome of his mission. He did so by using the language of the prophet Micah, which described the conditions preceding the Assyrian invasion of 722 BC. The meaning of the lesson, warning, or story is only fully understood by knowing the Old Testament context from which Jesus quoted. This is how the New Testament uses ancient biblical stories to draw attention to historical parallels and is highly impactful on how we are to understand many of its warnings.

Can this text have an application for a Christian today who encounters resistance within his or her own family because of their faith? Of course. However, the personal application of Jesus' words in contexts such as this should not obscure their relevant prophetic intent for Jesus' first-century audience. The text, as intended first for that audience, was one of many prophetic warnings meant to realign their expectations of his life, work, and the nature of his return. If our interpretation proceeds too quickly to satisfy our own need for immediate personal application, we bury the eschatological meaning intended for the disciples and miss a critical component of New Testament prophecy. We can easily lose sight of the meaning and significance of key eschatological texts and are eventually left with an underdeveloped theology of last things. We may find ourselves expecting Jesus to return any day (as many do) and missing the opportunities to engage the issues that are most relevant to the plan of God for our own time.

Setting the Historical Stage

The era ushered in by the Babylonian exile is known as the *times of the Gentiles* (referred to by Jesus in Luke 21:24). It is described as such because Israel ceased to be an independent political power after being conquered by Nebuchadnezzar of Babylon in the sixth century BC. From that time on, they would remain under the rule of several Gentile empires in succession. This era continued until Jesus established his kingdom in the first century AD. All of this is described prophetically in Chapters 2 and 7 of the Book of Daniel and will be further explained in our studies of the Olivet Discourse and the Book of Revelation.

Within the historical context of the times of the Gentiles, Judaism's *Second Temple Period* refers to their time under Persian, Greek, and Roman rule. Each of these empires, in turn, succeeded Babylon. The Persian period saw Jerusalem and the temple rebuilt two decades after Cyrus' decree, which allowed the Jews to return to their homeland after the Babylonian exile. Greece, led by the military conquests of Alexander the Great, succeeded Persia as the next major empire in the fourth century BC. This brought Greek language, culture, and philosophy (Hellenism) to the entire Mediterranean region and resulted in the translation of the Hebrew Bible into Greek (the Septuagint, or LXX). The translation was intended to accommodate the Greek-speaking Jews who remained dispersed after the exile. Despite its eventual loss of political dominance to Rome in the ensuing centuries, Greek language and culture remained a powerful influence, having a significant impact on both Judaism and Christianity.

After Alexander's death, the realm of Greek rule was parceled out to four generals and eventually consolidated into two major power centers: Egypt (the Ptolemies in the south) and Syria (the Seleucids in the north). Each controlled the land of Israel for a period of time. The era of Greek dominance ended in the second century BC, when the Jews revolted against Syria and its atrocious king, Antiochus IV Epiphanes. This uprising, called the Maccabean Revolt, resulted in a brief period of independence in the second and first centuries BC. Their independence under (Jewish) Hasmonaean rule lasted about 100 years and ended several decades before the birth of Jesus. The Second Temple Period continued through this era until the temple and the city's destruction in 70 AD by the Romans.

Enter Rome

Rome had long begun to rise as the preeminent power in the Mediterranean world. In 63 BC, the Roman general Pompey took control of Galilee and then Jerusalem, effectively ending Jewish independence. The land of Israel became a province of the now-established Roman Empire. In 37 BC, they appointed Herod, a half-Idumean Jew, to be King of Judea, and he was on the throne at the time of Jesus' birth. Over time, growing unrest among the Jews mounted against increasing Roman imposition into their civic and religious life, which was apparent at the time of Jesus. This unrest resulted in sporadic outbreaks of violent resistance by Jewish Zealots during the years of expansion of the early church and finally escalated into a full-scale revolt in 66 AD.

Nero commissioned the advance of Roman forces, led first by General Vespasian and then by Vespasian's son, General Titus. The multi-national armies of the empire marched through the land of Israel from the north, resulting in a bloodbath and destroying everything they encountered. The invaders burned cities and killed their inhabitants as they advanced toward the heart of Jewish life—Jerusalem. The devastation came within forty years, one generation after Jesus' prophecy concerning the ruin of the temple found in Matthew 24:3-34 (and parallels).

The war lasted from 66 to 73 AD; however, Rome's decisive victory came in 70 AD, three and a half years (42 months) after it began. The campaign began in February, 66 AD. Jerusalem and the temple were destroyed in August of 70 AD, as foretold in Luke and Revelation:

"But when you see Jerusalem surrounded by armies, then recognize that her desolation is near . . . and they will fall by the edge of the sword, and will be led captive into all the nations; and Jerusalem will be *trampled underfoot by the Gentiles until the times of the Gentiles are fulfilled*" (Luke 21:20-24).

. . . someone said, "Get up and measure the temple of God and the altar, and those who worship in it. Leave out the court which is outside the temple and do not measure it, for it has been given to the nations; and *they will tread underfoot the holy city for forty-two months.*" (Rev. 11:1-2).

During the siege, the horrific conditions within Jerusalem were beyond belief. The Roman armies finally broke through its walls, killing multitudes and burning everything to the ground. This occurred *on the very same day of the year that Nebuchadnezzar, King of Babylon, had done it centuries before, in 586 BC.* It has since been recognized as a solemn day of remembrance in Judaism, called the *Ninth of Av.* The destruction of the city and the temple was so thorough that no evidence remained that they ever stood there. The chronology of the times and detailed accounts of the war are furnished to us in the writings of *Josephus*, the first-century Jewish priest and eyewitness historian. Some have questioned the objectivity of Josephus' testimony because Rome commissioned his work. The potential for bias in favor of Rome would be obvious. However, his works remain a valuable source of information about the period. Josephus observed:

. . . the wall enclosed the city on the west side. This wall was spared, in order to afford a camp for such as were to lie in garrison [in the Upper City], as were the towers [the three forts] also spared, in order to demonstrate to posterity what kind of city it was, and how well fortified, which the Roman valor had subdued; but for all the rest of the wall [surrounding Jerusalem], it was so thoroughly laid even with the ground by those that dug it up to the foundation, that there was left nothing to make those that came thither believe it [Jerusalem] had ever been inhabited.[17]

This war, also known as the *First Jewish Revolt*, is rightfully acknowledged by many as a notable misfortune for the Jews in their history, and it is easy to view this as just another tragic war. Theologically, however, the Jewish-Roman war that brought the calamity of 70 AD was substantially more than that. From a biblical perspective, it was one of the most momentous events in redemptive history. Yet many (if not most) Christians know little or nothing about it or its importance. Again, Reformed scholar Kenneth Gentry has observed:

> Too often we tend to view Jerusalem's destruction as a horrible human tragedy befalling a helpless people under the crushing oppression of a mighty empire. But when we understand the event from the context of both Scripture's unfolding of redemptive history and from the religious history of the Jews, we gain a far deeper insight into its significance (underlined in original).[18]

Theological Implications

It is vital for us to recognize that the events leading up to and including the devastation of Jerusalem constituted the final removal of the standing vestiges of the Old Covenant, which included the city, the temple, its priesthood, and its sacrificial system. The New Testament presents it as having great theological implications. Many understand it to be a central theme of the Book of Revelation. This great catastrophe, the very judgment of God himself, was accomplished through the agency of the Roman armies and described in advance by Jesus in the Parable of the Wedding Feast, where those who were invited to celebrate the king's son persecuted and murdered his servants:

> "But the king was enraged, and he sent his armies and destroyed those murderers and set their city on fire" (Matt. 22:7).

This tragic episode, foreseen in this and other parables and prophecies, signaled the end of the age. It marked the conclusion of over 1400 years of redemptive history and the privileged nation status of the Jews under the economy of Moses. With the destruction of Jerusalem and the temple, God decisively affirmed that the New

Covenant was now in place. Jesus was not merely a deceased carpenter or once-popular itinerant rabbi from Nazareth. He was the resurrected Lord who had ascended to his heavenly throne as the firstborn of a new humanity and King Messiah, whose reign was being inaugurated. The cross of Christ finally and conclusively established that there was no room for the city and the temple that stood in opposition to God's long-awaited New Covenant economy.

All things related to the Old Covenant had served their purpose. Christ's atoning sacrifice was accomplished, and the subsequent forty years served as a probationary period for the Jews as a nation, which was their opportunity to embrace their Messiah and enter God's *true* rest. Unfortunately, their messianic hopes were misguided. The rest that God presented to them had nothing to do with political enemies or the geographical boundaries of their homeland. He offered rest from their labors under sin by receiving Christ's once-for-all atonement. The first-century conditions depict a remarkable parallel to their journey from Egypt to Canaan for those who received Christ:

From Egypt to Canaan in the Old and New Testaments

Old Testament (Type)	New Testament Parallel (Antitype)
Slavery in Egypt (Exo. 1:8-14)	Slavery to Sin (Rom. 6:17)
Passover (Exo. 12:1-51)	Christ: Our Passover (1 Cor. 5:7)
Crossing the Red Sea (Exo. 14:19-341)	Baptism by Water and Spirit (1 Cor. 10:2; Gal. 3:27)
40 Years in the Wilderness (Deu. 2:7)	40 Years' Probation (30–70 AD) (Heb. 3:7-12; cf. Rev. 17:3)
Entering the Land (Josh. 1:1-4)	Entering God's True Rest (Heb. 4:1-3)

Table 4.1

This was now the last opportunity for the Jews (as a nation) to acknowledge their Messiah and enter into the promise:

> Therefore, let us fear if, while a promise remains of entering His rest, any one of you may seem to have come short of it . . . since it remains for some to enter it, and those who formerly had good news preached to them failed to enter because of disobedience . . . Therefore, let us be diligent to enter that rest, so that no one will fall, through following the same example of disobedience (Heb. 4:1-11).

The calamities of the war signaled the removal of what was no longer necessary and was standing in opposition to the redemptive purpose of God in Christ. Jerusalem's fiery dissolution permanently freed the body of Christ from its identification with Jerusalem and the Law. It was the crucial event that ended the transition from the previous age and ushered in the Christian age. This was the era of freedom for the people of God, both Jews and Gentiles alike, who embrace the cross of Christ.

The city and temple's destruction rendered the definitive statement that the true city and temple of God, one made without hands, whose architect and builder is God, was now standing without rival (cf. Heb. 11:10).

The Great Separation

Decades earlier, the arrival of the Holy Spirit on the day of Pentecost (Acts 2:1ff) meant that the true dwelling place of God–the church–had finally been inaugurated. However, until the tragic events of 70 AD, the church was still viewed as a sect of Judaism. This was the common perception because many Jews began to receive Christ and studied their new "Jewish" faith using their Scriptures. The New Testament was only developing as letters and historical accounts. However, after the destruction of Jerusalem, the relationship of the two faiths was completely severed, as noted by historian Philip Schaff:

Henceforth the heathen could no longer look upon Christianity as a mere sect of Judaism, . . . The destruction of Jerusalem, therefore, marks that momentous crisis at which the Christian church as a whole burst forth forever from the chrysalis [cocoon] of Judaism, awoke to a sense of maturity, and in government and worship at once took its independent stand before the world.[19]

As Jesus declared in the parables, the tares were removed from the wheat (Matt. 13:24-30); the fish in the net were sorted and cast into the consuming fires of Jerusalem (Matt. 13:47-50). Our embrace of the historic significance of these realities affects our entire perspective of the cross of Christ and the eschatological outlook of the New Testament. This was the crisis foreseen in many prophetic texts in both the Old and New Testaments. In the Parable of the Tares and the Parable of the Dragnet, those rejected were cast into the *furnace of fire*. They also preview the harvest visions in Revelation 14:14-20:

"Allow both to grow together until the harvest; and in the time of the harvest I will say to the reapers, 'First gather up the tares and bind them in bundles to burn them up; but gather the wheat into my barn'" (Matt. 13:30).

"So it will be at the end of the age; the angels will come forth and take out the wicked from among the righteous, and will throw them into the furnace of fire; in that place there will be weeping and gnashing of teeth" (Matt. 13:49-50).

The Lord Jesus mined these word pictures from the Old Testament. They were not merely hatched from his imagination, as if he were saying, *"I think I'll describe it this way."* The furnace has specific reference to the prophetic imagery of Ezekiel, who refers to *Jerusalem* (not hell) as God's furnace (as does Isaiah in Isa. 31:9). Ezekiel warns of the razing of Jerusalem by Nebuchadnezzar in 586 BC, describing it as a *furnace* into which his disobedient people would be gathered. Observe how Matthew 13 uses the same Greek word, *kaminos*, which is translated furnace, in the Septuagint.

Let's see how Jesus alludes to Ezekiel's description of 586 BC to describe what was also coming in 70 AD. Although he changes the metaphor from *smelting* in Ezekiel to *fishing* in Matthew, the illustration is the same. Both prophecies point to a gathering to Jerusalem and the unfortunate suffering brought about by Babylon and Rome, respectively:

Ezekiel 22:18-22	Matthew 13:47-50
"Son of man, the house of Israel has become dross to Me; all of them are bronze and tin and iron and lead in the furnace [G2575]; they are the dross of silver. "Therefore, ... *I am going to gather you into the midst of Jerusalem.* 'As they gather silver and bronze and iron and lead and tin into the furnace [G2575] to blow fire on it in order to melt *it*, so *I will gather you* ... *and blow on you with the fire of My wrath,* ... 'As silver is melted in the furnace [G2575], so you will be melted in the midst of it;	"Again, the kingdom of heaven is like a dragnet cast into the sea, and gathering fish of every kind; and when it was filled, they drew it up on the beach; and they sat down and gathered the good fish into containers, but the bad they threw away. "So it will be at the end of the age; *the angels will come forth and take out the wicked from among the righteous, and will throw them into the furnace [G2575] of fire*; in that place there will be weeping and gnashing of teeth.

Table 4.2

The Lord foresaw opposing Jewish influences (not God-fearing Jews) seeking to deceive the fledgling congregations. They grew as tares (or weeds) among the churches (cf. Acts 15:1; Titus 1:10-11; Jude 1:4-5, 12). In Revelation 2, they are seen as *Balaam* and *Jezebel*, deceivers who caused the churches to stumble by introducing heretical ideas. These heresies allowed sexual promiscuity, reminiscent of Balaam's stumbling block during Israel's wilderness wanderings. They also promoted idolatry, as introduced by Jezebel in Elijah's time.

The letters allude specifically to Balaam and then Jezebel, who (as we shall see) is later identified with Jerusalem in Revelation 14:

'But I have a few things against you, because you have there some who hold the teaching of Balaam, who kept teaching Balak to put a stumbling block before the sons of Israel, to eat things sacrificed to idols and to commit acts of immorality' (Rev. 2:14).

'But I have this against you, that you tolerate the woman Jezebel, who calls herself a prophetess, and she teaches and leads My bond-servants astray so that they commit acts of immorality and eat things sacrificed to idols' (Rev. 2:20).

The tares would remain until the burning of Jerusalem and the temple by the Romans, which would finally separate Christianity from any perceived connection to Judaism or Jerusalem's jurisdiction.

But When Was It "Finished?"

Some rightly fear that overemphasizing the events of the Jewish-Roman war devalues what Christ accomplished at the cross and places undue theological importance on the events of 70 AD. I would maintain that the question is settled when we understand the character of the age in which the apostles lived.

The Letter to the Hebrews, one of the last books of the New Testament, was written just a few short years before the Jewish-Roman war broke out. The writer quotes the prophet Jeremiah (Jer. 31:31ff.) regarding the New Covenant and then makes a remarkable statement about the passing of the Old Covenant. First, from Jeremiah 31:31ff:

"Behold, days are coming, says the Lord, when I will effect a New Covenant with the house of Israel and with the house of Judah; not like the covenant which I made with their fathers on the day when I took them by the hand to lead them out of the land of Egypt . . . for I will be merciful to their iniquities, and I will remember their sins no more" (Heb. 8:8-12).

After quoting the text of Jeremiah, the writer adds:

When He said, "A New Covenant," He has made the first obsolete. But whatever *is becoming obsolete and growing old is ready to disappear* (Heb. 8:13).

The author states that the Old Covenant was *becoming obsolete* and *was ready (lit., near) to disappear*. Yet Jesus said, "*It is finished*" at the cross decades prior to this (John 19:30). Indeed, through his cross, resurrection, and ascension, Jesus brought about *the end of the* Law *as a covenantal basis for our relationship with God* (Col. 2:13-14). *However, the Law was also an age of time that remained in transition for forty years after the cross event,* as the following diagram illustrates:

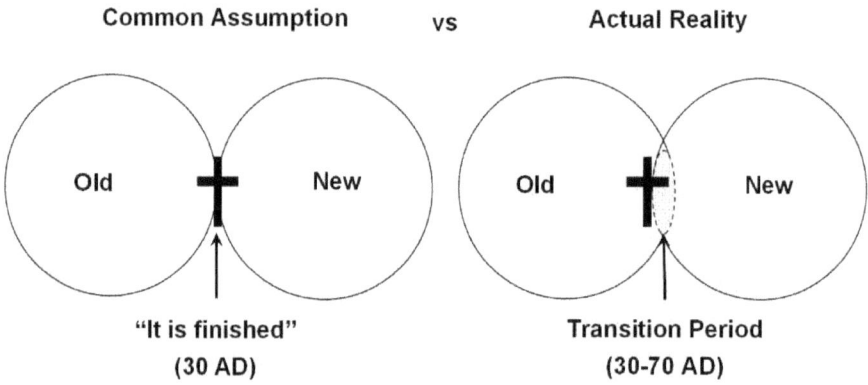

The Ages: A Critical Misconception Illustrated
"That which is old is getting ready to disappear"

Common Assumption   vs   Actual Reality

Old   New   Old   New

"It is finished"   Transition Period
(30 AD)   (30-70 AD)

Access to God was made available through the cross, yet the Old Covenant (as an age of time) continued for 40 years and finally concluded with the prophesied destruction of Jerusalem and the Temple

Why the Transition?

During this period of transition, God was fulfilling his covenantal obligations to Israel. He was bringing his promised remnant into the New Covenant, as explained in Paul's Letter to the Romans:

> God has not rejected his people whom he foreknew. Do you not know what the Scripture says of Elijah, how he appeals to God against Israel? "Lord, they have killed your prophets, they have demolished your altars, and I alone am left, and they seek my life." But what is God's reply to him? "I have kept for myself seven thousand men who have not bowed the knee to Baal." So too at the present time there is a remnant, chosen by grace. But if it is by grace, it is no longer on the basis of works; otherwise grace would no longer be grace. What then? Israel failed to obtain what it was seeking. The elect obtained it, but the rest were hardened (Rom. 11:2-7; cf. 1 Kings 19:10, 18).

Both Paul and the writer of Hebrews understood that God was completing his Old Testament business during the years of transition. This explains the statement in Hebrews that the Old Covenant was *ready* to disappear. Paul's reference in Romans 11:5 to t*his present time* was the apostle's present time. Just as a remnant existed in Elijah's own time, the first-century remnant existed in Paul's own time. The writer of Hebrews (8:13) unveiled the critical season during which the old system is passing away, but not before God's covenantal obligations concerning the remnant of Israel were accomplished. This was previously spoken by Isaiah the prophet when, in his remarkable vision of the heavenly throne room, he learns of the remnant:

> "Until cities are devastated and without inhabitant,
> Houses are without people
> And the land is utterly desolate . . .
> Yet there will be a tenth portion in it,
> And it will again be subject to burning . . .
> The holy seed is its stump"
> (Isa. 6:8-13).

Isaiah also announces:

"Then in that day
The nations will resort to the root of Jesse [Jesus] . . .
Then it will happen on that day that the Lord
Will again recover the second time with His hand
The remnant of His people, who will remain,
From Assyria, Egypt, Pathros, Cush, Elam, Shinar, Hamath,
And from the islands of the sea"
(Isa. 11:10-11).

"I will set a sign among them and will send survivors from them to the
nations: . . . Then they shall bring all your brethren from all the nations
as a grain offering . . ." (Isa. 66:19-20).

This second and true recovery from exile was of greater significance than their release from Babylon under Cyrus of Persia. It would be attributable to a leader arising from the root of Jesse (King David's lineage) who would bring true rest and freedom. In Christ, God would fulfill his covenantal promises to preserve a remnant. That season would close with the destruction of Jerusalem and the temple, so we now turn to the prophecy of Jesus relating to that event.

PART II

THE OLIVET DISCOURSE

CHAPTER 5

THE OLIVET DISCOURSE
APPROACH & OVERVIEW

In the Olivet Discourse, Jesus described to his disciples what they could expect in the decades leading up to the Jewish-Roman War and the fall of Jerusalem. His return (parousia), the end of the age, and the commencement of the age to come would be seen in the context of that impending military conflict. It would take place in the same manner as the cloud-presence of God was "seen" in the Old Testament, when he accomplished great power transitions through the agency of war. This is central to our understanding of the nature of the Lord's promised return. Our approach to this great discourse will be to examine Jesus' words in manageable segments, primarily from Matthew's account, considering context, historical data, and linguistic style.

The Olivet Discourse: Context

First, regarding its narrative and cultural contexts, Matthew Chapters 23–25 provide a unified narrative framework without interruption or thematic variation. There is no clear evidence or reason for a fundamental break from beginning to end. Matthew offers a more comprehensive base of information that is particularly relevant to a Jewish audience, which would have had an obvious vested interest in the fate of the city and the temple. It will also be appropriate to observe important contributions by Mark and Luke to our understanding of Jesus' discourse.

The broader setting begins in Matthew 21 with Jesus' triumphal entry into Jerusalem. The stage is being set for his last public confrontations with Jewish leaders, followed by his arrest and crucifixion. Several parables in Matthew 21–22 speak of the disinheritance of Israel and the approaching demise of Jerusalem in judgment:

Jesus Curses the Fig Tree (Matt. 21:18-19):

> Now in the morning, when He was returning to the city, He became hungry. Seeing a lone fig tree by the road, He came to it and found nothing on it except leaves only; and He *said to it, "No longer shall there ever be any fruit from you." And at once the fig tree withered.

The Parable of the Two Sons (Matt. 21:28-32):

> Jesus *said to them [Jewish leaders], "Truly I say to you that the tax collectors and prostitutes will get into the kingdom of God before you."

He alludes to Isaiah's *Song of the Vineyard* (Isa. 5:1-7) in his Parable of the Tenants (Matt. 21:33-45):

> ". . . when *the owner of the vineyard comes*, what will he do to those vine-growers?" . . . They *said to Him, "He will bring those wretches to a wretched end, and will rent out the vineyard to other vine-growers

who will pay him the proceeds at the proper seasons." . . . "Therefore I say to you, the kingdom of God will be taken away from you and given to a people, producing the fruit of it."

In the Parable of the Tenants, it is notable that the dissolution of Jewish privilege and the offer of the kingdom to new recipients (the church) occur *when the owner of the vineyard comes*. If that *coming* has not occurred, then the stewardship of the kingdom has not yet been transferred to the church. However, this coming has, in fact, already occurred, and according to Jesus, it marked the beginning, not the end, of the church age. This is also confirmed in parallel statements in Mark 12:9 and Luke 20:16, where, as in Matthew, it is distinctly indicated when and why the owner of the vineyard *comes*:

"What will the owner of the vineyard do? *He will come* and destroy the vine-growers, and will give the vineyard to others" (Mark 12:9).

"What, then, will the owner of the vineyard do to them? *He will come* and destroy these vine-growers and will give the vineyard to others" (Luke 20:15-16).

Observe how the sequence is the same in all three accounts:

1. The owner of the vineyard comes (Jesus).

2. The tenants (economy of first-century Israel) are destroyed.

3. The vineyard is given to new caretakers (the church).

Then, in Matthew Chapter 22, Jesus unmistakably warns of the destruction of Jerusalem by invading armies in the Parable of the Wedding Feast. The armies were the multinational forces of Rome:

"But the king was enraged, and he sent his armies and destroyed those murderers and set their city on fire" (Matt. 22:1-14).

The framework of the discourse itself begins in Chapter 23, which contains Jesus' thorough condemnation of the scribes and Pharisees.

This indictment in Matthew 23 is *Part One* of the entire discourse. It establishes the narrative context for Chapters 24–25. The hypocrisy of the scribes and Pharisees is clearly exposed before all in attendance. As it had occurred in their history, their unbelief would ultimately result in the persecution of those whom God would send (like their prophets) in Christ's name after his ascension. But Jesus doesn't stop there. Matthew's gospel captures the most shocking transition. The Lord closes his condemnation of them with the unsettling statement that Israel's house, which was their entire religious and political economy, would be abandoned by God, left in their own hands, and ultimately desolated:

> "Behold, your house is being left to you desolate [empty, waste, uninhabited]!" (Matt. 23:38).

As Matthew transitions to *Part Two* of the narrative in Chapter 24, it is apparent that the disciples didn't understand the implications of the things he had just spoken when Jesus said:

> "All these things shall come upon this generation" (Matt. 23:36).

Next, we see them walking with Jesus from the temple area and commenting on the beauty of the structure. In response, Jesus informs them that:

> "Not one stone standing here will be left" (Matt. 24:2).

This provokes the disciples to ask him *when* this would occur and what would be the sign that its time was approaching. Matthew 24:4–35 is Jesus' response. It is a description of the events that would occur in that generation, up to and including the fall of Jerusalem, and nothing more. *Part Three* of the discourse begins at Matthew 24:36 and continues through Matthew 26:1, where the writer concludes:

> When Jesus had finished all these words . . . (Matt. 26:1).

In this third section, Jesus assures the disciples of the permanence of his words despite the passing away of heaven and earth (or, *the heavens and the land*). We will see how that phrase refers to Israel's covenantal spaces and privileges, *not the sky and the planet*. Jesus gives the disciples illustrative warnings regarding readiness, personal responsibility, and the coming judgment that will distinguish his true flock. Remember, until Jerusalem fell, the Jews and their institutions remained (though transitionally) in covenantal status before God. As we are informed, his flock contained both sheep and goats, good fish and bad fish, wheat and tares, etc. (cf. 1 Pet. 4:17; Matt. 25:32; Matt. 13:47-50). These conditions would remain until the fall of Jerusalem, which brought about the end of the Old Covenant age. Additionally, we should note that although we are focusing on a particular first-century application, we must obviously recognize that such mixture has existed in the church throughout history.

In the entirety of the discourse (Matt. 23–25), there is contextually no transitional leap into a future second coming in Jesus' continuing remarks. Many notable scholars hold to a transition in the discourse beginning at or about Matthew 24:36 and continuing through all of Chapter 25. I hope to demonstrate that there is no such transition and that the Lord is still speaking in the context of the fall of Jerusalem and the final separation of the church from the Jewish system. This does not imply anything conclusively for or against a future return of Jesus or the end of the world. We are simply analyzing this specific discourse (in three parallel accounts) to determine what it says, what it does not say, and how it is constructed. Given that, there appears to be no valid reason to suggest that Jesus' teaching suddenly launches into a future that is beyond the scope of the disciples' generation.

We will also discover how the cultural context and worldview of the disciples would not have allowed for questions regarding the end of the world as we commonly understand it. Moreover, the notions of partial or double fulfillment of these prophecies, as well as the suggestion that they are typological of future events, are interpretive approaches that I do not support for reasons that will be enumerated.

The Olivet Discourse: Historical Data

Second, regarding historical data, we will see how an eyewitness, contemporary historians, and the New Testament describe the conditions of that time, confirming the signs Jesus foretold. These were historical realities in the first century, between the time of the Olivet Discourse in 30 AD and the fall of Jerusalem in 70 AD. They all transpired within a span of forty years (one generation), fulfilling the prophecy of Jesus. I have personally observed the shock on the faces of many Christians when, for the first time, they are presented with the historical realities of the decades following the resurrection of Christ. These historical accounts show how the words of Jesus were fulfilled in the very generation of which he spoke.

> *Although significant historical evidence exists, it isn't all that we depend on. Jesus' own words, if properly understood, provide sufficient evidence for the nature and timing of his prophecy.*

The Son of God made unambiguous statements that allow us to draw confident conclusions from the discourse itself. Our analyses must always be based on the Word of God and not on so-called *headline news*, whether it is ancient or contemporary.

The Olivet Discourse: Language

Third, the linguistic style employed by the Lord to describe his coming portrays neither world-ending events nor his appearance in the sky for all the world to see. Simple research into his manner of speech reveals that it was typical of the prophetic language and imagery employed by the ancient Hebrew prophets. They described

God's presence in rendering temporal judgments in history in the same dramatic form. Notably, it was the very *Spirit of Christ himself* who spoke through those prophets:

> As to this salvation, the prophets who prophesied of the grace that would come to you made careful searches and inquiries, seeking to know what person or time *the Spirit of Christ within them* was indicating as He predicted the sufferings of Christ and the glories to follow (1 Pet. 1:10-11).

> *Considering Peter's preceding statement, we must pose an important question: Why would Jesus in the days of his flesh (Heb. 5:7) use a different mode of speech through his own human voice than he used historically through the mouths of his prophets?*

The way his judgment-presence is described in the Olivet Discourse was precisely the style of communication heard regularly in their synagogues. In his description of his "return," Jesus sets himself forth as the very God of Israel, whose presence in the clouds is the same as described in their ancient texts.

"You" Doesn't Mean "They"

Imagine yourself for a moment, along with some close companions, ascending with Jesus to the Mount of Olives. He just condemned the religious establishment for their willful spiritual blindness and then stated clearly that the temple would be destroyed and their national economy desolated. You have rudimentary knowledge, having learned from your teachers what the temple's destruction means for the future of your country. As a first-century Jew, you're anxiously anticipating the coming age of Messiah, certain that Jesus is the one who will fulfill your hopes as the promised agent of God. Now, several of you inquire of Jesus. You find yourselves seated around him as he speaks of the things to come.

The discourse was not mere rhetoric spoken into empty air. You, in his immediate circle, would be absorbing the following words as they were being spoken to you. How would you have interpreted his warnings? What follows are the things you would have heard. They are the things Jesus said to his disciples regarding the end of their age, the birth of the Messianic age, and those who would witness it. All three gospel accounts reflect a common sequence and outcome. The following observations are from Matthew 24, where Jesus said to *his disciples*:

- See to it that no one misleads **you** (24:4).

- **You** will be hearing of wars and rumors of wars. See that **you** are not frightened (24:6).

- Then they will deliver **you** to tribulation, and will kill **you**, and **you** will be hated (24:9).

- When **you** see the abomination of desolation (24:15).

- But pray that **your** flight [from Jerusalem] will not be in the winter, or on a Sabbath (24:20).

- Then if anyone says to **you**, 'Behold, here is the Christ,' or 'There He is,' do not believe him (24:23).

- Behold, I have told **you** in advance (24:25).

- "So if they say to **you**, 'Behold, He is in the wilderness,' do not go (24:26).

- So, **you** too, when **you** see all these things, recognize that He is near, right at the door (24:33).

Then Jesus affirmed once more that the disciples would see and experience everything of which he spoke:

"Now learn the parable from the fig tree: when its branch has already become tender and puts forth its leaves, you know that summer is near; so, **you** too, when **you** see all these things, recognize that He is near, right at the door. Truly I say to you, this generation will not pass away until all these things take place" (Matt. 24:32-35).

With the rise of dispensational theology in recent history, Jesus' reference to the fig tree has commonly been taught as referring to Israel's becoming a nation in 1948. In their zeal to bring prophetic relevance into the contemporary world, the teachers of this theology have emphasized conditions in the Middle East relating to Israel as a key to the fulfillment of this prophecy.

Therefore, we have been told how the Olivet prophecy would be fulfilled in the generation that witnessed *that* event (or *that* generation). However, in our interpretation of the symbolism employed in the text, it is important to remember that:

Although the fig tree is often used as a symbol of Israel, biblical symbolism is not rigid but fluid and governed by the context in which it is presented. In this context, the budding of the fig tree is not Israel, but the presence of the signs in total. These signs have nothing to do with Israel again becoming a nation at a time far removed from the first century AD.

The Lord Jesus explained it in the immediate context:

"When you see *all* these things recognize that He is near, right at the door" (Matt. 24:33).

Luke further clarifies Jesus' meaning by adding these words to the fig tree illustration:

"Behold the fig tree *and all the trees*" (Luke 21:29).

The fig tree illustration is followed (in verse 36) by the affirmation that he didn't know the exact day or hour of his coming because it was known only by the Father. However, Jesus also clearly affirmed that *he knew* it would take place before that generation passed. Although this seems clear enough and the signs of which he spoke are verifiable, we must address the issue that is referred to as the *transgenerational you.*

This is a theological idea that is commonly imposed on the discourse to suggest that the reference to "you" can denote a wider audience than merely those in attendance.

Does "You" Mean "You?"

Is Jesus only referring to his contemporaries in the Olivet Discourse, or is he including future generations of people, especially the Jews? (See Vlach 2017 for a good and reasonable overview of this perspective.) [20]

Moses' remarks in Deuteronomy 28 provide an excellent example of transgenerational you. In Moses' address, *you* describes both Israel's then-current as well as future generations. For example:

> "Therefore, *you* shall serve your enemies whom the LORD will send against *you*, in hunger, in thirst, in nakedness, and in the lack of all things; and He will put an iron yoke on *your* neck until He has destroyed *you*. The LORD will bring a nation against *you* from afar, from the end of the earth, as the eagle swoops down, a nation whose language *you* shall not understand" (Deu. 28:48-49).

These events were well into the nation's future, yet Moses addresses Israel as a collective, inclusive of their future generations. However, by examining the entire context of Moses' farewell address to Israel, we see a distinction between the prophecies of Moses and Jesus. Christ's words are not seen as extending to future generations, whereas Moses' remarks were clearly stated as inclusive:

> "You shall have *sons and daughters* but they will not be yours, for *they* will go into captivity . . . So all these curses . . . shall become a sign and a wonder *on you and your descendants* forever" (Deu. 28:41-46).

> "Now not with you alone am I making this covenant and this oath, but both *with those who stand here* with us today in the presence of the LORD our God *and with those who are not with us here today*" (Deu. 29:14-15).

Moses' statements in Deuteronomy Chapter 4 are also inclusive of their future generations:

"When you become the father of children and children's children and have remained long in the land, and act corruptly, and make an idol in the form of anything, and do that which is evil in the sight of the LORD your God so as to provoke Him to anger"* (Deu. 4:25).

As well as those living in the latter days:

"When you are in distress and all these things have come upon you, *in the latter days you will return* to the LORD your God and listen to His voice" (Deu. 4:30).

The first half of Leviticus 26 includes the transgenerational you:

"Then the land will enjoy its sabbaths all the days of the desolation, while you are in your enemies' land . . . the days of its desolation it will observe the rest which it did not observe on your sabbaths, while *you* were living on it." (Lev. 26:34-35).

But Moses' warnings transition to future generations as his focus changes from *you* to *they:*

"If *they* confess their iniquity and the iniquity of their forefathers, in their unfaithfulness which *they* committed against Me, and also *in their* acting with hostility against Me—I also was acting with hostility against *them*, to bring *them* into the land of their enemies—or if *their* uncircumcised heart becomes humbled so that *they* then make amends for *their* iniquity . . ." (Lev. 26:40-41).

It is apparent that the entire scope of Moses' prophetic vision included both Israel's contemporary *and* future generations. This does not at all appear to be the prophetic scope of Jesus' remarks. In stark contrast, nothing we have seen in Jesus' statements gives the impression that the noted events go beyond his contemporary generation. The entire context of the discourse involves the things that they, the disciples present, would see and experience. Even the singular occurrence of the word *they*, which occurs in Matthew 24:30 (cf. Mark 13:26), is a reference to the great mourning and the agony of the Jews when they witnessed the destruction of their city and temple as the Son of Man came to judge:

> "And then the sign of the Son of Man will appear in the heavens. And then all *the tribes of the land will wail*. And they will see the Son of Man coming on the clouds of heaven with power and much glory."
> (Matt. 24:30, LITV).

The disciples would not be given to such mourning. They would be enlightened by the Holy Spirit, whom Jesus was going to send to them, and would show them and give them an understanding of the things that were coming upon the nation. (John 16:12-15). The Spirit would bring to their remembrance all that Jesus' said. The event was inevitable, fast approaching, and the divine purpose behind it included their own deliverance and the birth of the new age:

From Jamieson-Fausset-Brown's respected commentary:

> If the reader will turn to Dan. 7:13, Dan. 7:14 . . . He seems to us, by "the Son of man . . . coming in the clouds with great power and glory," to mean, that when judicial vengeance shall once have been executed upon Jerusalem, and the ground thus cleared for the unobstructed establishment of His own kingdom . . . it can hardly be understood of anything else than the full and free establishment of the kingdom of Christ on the destruction of Jerusalem.[21]

We will consider additional data supportive of a historical fulfillment, but for now, we'll proceed with reasonable confidence that he spoke to a specific group of men and their historical context:

- They would see false messiahs and false prophets.
- They would hear of wars and rumors of wars.
- They would witness outbreaks of famine.

- They would see cities devastated by earthquakes.

- They would be persecuted, causing some believers to stumble in fear and depart from the faith. This would cause diminishing love, leading to increasing fear, self-preservation, and betrayal. Those who endured would be delivered.

- Despite the persecutions and turmoil of the era, they would take the gospel into all the world before the age of the Law came to an end.

Then, as the time of the temple and the city's destruction grew near:

- They would see the abomination of desolation, and immediately any faithful Christians in Jerusalem and its vicinity would have to flee to safety.

- They would stand at a time of unparalleled tribulation culminating in a great power transition in the heavens and the sign that Christ, the Son of Man, was coming on the clouds of heaven, as prophesied by Daniel (Dan. 7:13-14). That sign (*not a visible sign in the sky*) would be the fall of Jerusalem, the temple, and the Jewish economy, all of which had historically represented God's testimony to humanity. It would be the sign that the dominion of the Son of Man was now established.

- At the sight of the city and temple's destruction, there would be great despair and agony; *the tribes of the land would mourn greatly.*

In other words, everything of which Jesus warned concerning the end of the age was about to take place before the passing of that generation. His use of imagery is consistent with prophetic speech, the relevant audience is identified, and the conditions he described can be historically authenticated.

Gems from Matthew 13:
The Disciples Understood

A seemingly convincing argument offered by many is that Jesus' words were meant for a future generation, which might make some sense if interpreted in a wooden, literal manner. However, we cannot overlook that the subsequent New Testament teachings of the apostles affirmed their understanding of what Jesus taught them. They expected those things to occur in their own time. The apostles were never mistaken about the nature and timing of these events. Nor did they, as we will see, anticipate a centuries-long delay in their fulfillment.

Observe their response to Jesus in Matthew 13, prior to the Olivet Discourse, concerning the end of the age in parables:

> "The harvest is *the end of the age*, and the reapers are angels" (Matt.13:39).

> "Just as the weeds are gathered and burned with fire, so will it be at *the end of the age*" (Matt.13:40).

> "So it will be at *the end of the age*. The angels will come out and separate the evil from the righteous" (Matt. 13:49).

After Jesus stated the preceding, the following simple but significant exchange took place between him and his disciples:

> "Have you understood all these things?" *They said to Him, "Yes."* (Matt. 13:51).

The gospel writers are candid about the disciples' frequent misinterpretations of Jesus' words. There are many recorded instances in their accounts where this is seen. In some instances, it was almost comedic. When they were wrong, he let them know. Here, the Lord did not contest their response. The end of the age was consistent with their Jewish training, and Jesus had just told them:

Jesus answered them, *"To you it has been granted to know the mysteries of the kingdom* of heaven, but to them [probably the Jews and their leaders in attendance: v.14-15] it has not been granted" (Matt. 13:11).

As we will see, their concept of Messiah and the end of the age had to do with his mission and victory in the season of his presence in Israel. Jewish theology of the time offered no *futuristic* ideas regarding a messianic return from heaven to earth at a distant time. Israel's hope rested on the fact that Messiah's entire mission was to be completed at the time of his rise to power. We will examine this further in our discussion of the ages.

Returning to Matthew 13, in this same context, Jesus followed up with the illustration that both the Old Testament and the coming revelation by the Holy Spirit would be sources of insight for them:

"And Jesus said to them, Therefore every scribe who has become a disciple of the kingdom of heaven is like a head of a household, who brings out of his treasure things new and old" (Matt. 13:52).

It is remarkable, considering the premise of our study, that in the context of teaching about the end of the age in Matthew 13, Jesus tells his disciples (note: only in Matthew) that the Old Testament would be a treasure chest of knowledge in matters of eschatology!

Matthew 13:52 tells us that their own history would provide clues as to what was about to befall the nation as God's redemptive story transitioned to the messianic age. Later, at the Last Supper, Jesus promised his disciples that:

"When He, the Spirit of truth, comes, He will guide you into all the truth . . . He will disclose to you what is to come" (John 16:13).

Jesus promised the disciples that not only their historical texts but also the Holy Spirit, who was to be given to them, would bring clarity concerning things to come. Through Pentecost, they received the essential understanding and were not mistaken in their expectations concerning the nation's last days, the day of the Lord, and Jesus' return. At Pentecost, Peter announced to the Jews in Jerusalem, who were gathered there from the nations, that:

> ". . . *this is what was spoken* of through the prophet Joel: 'and it shall be *in the last days*,' God says, 'THAT I WILL POUR FORTH OF MY SPIRIT ON ALL MANKIND . . . THE SUN WILL BE TURNED INTO DARKNESS AND THE MOON INTO BLOOD, BEFORE THE GREAT AND GLORIOUS DAY OF THE LORD SHALL COME. 'AND IT SHALL BE THAT EVERYONE WHO CALLS ON THE NAME OF THE LORD WILL BE SAVED'" (Acts 2:16-21).

The events described in the Olivet Discourse are those leading up to the desolation of the temple and Jerusalem, not the end of the world. The prophesied events can all be historically authenticated. The destruction of Jerusalem by the Romans was looming on the horizon, and the apostles understood this and communicated it to the churches.

CHAPTER 6

THE OLIVET DISCOURSE
NARRATIVE AND CULTURAL CONTEXT

Jesus' predictions concerning the destruction of Jerusalem and the temple constitute the entire framework of the Olivet Discourse, as recorded for us in Matthew 24:2-3, Mark 13:1-4, and Luke 21:5-7. It would seem that the prophecy straightforwardly referred to that event, as well as the conditions in the decades leading up to it. In Matthew 23 (Part I of the Discourse), we see that Jesus severely rebuked the Pharisees, who were guilty of gross failures regarding the truth of God, just like their ancestors. He then declared to them that judgment was coming upon their generation and that their house was to be left to themselves and desolate.

The Pharisees and their scribes were a separate faction from the Sadducees. The Sadducees were the wealthiest and most powerful sect and controlled the Sanhedrin (the supreme council in Judaism). They maintained their power center in Jerusalem, were religious rationalists, and were also sympathetic to Rome. Jesus has nothing to say to them in this indictment. He knew this sect was soon to vanish, and it did. The sect of the Sadducees disappeared from history after the Jewish-Roman war. We'll see a likely reference to the Sadducees and their elite associates in the Book of Revelation.

In contrast, the party of the Pharisees were the leading keepers and instructors of the Law, the Prophets, and the oral traditions passed down through their generations. Their scribes managed many of their administrative tasks. Jesus confronts them both in Matthew 23:

> "Woe to you, scribes and Pharisees, hypocrites! . . . how are you to escape being sentenced to hell [gehenna]? Therefore, I send you prophets and wise men and scribes, some of whom you will kill and crucify, and some you will flog in your synagogues and persecute from town to town, so that on you may come all the righteous blood shed on earth [*or, Greek: "*the land*"] . . . Truly, I say to you, all these things will come upon this generation. O Jerusalem, Jerusalem, the city that kills the prophets and stones those who are sent to it! How often would I have gathered your children together as a hen gathers her brood under her wings, and you would not! See, your house is left to you desolate [cf. Jer. 22:5]. For I tell you, you will not see me again, until you say, 'Blessed is he who comes in the name of the Lord'" (from Matt. 23:1-39; *The Jewish people of that generation were obviously not responsible for all bloodshed on the whole earth).

Immediately following his rebuke of the scribes and Pharisees and the declaration of Jerusalem's demise, we are told in Scripture that:

> As He was going out of the temple, one of His disciples said to Him, "Teacher, behold what wonderful stones and what wonderful buildings!" (Mark 13:1; cf. Matt. 24:1; Luke 21:5).

The words that Jesus had just spoken concerning their house clearly meant that their city and temple were being abandoned by God and subjected to the Roman forces about to descend upon them. The disciples' subsequent remarks regarding the beauty of the temple in Jerusalem prompted Jesus' initial retort about its certain destruction. This became the catalyst for their questioning of him. The Olivet Discourse is Jesus' response to their inquiry. As we observed in Matthew 13, the disciples had a rudimentary understanding of *what* Jesus meant by *the end of the age*. Now they were going to question how they would know it was about to occur.

Understanding the Disciples' Inquiry

We must not allow the chapter division between Matthew 23 and 24 to interrupt the continuity of the narrative. Their questions arose from a specific context in Matthew 23, and therefore, if we don't account for that context and the nature of their inquiry, we will not fundamentally understand what the Lord Jesus was preparing them for. The Lord responded to them by declaring that the temple complex (the very one they were looking at) would be utterly destroyed:

And He said to them, "Do you not see all these things? Truly I say to you, not one stone here will be left upon another, which will not be torn down" (Matt. 24:2).

And Jesus said to him, "Do you see these great buildings? Not one stone will be left upon another which will not be torn down" (Mark 13:2).

"*As for* these things which you are looking at, the days will come in which there will not be left one stone upon another which will not be torn down" (Luke 21:6).

Upon hearing his words, the most obvious questions on the minds of his disciples would be, "When?" "How will we know?" "What will be a warning that this is about to happen?" Here, we must see their inquiry from the perspectives of each of the Gospels. The distinctions in how each framed the questions are important for our understanding:

Beginning with Mark:

And as He was sitting on the Mount of Olives opposite the temple, Peter and James and John and Andrew were questioning Him privately, "Tell us, when will these things be, and what will be the sign when all these things are going to be [lit., *about to be*] fulfilled? (Mark 13:3-4).

Then Luke:

They questioned Him, saying, "Teacher, when therefore will these things happen? And what will be the sign when these things are about to take place?" (Luke 21:7).

Mark and Luke record two entirely connected questions: "When will these things happen?" "Will there be a sign that they are *about to take place?*" There is little doubt as to what they had in mind. The questions focused on the timing and events surrounding the temple's destruction, as Jesus had just described. However, Matthew's account adds a dimension that is highly relevant and the topic of much scholarly debate because it is alleged that Matthew records three distinct questions:

As He was sitting on the Mount of Olives, the disciples came to Him privately, saying, "Tell us, when will these things happen, and what will be the sign of your coming, *and of the end of the age?*" (Matt. 24:3).

The word translated as *coming* is the Greek word *parousia*. Klaus Berger sums up its meaning and origin more precisely than our first mention of the term in Chapter 1:

The Hellenistic term "parousia" means the arrival, visit and presence of armies, officials, rulers and gods. There is no equivalent in the [Old

Testament] . . . the term is used in Jewish apocalyptic in Greek, in the *Testaments of the Twelve Patriarchs* and the *Testament of Abraham*. In the [New Testament] too, ancient Greek elements: are linked with [Old Testament] notions of the Day (of judgment) of Yahweh.[22]

Close, Yet Miles Apart

There is significance in the slight differences in how the disciples' questions are recorded. These variations in the gospel narratives can be troubling for some, but they are not accidental or contradictory. Dennis Bratcher insightfully explains:

> Even in the Gospels, there are places where the writers stop and explain Jewish customs (e.g., Mk 7:3), an indication that the people to whom they were writing were not familiar with them . . . Jews would need to hear the message in one way, while Greeks with different interests, background, and concerns would need to hear it in a different way. Even among Jews, traditional Palestinian Jews most likely needed to hear it in different terms than Hellenistic Jews . . . we might ask which version was the 'original' version, and therefore which one was 'true' . . . The better question is: 'What was this author trying to say by telling us the tradition in this way? . . . They [the Gospel writers] were not simply editors or compilers who passed on what they had heard without comment. They took an active role in trying to bring the Gospel tradition alive within a certain context and for a certain purpose and likely for a certain audience.[23]

The Holy Spirit purposefully arranged the accounts through our gospel writers so that their audiences would understand. Neither Mark nor Luke mentioned anything about an end of the age, which was a concept unique to the audience of Matthew's gospel. The phrase is not found in any other gospel, yet it occurs five times in Matthew (13:39; 40; 49; 24:3; 28:20). Jesus' disciples were anticipating the end of the Mosaic age, which would usher in the Messianic age, *not the destruction of the planet*. Yet, in apparent contrast to this, the popular *futurist* view is that the disciples asked *three* questions, which creates a problem:

- Tell us, when will these things happen?
- and what will be the sign of your coming?
- and [what will be the sign(s)] of the end of the age?

First, Matthew does not present a third question besides those recorded by Mark and Luke. He merely places the disciples' identical inquiry into a framework suited to his target audience. This is the beauty of the fourfold gospel. Each was tailored to meet inquiries from different cultural milieus. This is not to suggest that these distinctions should be rigidly imposed upon the text, because the four accounts also hold much material in common. There are, however, clearly unique characteristics of Jesus' story in each gospel that relate to a specific audience.

These principles are commonly understood and typically taught in Bible studies and seminaries concerning the nature of the Gospels. It is unfortunate that they are so rarely employed in the actual process of interpretation. For Mark and Luke, the questions are clearly to be understood as to "when" and "what conditions (signs)" would accompany or foreshadow the destruction of the temple. However, the unique phrase *end of the age* is mentioned only by Matthew because both Jesus' disciples and the audience to whom Matthew would tailor his gospel would possess a unique interest in what the temple's destruction would mean. Among the prevailing beliefs concerning the age to come were their anticipation of the construction of a third temple and the rebuilding of Jerusalem. So, their inquiry related to the *end of the age (aion)* in Matthew's account. It was specifically tied to their eschatological hopes of Messiah's defeat of Rome and the restoration of the kingdom of Israel as head of the nations.

Second, neither Jesus nor the disciples mention the end of the world (Greek: *kosmos,* the whole harmonious order of the creation). They inquired about the end of the age. Some older Bible versions have unfortunately mistranslated the term aion (age) as world.

The Ages

The rabbis, although having diverse opinions, taught that there would be much turmoil associated with the coming Messianic age. It was to be a transition period that ushered in a new world order called the age (or world) to come. In Hebrew, it is called *olam haba*. This would bring an end to the present age (or world system), called *olam hazeh*. It was believed that many wonders would occur at this time, including the resurrection of the dead and, as some held, the reconstitution of the world system under Judaism.

The earliest known source in which the phrase olam haba occurs is the Book of Enoch, which arose out of Second Temple Judaism sometime during the three centuries before Christ (scholarly opinions vary concerning its date). Robert Charles' translation reads:

> And he said unto me: 'He proclaims unto thee peace in the name of the world to come [olam haba]; For from hence has proceeded peace since the creation of the world, And so shall it be unto thee for ever and for ever and ever.[24]

The Lord Jesus recognized, or at the very least accommodated, this two-age Jewish worldview:

> "Whoever speaks a word against the Son of Man, it shall be forgiven him; but whoever speaks against the Holy Spirit, it shall not be forgiven him, either in this age [olam hazeh] or in the age to come [olam haba]" (Matt.12:32; cf. Mark 13:29).

When is this "Age to Come?"

Christians commonly misunderstand the phrase *age to come* in the New Testament. However, understanding it correctly can entirely change how we see the first century and the New Testament itself. As a first consideration, we must understand that the New Testament teaches that Jesus was born in the age of law:

> But when the fullness of the time came, God sent forth His Son, born of a woman, *born under the Law* (Gal. 4:4).

As previously seen in our two-age diagram, the age in which the first century church lived was a period of transition out of the age of the Law and its controlling powers, which were sin and death. The covenantal spaces and practices of the old system (the land, the city, the temple, and the priestly offerings) had been judicially abolished and rendered obsolete at the cross. Now they were about to be physically removed from their place in God's economy, as we saw in the Letter to the Hebrews:

> When He said, A New Covenant, He has made the first obsolete. But whatever *is becoming obsolete and growing old is ready to disappear* (Heb. 8:13).

Therefore, if we recognize that the disciples understood the temple's destruction to mean the end of the age, then the *age to come* from the standpoint of the New Testament *must be the church age*. This may shock some who think that the age to come is (strictly) heaven or an alleged future millennial golden age. It is not, as we will see in Revelation. This corresponds to the Jewish olam haba. The long-anticipated olam haba was to be ushered in at the time of the presence (*parousia*) of Messiah. Again, we read:

> And when he is sitting on the Mount of the Olives, the disciples came near to him by himself, saying, "Tell us, when shall these be? and what is the sign of thy presence [*parousia*], and of the full end of the age?" (Matt. 24:3 YLT).

The word *parousia* (coming; arrival) is employed in the text. We have just observed that it has no equivalent in the Old Testament. The significance of the fact that the term is rooted in Jewish second-temple literature must not be underestimated. It clearly suggests that the disciples were inquiring in the context of learned rabbinical traditions of their time. The question of the disciples had everything to do with the ushering in of the expected age of Messiah and the olam haba in the first century AD, as eminent New Testament scholar N. T. Wright observes:

> . . . within the mainline Jewish writings of this period, covering a wide range of styles, genres, political persuasions and theological perspectives, there is virtually no evidence the Jews were expecting the end of the space-time universe . . . They believed that the present world order would come to an end . . . in which pagans held power, and Jews, the covenant people of the creator God, did not.[25]

Third, as previously mentioned, the disciples had no concept of Jesus returning to earth at a far-off future end of the world because they didn't even understand he was about to die, rise from the dead, and ascend to heaven. Despite the earlier disclosure concerning their knowledge of the end of the age, the disciples did not understand that it would come about through Jesus' death and resurrection.

Let's observe how the Gospels provide strategically placed references to their blindness about Jesus' destiny. This greatly impacts our understanding of their Olivet inquiry:

Prior to the Olivet Discourse, the twelve did not comprehend Jesus' impending death and resurrection:

> For He was teaching His disciples and telling them, "The Son of Man is to be delivered into the hands of men, and they will kill Him; and when He has been killed, He will rise three days later." But *they did not understand* this statement, and they were afraid to ask Him. (Mark 9:31-32).

After the Olivet Discourse (and even after his resurrection), they did not comprehend his resurrection:

> *For as yet they did not understand* the Scripture, that He must rise again from the dead (John 20:9).

During his post-resurrection appearances, he rebuked the disciples for not understanding his death and resurrection:

> And He said to them, "O foolish men and *slow of heart to believe* in all that the prophets have spoken! Was it not necessary for the Christ to suffer these things and to enter into His glory?" (Luke 24:25-26).

These gospel texts show the disciples' fundamental blindness to Jesus' pending death, resurrection, and ascension. How, then, is it possible that just prior to his sacrifice on the cross, they would question him on the Mount of Olives concerning a second coming from heaven at the end of the world? Such a notion was not even remotely in their worldview. It would have been like asking Jesus how long before George Washington would be President of the United States!

Their inquiry was entirely related to the things he had just said to them pertaining to the fall of Jerusalem and the end of the Mosaic era. According to their Jewish understanding, these events were related to the *days of Messiah* and ultimately the *age to come*. This was all to take place, not at a future time but at the precise time of Messiah's life and ministry, as Wright explains:

> . . . There was no reason, either in their [disciples'] own background or in a single thing that Jesus had said to them up to that point, for it even to occur to them that the true story of the world, or of Israel, or of Jesus himself, might include either the end of the space-time universe, or Jesus or anyone else floating down to earth on a cloud.[26]

There were and have always been diverse views among the Jews regarding the time and events relating to the Messiah. To examine the context of Judaism with any accuracy would require far too much space in this work. Yet, there appears to have been no connection in the minds of these Jewish disciples between the destruction of the temple in Jerusalem and a post-ascension return of Messiah from heaven. The disciples simply had no such perception.

The great Alfred Edersheim, a renowned Hebrew scholar of the nineteenth century, penned the following insights. He explains how the *time (or days) of Messiah* stood in transition between the end of their current age and the birth of the new age. According to Edersheim (who references relevant Jewish source material), the following scenario captures what was likely to have been in the minds of the disciples when they questioned Jesus on the Mount of Olives:

> . . . according to general opinion, the birth of the Messiah would be unknown to His contemporaries; that He would appear, carry on His work, then disappear–probably for forty-five days; then reappear again, and destroy the hostile powers of the world, notably 'Edom,' 'Armilos,' the Roman Power - the fourth and last world-empire . . . We have now reached the period of the 'coming age' . . . All the resistance to God would be concentrated in the great war of Gog and Magog, and with it the prevalence of all the wickedness be conjoined [combined] . . . Three times would the enemy seek to storm the Holy City. But each time would the assault be repelled - at the last with complete destruction of the enemy. The sacred City would now be wholly rebuilt and inhabited . . . And with a view to [a] new Law, which God would give to his world through the Messiah . . .[27]

As you can see, the disciples, who were rooted in Jewish thought, would not have expected Jesus' death, or return from heaven. Their worldview most likely allowed for the short-term disappearance of Messiah (probably 45 or 90 days), then for him to return within that time frame as their military leader in the war against Rome. His great victory would re-establish Israel as the head of the nations. According to Kohler, who also references Jewish sources in the *Jewish Encyclopedia*, his brief disappearance was to be like that of Moses (see Exo. 24:1-18; Deu. 18:15):

Renewal of the Time of Moses.

> . . . manna will again be sent down from heaven (Ps. lxxii. 16; comp. Ps. lxxviii. 24; Syriac Apoc. Baruch, xxix. 8); and water rise from

beneath by miraculous power (Joel iv. [A. V. iii.] 18; comp. Ps. lxxviii. 15 et seq.; Eccl. R. i. 9). Like Moses, the Messiah will disappear for 90 or 45 days after his appearance.[28]

Further along, Jesus even alludes to this misunderstanding in a parable. He debunks the notion of a speedy return, knowing there was likely to be as much as a forty-year wait. He told the disciples:

"Now *after a long time* the master of those slaves came and settled accounts with them" (Matt. 25:19).

The "long time" to which Jesus refers does not have to be a period of 2000 years or more, as is popularly understood. Forty years is a long wait if you're expecting someone in 45 days. The common interpretation that a long time must encompass the entire church age is based on presumption and is nowhere suggested by the text.

The disciples expected that Messiah's disappearance would end in less than three months. His return and presence would mean Rome's defeat and the restoration of Israel as the head of the nations in the age to come. We have seen that the twelve did not understand his death and resurrection either before or after this discourse. One would have to reject the clear testimony of the Gospels to believe they were asking him about a far-off, future return from heaven.

Fourth, we must consider the use of the Greek word *kai* in Matthew's version of the question as it relates to Jesus' parousia:

"Tell us, when will these things happen, and what *will be* the sign of Your coming, and [*kai: even; which is to say*] of the end of the age?" (Matt. 24:3)

As we will occasionally see, this common Greek word not only means *and or also,* but has an explicative sense, meaning "which is to say"(the end of the age). It strengthens and clarifies the preceding expression. Reading Matthew 24:3 in that manner eliminates the phrase *the end of the age* as a *third* question. Instead, it links to it as an explanation of the preceding questions from a Jewish perspective. The signs, his parousia, and the end of the age make up one series of events. There is no need to look out into our future for an alleged "end of the age" in this discourse.

Misplacing 1ˢᵗ Century AD Events?

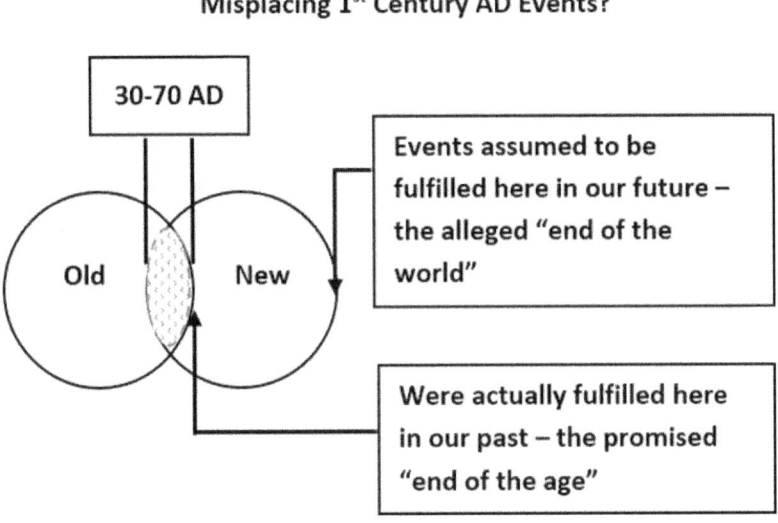

Let's Summarize

1. In Matthew 23, Jesus condemned the contemporary Jewish establishment for their hypocrisy and declared that their economy and treasured institutions would be destroyed. This would occur before that generation passed.

2. In Matthew 24, Mark 13, and Luke 21, as the disciples were admiring the temple complex, Jesus again affirmed the certainty of its destruction. The disciples inquired as to the timing of the event and the signs or indications by which they would know it was about to occur. There is no indication that their inquiry related to anything other than their current age, the olam hazeh.

3. Matthew's account uniquely employs a particular Jewish theological reference to the *end of the age* not mentioned by Mark or Luke because it was far less relevant to, or understood by, the audiences of those two writers. This reference had a specific meaning to Palestinian Jews regarding the end of the Mosaic era, the time of Messiah, and the dawning of their long-awaited age to come.

4. In Matthew's account, the disciples did not ask a *third* question regarding Jesus' return at the end of the world. They clearly did not understand what was about to take place, specifically his death, resurrection, and ascension. Therefore, they had no concept of his going to heaven and returning at a distant future time. This was a question that they were incapable of raising. They asked concerning his arrival, which corresponded to the end of their current age.

5. In Matthew 25 (which we will examine in Chapter 10), the references to his disciples' waiting a long time for Jesus' return must be understood in the context of the expectation that their Messiah was to briefly disappear then physically return within a short time (45–90 days). Jesus corrected this expectation that was founded in their Jewish learning. He admonished them that it could be as much as forty years rather than two or three months, which, in fact, occurred.

Hopefully, this has provided you with a better understanding of the key elements of the narrative and cultural contexts of Jesus' Olivet Discourse. Let us now turn to the evidence of history to determine to what extent it substantiates his predictions concerning the times his disciples were about to face in their generation.

CHAPTER 7

THE OLIVET DISCOURSE
HISTORICAL DATA: THE EMPIRE

Although it is unknown to many Christians, there is a considerable amount of historical and biblical data relating to the various signs and events of Jesus' prophecy on Mount Olivet. I would encourage anyone who thinks that these things of which Jesus spoke did not occur in the lifetime of the disciples to do some personal research. There is an abundance of historical data in books and free, reputable online resources.

The Prophetic Ministry of Jesus

Among the many purposes to be accomplished by the Son of God through his journey into humanity was to serve as a prophetic voice to the nation of Israel. As God in the flesh, he visited this planet first and foremost to surrender his life on the cross once and for all to destroy the power of sin and death. However, at the same time, there was another purpose. He had unfinished business concerning his historical people, the Jews. This is clear in the gospel narratives:

> But He answered and said, "I was sent only to the lost sheep of the house of Israel" (Matt.15:24).

This was the time of their promised ingathering, but it was also a final warning to Israel that the day of reckoning was near. Jesus came as their Messiah, bringing healing, deliverance, and many signs and wonders. Yet, relatively few received him. The certainty of this imminent day of judgment was present in many of his parables, especially during encounters with Jewish leaders. However, a promised remnant was being gathered to his new nation, the church. That new nation would bring forth the fruits of the kingdom. However, for Israel as a whole, the coming days would bring about unparalleled destruction. That destruction would cause the final, irreversible expulsion from their privileged status as the holy nation of God:

> "Therefore, I say to you, the kingdom of God will be taken away from you and given to a people, producing the fruit of it" (Matt. 21:43).

Historical and Biblical Evidence

As Jesus departed from his confrontation with the Jewish leaders in Matthew 23, he immediately prophesied to his disciples (in Matthew 24) regarding when and how this transference of the privileges of citizenship in God's kingdom would take place. What follows are selected observations, all of which occurred in the four decades after

Christ's resurrection in the generation of the apostles. These observations parallel Chapter 5, our earlier list of what the disciples would witness.

Historians, biblical scholars, and non-sympathetic witnesses furnish the relevant historical data. Non-Christian sources of history, such as Josephus or Tacitus, were obviously not attempting to validate the prophetic statements that Jesus made. However, their recorded accounts substantiate elements of the Lord's prophecy, demonstrating the occurrence of what Jesus foretold. In some instances, the New Testament itself furnishes or confirms the history.

> *The reader should recognize that it is unnecessary for every minor historical detail of that century to fulfill Jesus' words. Exhaustive proofs of how "this fulfills that" can be both tedious and unnecessary. The historical records of the time (including those of the New Testament) clearly provide sufficient evidence of conditions that correspond to his prophetic statements.*

The samples of historical data that we will observe are not in any way exhaustive. However, I am confident that they are adequate to demonstrate to the reader that there is ample historical and New Testament evidence of the first-century fulfillment of the things that Jesus foretold.

Upon concluding his indictment of the religious leadership of the Jews and declaring that the temple would be destroyed, Jesus proceeded to inform his disciples of the historical conditions that would arise in their generation:

1. **False messiahs and false prophets would arise.**

And Jesus answered and said to them, "See to it that no one misleads you. For many will come in My name, saying, I am the Christ, and will mislead many" (Matt. 24:4).

Historical Data:

Josephus:

. . . these impostors and deceivers persuaded the multitude to follow them into the wilderness, and pretended that they would exhibit manifest wonders and signs . . . [29]

The Book of Acts:

For some time ago Theudas rose up, claiming to be somebody, and a group of about four hundred men joined up with him . . . After this man, Judas of Galilee rose up in the days of the census and drew away some people after him . . . (Acts 5:36).

Then you are not the Egyptian who some time ago stirred up a revolt and led the four thousand men of the Assassins out into the wilderness? (Acts 21:38).

Thomas Newton:

. . . in the reign of Nero, and under the procuratorship of Felix, these impostors arose so frequent, that many of them were apprehended and killed every day. They seduced great numbers of the people. [30]

2. Military conflicts would erupt.

"You will be hearing of wars and rumors of wars. See that you are not frightened, for those things must take place, but that is not yet the end. For nation will rise against nation, and kingdom against kingdom" (Matt. 24:6-7).

Historical Data

Tacitus:

Despite the *Pax Romana* (Roman Peace), Tacitus wrote that many conflicts arose in the empire leading up to 70 AD. He mentions Germany, Africa, Thrace, Gaul, the Parthians, the war in Britain, and war in Armenia.[31]

The following is a list of just some of the Roman wars and civil uprisings that occurred between 36 and 66 AD during the decades following Jesus' resurrection:

First Century Roman Conflicts

36-66 AD	Conflicts
36	Revolt of the Cietae in Cappadocia: revolt suppressed by Marcus Trebellius
38 & 40	Alexandrian riots
40 - 44	Revolt of Aedemon and Sabalus in Mauretania: revolt suppressed by Gaius Suetonius Paulinus and Gnaeus Hosidius Geta
41	Caligula overthrown by the Praetorian Guard, senators, and courtiers. Claudius proclaimed emperor
42	Failed usurpation of Lucius Arruntius Camillus Scribonianus in Dalmatia
43	The Roman conquest of Britain (43–96)
46	Revolt in Thrace–revolt suppressed
46 - 48	Jacob and Simon uprising in the Galilee: revolt suppressed
58-63	The Roman and Parthian War
60 - 61	Boudica's uprising in Britain: revolt suppressed by Gaius Suetonius Paulinus

Table 7.1
From Wikipedia: Roman Wars, Edited to Suit[32]

3. There would be outbreaks of famine.

". . . and in various places there will be famines" (Matt. 24:7).

Historical Data:

Christian Historian, Eusebius:

Under [Claudius Caesar] the world was visited with a famine, which writers that are entire strangers to our religion have recorded in their histories. And thus the prediction of Agabus recorded in the Acts of the Apostles [Acts 11:28], according to which the whole world was to be visited by a famine, received its fulfillment.[33]

4. Earthquakes would occur.

". . . and in various places there will be . . . earthquakes" (Matt. 24:7).

Historical Data:

Holford:

In the reign of Claudius there was one at Rome and another at Apamea in Syria . . . latter . . . was so destructive; that the emperor. . . remitted its tribute for five years . . . There was one also . . . in Crete. This is mentioned by Philostratus, in his *Life of Apollonius*, who says, that 'there were others at Smyrna, Miletus, Chios, and Samos . . . In the reign of Nero there was an earthquake at Laodicea. Tacitus records this also. It is likewise mentioned by Eusebius and Orosius, who add that Hierapolis and Colossae, and Laodicea, were overthrown by an earthquake [see Col. 4:12-13 – Paul mentions a concern for these cities in advance of the event] There was also one in Campania . . . (of this both Tacitus and Seneca speak; and another at Rome in the reign of Galba, recorded by Suetonius).[34]

Tacitus (describes an earthquake and famine):

. . . houses were overturned by repeated shocks of earthquake, and, as the panic spread . . . A shortage of corn, again, and the famine which resulted, were construed as a supernatural warning . . .

Claudius, sitting in judgement, was surrounded by a wildly clamorous mob . . . It was established that the capital had provisions for fifteen days, no more.[35]

5. **Jesus' disciples would be persecuted; some followers would stumble in fear and depart from the faith. There would be widespread hatred and betrayal. However, those who endured would be delivered.**

"Then they will deliver you to tribulation, and will kill you, and you will be hated by all nations because of My name. At that time many will fall away and will betray one another and hate one another . . . Because lawlessness is increased, most people's love will grow cold. But the one who endures to the end, he will be saved" (Matt. 24:10-13).

Historical Data:

The Book of Acts:

And on that day a great persecution began against the church in Jerusalem . . . Saul began ravaging the church, entering house after house, and dragging off men and women, he would put them in prison (Acts 8:1-3).

First Thessalonians:

. . . you also endured the same sufferings at the hands of your own countrymen, even as they did from the Jews (1 Thes. 2:14).

Tacitus:

. . . to stop the rumor [that he had set Rome on fire], Emperor Nero falsely charged with guilt, and punished with the most fearful tortures, the persons commonly called Christians . . .

. . .first those were arrested who confessed they were Christians; next on their information, a vast multitude were convicted, not so much on the charge of burning the city, as of "hating the human race."[36]

6. **The gospel would go out into all the world.**

"This gospel of the kingdom shall be preached in the whole world [*oikoumene: inhabited world; empire*] as a testimony to all the nations, and then the end will come." (Matt. 24:14).

Historical Data:

Paul to the Colossians:

All over the world [*oikoumene*] this gospel is bearing fruit and growing . . . This is the gospel that you heard and that *has been proclaimed to every creature under heaven* (Col. 1:6, 23).

And to the Romans:

. . . I thank my God through Jesus Christ for you all, because your faith is being proclaimed throughout the whole world (Rom. 1:8)

Excursus:
The Significance of Matthew 24:14

Jesus' words regarding the spread of the gospel to the whole world (*oikoumene*) were fulfilled in the first century, before the *end* came (the destruction of Jerusalem). However, this does not imply that it would then cease to be spread. Jesus declared that the great ingathering foreseen by the prophets would be fulfilled in the lifetime of the apostles.

As we have seen, Isaiah prophesied concerning a time to come when there would be a great ingathering of Jews and Gentiles throughout the world *during that time in history*. The Jewish remnant was the company of *survivors* who would come to faith in Christ:

"The time is coming to gather all nations and tongues. And they shall come and see My glory. I will set a sign among them and will send survivors from them to the nations . . . And they will declare My glory among the nations. Then they shall bring all your brethren from all the nations as a grain offering to the LORD, on horses, in chariots, in litters, on mules and on camels, to My holy mountain Jerusalem, says the LORD, just as the sons of Israel bring their grain offering in a clean vessel to the house of the LORD. I will also take some of them for priests and for Levites, says the LORD. For just as the new heavens and the new earth Which I make will endure before Me, declares the LORD, So your offspring and your name will endure" (Isa. 66:18-22).

The New Testament contains time indicators that relate to Isaiah's prophecy. In his Letter to the Romans, the apostle Paul sees his own first-century ministry as a "survivor." His ministry is *priestly*, and his churches are his *offering* to the Lord:

But I have written very boldly to you on some points so as to remind you again, because of the grace that was given me from God, to be a minister of Christ Jesus to the Gentiles, ministering as a priest the gospel of God, so that my offering of the Gentiles may become acceptable, sanctified by the Holy Spirit (Rom. 15:15).

Also, the Letter to the Hebrews informs its Jewish readers that they had arrived at Isaiah's holy mountain, Jerusalem, as prophesied in Isaiah 66:20. However, they needed to understand that it was *a heavenly and not an earthly mountain city*:

For you have not come to a mountain that can be touched . . . But *you have come to Mount Zion* and to the City of the living God, the heavenly Jerusalem, and to . . . the church of the firstborn who are enrolled in heaven (Heb. 12:18-23).

The same remnant is revealed in the Book of Revelation, which suggests that John did not see something far off in the future but the same first-century remnant. They were the promised *first fruits* of God's harvest:

Then I looked, and behold, *the Lamb was standing on Mount Zion, and with Him one hundred and forty-four thousand* . . . These have been purchased from among men as first fruits to God and to the Lamb (Rev. 14:1-4).

The Jewish remnant was being gathered at the time of the apostles. It was in their *present* time, just like the remnant in Elijah's own time (1 Kings 19:18). Isaiah 66 foresees the empire-wide spread of the gospel to gather that remnant to Christ before the end of the age.

> "I will . . . send survivors from them [Israel's remnant] to the nations" (Isa. 66:19).

James also explains this at the first church council in Jerusalem, recorded in Acts 15. He quotes from Amos 9:11-12, demonstrating that the restored remnant would be a nucleus to nurture the influx of Gentiles:

> . . . just as it is written, "AFTER THESE THINGS I WILL RETURN, AND I WILL REBUILD THE TABERNACLE OF DAVID WHICH HAS FALLEN, AND I WILL REBUILD ITS RUINS, AND I WILL RESTORE IT, SO THAT THE REST OF MANKIND MAY SEEK THE LORD, <u>AND</u> [*kai: "which is to say"*] ALL THE GENTILES WHO ARE CALLED BY MY NAME" (Acts 15:14-19).

"[And] all the Gentiles" is probably best understood from the context and the use of the Greek word, *kai*, to read as:

> ". . . *which is to say*, all the Gentiles . . ."

The ingathering would create a core of Jews to serve as Bible teachers for the ingathered Gentiles, who had little knowledge of Israel's God, the Scriptures, or the Messianic hope.

The Implications of Acts: 15:14-19

James' assessment contradicts the commonly alleged ingathering of Jews to Christ at the end of the world. James cites the prophet Amos as foreseeing the great ingathering so that the Gentiles may seek the Lord. It does not occur after the Gentiles have sought the Lord throughout the church age. It reflects the beginning of the gospel era, not its mischaracterized conclusion.

CHAPTER 8

THE OLIVET DISCOURSE
HISTORICAL DATA: THE ABOMINATION OF DESOLATION

Jesus' prophecy continues with a new focal point as the prophetic spotlight moves away from events occurring throughout the approaching four decades, 30–66 AD. He now brings the disciples' attention to the final 3½ years, when the Jewish war against Rome would occur, resulting in the siege and fall of Jerusalem. Luke's version of the discourse describes the conditions that the disciples are to be ready for:

> "But when you see Jerusalem surrounded by armies, then recognize that her desolation is near" (Luke 21:20).

(Continued from Chapter 7)

7. **They (the disciples) would see the abomination of desolation and immediately need to flee Jerusalem and its vicinity.**

> "Therefore, when you see the abomination of desolation which was spoken of through Daniel the prophet, standing in the Holy place (let the reader understand), then those who are in Judea must flee to the mountains. Whoever is on the housetop must not go down to get the things out that are in his house. Whoever is in the field must not turn back to get his cloak. But woe to those who are pregnant and to those who are nursing babies in those days! But pray that your flight will not be in the winter, or on a Sabbath" (Matt. 24:15-20; Mark 13:14-20; Luke 21:20-24; cf., Dan. 9:24-27).

Regarding the abomination of desolation, Jesus warned his disciples that it was something *they would see*. In Matthew, it would be something occurring in relation to Jerusalem and the temple, that is, in *a* holy location. The definite article (*the*), referring to *the* holy place, may be implied but is not actually in the text:

> "Therefore when you see the abomination of desolation which was spoken of through Daniel the prophet, standing in [the or a] holy place" (Matt. 24:15).

Mark may have had Jews in the regions distant from Jerusalem in mind, as his rendering informs us that the abomination is *standing where it should not be*. This may refer to the approach of the Roman armies in the northern and central regions of the holy land. They would have been visible well before they arrived and surrounded Jerusalem. He also warns those on the housetops in Jerusalem and throughout the land. These housetops were typically flat and accessible from outside the home. They were commonly used for gathering and recreation. They also may have offered a good vantage point from which the Judean countryside could be seen:

"But when you see the abomination of desolation standing where it should not be, The one who is on the housetop must not go down, or go in to get anything out of his house; and the one who is in the field must not turn back to get his coat" (Mark 13:14-16).

The sight of the approaching armies was to be a signal to the faithful that it was time to leave everything behind and flee to safety. Mark does not mention the temple or its holy place in his account; he only says that something is standing where it doesn't belong.

Three Accounts: One Series of Events

Some suggest that Matthew and Mark point to a world-ending tribulation, whereas Luke speaks of the events of the first century. I do not agree that this is a justifiable interpretation. The following tables parallel the three gospel accounts. I have aligned key statements side by side for the reader's benefit. It is not difficult to see that the inspired authors are speaking of the *same events with slight variations suitable to their audiences*:

Gospel Harmony:
The Abomination of Desolation

Matthew 24	Mark 13	Luke 21
15 "Therefore when you see the abomination of desolation which was spoken of through Daniel the prophet, standing in [the] holy place (let the reader understand),	14 "But when you see the abomination of desolation standing where it should not be (let the reader understand),	20 "But when you see Jerusalem surrounded by armies, then recognize that her desolation is near [*Verse 20 is Luke's equivalent to Matthew and Mark*]

Table 8.1

Gospel Harmony:
Further Alignment of the Olivet Discourse

16 then those who are in Judea must flee to the mountains.	then those who are in Judea must flee to the mountains.	21 Then those who are in Judea must flee to the mountains,
17 Whoever is on the housetop must not go down to get the things out that are in his house.	15 "The one who is on the housetop must not go down, or go in to get anything out of his house;	and those who are in the midst of the city must leave, and
18 Whoever is in the field must not turn back to get his cloak.	16 and the one who is in the field must not turn back to get his coat."	those who are in the country must not enter the city;
		22 because these are days of vengeance, so that all things which are written will be fulfilled."

Table 8.2

The Abomination of Desolation:
Luke to the Rescue

In Luke 21:20, note how his account brings clarity to Jesus' statement regarding the timing of the abomination of desolation for a non-Jewish audience:

> "But when you see Jerusalem surrounded by armies, then recognize that her desolation is near" (Luke 21:20; cf. Matt. 24:15; Mark 13:14).

The presence of the pagan armies of Rome may have merely signaled the timing of the *abomination of desolation*, but it is also a popular position among partial and full preterists that it was the very event of which Jesus spoke. A major reason is that the pagan Roman armies and their idolatrous ensigns surrounded the "holy ground" of

Jerusalem as they prepared to bring destruction upon it. Luke, as shown in the parallel verses in the preceding tables, speaks of the same events in the same period as Matthew and Mark. His record may simply identify the timing of the abomination of desolation in the temple as occurring at the same time Jerusalem was being surrounded by armies. Later in this chapter, we will briefly address the disgraceful (abominable) Zealot activities in the temple.

Observe how Matthew and Mark make special note of a sign that needed to be discerned, most likely by Jews in Jerusalem and Judea, which was not necessary for Luke's audience:

(". . . let the reader understand." -Matt. 24:15; Mark 13:14).

The phrase abomination of desolation would have had little value for Luke's non-Jewish audience. Therefore, he describes the scene appropriately for his own readers. Once again, we see how distinctions in the gospel accounts have much to do with each writer's audience. Luke's readers needed no special discernment to recognize an army approaching and surrounding Jerusalem.

I would urge that the entire context of the three accounts be understood as having a common historical reference. Unfortunately, some otherwise excellent harmonies of the four Gospels choose to realign Luke 21:20–Jerusalem *being surrounded by armies*–out of parallel configuration with Matthew and Mark's statements regarding the abomination of desolation. The decision was apparently made to place it out of parallel with the common statements in Matthew 24:15 and Mark 13:14 (for example, see Robertson 1922).[37]

The presence of the Roman armies at the onset of the war, which is Luke's description of the time of the abomination of desolation, is shown as being something historically distinct from what I would submit to be clearly parallel events in Matthew and Mark. The following table illustrates this misalignment:

Gospel Harmony:
Misalignment of the Abomination of Desolation

Matthew 24	Mark 13	Luke 21
15 *"Therefore* when you see the ABOMINATION OF DESOLATION *which was spoken of through Daniel the prophet, standing in [the] Holy place*	**14** "But *when you see the* ABOMINATION OF DESOLATION *standing where it should not be*	*[v. 20 below should be placed [here]. Instead, it is placed out of parallel alignment [below]*
		20 *"But* when you see Jerusalem surrounded by armies, *then recognize that her desolation is near."*
(let the reader understand)."	*(let the reader understand.)."*	

Table 8.3

The Past Great Tribulation

The preceding is not the only unfortunate misalignment. We also find that in addition to Luke 21:20, the second part of Luke 21:23, which mentions *great distress,* is shown as being out of parallel with Matthew 24:21 and Mark 13:19, where the *great tribulation* is mentioned. However, as in Luke 21:20, I would strongly suggest that the context requires that they describe the same historical events. We have already seen sufficient parallel declarations from the lips of Jesus to substantiate that the three descriptions captured by our gospel writers affirm that Matthew, Mark, and Luke all have conditions in the first century leading up to the invasion of Rome and the destruction of Jerusalem and the temple in view. The following table demonstrates the misplacement of Luke 21:23:

Gospel Harmony:
Misalignment of the Great Tribulation

Matthew 24	Mark 13	Luke 21
21 "For *then there will be a great tribulation,* such as has not occurred since the beginning of the world until now, nor ever will."	19 "For *those days will be a time of tribulation* such* as has not occurred since the beginning of the creation which God created until now, and never will."	*[v. 23b-24 below should be placed here] Instead, it is placed out of parallel alignment [below]*
		23b "for *there will be great distress* upon the land and wrath to this people; 24 and they will fall by the edge of the sword, and will be led captive into all the nations; and Jerusalem will be trampled underfoot by the Gentiles until the times of the Gentiles are fulfilled.

Table 8.4

The alignments in the three accounts shown in the preceding tables are apparently designed to suggest that Luke refers to the destruction of Jerusalem, whereas Matthew and Mark speak of the end of the world. I certainly respect those who propose this alignment, recognizing that gospel harmonies require diligent effort by their authors. They are valuable tools for study, but they are *not infallible.*

Although the texts themselves are the *gospel,* their alignment and chronological ordering represent the chronicler's best efforts. I would respectfully submit that what we have observed is an unfortunate misalignment of what appear to be parallel prophetic assertions. Every statement of Jesus in the three accounts is almost identical and relates to the same period and events. I would hold that the Holy Spirit guided

Luke to explain the timing of all three accounts and clarify the statements of Matthew and Mark for his Gentile audiences. Given the utterly clear parallel language of the three accounts, if Luke speaks of first-century events, then so must Matthew and Mark. They all speak of Rome's invasion of Jerusalem, and Luke adds the resulting exile of the Jews from their homeland. I invite the reader to review the preceding tables once more and determine for yourself if these three accounts speak of different periods that are two or more millennia apart, or are they simply describing the same first-century events in a manner that is suitable to their audiences?

What is the Holy Place?

We have already noted that in Mark 13:14, the abomination of desolation is *standing where it should not be*. Although I have offered a plausible explanation, this reference by itself does not provide the clarity we need because it is not as specific as the other two gospel accounts. Matthew's record, however, provides further clarity, especially if we remember that it has a unique application for a Jewish reader:

> "Therefore, when you see the abomination of desolation which was spoken of through Daniel the prophet, standing in [the; a] Holy place (let the reader understand)" (Matt. 24:15).

An *abomination was* typically something disgusting (in this case, to God); something filthy, immoral, or idolatrous:

> "The graven images of their gods you are to burn with fire; you shall not covet the silver or the gold that is on them, nor take it for yourselves, or you will be snared by it, for it is an abomination to the Lord your God" (Deu. 7:25).

Jesus' phrase is probably best understood as the abomination *causing or resulting in* desolation. It is mentioned three times in the

Book of Daniel. Its reference in Daniel 9 is specific to the events that would occur after Messiah's death and bring about the final desolation of the city, the temple, and the nation:

> "Then after the sixty-two weeks the Messiah will be cut off and have nothing, and the people of the prince who is to come will destroy the city and the sanctuary. And its end will come with a flood [a military invasion]; even to the end there will be war; desolations are determined. And he will make a firm covenant with the many for one week [or: one week shall establish the covenant], but in the middle of the week he will put a stop to sacrifice and grain offering; and on the wing [army] of abominations will come one who makes desolate, even until a complete destruction, one that is decreed, is poured out on the one who makes desolate" (Dan. 9:26-27; cf. Luke 21:23-24).

The prophecy foretold that events of redemptive significance would be accomplished prior to this abomination, during seventy weeks (or *seventy sevens*) of years. That is a total of 490 years, which was literally fulfilled, starting with the Persian decree to release the Jews (Dan. 9:24). The prophetic period would reach its fulfillment in the first century, encompassing the life and ministry of Jesus and the final determination concerning the destruction of Jerusalem. (There is some fascinating chronology pertaining to this period, but it is beyond the scope of this present study.) Jesus said that the abomination spoken of by the prophet would stand in *a holy place*. Let us now consider why this may or may not be the holy place within the temple.

The Design of the Tabernacle and the Temple

The tabernacle (the portable tent structure) was constructed in the time of Moses. It was a mobile complex and served as the habitation and throne of Israel's God. It was the center of Israelite worship and sacrifice during their forty years in the wilderness and the subsequent centuries of the rule of their judges. The tabernacle moved in and out of the Old Testament storyline until Solomon built the permanent temple in the tenth century BC. The Babylonians destroyed this temple in 586 BC. The Jews rebuilt it after their return from exile, later in the sixth century BC. It is commonly referred to as Herod's temple because of the massive reconstruction of the complex during his reign at the time of Jesus. The original tabernacle, Solomon's temple, and Herod's temple were designed with two major divisions: 1) the outer courts, and 2) the sanctuary proper.

The Tabernacle in the Wilderness

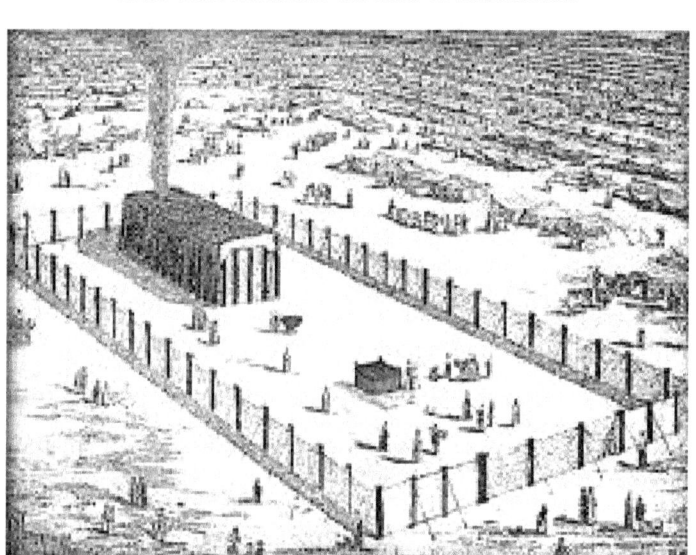

The tabernacle in the wilderness, its enclosure, and miles of tents.
Wellcome Collection. Public Domain Mark

The sanctuary was separated from the outer court area and had two compartments. The first was the *holy place.* There, the priests offered the showbread (bread of the presence), kept the golden candlestick lit, and maintained the altar of incense. The second was the innermost sanctuary, the *holy of holies,* which was separated by a veil. It was entered annually on the Day of Atonement (Yom Kippur), by the high priest to present sacrificial blood to atone for the sins of the nation.

Cutaway of the Inner Courts
of the Tabernacle and the Temple

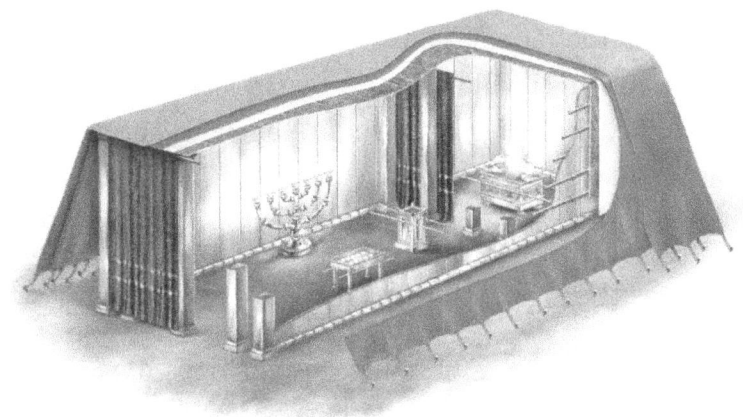

Sanctuary Cut-Away; Artist/Photographer: Phil McKay; Image ID: pcmas0123
Licensed by www.goodsalt.com

This holy of holies also housed the ark of the covenant, which was a gold chest with the mercy seat as its lid (see Heb. 9:1ff). The mercy seat was the throne of the God of Israel, upon which rested two great winged cherubim.

The Greek phrase for holy place in Matthew 24:15 is *topho hagio.* In the Septuagint, it referred to anything from the courtyard of the tabernacle or temple (Lev. 6:16) to the ground of God's presence on which Moses or Joshua stood (Exo. 3:5; Josh. 5:15). Although not the exact phrase, it also refers to the area surrounding Jerusalem, as noted in Ezekiel 43:12. *Topho hagio* is not used in the Septuagint or the New Testament to describe either the holy place or the holy of holies. Despite this, some interpreters assume that Jesus said the abomination would appear in the inner courts of the temple in Jerusalem. However, in Hebrews 9:2-3 and 9:24-25, the holy place of the temple is referred to in Greek as simply *hagia* (lit., *holies*). The holy of holies is termed *hagia hagion* (lit., holies of holies). These expressions are also similar to the Greek Old Testament terminology (see Exo. 26:33 LXX).

Given the terminology used, the Greek text of Matthew might allow for the abomination to be the presence of Roman armies surrounding the holy area, ground, or overall landscape of Jerusalem and the temple. The interpretation of this section of the discourse suggesting that a future antichrist will one day arrive in Jerusalem and sit in the holy place or holy of holies in a (rebuilt) temple is neither warranted by the original text nor its narrative context. *Most importantly, Jesus told his disciples that they would see it.*

Historical Insight

John Gill offers the following insight regarding Jesus' Old Testament reference to the abomination of desolation (Dan. 9:27):

> Armies are called wings, (Isa. 8:8) and the Roman armies were desolating ones . . . not only because they consisted of heathen men . . . but chiefly because of the images of their gods, upon their ensigns.[38]

Gill's explanation agrees entirely with the clarification supplied in Luke's version of the Olivet Discourse (Luke 21:20). The abomination of desolation was, or was at least concurrent with, the presence of the Roman armies surrounding Jerusalem at the onset of the siege. It was an unambiguous sign that it was time for Christians to escape.

Additionally, Matthew's use of topho hagio rather than hagia hagion is not incidental. It may have been intended to provide a subtle theological hint by establishing a linguistic connection between his account and Luke's. Luke describes armies surrounding Jerusalem, which would be "holy topography." Matthew's choice of a seemingly uncharacteristic Greek expression for the holy place of the temple accommodates Luke's description. This further supports the proposition that they both describe the same first-century event.

Another Important Perspective

First Corinthians 13:9 reminds us that we all know in part. Therefore, if the prophecy requires an idolatrous abomination in the inner sanctuary of the temple (at the time of the war), there remains historical evidence of that as well. Josephus informs us that Jewish rebel leaders retreated into the holy of holies of the temple during the war, where it became their military stronghold. This was the very room where God's glory rested on the mercy seat on Israel's annual Day of Atonement. No one was allowed inside except the high priest, and then only with atoning blood on that holiest of days. The rebels used the holy wine and oil for drinking and anointing themselves in total disregard for the holiness of God. They also mercilessly shed the blood of the priests of the sanctuary. I cannot imagine, especially in that day, a more repugnant sacrilege. According to the historian:

> When any of the zealots were wounded, he went up into the temple, and defiled that sacred floor with his blood, insomuch that one may say it was their blood alone that polluted our sanctuary . . . for that (the temple) is now made their receptacle and refuge, and the fountain-head whence their preparations are made against us. And this place, which is adored by the habitable world . . . is trampled upon by these wild beasts born among ourselves.[39]

What could be more idolatrous than exalting Jewish nationalism (or *any* nationalistic pride) above the holiness of God himself? Aaron's sons Nadab and Abihu arrogantly entered the holy of holies, and God consumed them by fire for their presumption (Lev. 10:1-3). God called it *strange fire*. The Zealot presumption and arrogance in the first century was no less a strange fire that resulted in God's consuming blaze that engulfed the once-holy city. Reformed scholar James Jordan observes how this first-century abomination was something of which the Jews themselves were guilty during the revolt. It was similar to their history:

Returning to the time of the Maccabees and Daniel 11, we need to ask who were the "forces from him" that desecrated the sanctuary and set up the desolating sacrilege? They were the reigning High Priests Jason and Menelaus, who apostatized to Greek religion, and who invited Antiochus to help them take over Jerusalem for their own purposes.[40]

Like their ancestors in the second century BC incident involving Antiochus IV Epiphanes, the Jewish Zealot leaders admitted Idumaean soldiers into Jerusalem to help them take control of the city. These were descendants of Esau, who were from Edom in southern Palestine. This exacerbated an already blasphemous situation. Luke's statement about Jerusalem being *surrounded by armies* may or may not have been the actual abomination, but at the very least, it *signaled to those on the outside that the prophesied event was occurring within the temple*. These events may also provide insights into Paul's remarks to the Thessalonians:

[The Day of the Lord] will not come unless the apostasy [revolt; rebellion] comes first, and the man of lawlessness is revealed, the son of destruction [perdition], who opposes and exalts himself above every so-called god or object of worship, so that he takes his seat in the temple of God, displaying himself as being God (2 Thes. 2:3-4).

There are two distinct hints that Paul was writing to the Thessalonians concerning the approaching Zealot-led revolt and the pollution of the temple, and *not* a future antichrist. First, he uses the Greek term *apostasia*, which is not necessarily a falling away or religious apostasy (by the end-time church), which is a common view of those who hold a *futurist* view of eschatology. That is how Paul's statement is understood as referring to a great tribulation believed to be in *our* future. However, this same Greek word is used by Josephus when referring to the Jewish *revolt* against Rome. This word definition is recognized and employed in more recent Bible translations:

Let no one deceive you in any way. For that day will not come, unless *the rebellion* [apostasia] comes first, and the man of lawlessness is revealed, the son of destruction . . . (2 Thes. 2:3 ESV; cf. NIV).

This strongly suggests that *the man of lawlessness,* who is also the son of destruction, was someone of significance in the Jewish revolt against Rome. Also, the Greek phrase son of destruction *(son of perdition or lawlessness)* is found only one other time in the Bible, where Jesus describes Judas Iscariot, the infamous *Jewish* traitor:

". . . and I guarded them and not one of them perished but the son of perdition, so that the Scripture would be fulfilled" (John 17:12).

Second Thessalonians describes a contemporary Jewish leader, almost two decades before the revolt. He is not referring to someone coming in *our* future, but most likely to one of the Zealot leaders. Some suggest he is one of two powerful individuals: John of Gischala or Eleazar. Each of these, in turn, commandeered and polluted the temple sanctuary during the revolt with total disregard for the holiness of God. In doing so, that leader would have been exalting himself above Israel, Rome, and the holiness of God when he and his faction took up residence in the holy of holies. This was the most revered place on earth. This leader is the one whom Paul described as:

. . . [the one] who opposes and exalts himself above every so-called god or object of worship, so that he takes his seat in the temple of God, displaying himself as being God (2 Thes. 2:4).

Summarizing the Abomination of Desolation

To take a position in the holy of holies, which was God's historical throne room, would effectively elevate oneself *as God.* There is no reason to suggest that any New Testament writings refer to a future antichrist who will be purportedly enthroned in a rebuilt temple in Jerusalem. Paul's letter to Thessalonica complements Jesus' warning concerning the abomination of desolation. In the Olivet Discourse, Jesus gave his disciples a critically important panoramic view of this signal event from differing vantage points. Anyone remaining in Jerusalem would have witnessed the horrific sacrilege taking place within the temple by the raging anti-Roman Zealots. Those outside the city who could not see the inner chambers of the holy house would have witnessed the earlier approach and surrounding of Jerusalem by pagan Roman armies. From our retrospective vantage point, the abomination of desolation does not have to be particularly identified as *this* or *that*. The overall scenes both in and around Jerusalem conclusively satisfy the intent of both the abomination of desolation and Paul's Jewish man of sin taking his seat in the temple. The prophecy of Jesus, therefore, offered a visible, tangible warning to escape, regardless of the location of the hearer or reader in relation to Jerusalem and its impending desolation.

Our focus has been on how the eschatological outlook of the Olivet Discourse finds its fulfillment in the events relating to the Jews and the conditions that led to their exile. The things we have observed are historical, and that is a critical component of our understanding of eschatology. It is unfortunate that the texts we are examining have been speculatively catapulted by many into our future when they are, in fact, episodes of the past.

Then Who is the Antichrist?

Much has been told through the centuries of the Christian church regarding a future world leader called the *antichrist*. This individual, who is alleged to be the personification of the devil, is predicted to rise as a favored leader from among the nations in the so-called last days. He will assume control of a one-world government and enthrone himself in the holy of holies of a rebuilt temple in Jerusalem. There, he will demand to be worshipped throughout the world. It is alleged that these events will usher in, or be central to, the *great tribulation* as the world enters its final seven years before the return of the Lord Jesus from heaven. All of this will allegedly usher in a literal one-thousand-year reign of Christ with his glorified saints. As just observed, the antichrist figure is often associated with the man of sin in 2 Thessalonians 2:1-4 and a world-ruling beast who is introduced in Revelation 13. All of this makes for grand theater, but is it a biblically accurate description of the antichrist?

In contrast to all that has been formulated in so-called Christian teachings about this horrific figure and the events associated with his appearance, the Bible itself says very little. As a matter of fact, there are only two letters, both from the apostle John, in which the subject is even mentioned. They are First and Second John. In these two brief letters, the apostle paints a simple and clear portrait of antichrist. Let us briefly look at his description.

John's Portrait of Antichrist

First, the apostle tells us that antichrist's appearance was in his own time, the last hour of the Jewish age. His readers had heard about a coming antichrist, but John informs them that there were many, not a solitary figure:

> Children, it is the last hour; and just as you heard that antichrist is coming, even now *many antichrists* have appeared; *from this we know* that it is the last hour (1 John 2:18).

Second, he informs his readers that these many antichrists *went out from us* (the first-century church), meaning they departed to serve their own purposes. They never really belonged to Christ:

> They went out from us, but they were not *really* of us; for if they had been of us, they would have remained with us; but *they went out, so that it would be shown that they all are not of us* (1 John 2:19).

Third, their doctrine denied the nature and work of Jesus. They denied not only the Son but also the Father who sent him:

> Who is the liar but the *one who denies that Jesus is the Christ? This is the antichrist,* the one who denies the Father and the Son. Whoever denies the Son does not have the Father; the one who confesses the Son has the Father also (1 John 2:22-23; cf. John 5:23).

Fourth, in 1 John 4:1-6 (below), the apostle John provides the following clear, fourfold description of the true character of this faction:

- They were under the influence of a lying spirit (antichrist).

- They denied that Jesus, God the Son, came in flesh (possibly fostered by the Gnostics, a conglomeration of religion and Greek philosophy).

- This spirit was already influencing many in John's own time.

- It is the spirit of error that seduces with false doctrine.

> Beloved, do not believe every spirit, but test the spirits to see whether they are from God, because many false prophets have gone out into the world. By this you know the Spirit of God: every spirit that confesses that Jesus Christ has come in the flesh is from God; and *every spirit that does not confess Jesus is not from God; this is the spirit of the antichrist,* of which you have heard that it is coming, and now it is already in the world. You are from God, little children, and have overcome them; because greater is He who is in you than he who is in the world. They are from the world; therefore, they speak *as* from the world, and the world listens to them. We are from God; he who knows God listens to us; he who is not from God does not listen to us. By this we know the spirit of truth and the spirit of error. (1 John 4:1-6).

Then, conclusively, an element of this heresy involved a false teaching regarding the true nature of Christ:

For many deceivers have gone out into the world, those who do not acknowledge Jesus Christ as coming in the flesh. <u>This is the</u> <u>deceiver</u> <u>and the antichrist</u> (2 John 1:7).

Antichrist: Let's Summarize

1. Antichrist was not a person but a spiritual influence already manifesting in the waning hours of the Old Covenant age. (1 John 2:18; 1 John 4:3).

2. This spirit (or spirits) seduced those who were apparently false Christians to leave the churches (1 John 2:19; 1 John 4:3). They were deceived into believing that there was a better and more philosophically attractive doctrine concerning Christ.

3. The deceived ones forsook the opportunity to learn the truth of God. Instead, they embraced heresy, especially in relation to the person and work of the Lord Jesus Christ (1 John 2:22; 1 John 4:3).

4. Their heretical doctrine had several facets:

   - It denied that Jesus was the Messiah (1 John 2:22).
   - It denied the mediatory work of Christ, which is to say that it denied that Jesus is the only mediator between God and man (1 John 2:22-23; cf. 1 Tim. 2:5).
   - It denied the incarnation: that Jesus, who is God himself, took on human flesh and blood (1 John 4:2; 2 John 1:7; John 8:24; John 14:8-9; Phil. 2:5-8).

John's portrait is the sole explicit description given in the Bible regarding antichrist. It was, and has been throughout church history, a lying and seductive spiritual influence. It emerged in the time of the apostles and has undoubtedly remained throughout our history, seeking to entice God's people away from the truth.

CHAPTER 9

THE OLIVET DISCOURSE
HISTORICAL DATA: JUDEA AND JERUSALEM

The people of God were to be alert and watchful. As the great abomination began to take place, an opportunity would arise to quickly depart from the city so as not to be *trapped* in the siege. The first opportunity occurred in 66 AD. However, after Nero's death in 68 AD and the temporary suspension of the war, there would be a temptation to return. The Jews, carrying on with their worldly affairs, were unaware that Jerusalem was going to be sealed up by both the Zealots within and the Romans without. Note Luke's chilling allusion to being *trapped* in the siege:

> "Be on guard, so that your hearts will not be weighted down with dissipation and drunkenness and the worries of life, and that day will not come on you suddenly like a trap" (Luke 21:34).

Continued from Chapter 8

8. Departure from the City

"Then those who are in Judea must flee to the mountains. Whoever is on the housetop must not go down to get the things out that are in his house. Whoever is in the field must not turn back to get his cloak. But woe to those who are pregnant and to those who are nursing babies in those days! But pray that your flight will not be in the winter, or on a Sabbath" (Matt. 24:16-20).

In the early stages of the war, the door of opportunity would open and close very quickly, so there was no time for delay. In addition, they were to pray for favorable travel conditions for those in flight. Winter difficulties, Sabbath travel restrictions, pregnancy, or nursing would create difficult circumstances for hasty departure and travel. Matthew uniquely mentions Sabbath travel to his Jewish audience because Jewish customs only allowed limited distances to be traveled on the Sabbath. Mark and Luke entirely omit this. In any case, this would not be a time to be thinking about marital bliss and a charming little home in the suburbs (see 1 Cor. 7:26-31).

Historical Data:

As a matter of historical record, there was a miraculous turn of events relating to the initial surrounding of Jerusalem by Cestius Gallus, the Roman military commander. This occurred in September of 66 AD. His campaign came to an abrupt and unexpected end after he marched into Judea with a reported force of over 30,000 men. We are informed by Josephus that Cestius' troops surrounded the city, could have taken it, and quickly brought the rebellion under control.

Suddenly, and for no apparent reason, he retreated. Some suggest that he perceived that there were insufficient armaments to engage in a conflict. Whatever his reasons, the retreat offered a brief window of opportunity that allowed many in Jerusalem to escape while the Zealot forces left the city in pursuit of the departing Romans. Various historians and scholars note this:

Josephus:

> It then happened that Cestius . . . recalled his soldiers from the place, and by despairing of any expectation of taking it, . . . he retired from the city, without any reason in the world.[41]

Eusebius provides the additional detail that, before the revolt, the Jerusalem Christians migrated to Pella, east of the Jordan River:

> But the people of the church in Jerusalem had been commanded by a revelation, vouchsafed to approved men there before the war, to leave the city and to dwell in a certain town of Perea called Pella.[42]

Pella appears to have been a place of refuge for at least some Jerusalem Christians. There is evidence of the presence of Jewish Christian groups in the area in the early part of the second century AD. The main point is that the faithful fled Jerusalem. The precise location to which they fled is secondary to the point. As to Jesus' reference to being *trapped*, there was a final approach to the city that is not always accounted for.

"They Will Not Escape"
A Chilling Prophetic Reference

After the suspension of the war effort when Nero committed suicide, the absence of military presence left the Jews with a false sense of security:

> For you yourselves know full well that the day of the Lord will come just like a thief in the night. While they are saying, "Peace and safety!" then destruction will come upon them suddenly like labor pains upon a woman with child, and they will not escape (1 Thess. 5:2-3).

In the spring of 70 AD, thousands of Jews returned to the city, thinking that it was now safe to return to Jerusalem to celebrate Passover. *However, Jesus had warned his disciples to stay clear of Jerusalem.* Three days before the commencement of Passover, Titus, now leading the war effort after Vespasian was crowned emperor, returned with his armies to re-engage the offensive. He surrounded the city, leaving the entire multitude tapped within, as Josephus notes:

> . . . they had come up from throughout the country to the Feast of Unleavened Bread . . . and were suddenly shut up by an army, which immediately occasioned so great distress among them that there came a pestilential destruction, and soon afterward a famine that destroyed them even more swiftly.[43]

9. **There would be a time of unparalleled tribulation culminating in a great power transition in the heavenly domain and the sign that Christ, the Son of Man, was coming on the clouds of heaven, as prophesied by Daniel.**

(We will first examine the great tribulation, then later address Christ's coming on the clouds.)

> "For then there will be a great tribulation, such as has not occurred since the beginning of the world until now, nor ever will" (Matt. 24:21).

Jesus declared that this time of great tribulation would be unequaled since the beginning of the world and never be equaled again. Popular interpretations of Jesus' words tell us that the death tolls of the twentieth-century Nazi Holocaust far exceeded the calamities of 66–70 AD. Given the significantly greater levels of those atrocities, the *great* tribulation could not possibly have occurred in the first century AD. Therefore, Jesus could not have been referring to the coming destruction of Jerusalem. *Let's examine the flaws in this thinking.* The first two points will be helpful, but I believe the third explanation is most essential to our understanding of the text.

Comparisons Miss the Point

First, it is true that the death toll reached approximately 6 million under Hitler, yet *only* 1.1 million during the Roman invasion.[44] However, we should not overlook the fact that, besides the Jews who died in the Jewish war, the gospel was seeded by the blood of innumerable Christian martyrs in the years preceding the war under Nero's reign of terror. Therefore, precise death tolls cannot be ascertained. Of course, the data in either case is horrific but should never be viewed as the ultimate arbiter of the words of Jesus. As biblical people, we must consider such things from a theological perspective, as our second and third points explain.

Second, from a theological or redemptive perspective, the tribulation of 66–70 AD marked the close of the 1400-year era of God's miraculous dealings with the Jews under the Mosaic economy. This time of tribulation was the birth pangs of a new era in God's plan. It was a unique period, never to be repeated. To appreciate this, we must step away from our emotional tendencies to evaluate things from the standpoint of human tragedy. We don't devalue such misfortune, but we must see these things from a divine perspective. It is important to measure the significance theologically, from God's perspective and not our own.

Third (and this is why comparisons miss the point), Jesus' words were a dramatic expression used for emphasis. Similar language is used to describe a pair of highly regarded kings of Judah who lived two generations apart. Each is said to have been without equal, prior to and after their time:

Regarding King Hezekiah of Judah (c. 700 BC), it is written:

[Hezekiah] trusted in the LORD, the God of Israel; so that after him there was none like him among all the kings of Judah, nor among those who were before him (2 Kings 18:4-5).

Seventy years later (c. 630 BC), regarding Josiah, we read:

Before him [Josiah] there was no king like him who turned to the LORD with all his heart and with all his soul and with all his might, according to all the Law of Moses; nor did any like him arise after him (2 Kings 23:24-25).

So, who's the greatest, Hezekiah or Josiah?

Beloved ones, that isn't the point. These texts obviously contradict one another if we assume the author of Second Kings was providing literal assessments. That is not the case. The statements reflect ancient modes of speech. They were chronicled hundreds of years before the time of Jesus, in a culture whose manner of expression was far different from ours today. It is a rhetorical device, a form of hyperbole (exaggeration; overstatement), used to highlight or emphasize the distinctiveness of each of these kings in their own time. If understood that way, we have no issue.

The language employed by the inspired Old Testament chronicler provides a basis for understanding Jesus' use of this same ancient form of emphasis. Again, I remind the reader that the New Testament's use of the Old Testament and its literary styles is critical to our analytical process. Failure to do so results in all kinds of strange, arbitrary, and faulty interpretations.

False Signs and Wonders

"Unless those days had been cut short, no life would have been saved; but for the sake of the elect those days will be cut short. Then if anyone says to you, 'Behold, here is the Christ,' or 'There He is,' do not believe him. For false christs and false prophets will arise and will show great signs and wonders, so as to mislead, if possible, even the elect. Behold, I have told you in advance. So, if they say to you, 'Behold, He is in the wilderness,' do not go out, or, 'Behold, He is in the inner rooms,' do not believe them" (Matt. 24:22-26).

Jesus mentions false christs a second time (the first was Matt. 24:5). As I have suggested, this redundancy supports the idea that his focus has shifted from the events of the previous decades to the sacking of Jerusalem. His use of *then*, or *at that time* (Matt. 24:23), also supports this. In Jerusalem, many false prophets prophesied a false hope of deliverance for the Jews.

Historical Data

The Book of Acts:

The Lord warned his disciples not to be deceived at the time of this great tribulation by the appearance of false prophets performing "miraculous" signs. What kind of signs? Can examples be found in history? The answer is yes. Various phenomena existed. Rodney Thomas' *Magical Motifs in the Book of Revelation* provides examples from early Roman history of talking statues of emperors and various phenomena involving images that exhibited lifelike behavior. [45] We are also informed in the Book of Acts that magical arts were commonplace:

> Now there was a man named Simon, who formerly was practicing magic in the city and astonishing the people of Samaria, claiming to be someone great; and they all, from smallest to greatest, were giving attention to him, saying, "This man is what is called the Great Power of God." And they were giving him attention because he had for a long time astonished them with his magic arts (Acts 8:9-11).

We also find in Josephus a focus on false prophets in Jerusalem at the time of the siege:

> [Nor] did any one of them escape with his life. A false prophet was the occasion of these people's destruction, who had made a public proclamation in the city that very day, that God commanded them to get up upon the temple, and that there they should receive miraculous signs of their deliverance. Now, there was then a great number of false prophets suborned [bribed] by the tyrants [Zealot leaders] to impose

upon the people . . . that they should wait for deliverance from God: and this was in order to keep them from deserting, and . . . be buoyed up above fear . . . Now, a man that is in adversity does easily comply with such promises; for when such a seducer makes him believe that he shall be delivered from those miseries which oppress him, then it is that the patient is full of hopes of such deliverance. Thus were the miserable people persuaded by these deceivers.[46]

How gravely unfortunate it was for those who refused to hear the admonition from Jesus and, subsequently, his apostles. They chose not to flee the city, as warned. They listened to the voices of the false prophets and remained, expecting a miraculous deliverance. But there would be no deliverance. They were trapped and mercilessly destroyed in the siege by famine, the Zealots, fire, and the Roman army.

Lightning from the East to the West

"For just as the lightning comes from the east and flashes even to the west, so will the coming [*parousia*] of the Son of Man be. Wherever the corpse is, there the vultures [or eagles] will gather." (Matt. 24:27-28).

In contrast to the appearances of the false messiahs and prophets, Jesus informs the disciples that his own arrival would be contrary to what these impostors fostered as they preyed upon contemporary Jewish beliefs. He dispelled what their Jewish leaders taught regarding Messiah's arrival as a military leader (in 45–90 days). His presence would not be earthly and bodily, but in a manner consistent with God's presence in judgment as described in the Old Testament. Jesus would be present as a military leader, but as the Lord of Hosts, leading the *heavenly* hosts. He vividly describes to his disciples how lightning-like judgments would flash through the east in the land of Israel (the eastern part of Rome's empire) and also flash into Rome in the west. It would sweep through the national centers of both Israel and Rome, touching both Israel and the empire bent on her destruction.

Historical Data:

As Roman General Vespasian's troops were invading the region of Galilee in the land of Israel with devastating force (in the east), Emperor Nero is believed to have set fire to Rome. He proceeded to blame Christians for the fire and horribly execute many. He came under public suspicion as the true perpetrator of the fire, and in 68 AD, Nero committed suicide. Subsequently, Rome (in the west) would see the rise and fall of three short-lived emperors and come to near collapse. Because of this, the war against Israel had to be temporarily suspended. Historians refer to 69 AD as *the Year of the Four Emperors.*

Holford writes:

> While these destructive contests prevailed in the *East,* the *western* parts of the Roman empire were rent by the fierce contentions of Galba, Otho, and Vitellius . . . three emperors . . . they all, together with Nero, their immediate predecessor, died a violent death.[47]

An Amazing Old Testament Reference

Holford's historical remarks afford us an opportunity to consider a relevant prophetic vision from the Book of Ezekiel. The prophecy to which Jesus alludes involves the striking image of God's sword of judgment, removed from its sheath, polished, and crackling like the brightness of *lightning* as it reflects his own incredible glory. The sword is then given to Nebuchadnezzar (the slayer) as he advances upon Jerusalem to carry out God's judgment:

> "Son of man, set your face toward Jerusalem, and speak against the sanctuaries and prophesy against the land of Israel; And say to the land of Israel, 'Thus says the LORD, "Behold, I am against you; and I will draw My sword out of its sheath . . ."" "Son of man, prophesy and say, 'Thus says the LORD.' "Say,
> A sword, a sword sharpened And also polished!

Sharpened to make a slaughter,
Polished to flash like lightning! . . .
It is given to be polished, that it may be handled; the sword is
sharpened and polished, to *give it into the hand of the slayer* . . . that
their hearts may melt, and many fall at all their gates. I have given the
glittering sword. Ah! *It is made for striking like lightning.* Show yourself
sharp, *go to the right*; set yourself; *go to the left*, wherever your edge
is appointed . . . As for you, son of man, make two ways for the sword
of the king of Babylon to come" (Eze. 21:2-19).

Jesus drew on the remarkable imagery of God's sword of judgment, thoroughly polished and prepared. As it is removed from its sheath, it explodes with a blinding crackle of light, like a great bolt of lightning striking Israel's land. This testimony of Ezekiel pertains to the attack on Jerusalem by Nebuchadnezzar of Babylon in 586 BC. The nearly identical circumstances from centuries earlier provide the basis for understanding Jesus' words. In his first-century application of the imagery, his great sword would sweep into the eastern empire, striking Israel's land of inheritance, including Judea and Jerusalem. From there, it would sweep across the western empire, where Rome was situated.

The sword struck both the Jews in the east and brought great national disturbances to the west. As in Ezekiel, it would go both "to the right and to the left" as directed by God (Eze. 21:16). In Scripture, judgments carried out by invading armies often came out of the north of Israel, such as Babylon. The two-edged sword of judgment would swing both right and left and pass through Rome in the west and Israel in the east. The upheavals in Rome were of incredible magnitude. According to Josephus, the attack on Jerusalem had to be suspended:

Vespasian had returned to Caesarea and was preparing to march in full strength upon Jerusalem itself, when the news reached him that Nero was slain." [68 AD] Therefore Vespasian "deferred his expedition against Jerusalem, anxiously waiting to see upon whom the empire would devolve after Nero's death.[48]

In 69 AD, after over a year of civic turmoil, the Roman senate acknowledged Vespasian as Caesar. The offensive against Jerusalem resumed under the new emperor's son, General Titus. Forty years earlier, Jesus provided an eerie description of the armies of Titus surrounding Jerusalem. Matthew records:

> "Wherever the corpse is, there the vultures [or eagles] will gather" (Matt. 24:28).

Once the city was surrounded, the Roman ensigns, which were symbols of eagles and carried by their soldiers, were seen everywhere around the now-dead carcass of Jerusalem. The image of birds of prey swirling for five months around the carcass of the once-holy city of God is a vivid one.

Summary

Jesus declared that the years leading up to and including the events of 70 AD were to be marked by convulsive birth pains in the civilized world, which, as history shows, did occur. The table on the following page summarizes what we have seen from both biblical references and credible historical accounts.

Historical Fulfillments of the Olivet Discourse

Jesus' Prediction	Observations: 30–70 AD
False Christs (Messiahs)	There were numerous false messiahs up to and including the siege of Jerusalem.
Wars and Rumors of Wars	Wars and civil disturbances throughout the period disrupted the great Pax Romana (Roman peace).
Famines	Many occurred in the region and were recorded during the period.
Earthquakes	Many major earthquakes were recorded during this period.
Pestilences	The natural consequences of famines, earthquakes, and wars, possibly from a lack of disposal of multitudes of dead bodies.
False Messiahs (in Jerusalem)	Many in the region throughout the period and during the siege deceived the masses with promises of deliverance.
Abomination of Desolation	Jerusalem was besieged by the Roman armies, and the temple was desecrated by the Jewish Zealots, who used it as a military stronghold.
The Temple's Destruction	Unquestioned historical event: it occurred in 70 AD, forty years after Jesus' prophecy on Mount Olivet.
The Great Tribulation	The madness of the time was unparalleled. Consider hyperbole based on the Old Testament accounts of Hezekiah and Josiah.
The Apostles' Generation	All these things occurred just as Jesus promised, before that very generation (biblically, forty years) passed into history.

Table 9.1

CHAPTER 10

THE OLIVET DISCOURSE
THE LANGUAGE OF BIBLICAL PROPHECY

Thus far, we have examined the literary and cultural contexts of Jesus' great prophetic discourse. We have also seen a sampling of the biblical and historical data that supports his prophecy being fulfilled in the generation of his contemporaries, just as he promised. Now, since we have proposed that Jesus' prophecy was not about the end of the world but the end of the Jewish age, we must reasonably account for the extremely dramatic language he used to describe his return.

In Chapter 9, we saw that his coming, or presence in judgment, was to be like *lightning flashing from east to west*. Hopefully, that has been adequately explained, but there is more. Jesus said that, in connection with his parousia, the following *cosmic* phenomena would also occur in *that* generation:

> "But immediately after the tribulation of those days THE SUN WILL BE DARKENED, AND THE MOON WILL NOT GIVE ITS LIGHT, AND THE STARS WILL FALL FROM THE SKY, and the powers of the heavens will be shaken. And then the sign of the Son of Man will appear in the sky, and then all the tribes of the earth will mourn, and they will see THE SON OF MAN COMING ON THE CLOUDS OF THE SKY with power and great glory. (Matt. 24:29-30; cf. Isa. 13:10, Dan. 7:13-14).

As we begin our journey into the linguistic style of the Lord Jesus, let's consider the following excerpt written by contemporary Orthodox Jewish Rabbi Jack Abramowitz. As of this writing, he is the Torah Content Editor at the Jewish Orthodox Union, headquartered in New York City. The rabbi beautifully explains the highly charged and imaginative language of prophetic discourse. Please note that the following does not have specific reference to Jesus' words, but biblical interpretation in general:

> If you hear someone speaking a language you've never heard before, you would still recognize the sounds coming out of his mouth as speech. In the stranger's language, you may perceive a word here and there that sound like words in your own language. Not only might these words mean different things to the two of you, that particular set of syllables might mean the exact opposite to each of you! For example, to table a discussion in American English means to put it aside, while in British English, it means to deal with it . . . This, the Rambam [Maimonides, influential 12th century Jewish scholar] tells us, is what many people experience when reading the words of the prophets. [II, 29] They either don't understand their words at all or they completely misconstrue them. . . For example, to describe the downfall of a kingdom, Isaiah employs such metaphors as 'the stars have fallen,'

'the heavens have been overthrown,' 'the sun has gone dark,' etc. Sometimes, the prophets refer to 'mankind' even though they are speaking only of the inhabitants of a particular land, as in 'God will remove man to far away' (Isaiah 6:12) and 'I will cut off man from upon the Earth' (Zephaniah 1:3), even though these verses are speaking only of the kingdom of Judah . . . When Isaiah foretells the downfall of Nebuchadnezzar, he says such things as, 'the stars of Heaven and the constellations will not give their light, the sun will be darkened in its going forth and the moon will not let her light shine' (Is. 13:10). He also says, 'I will shake the heavens and Earth will be moved from its place' (13:13). The Rambam asks: 'is anyone so foolish, so willfully ignorant, or so enamored of literalism that they would take such verses to mean that when Babylonia fell, the nature of the sun, moon and stars changed, or that the Earth changed orbits? Clearly these are metaphors! These phrases speak to the bitterness of the conquered nation, not to a fundamental change in the fabric of the universe.'[49]

It is important to understand that the fall of Jerusalem and the temple was a significant upheaval and a transition of power in both the seen and unseen structures of authority. That is why Jesus described it with universe-obliterating imagery. He spoke of the fall of the city, the temple, the Jewish economy, and the diabolical, unseen powers behind Rome. He did so in a manner that was entirely familiar to the disciples because it was identical to the language employed by their great prophets of old. In addition to his allusion to Isaiah's description of Babylon's downfall (Isa. 13:1ff), it is significant that he quotes directly from Daniel 7:13-14, where the Son of Man's cloud-coming is not one of an arrival upon the earth but of an arrival in heaven to receive dominion:

I kept looking in the night visions,
And behold, with the clouds of heaven
One like a Son of Man was coming,
And He came up to the Ancient of Days
And was presented before Him.
And to Him was given dominion,

Glory and a kingdom,
That all the peoples, nations and *men of every* language
Might serve Him.
His dominion is an everlasting dominion
Which will not pass away;
And His kingdom is one
Which will not be destroyed.
(Dan. 7:13-14)

Daniel's vision describes how, upon defeating his enemies, Messiah comes *with the clouds of heaven up to the Ancient of Days and is given dominion.* I strongly suggest that any translation portraying this part of Jesus' discourse as "the sign of the Son of Man will appear in the *sky*" violates the spirit of Daniel 7 and the nature of this event. The reference is to the sign of the Son of Man in heaven, in the presence of the Ancient of Days.

> *In Matthew 24:29-30, Jesus combined the prophecy of the fall of Babylon, which is how Jerusalem is characterized in Revelation, with Daniel's vision of the Son of Man being given dominion. In so doing, he established the indisputable connection between these two events. He provided the disciples, who asked for a sign, with the quintessential sign. When Jerusalem and the temple fall, the old order, with its governing principalities and powers, will have been demolished. The Son of Man, the Messiah, will have been given dominion by the Ancient of Days.*

Daniel's vision also portrays the rise of the Roman beast and the final destruction of the unholy forces behind it. As this is accomplished and the Son of Man ascends on the cloud to receive dominion from the Ancient of Days, the result is that Satan is bound. We will examine this in Revelation 19–20. Although I do not suggest or recommend a rigid compartmentalization of the following points, it may be helpful to see how Jesus' first-century mission unfolded as God became one of us to redeem and restore his creation. It began with his virgin birth in Bethlehem, a sinless earthly life, and the anointing by the Holy Spirit at his baptism. Then:

- He bore our sins and destroyed the condemning force of the Law in his crucifixion (Col. 2:13-14).

- He conquered the power of death in his resurrection (Rev. 1:18; 2 Tim. 1:10).

- He ascended as High Priest to cleanse the heavenly sanctuary from the stains of sin and the adversary's presence with his own blood (Heb. 9:19-24).

- He offered Israel a probationary period (40 years) to repent and acknowledge Jesus as their Messiah, while at the same time preserving a remnant according to his promise to the fathers of the nation (Rom. 11:1-6; Rom. 15:7-9).

- He came in the clouds to destroy his enemies, then returned to the Father to receive the dominion (Matt. 24:29-30; in Rev. 2:26-27, it is seen proleptically (as certain, about to be accomplished); also portrayed in Rev. 14:14-18, and in Dan. 7:13-14).

Concerning Christ's Dominion

At the time of his ascension in Matthew 28:18, the reader will recall how Jesus declared to his disciples that "all authority" was given to him. Why then are we told that Jesus was not given dominion over the nations until forty years later, at the destruction of Jerusalem? This can be reasonably explained through the lens of an Old Testament storyline. Remember that the ancient people, stories, and institutions served as *types* that prefigured Christ and the glorious realities of the

New Testament (1Cor. 10:1-6; Col. 2:16-17). The helpful storyline is that of David's rise to the throne of Israel. David was a type or foreshadow of the Lord Jesus. He was first anointed king by Samuel the Prophet, while Saul, who had fallen out of God's favor, was still Israel's king (1 Sam. 16:13). Saul may be seen typologically as the waning authority of the Jewish order that yet remained established at the time of Jesus (Heb. 9:8-9). Upon Saul's death (foreshadowing the demolition of the Old Covenant order in 70 AD), David became fully established as king, first over Judah (2 Sam. 2:4), then all of Israel (2 Sam. 5:3). David was proclaimed with certainty as the rightful king while Saul was still in power, but he wasn't fully established after Saul's death. Of course, it is only a scant portrayal of the relevant circumstances. Despite that, I would hope that this glimpse into David's rise to the throne of Israel helps to clarify the potentially confusing portrayal of Christ's reception of universal dominion, which seems to occur under two separate historical circumstances.

Sometimes, Prose Just Isn't Adequate

Prose, which is language in its ordinary form, is most often inadequate to describe biblical events of enormous theological significance. Great transitions of power in both the visible and invisible worlds are typically described in prophetic Scripture in highly poetic forms of speech. Jesus' descriptions of the fall of Jerusalem are not the first occurrences in the Bible that depict power transitions in this manner. They frequently occur in the Old Testament. Consider King David's words in 2 Samuel 22:8ff (which is also Psalm 18):

Then the earth shook and quaked;
And the foundations of the mountains were trembling . . .
He also bowed the heavens down low, and came down
With thick darkness under His feet.
He rode on a cherub and flew;

And He sped on the wings of the wind.
He made darkness His hiding place,
His canopy around Him . . .
He sent out His arrows, and scattered them,
And lightning flashes in abundance, and routed them.
Then the channels of water appeared,
And the foundations of the world were exposed
By Your rebuke, LORD,
At the blast of the breath of Your nostrils . . .
He saved me from my strong enemy.

Given David's grand descriptions, one might think the world was being turned upside down by the visible presence and power of God. It was, but not in the way you or I might imagine. The introduction to Psalm 18 is found in 2 Samuel 22:1 and provides a time reference that establishes its meaning. Although Psalm headers are not typically considered inspired, Psalm 18's header is a duplicate of the historical text in Second Samuel. The following *is the inspired* header for David's declarations in Psalm 18:

David spoke the words of this song to the LORD in the day that the LORD delivered him from the hand of all his enemies and from the hand of Saul (2 Sam. 22:1; Psa. 18:1).

Remarkably, David's dynamic, universe-demolishing language was *describing a change of kings in Israel.* Upon the death of the evil Israelite King Saul, the nation and the land, which constituted the Old Covenant domain of God, were being divinely delivered from a self-serving monarch. They were being transitioned into the hands of the forefather of the Lord Jesus, King David. Very remarkable *indeed*!

Heavenly power transitions such as these need to be understood from God's eternal perspective. They can only be adequately described by imaginative, highly charged, poetic forms of speech that were common in the ancient Near East. God is seen *coming down* (Psa. 18:9) to alter the state of things. The very foundations of civilization are being laid bare and reestablished by divine power and directive. These events, very often the result of war, are frequently described this way. Our text, Psalm 18, is David's reflection on the 1 Chronicles 10:1-4 storyline, where King Saul died in battle against the Philistines, bringing deliverance to David from his evil oppressor.

The following table contains examples of how biblical imagery is employed; however, it is important to understand that such metaphors are fluid and contextual. Images and symbols do not always mean precisely the same thing. They have basic associations that may be applied in different ways. For example, in 1 Corinthians 5:8, Paul uses *leaven* as a symbol of the undesirable spread of *malice and wickedness* in the church. However, in Matthew 13:33, Jesus used the same symbol to describe the expansion and influence that the kingdom of God would have throughout the world, despite its small beginnings.

Samples of Imagery in the Prophets

Phrase / Imagery	Typical Meaning
The Day of the LORD (frequent in Bible history)	God arising to make things right, bringing justice and salvation to the world's social and political arrangements, especially for his people.
The sun darkened; the moon turns dark or as blood	God's judgment upon governments and economies. Leaders and legal systems are demolished. Chaos and bloodshed result from war and civil unrest.
Stars fall from the heavens	God causes religious and/or civil rulers to be toppled from their seats of power.
Darkness and confusion reign	Chaos resulting from war or civil unrest.
Waves of the sea roar	The uproar of pagan Gentile nations and their armies as they prepare to invade.
God coming in or on a cloud	The obscured, invisible presence of God in judgment (as the commander of an invading army), coming as "The LORD of Hosts."

Table 10.1

Time Texts, Prophecy, and Imagery

Time texts, also called time stamps or time indicators, as we just observed in 2 Samuel 22:1 and Psalm 18:1, are common in the Bible's prophetic literature. They are statements embedded in the context of a prophecy that identify, or at least offer clues to, the meaning or historical time frame of its fulfillment. The following are examples of both prophetic language and its associated time texts. We have previously observed the fall of Babylon in Isaiah 13 (see page 9), but also note Isaiah 19:

Isaiah 19:1-3 According to Keil and Delitzsch's Old Testament Commentary, civil war broke out in Egypt c. 695 BC, in Isaiah's lifetime.[50] Isaiah speaks of God *about to come* to Egypt on a cloud, and the great civil disturbance it would cause. Note how this event is described by the prophet:

- The LORD, riding on a swift cloud is about to come to Egypt
- The idols of Egypt will tremble at *His presence*
- And the heart of the Egyptians will melt within them
- I will incite Egyptians against Egyptians (i.e., civil war)

Micah 1:3-6 Micah describes the fall of Samaria (the capital city of Israel's northern kingdom) to Assyria:

- For behold, the LORD is coming forth from His place
- *He will come down* and tread on the high places
- Mountains will melt under Him And the valleys will be split

The time text:

"For I will make Samaria a heap of ruins . . . I will pour her stones down into the valley. And will lay bare her foundations" (Mic. 1:6).

History informs us that this occurred at the hands of the Assyrians in 722 BC (also 2 Kings 17:6). Micah, a contemporary of Isaiah, prophesied prior to that event. Notice that *God came down.*

Nahum 1:1-5 describes the fall of Nineveh (the capital city of Assyria) at the hands of the Babylonians in 612 BC. Again, we see world-collapsing language:

- The oracle of [concerning] Nineveh [*the time text*]
- Mountains quake, hills melt, the earth [*land*] is burned
- The world [their political arrangements], and all that dwell there

Hopefully, the reader can see the importance of the time and location references that aid us in interpretation. As we have previously noted, 1 Peter 1:11 tells us the prophets spoke of *the sufferings of Christ and the glories to follow,* but they were not entirely detached from contemporary world events. This is especially true of Israel and its relationships with the nations. Since the rise and fall of nations were described in this manner, why would we assume that such language as Matthew 24:29 must now be taken literally as describing the destruction of the physical universe? Such interpretation violates sound principles of interpretation, especially that *Scripture both interprets Scripture and teaches us how to read and interpret Scripture.*

Jesus' depictions of the cosmic chaos attending his parousia are consistent with those employed by the same Holy Spirit (the Spirit of Christ) who spoke through the prophets of old. In his earthly life, he used the same vernacular that he employed throughout biblical history. The era of Israel's national privilege was giving way to the emerging kingdom of God in the world. Given the linguistic heritage of the prophets, there is no reason to take these depictions literally.

The following is a well-articulated quote from Christian author Andrew Perriman, who writes concerning Jesus' use of such imagery:

There is no reason to think that Jesus, as a first century Jewish prophet with a familiarity and inclination toward apocalyptic imagery, was suddenly playing by an entirely different set of linguistic rules . . . I don't see anything in the Synoptic Gospels to suggest that the writers [of the Gospels] thought Jesus made a significant break with his natural biblical-Jewish linguistic context. Historically, it is reasonable to assume that he used language, including prophetic and apocalyptic language, like other Jews of his time.[51]

The apostles came to understand Jesus' meaning under the Spirit's guidance (John 14:26 and 16:13), and the manner of speech was part of their own tradition. Therefore, they could prepare the churches for what was about to come. This language is not mystery wrapped in a shroud but plainly heard in the voices of Israel's great prophets of old. They were inspired by the same Holy Spirit who spoke through the Lord Jesus and the apostles who carried the message to the nations.

Jesus' Critical Time Text

Just as he gave time indicators through his prophets, Jesus himself offered his disciples the same. Although he did not know *the day or the hour,* we have seen that he specified the *generation* in which his arrival in judgment would occur. His reference to *this generation* (Matt. 24:34) seems very clear as being the very one existing in his own time, not a future generation. Note the following from Matthew's Gospel:

11:16 but whereunto shall I liken *this generation*?

12:41 men of Nineveh shall rise . . . with *this generation*

12:42 the Queen of the South shall rise . . . with *this generation*

23:36 all these things shall come upon *this generation.*

The events were clearly coming upon that specific generation (Matt. 24:30), not the Jews as a *race* of people or a future generation. The following pages now continue our illustration of the parallels in all three synoptic accounts of the Olivet Discourse:

Gospel Harmony

Matthew 24	Mark 13	Luke 21
29 "But immediately after the tribulation of those days THE SUN WILL BE DARKENED, AND THE MOON WILL NOT GIVE ITS LIGHT,	24 "But in those days, after that tribulation, THE SUN WILL BE DARKENED AND THE MOON WILL NOT GIVE ITS LIGHT,	25 "There will be signs in sun and moon and stars, and on the earth dismay among nations, in perplexity at the roaring of the sea and the waves,
		26 men fainting from fear and the expectation of the things which are coming upon the world;
and the stars will fall from the sky,	25 and the stars will be falling from heaven,	
and the powers of the heavens will be shaken.	and the powers that are in the heavens will be shaken.	for the powers of the heavens will be shaken.
30 And then the sign of the Son of Man will appear in the sky, and then all the tribes of the earth [land] will mourn,		
and they will see THE SON OF MAN COMING ON THE CLOUDS OF THE SKY with power and great glory.	26 Then they will see THE SON OF MAN COMING IN CLOUDS with great power and glory.	27 Then they will see THE SON OF MAN COMING IN A CLOUD with power and great glory.
31 And He will send forth His angels with A GREAT TRUMPET AND	27 And then He will send forth the angels, and	
THEY WILL GATHER TOGETHER his elect from the four winds, from one end of the sky to the other."	WILL GATHER TOGETHER His elect from the four winds, from the farthest end of the earth to the farthest end of heaven."	28 But when these things begin to take place, straighten up and lift up your heads, because your redemption is drawing near.

Table 10.2 (continued on next page)

Gospel Harmony

Matthew 24	Mark 13	Luke 21
32 "Now learn the parable from the fig tree:	28 "Now learn the parable from the fig tree:	29 Then He told them a parable: "Behold the fig tree and all the trees;
when its branch has already become tender and puts forth its leaves, you know that summer is near;	when its branch has already become tender and puts forth its leaves, you know that summer is near.	30 as soon as they put forth leaves, you see it and know for yourselves that summer is now near.
33 so, you too, when you see all these things, recognize that He is near, right at the door.	29 Even so, you too, when you see these things happening, recognize that He is near, right at the door.	31 So you also, when you see these things happening, recognize that the kingdom of God is near.
34 Truly I say to you, this generation will not pass away until all these things take place.	30 Truly I say to you, this generation will not pass away until all these things take place.	32 Truly I say to you, this generation will not pass away until all things take place.
35 Heaven and earth will pass away, but My words will not pass away.	31 Heaven and earth will pass away, but My words will not pass away.	33 Heaven and earth will pass away, but My words will not pass away."
36 But of that day and hour no one knows, not even the angels of heaven, nor the Son, but the Father alone."	32 But of that day or hour no one knows, not even the angels in heaven, nor the Son, but the Father alone. "	

Table 10.2

A Shadow of Future Fulfillment?

There are some who believe, or at least consider the possibility that the texts of the Olivet Discourse are subject to double fulfillment. I find it difficult to justify any suggestion that the prophecy serves as a mere partial fulfillment, type, prefiguration, or shadow of future events at a future time (an end of the world). There does not appear to be any indication that Jesus' words find their final and complete fulfillment anywhere but in the first century. Let's examine why:

First, from a typological perspective, the nature of biblical typology is that it provides coherence between the Old Testament and the New Testament, not between the New Testament and a perceived future, which is often based upon our theological precommitments. The New Testament fulfills types *but does not create them*. As previously noted about David and Saul, typology is a method of biblical interpretation whereby a story, person, institution, nation, or event found in the Old Testament prefigures a New Testament reality. The old is called the *type*, and the new (its fulfillment) is called the *antitype*. Ramm offers:

> Typological interpretation is specifically the interpretation of the Old Testament based on the fundamental theological unity of the two Testaments whereby something in the Old shadows, prefigures, adumbrates [sketches or outlines] something in the New. Hence, what is interpreted in the Old is not foreign or peculiar or hidden, but arises naturally out of the text due to the relationship of the two Testaments.[52]

This relationship exists uniquely between texts in the two testaments of the Bible. It is not a speculative forecast based on New Testament characters or events. Ramm's use of *shadow* and *substance* is significant because it echoes the words of Paul to the Colossians:

> Therefore let no one pass judgment on you in questions of food and drink, or with regard to a festival or a new moon or a Sabbath. These are a shadow of the things to come, but the substance *belongs to [is]* Christ (Col. 2:16-17 ESV).

Types are the shadows of lesser significance in the Old Testament. They prefigure things to come. Antitypes are fulfillments in the New Testament by something greater. The greater is final, conclusive, and supreme, both in this world and the next. This is the very nature of typology. Christ and the New Covenant are the substance. They are not, nor do they create foreshadowings of something more substantive. In Christ, the future to which the Old Testament pointed has arrived. He has conquered death. The new Jerusalem has come down from heaven, unseen yet coexisting with the physical world, ready to receive each of us as we pass from death to life.

If the New Testament creates new types, what other realities found within its pages must be considered as types of the future? Where are they explicitly stated as such? Are there accepted hermeneutical parameters that govern this method of interpretation? If such parameters exist, are they human-engineered models by which the types are affirmed, or are they derived from the Scriptures themselves? As for the Old Testament, it attests to its own typological nature in texts such as:

Moses' declaration to Israel that Yahweh would raise up a future prophet like himself. The Lawgiver was a type of Christ:

> The LORD your God will raise up for you a prophet like me from among you, from your countrymen, you shall listen to him (Deu.18:15).

Zechariah's post-exilic courtroom vision, where we are informed of the symbolic character of the priests alongside Joshua, the high priest. They are *mopheth* (a wonder or sign) said to foreshadow something greater relating to the Branch (Jesus, the Messiah):

> Now listen, Joshua the high priest, you and your friends who are sitting in front of you—indeed they are men who are a symbol [Heb., mopheth], for behold, I am going to bring in My servant the Branch (Zec.3:8).

Second, nowhere in Scripture did Jesus, the apostles, or the prophets employ the language of cosmic collapse to describe the destruction of the physical universe. The prophets first used such hyperbole to describe the fall of political powers throughout the course of biblical history. The proposition that this discourse is the partial or typological fulfillment of a future cosmic collapse is an interpretation that I suggest must be imposed upon the texts. One must begin with an assumption concerning a cataclysmic destruction of the space-time universe, then seek a hermeneutical method, such as typology or repeat fulfillment, to support it from texts that offer no such indication.

It is evident that the destruction of the physical order is presumed to be seen in prophecies whose fulfillments are now recorded history. Close examination of statements that appear to describe the future destruction of the planet shows that they, in fact, do not. They depict an imminent, local, divine intervention into the world of the first century in the New Testament in the same manner that prior judgments of nations were described by the ancient prophets. With that, it becomes necessary to ask: Where does the Bible explicitly describe these kinds of calamities in relation to an actual end of the world? I will concede that biblical references such as "then comes the end" (1 Cor. 15:24) and events that occur "when the thousand years are completed" (Rev. 20:7-9) *may* describe a "final" end. However, the universe-obliterating language that is used in the typical Old and New Testament descriptions of judgments is conspicuously absent from these texts. Nothing familiarly catastrophic is explicitly stated about "stars falling" and "mountains crumbling" that might refer to a final, universal collapse. We find only *alleged* typological images and texts taken entirely out of context, but never unambiguous descriptions of a catastrophic dissolution of the planet. Other than highly symbolic ideas from the Book of Revelation, there is no definitive statement in the Bible indicating that *this is the calamity that ends the world*, from which one can derive types or repeat fulfillments. I would also question any suggestion that Revelation's catastrophes describe the collapse of the physical universe. We will examine this in more detail in Part IV.

Consider this in contrast to how other types are presented. Jesus was sacrificed for our sins, and the New Testament points us to the sacrificial lamb that is seen at Passover and the various sacrifices in the Old Covenant. We are taught to be baptized and told how Old Testament images of flood waters, such as Noah and the Red Sea narratives, display its meaning and value. Flood waters also describe invading armies (e.g., as pointing to Rome in the first century). We have seen how Paul alludes to the Babylonian invasion in Acts 13 as a foreshadowing of similar events that occurred in 66–70 AD. In each case, there are concrete and explicit reference points from which the antitype or secondary fulfillment can be derived. This leads me to ask: Where is the unambiguous statement concerning global destruction that provides the basis for the proposition that the Olivet Discourse is a partial fulfillment or type of a far-future end of the world?

Third, the principle of audience relevance requires that this discourse be understood as having been presented to a specific audience for a specific season of incredible redemptive significance. The entire prophecy offers a degree of specificity regarding the events and conditions leading up to and including the destruction of Jerusalem and the temple.

It answers fundamental interpretive inquiries such as *when, who, what, and why,* for example:

"Tell us, when will these things be, and what will be the sign *when all these things* are going to be fulfilled?" (Mark 13:4).

". . . these *are days of vengeance,* so that all things which are written will be fulfilled." (Luke 21:22).

"But *in those days,* after that [*ekeinos:* that one] tribulation . . ." (Mark 13:24)

"For this reason, *you* [Jesus' disciples in the first century] also must be ready; for the Son of Man is coming at an hour when *you [those same disciples]* do not think He will" (Matt. 24:44).

Fourth, we must distinguish between the specific historical fulfillments of a prophecy and the ongoing application of ethical lessons available in those same texts. The details of a prophecy are not likely to be applicable at all times to all. It cannot be overemphasized that although all Scripture is both inspired and profitable for all, specific aspects of prophecies have intended audiences. It is critically important that we make that distinction; otherwise, it raises serious questions about specific time and location references in all prophetic literature.

John Edwards offers an excellent illustration of how time-bound communication with a specific "fulfillment" may have broadened or even universal application:

> Imagine that you searched the attic in your grandmother's house and found an old letter which your great-grandfather had written to your great-grandmother . . . promising to return . . . after the War and marry her. As you read it, you may feel inspired to apply some of your great-grandfather's examples of faith and love to your own present-day relationships. But there's a difference between applying the letter and fulfilling it. Your great- grandfather's letter had one and one only historical fulfillment, and that was on the day he married your dear great-grandmother! Thereafter your great-grandparents may have kept the letter knowing that their children and their children's children may someday find it interesting or even helpful . . . If we allow for a 'double fulfillment' of the predictions made by Jesus in Matthew chapter 24 even though no precedent seems to exist for such a hermeneutic, then what is there to stop anyone allowing for a third, fourth or fifth 'fulfillment'? It means even though we may witness an exact repeat of the very same events which Jesus predicted, happening before our very own eyes in our own generation, we would have no way of knowing whether what we are seeing is the final fulfillment of the prophecy or not. It could be that today's event is no more a sign of the end than what happened in 1967, or 1948, or in AD70. In other words, we wouldn't know whether it was a sign of the end or not. The events Jesus described would lose any value as a 'sign' that the end is near.[53]

Summary

In his discourse on Mount Olivet, we have seen how Jesus revised the deeply entrenched expectations of the disciples by explaining not only the timing of his presence (parousia) but also its nature.

It is evident that Jesus (as God) was not returning in a month or two as a physically present Messiah to defeat Rome. Neither was he speaking of a far-future coming to destroy the world. He was returning in a (very real) cloud-presence to judge Jerusalem. His agent of destruction was the Roman Empire. The language of his return was consistent with the linguistic style of the ancient prophets of Israel, through whom he spoke in times past. Once the judgment on Israel was accomplished, he would also destroy (unseen by man) the demonic principalities at work behind Rome, as we shall see in the Book of Revelation.

Let's now recap what we have seen in Matthew 24. It will help us understand the contextual flow of Matthew 24 as it transitions to his teaching in Matthew 25, the third part of this great discourse. We will seek to determine whether Jesus' teaching continues to describe the events of the first century or if, as some believe, he transitions to an explanation of things relating to future events beyond the time of the disciples. What we have examined thus far in the discourse can be summarized as follows:

24:1-3   The Disciples' Inquiry

The disciples had just heard Jesus denounce the Pharisees, pronounce judgment upon them, and declare that the desolation of their national economy was certain (Matthew 23). While the disciples were admiring the temple, Jesus announces that it would be destroyed. Based on their prior learning, the disciples associate this with the end of their present age and inquire as to when this will take place. Their Jewish training had taught them that a brief disappearance and return of Messiah would usher in the age to come (olam haba). Our awareness of their worldview is a critical aspect of interpreting Jesus' response to their questions.

24:4-8   Jesus' Initial Response

He informs the disciples not to be frightened or misled by the natural disasters and geopolitical disorder that they will witness in the coming decades. These disturbances must come to pass, and they are the beginning of the birth pangs of the arrival of his kingdom. Again, it should be emphasized how Jesus consistently informs the disciples that *they* would see all these things. The context of the discourse does not support the notion that he had any far-off, future audience in mind. There is no "transgenerational you" to be interpreted from the text that would suggest its inclusion of any future audience beyond those addressed.

24:9-14   Heightened Persecution, Betrayal, and Chaos

A great persecution of the church would arise (a possible reference to the persecution under Nero and by their fellow Jews). Faced with this, many believers would deny their faith and betray one another. The Jews would also be persecuted. False prophets would continue in the land and lawlessness would abound. Martyrdom awaited many of them and steadfast endurance in the face of unimaginable circumstances would be necessary.

Despite these overwhelming obstacles, the gospel would continue to spread throughout the civilized world. Once the latter-day remnant of Israel was gathered into the church and sealed by the Holy Spirit, the events that would bring about the end of the age (of law) would ensue and the church age would commence.

24:15-22 The Abomination of Desolation and the Flight of the Faithful from Jerusalem

The focus narrows to events related to Jerusalem. They would witness the desolating sacrilege in and around the holy region of the city, within its walls, and within the temple. Luke 21:20 informs us that this event would be (or at least be concurrent with) the surrounding of Jerusalem by pagan armies. This would be the signal for Christians to flee Jerusalem and the neighboring areas. It would be a brief window of opportunity. There would be no time to even gather up earthly belongings. They needed to flee to safety because a time of tribulation bringing atrocities that exceeded anything they could imagine was about to begin.

24:23-28 The *Parousia* of Christ

Jesus warns of false prophets in the city who would claim to prophesy deliverance from God. They would even perform false wonders. Some would claim to be the Messiah. In response to their original question regarding his *parousia*, Jesus again affirms that it would not be a bodily appearance as they had been previously taught concerning their Messiah-Deliverer. He draws upon Ezekiel's prophetic imagery (Eze. 21:9ff; cf. Zec. 9:14) to describe his presence as the sword of judgment flashing like lightning from the east–Israel– to the west–Rome. Jesus' imagery characterizes how Rome's invasion of the land had to be suspended in 69 AD upon news of Nero's death. His burning of Rome and subsequent suicide caused great civil unrest that erupted in Rome, which brought it to near collapse. God was shaking both the empire and the land of Israel. However, order was eventually restored, and the Roman armies re-engaged the assault. They descended upon the land like vultures, then finally and mercilessly upon the dead carcass of Jerusalem. It was destroyed from within by the Zealots and from without by Rome.

24:29-31 The Fall of Jerusalem

The apostles understood the meaning of the "cosmic" imagery. Stars falling, the lights of the sun and moon failing, and similar images were part of their prophetic history. The last vestiges of the age of the Law of Moses would be destroyed. Daniel's prophecy (Dan. 7:13-14) would be fulfilled. The Son of Man will have been given dominion and passed judgment in favor of the saints, having vanquished the generation of his enemies. Jesus promised that he would gather* his own to safety from wherever they were during this period of great destruction (cf. Rev. 7:1-8). This gathering may have included the resurrection of the Old Testament saints (cf. Matt. 27:51; Rev. 11:18).

24:32-36 The Timing of the Events

The generation of the disciples would witness Jesus' prophecy. The destruction of Jerusalem, the land, and the temple is described as the *passing away of heaven and earth* (the heavens and the land). These had once been the sacred spaces under the Old Covenant, the replica of heaven on earth. He assures them that although these were passing away, his words would endure. Jesus knew only the generation. The precise day (*that day*) was known by the Father alone.

*Special note concerning Matthew 24:31

With respect to the gathering of the elect, there is a small minority of full preterist Christians (cf. p. 48) who hold that this event (not a future one) included the rapture of the saints living at that time, concerning which Paul may refer in 1 Thessalonians 4:13-18. I find this to be an intriguing proposition, however, one that I currently neither endorse nor condemn. It has been observed that due to the vast devastation, turmoil, chaos, and death that Josephus describes as occurring during the war of 66–70 AD, it is conceivable that the disappearance of multitudes of believers might not have been noticed. Also, the event occurs at the sound of the trumpet both in Matthew 24:31 and 1 Thessalonians 4:16, both texts having reference to the first century AD (not the end of the world). Therefore, I personally consider it a proposition that is within the realm of possibilities.

CHAPTER 11

THE OLIVET DISCOURSE
MATTHEW 24-25: CONTINUITY OR TRANSITION?

We now come to Part Three of the discourse, beginning in Matthew 24:35-36 and ending in Matthew 26:1, where the gospel writer states:

"When Jesus had finished all these words . . ."

Many notable scholars view this section of the discourse as a *transition* from events in the first century to a *future* return of Jesus. This view is held even among some of those who would generally agree with many of the perspectives I have offered thus far on the Olivet Discourse. However, they believe that the focus of Jesus' teaching shifts to a future, final return of the Lord at the end of history.

"Ok Boys, Now Let's Talk About a Different End" (?)

"Now learn the parable from the fig tree: when its branch has already become tender and puts forth its leaves, you know that summer is near; so, you too, when you see all these things, recognize that He is near, right at the door. Truly I say to you, this generation will not pass away until all these things take place. Heaven and earth will pass away, but My words will not pass away. *But of that day* and hour no one knows, not even the angels of heaven, nor the Son, but the Father alone" (Matt. 24:32-36).

Although there are minor differences of opinion, the phrase, *but of that day*, is often said to represent a transition in the discourse. It is alleged that from this point on, the teachings describe events beyond the time of the disciples; a future return of Jesus and a series of end-of-the-world judgments. I would suggest otherwise. Although there is an acknowledged transition away from the conditions and signs just enumerated, the notion that Jesus suddenly launches into far-future events seems entirely inconsistent with the context of the discourse. There are also reasonable indications in the text that Jesus has not changed the topic or the time frame of his prophecy. In other words, he continues his discourse regarding 70 AD and its consequences. We will now seek to establish key points for reflection as to why

In considering the following, it is important for the reader to recognize that the overriding strength of my rejection of the transition theory is based on the principle of *audience relevance*. As we have seen in other parts of this book, we often make assumptions about the knowledge base of the disciples of Jesus. We assume they understood theological matters the same way we do, when, in fact, they did not. They were first-century Jews who thought and acted as such. They had their own norms and traditional understandings that were largely rooted in rabbinical thinking passed down from their spiritual leaders. Recognizing this will help us see why the Olivet Discourse only has one return of Jesus in view, which occurred in the period of 66–70 AD.

First, why is a transition or change in subject after Matthew 24:34 even necessary? Jesus continues his prophecy with warnings to his attending disciples and turns his focus to the *consequences* relating to the unbelief of the Jewish nation and the fall of Jerusalem. What we have seen in Matthew 24 addresses the *historical circumstances* surrounding his return. Following that, he prepares his disciples concerning the *implications* of the events, especially for the nation of Israel, which was divided over Christ:

> Do you suppose that I came to grant peace on earth [or, *the land*]? I tell you, no, but rather division; for from now on five *members* in one household will be divided, three against two and two against three. They will be divided, father against son and son against father, mother against daughter and daughter against mother, mother-in- law against daughter-in-law and daughter-in-law against mother- in-law."
> (Luke 12:52-53).

He had just recalibrated their understanding of the nature of his return (see Chapter 6). Now, the outcomes of that return would also be a departure from their prior learning. With that, Jesus could only affirm the generation of his *parousia* (v. 34). His disciples would see and experience all of which he spoke, but the precise day and hour of the passing away of the Jewish system were known only by the Father (v. 36). It would make sense, therefore, that Jesus would refer to the specific day as *that day and hour.* In addition, as we saw in our previous chapter, if we approach the discourse with a theological precommitment that there is a future return of Jesus in the prophecy, we are assuming the disciples had knowledge of future events concerning which Jesus did not provide them prior to this discourse.

I would suggest that the whole transition argument starts with a presupposition regarding things concerning which Jesus never spoke, then seeks to establish them in the remainder of his narrative. Scholarly explanations of the alleged transition in content often present elaborate (and quite impressive) explanations of nuances in the Greek text that characterize a transition. However, a fundamental issue demands consideration. When did the disciples become familiar with, or at some point inquire about a future end of the world, *a that day*? It was not even in their worldview at any time during Jesus' earthly ministry. Anything beyond the end of their present age and the birth of the age to come was nowhere in view (see Chapter 2). Nothing in the context requires a change in topic. They had inquired concerning the end of *their* age–the end of olam hazeh. The *parousia* of Jesus, their Messiah, meant that the long-awaited olam haba, the age to come, would arrive with all its attendant glories. That launched the entire discourse, and that alone is precisely what Jesus answered and described. He spoke only concerning the end of the Mosaic age, the dawning age, and the eternal life pertaining to it.

Second, the passing away of heaven and earth, or "the heavens and the land," in verse 35 is not the sky and the planet. It was the collapse of the Jewish economy, the city, and the temple. Jesus stated that heaven and the land would pass away, but his words would never pass away. In ancient Jewish cosmology (the origin or make-up of the universe), Israel's land, Jerusalem, and the temple comprised their God-given creation. It was his covenant domain. Beyond Israel's borders were the raging seas–the stormy, unsettled regions of the Gentile nations–beautifully illustrated in Isaiah, who uses poetic parallelism and repetition:

> Oh, the uproar of many peoples
> Who roar like the roaring of the seas,
> And the rumbling of nations
> Who rush on like the rumbling of mighty waters!
> The nations rumble on like the rumbling of many waters . . .
> (Isa. 17:12-13).

- peoples . . . roar like seas
- nations . . . rush like mighty waters
- nations . . . rumble like many waters

In contrast, the land, with its city and sanctuary, was the place of God's *shalom* (Heb. peace; rest) and his enthronement. It was his own creation. Isaiah spoke again in his prophecies of post-exile hope, saying that it was God who stirred up the nations (seas) against them, causing their exile. Yet he assures them he intends to establish his heavenly reign once again in the land:

> "For I am the LORD your God, who stirs up the sea and its waves roar (the LORD of hosts is His name). I have put My words in your mouth and have covered you with the shadow of My hand, to establish [lit., plant] the heavens, to found the earth [*eretz*: land], and to say to Zion, 'You are My people'" (Isa. 51:15-16).

Isaiah describes the entire scope of Israel's privileges. In settling the nation in their land, giving them his word, and establishing the holy city and temple, God was *planting heaven on earth*. He prepared an environment in a world plagued by the corruption of the powers of sin and death where he could dwell among them. Jesus uses this same imagery in Matthew 13, where he explains how the kingdom is planted like a seed in the earth:

> "The kingdom of heaven is like a mustard seed, which a man took and sowed in his field" (Matt. 13:31).

Also, in the Lord's Prayer, he petitions the Father that the realities of his kingdom be reflected on earth:

> 'Your kingdom come.
> Your will be done,
> On earth as it is in heaven'
> (Matt. 6:10).

The context in which Jesus had just spoken regarding the collapse of these ancient sacred spaces in Matthew 24:1-34 leads me to believe that he is still talking about those very things. All that Israel had known before—the *planted* heavens and the land—which was the covenantal domain of God, would pass away with the Old Covenant. His own teaching would remain and endure. The physical things, as observed by the writer of Hebrews, were about to be shaken and destroyed. Only the eternal, unshakable kingdom of God would remain (Heb. 12:26-27).

The Temple as a Microcosm of the Universe

Dr. Paul Penley explains the meaning behind the temple in ancient Jewish thought:

> . . . the Jerusalem temple had been built to look like a microcosm of the universe . . . According to Josephus, two parts of the tabernacle were "approachable and open to all" but one was not. He explains that in so doing Moses "signifies the earth and the sea, since these two are accessible to all; but the third portion he reserved for God alone because heaven is inaccessible to men" (Ant. 3:181, see 3:123).

> In Talmudic tradition, Rabbis described how the inner walls of the temple looked like waves of the sea (b. Sukk. 51b, b.B.Bat. 4a). From heaven and earth inside the temple, you looked out at the sea surrounding the world. Why? Ancients believed the earth had one giant land mass surrounded by sea. The temple reflected that cosmology . . . Isaiah used the same language of "heaven and earth" to depict Jerusalem and her citizens in Isaiah 65:17-18.

> "For behold, I create new heavens and a new earth; and the former things will not be remembered or come to mind. But be glad and rejoice forever in what I create; For behold, I create Jerusalem* for rejoicing and her people for gladness."

> He uses Hebrew parallelism to equate the creation of "new heavens and a new earth" with the restoration of Jerusalem . . .[54]

This same understanding of the temple, its functions, the elements of the Law, and the land is found in Peter's description of the soon-coming day of the Lord. He tells his readers to be prepared, as these foundations of their Jewish heritage were about to be consumed by fire in the Roman invasion (note the imagery drawn from Psalm 18:7, 15):

But the day of the Lord will come like a thief, in which the heavens will pass away with a roar and the elements will be destroyed with intense heat, and the earth [*land*] and its works will be burned up. Since all these things are to be destroyed in this way, what sort of people ought you to be in holy conduct and godliness, looking for and hastening the coming of the day of God, because of which the heavens will be destroyed by burning, and the elements will melt with intense heat! (2 Pet. 3:10-12).

Third, **audience relevance matters.** Nothing in the words of Jesus indicates that he suddenly began to describe something future with which his disciples had no familiarity. The entire context of Matthew 24:36-51 has to do with the expectations and preparedness *of his immediate audience*. We often forget that Jesus was speaking directly to a group of men in front of him. He wasn't pontificating into mid-air.

All three gospel writers affirmed that only the Father knew the exact day and hour. Then they each recorded how Jesus admonished the disciples to be in readiness.

What would be the point of the following warnings if they referred to something well beyond the lifetimes of these disciples? These are his words *after* the so-called transition in Matthew 24:36:

"Therefore, be on the alert, for *you* [the disciples] do not know which day your Lord is coming" (Matt. 24:42).

"For this reason, *you* [the disciples] also must be ready; for the Son of Man is coming at an hour when *you* [the disciples] do not think He will" (Matt. 24:44).

"Be on the alert then, for *you* [the disciples] do not know the day nor the hour" (Matt. 25:13).

Upon consideration of these statements, I must appeal to those who hold the transition theory. It is alleged that there are expressions in the original Greek text that support a transition. However, we must ask: *Who was Jesus talking to?* The obvious answer is *the disciples*. If his disciples understood (or were being given new understanding) that he was talking about the end of the world, which was far removed from their present time, why would they be exhorted to *be on the alert*?

> *If Jesus wasn't addressing issues relating to the fall of Jerusalem but rather the end of the world, then we are left with the absurd notion that he warned them to prepare for the possibility that the world might end before the Roman invasion of 66-70 AD, which is obviously untenable.*

Only in Matthew

Most of the text in Matthew 24:35–26, which is Part Three of the discourse and includes the parables of the virgins and the talents, and the judgment of the sheep and goats, is included *only in Matthew's Gospel.* That information, in this context, is directed toward a decidedly Jewish audience. It pertained to their people, land, city, and temple. Mark 13 and Luke 21 offer only minimal portions of this material regarding Jesus' remarks on readiness. In Luke 17, he mentioned the days of Noah, but even there he spoke to his disciples and in the presence of the Pharisees (Luke 17:20). The less "Jewish" versions of the discourse in Mark and Luke most likely omit these additions because they would not have the same relevance to Gentiles as they would to Jews.

However, this begs an interesting question. If Jesus spoke about the end of the world, why would these detailed instructions not be included in the other versions of the prophecy offered by Mark and Luke? Would it not have been just as important to them? Admittedly, we can't underscore what the Bible doesn't say or the audience to whom it doesn't speak. Nevertheless, the interpretive principle of audience relevance suggests that this at least be considered a significant question.

Fourth, the parousia (a single event in this context) is described in the same manner before and after the so-called transition text. Jesus states in both contexts, "and so will be the coming [parousia] of the Son of Man." In Matthew 24:37, the apostle records precisely the same Greek expression appearing in Matthew 24:27. If verse 27 is specific to his coming in judgment in 70 AD, how does that identical language referring to his coming in the first century now mean something two millennia or more in the future? The same coming [*parousia*] of the Son of Man is mentioned as follows:

> "For as the lightning comes from the east and shines as far as the west, so will be the coming of the Son of Man" (Matt. 24:27 ESV; referring to 70 AD).

> For as were the days of Noah, so will be the coming of the Son of Man (Matt. 24:37 ESV; does it now mean the end of the world?)

Observe the Greek of Matthew 24:27 and 24:37. You can see that the Greek text (transliterated for the non-Greek reader) is identical in both cases:

> Matt. 24:27 outos estai [kai] he parousia tou uiou tou anthropou

> Matt. 24:37 outos estai [kai] he parousia tou uiou tou anthropou

> Translation: "so will [also] be the presence [*parousia*] of the son of man" (the Received Text [KJV] adds *kai*: translated "also").[55]

There is nothing distinct in either verse in Matthew's record regarding the phrase, *the parousia.* There is no hint that the first statement is "a" *parousia* and the second is "the" or "another" *parousia* referring to a future time. Why would we be asked to believe that these events are centuries apart?

Fifth, Jesus' following references in Matthew 24–25 to a delay or a long time should not be assumed to mean his parousia might be two thousand years or more in the future of his disciples:

"But if that evil slave says in his heart, 'My master is not coming for a long time,' and begins to beat his fellow slaves and eat and drink with drunkards . . ." (Matt. 24:48-49)

"Now while the bridegroom was delaying, they all got drowsy and began to sleep" (Matt. 25:5).

"Now after a long time the master of those slaves *came and *settled accounts with them" (Matt. 25:19).

In the Parable of the Servants, the delay is merely *a perception* on the part of the servant. In the two parables that follow, it is stated as an actual delay or long time. Regarding these descriptions of the delay, consider the following:

It is regrettably presumptuous and theologically biased on our part to assume that the phrases describing the Lord's time away (delay; long time) must refer to several thousand years or more. The phrase "a long time" is not an absolute measure of time, and neither is the "delay" in the teachings of Matthew 24–25. These expressions must be understood relative to the expectations of those who heard his words.

Let's say, for example, that, when a friend and I were at the tender age of twenty, he left the U.S.A. for Europe, planning to return in a couple of months. Forty years later, when he finally returned, I was a 60-year-old grandfather. I strongly doubt anyone would disagree that he was away for a *long time*! It cannot be underestimated how deeply disciples' expectations were ingrained in their understanding of Messiah's role. Jesus would disappear and then return from seclusion in a couple of months. It was so deeply rooted that they were still asking about it, right up to the time of his ascension!

So when they had come together, they were asking Him, saying, "Lord, is it at this time You are restoring the kingdom to Israel?" (Acts 1:6).

Given that expectation, we could safely assume that a 20, 30, or 40-year wait would certainly qualify as a long time. Note how the phrase *long time* is used in other New Testament contexts:

> A man was there who had been ill for *thirty-eight years*. When Jesus saw him lying there, and knew that he had already been *a long time* in that condition, He *said to him, "Do you wish to get well?" (John 5:5-6).

> Now Herod was very glad when he saw Jesus; for *he had wanted to see Him for a long time*, because he had been hearing about Him and was hoping to see some sign performed by Him (Luke 23:8).

As we saw in Chapter 6, a messianic trip to heaven and return in the distant future were beyond the scope of their worldview. Most importantly, the context of the discourse does not support it. Given that, and although I have elected not to delve into the matter at any length, I believe the preceding explanation provides a decisive counterargument to the common scholarly theory that there was a *delay in the parousia*. That is to say, Jesus' return was expected in the first century but delayed for some unstated reason (although some have attempted to explain why). However, if we acknowledge that the delay as it is described in the Olivet Discourse pertains to a possible forty-year wait as opposed to the disciples' anticipation of 45–90 days, then the dilemma is resolved. Jesus promised to return in the lifetimes of the disciples, but not in the timeframe or manner that Judaism had taught them. There would be an interval (or delay) of as much as forty years, one biblical generation.

The Days of Noah: Rapture or Invasion?

> "For the coming of the Son of Man will be just like the days of Noah. "For as in those days before the flood they were eating and drinking, marrying and giving in marriage, until the day that Noah entered the ark, and they did not understand until the flood came and took them all away; so will the coming of the Son of Man be. Then there will be

two men in the field; one will be taken and one will be left. Two women will be grinding at the mill; one will be taken and one will be left" (Matt. 24:37-41).

Matthew's version of the Olivet Discourse alone includes Jesus' reference to the days of Noah. The people did not heed Noah's warnings and carried on with life as usual. Luke mentions it in another setting, but also to a Jewish audience, in Luke 17:26ff. To their utter horror, the unsuspecting Jews were tragically taken away in judgment by the flood. Only this time, they would be taken by the flood of Rome's invading armies. The coming prince in the following text from Daniel was General Titus, who led the Roman forces in Jerusalem's destruction. Notice the flood imagery:

> . . . the people of the prince who is to come will destroy the city and the sanctuary. *And its end will come with a flood*; even to the end there will be war; desolations are determined . . . on the wing of abominations *will come* one who makes desolate (Dan. 9:26-27).

These are the concluding words from Daniel 9:24-27, where the prophet is given a 490-year timeline that begins with the Persian decree to release the Jews to rebuild their city and temple. It continues through the life and work of the Lord Jesus and concludes with God's determination that Jerusalem will be desolated, likening it to a flood. Although it deserves more than a mere mention, the timeline was literally fulfilled.

Many suggest that there is a *rapture* in Matthew's statements, distinguishing *those taken from those left*. However, such a proposal reverses the outcome of the story of Noah in Genesis. In the account to which Jesus refers, *Noah and his family were left, not taken*:

> Thus, He blotted out every living thing that was upon the face of the land, from man to animals to creeping things and to birds of the sky, and they were blotted out from the earth; and *only Noah was left, together with those that were with him in the ark* (Gen. 7:23).

". . . just like the days of Noah . . . the flood came and took them all away . . . one will be taken and *one will be left*" (Matt. 24:37-41).

Those who refused to believe Jesus were swept away by the flood, that is, the rushing waters of the invading Romans. The only similarity to Noah's day is that people would conduct their lives as if nothing of consequence was about to occur. Then suddenly, the day would arrive like a flood (cf. Dan. 9:26).

According to Josephus:

> Now the number of those that were taken captive during the whole war was calculated to be ninety-seven thousand, and those that perished during the siege one million one hundred thousand. Of these, the greater part were indeed of the same nation but did not live in the city itself, for they had come up from throughout the country to the Feast of Unleavened Bread . . . [56]

Those who believed Jesus' words were prepared and preserved, having left the city and its environs when the presence of the Roman Army first appeared. Those who were unprepared were swept away in judgment. The focus now shifts to warnings to *his own disciples* not to be distracted by the issues of this life during his absence but to be ready for his return in their generation. His next words to *them* were:

"Therefore, be on the alert."

CHAPTER 12

THE OLIVET DISCOURSE
MATTHEW 25: CONCERNING READINESS AND JUDGMENT

As we proceed to Matthew 25, it is necessary to determine if the parables, illustrations, and warnings can reasonably fit into a first-century context. Remember that in the Olivet Discourse, the parables of the *Ten Virgins, the Talents, and the judgment scene of the Sheep and the Goats are exclusive to Matthew's Gospel.* However, the Parable of the Talents appears in Luke 19:11-27, in a different setting. The most important question to ask is whether these teachings of Jesus can reasonably be interpreted as thematically and historically continuous with his dialogue in the first two parts of the discourse or whether they must be thrust speculatively into the future of the disciples as world-ending scenes.

The Parable of the Ten Virgins

In Matthew 25:1, Jesus continues his discourse on various aspects of the pending judgments. He has just warned the disciples to be prepared. Now he allows us to see the state of God's household in the period of transition from 30 to 70 AD:

> "Then the kingdom of heaven will be comparable to ten virgins, who took their lamps and went out to meet the bridegroom. Five of them were foolish, and five were prudent. For when the foolish took their lamps, they took no oil with them, but the prudent took oil in flasks along with their lamps. Now while the bridegroom was delaying, they all got drowsy and began to sleep. But at midnight there was a shout, 'Behold, the bridegroom! Come out to meet him.' Then all those virgins rose and trimmed their lamps. The foolish said to the prudent, 'Give us some of your oil, for our lamps are going out.' But the prudent answered, 'No, there will not be enough for us and you too; go instead to the dealers and buy some for yourselves.' And while they were going away . . . the bridegroom came, and those who were ready went in with him to the wedding feast; and the door was shut. Later the other virgins also came, saying, 'Lord, lord, open up for us.' But he answered, 'Truly I say to you, I do not know you.' Be on the alert then, for you do not know the day nor the hour" (Matt. 25:1-13).

There are not merely ten virgins, but *two groups of five*. This speaks of the first-century conditions under which Israel and the church co-existed. We have seen that the period was a forty-year probationary transition during which God gave Israel the opportunity to repent and receive the gospel. During this time, there were two covenantal peoples (symbolized as virgins) and two ages of time existing simultaneously in the world. As the darkness and shadows of the Old Covenant were quickly disappearing, the light of the New Covenant age in Christ (and his body) was beginning to shine. As we have seen, the apostolic era was the unique transition during which both periods intersected. In a vision of the period, Zechariah prophesied:

For it will be a unique day which is known to the Lord, neither day nor night, but it will come about that at evening time there will be light. (Zec. 14:7).

The distinction between the two companies of virgins was that there were those who embraced the New Covenant and those who did not. Other details in the parable reinforce this as well. In the Old Testament, the *oil* typically refers to the Holy Spirit's anointing for special service. In the New Testament, God gives the Spirit to those who receive Jesus, just as Peter declared in Acts 2:38, on the day of Pentecost. Those who repented and were baptized received the Spirit as a gift. God's patience allowed for an opportunity for the Jews to repent and receive the gospel before the door would be shut. Those Jews who were ready had oil in their lamps, meaning they had the Spirit in their inner being through faith in Christ. They were received by the Lord when the bridegroom came.

In Revelation 14:1-5, they are seen standing on Mt. Zion, which is New Covenant imagery. They were the remnant of Israel, and as we shall see in Part IV, they were first fruits and, notably, *"virgins" who follow the lamb."* These were the first Jews of God's great gospel harvest that continues through the church age, as James wrote to his first-century Jewish audience (see Jas. 1:1):

In the exercise of His will, He brought us forth by the word of truth, so that we would be a kind of first fruits among His creatures (Jas. 1:18).

Those who remained entrenched in the Old Covenant possessed no oil and were consequently left out when Jesus came and destroyed the temple and its system of worship. They would not enter the promised new age of Messiah. Those who were ready for entrance into the dawning era of the New Covenant, characterized as the wedding feast (cf. Rev. 19), had received the indwelling Holy Spirit through faith in Christ. This meant that their lamps would be lit when the time arrived.

In the meantime, the old oil of the previous covenant had run out for the others. Israel's era of national privilege was coming to an end. The disciples needed to be made aware that not all Israelites would participate in the age to come. Not all Israelites would enjoy the refreshing comfort of the promised Spirit. Faith in Christ had divided the virgins into two camps. This was not an exclusion of only the most derelict of their nation, as was the common understanding offered by their rabbis. It was the disentitlement of even the most noble among them who refused Christ's offer of redemption. There was no place for presumptuousness about their natural heritage. The time of the Mosaic era was now expiring, and its regulations could not light the way or adequately clothe the unbelieving ones for the great wedding of Christ and his bride.

Readiness in this parable meant being filled with the Holy Spirit and clothed with the righteousness that comes only through faith in Christ. Given these realities, the disciples were to be prepared for what was about to transpire in their generation. They needed to be diligent and not slip into complacency or turn back to their cultural and religious comfort zone of Judaism (cf. Heb. 6:4-8). This would be a major temptation when Jesus did not return according to their prior expectations.

The Parable of the Talents

Like the Parable of the Virgins, this parable establishes that ethnicity would no longer be the determining factor in covenant blessing and membership. These *privileges were to be based on personal responsibility and not an exclusive benefit of their Jewish heritage.*

"For it is just like a man about to go on a journey, who called his own slaves and entrusted his possessions to them. To one he gave five talents, to another, two, and to another, one, each according to his own ability; and he went on his journey. Immediately the one who had received the five talents went and traded with them, and gained five more talents. In the same manner the one who had received the two talents gained two more. But he who received the one talent went away, and dug a hole in the ground and hid his master's money. Now after a long time the master of those slaves *came and *settled accounts with them. The one who had received the five talents came up and brought five more talents, saying, 'Master, you entrusted five talents to me. See, I have gained five more talents.' His master said to him, 'Well done, good and faithful slave. You were faithful with a few things, I will put you in charge of many things; enter into the joy of your master.' Also the one who had received the two talents came up and said, 'Master, you entrusted two talents to me. See, I have gained two more talents.' His master said to him, 'Well done, good and faithful slave. You were faithful with a few things, I will put you in charge of many things; enter into the joy of your master.' And the one also who had received the one talent came up and said, 'Master, I knew you to be a hard man, reaping where you did not sow and gathering where you scattered no seed. 'And I was afraid, and went away and hid your talent in the ground. See, you have what is yours.' But his master answered and said to him, 'You wicked, lazy slave, you knew that I reap where I did not sow and gather where I scattered no seed. 'Then you ought to have put my money in the bank, and on my arrival I would have received my money back with interest. 'Therefore take away the talent from him, and give it to the one who has the ten talents.' For to everyone who has, more shall be given, and he will have an abundance; but from the one who does not have, even what he does have shall be taken away. Throw out the worthless slave into the outer darkness; in that place there will be weeping and gnashing of teeth" (Matt. 25:14-30).

Here, as in his parables in Matthew 13, he repeats similar lessons with differing illustrations (wheat and tares, good fish and bad fish, etc.). Jesus uses a different example to affirm that the rewards of the kingdom would not be determined by their Jewish ethnicity but by their personal stewardship over God's resources. This is a major departure from the prior covenant, as John the Baptist had also previously declared:

And do not suppose that you can say to yourselves, We have Abraham for our father; for I say to you that from these stones God is able to raise up children to Abraham (Matt. 3:9).

Under the Old Covenant, privilege was based on Jewish heritage. This was established when the Israelites were formed into a nation at Mt. Sinai (Exodus 19:5; 24:7, 8; 34:10; 34:27-28). In this national covenant, the individual had standing, but only as a member of the elect nation—those born from the patriarchs Abraham, Isaac, and Jacob. However, John the Baptist called the people to individual, personal repentance:

Indeed, the axe is already laid at the root of the trees; so every tree that does not bear good fruit is cut down and thrown into the fire. (Luke 3:8ff).

This is echoed by Paul in Romans:

. . . for we have already charged that both Jews and Greeks are all under sin; as it is written, THERE IS NONE RIGHTEOUS, NOT EVEN ONE (Rom. 3:9-10; cf. Psa. 14:3).

Repentance, personal stewardship, and personal responsibility would be the determining factors in the approaching national judgment. These were the *good fruits* of which the baptizer spoke. The lesson is universal, yet at the same time, it fits well into the conditions of the first century. Obtaining covenantal privileges based merely on natural (Jewish) heritage was no longer a valid assumption. This is especially significant considering the disciples' expectation that Israel was about to assume her role as the head of the nations. Jesus concludes with the casting out of the worthless slave. Outer darkness is an image of someone being removed from the well-lit, joyous feast and cast into the surrounding darkness to face whatever peril may be lurking. It speaks unambiguously, to their surprise, of exclusion. After all, the citizens of the nation were destined for greatness.

In addition to the preceding, this parable bears a strong resemblance to the Parable of the Minas (sums of money) in Luke 19:11-27. Although under different circumstances, both parables address the issue of the nation's stewardship of divinely distributed resources. In Luke's account, Jesus addresses a first century Jewish audience *because he was near to Jerusalem, and because they supposed that the kingdom of God was to appear immediately* (19:11 ESV). In both parables, the stewards who were not faithful in the use of resources are rejected, regardless of their national heritage. Significantly, a major component of both versions (Luke 19:14-15 and Matthew 25:19) is the mention that they are called to give account upon Jesus' return. Luke also notes that those who received the resources rejected his reign. Both the details of this parable and those of Matthew's similar version addressed to the disciples end with the rejection of those Jews who did not act responsibly with God's resources. They would not inherit the kingdom. Both accounts warrant consideration for first–century application.

Sheep and Goats:
A Single, Mixed Flock

"But when the Son of Man comes in His glory, and all the angels with Him, then He will sit on His glorious throne. All the nations will be gathered before Him; and He will separate them from one another, as the shepherd separates the sheep from the goats; and He will put the sheep on His right, and the goats on the left. Then the King will say to those on His right, 'Come, you who are blessed of My Father, inherit the kingdom prepared for you from the foundation of the world. For I was hungry, and you gave Me something to eat; I was thirsty, and you gave Me something to drink; I was a stranger, and you invited Me in; naked, and you clothed Me; I was sick, and you visited Me; I was in prison, and you came to Me.' . . . 'Truly I say to you, to the extent that you did it to one of these brothers of Mine, even the least of them, you did it to Me.' Then He will also say to those on His left, 'Depart from Me, accursed ones, into the eternal fire which has been prepared for the devil and his angels; for I was hungry, and you gave Me nothing to eat; I was thirsty, and you gave Me nothing to drink; I was a stranger, and you did not invite Me in; naked, and you did not clothe Me; sick, and in prison, and you did not visit Me . . . to the extent that you did not do it to one of the least of these, you did not do it to Me.' These will go away into eternal punishment, but the righteous into eternal life" (Matt. 25:31-46).

In Parts III and IV, we will examine the judgment of eternal fire pronounced upon the goats in Matthew 25:41-46. I have elected to reserve that portion for when we survey eternal conscious torment.

In Matthew 25:31, we see the Son of Man coming (in glory), and again, there are two groups gathered for judgment. One major reason I suggest that this points to the first century is that it has Ezekiel 34:17 as its apparent reference. There, God declares he will *divide his own flock in judgment*:

"As for you, My flock, thus says the Lord GOD, Behold, I will judge between one sheep and another, between the rams and the male goats" (Eze. 34:17).

Peter informed us that, at the time of his writing, it was *time for judgment to begin with the household of God* (1 Pet. 4:17). He wrote his letter to the exiles, or sojourners, of the dispersion (1 Pet. 1:1). These were the scattered Jewish tribes who lived among the nations. He saw an imminent separation on the horizon that would divide people in God's household. As Ezekiel had previously declared, the division would be between sheep and goats *within God's own flock*. Jesus' reference to the nations would likely have the pagan world in view (but could also include the various jurisdictions of the land of Israel). It could easily include the Jews who were scattered throughout the empire. There were sheep and goats in every nation. We will see how Jesus illuminates the reasons for that distinction in the judgment scene due to its similarity to what we have just seen regarding the two groups in the Parable of the Ten Virgins. This further convinces me that this is not a judgment that separates entire nations of people at the end of the world. To that point, Jesus employed *God as shepherd* and *people as flock* imagery. In the Bible, this is exclusive to God and his own people, either Israel or the church, depending on the context. As Ezekiel informs us, that flock can and did contain mixed company. We also saw this illustrated in Jesus' parables in Matthew 13. Although the metaphors vary, his judgments in those parables pertain to the mixture among his people at the end of the age:

> "So just as the tares are gathered up and burned with fire, so shall it be at the end of the age. "The Son of Man will send forth His angels, and they will gather out of His kingdom all stumbling blocks, and those who commit lawlessness, and will throw them into the furnace of fire; in that place there will be weeping and gnashing of teeth." (Matt. 13:40-42).

> "Again, the kingdom of heaven is like a dragnet cast into the sea, and gathering fish of every kind; and when it was filled, they drew it up on the beach; and they sat down and gathered the good fish into containers, but the bad they threw away. "So it will be at the end of the age; the angels will come forth and take out the wicked from among the righteous, and will throw them into the furnace of fire; in that place there will be weeping and gnashing of teeth" (Matt. 13:47-50).

There is also an allusion to the seventh chapter of Daniel. The events mentioned in Jesus' judgment scene contain the same elements as those in Daniel's vision. *They are also located historically at the time of the fourth beast, which, as we will see in Revelation, was the Roman Empire. Both Daniel and* Matthew describe a great judgment scene involving:

1. the enthronement of the King
2. judgment being passed in favor of the saints, and
3. their reception of the inheritance of the kingdom

. . . the Ancient of Days came and *judgment was passed in favor of the saints* of the Highest One, and the time arrived when the saints *took possession of the kingdom.* "Thus he said: 'The fourth beast will be a *fourth kingdom on the earth* . . . 'But *the court* will sit for judgment . . . 'Then the sovereignty, the dominion and the greatness of all the kingdoms under the whole heaven will be *given to the people of the saints* of the Highest One; *His kingdom will be an everlasting kingdom,* and all the dominions will serve and obey Him" (See Dan. 7:22-27).

The Treatment of His Brothers

The gospel narratives identify those whom Jesus calls his brothers and the judgment upon those who mistreat them:

Someone said to Him, "Behold, Your mother and Your brothers are standing outside seeking to speak to You." But Jesus answered the one who was telling Him and said, "Who is My mother and who are My brothers?" And stretching out His hand toward His disciples, He said, "Behold My mother and My brothers! "For whoever does the will of My Father who is in heaven, he is My brother and sister and mother" (Matt. 12:46-50).

To assume that the poor, the imprisoned, and the hungry in the narrative of the sheep and goats automatically qualify as Jesus' brothers is, in my opinion, unfortunately not entirely accurate. Nor are these poor and afflicted "brothers" to be understood as Jews. This does not by any means excuse the church from caring for the needy, visiting the poor, the sick, and those in prison, and being ministers of mercy to *any* ethnicity and without partiality. That is central to the mission of the church and reflective of true faith in Christ. There are other texts that command us to show mercy to the poor, the outcast, and those who cannot give us anything in return. Therefore, there is no excuse to abandon a clearly stated charge to the church. However, it does not mean that in Matthew 25:31ff, Jesus makes his mandate to do works of mercy the basis by which someone is awarded eternal life or sent away to eternal separation from God. Many sincere Christians fall short of the goal of charitable deeds. Although that is less than desirable in the eyes of God, it does not negate the work of Christ in someone's life and consign them to eternal separation from God. Yet, this would be the case if we interpret all the poor as his brothers. Therefore, I suggest that in this narrative, Jesus addresses those Jews who received the church and supported it when it was under persecution. The Lord received them because they recognized his disciples as legitimate children of God. They recognized the ambassadors of Jesus, effectively affirming what Jesus had promised in his condemnation of the Pharisees in Matthew 23:39:

> "For I say to you, from now on you will not see Me until you say, 'BLESSED IS HE WHO COMES IN THE NAME OF THE LORD!'"

This was consistent with his preparatory remarks to his disciples as he sent them out, two by two, on their first (trial) mission. They were to declare the arrival of the kingdom through the cities of Israel:

> These twelve Jesus sent out after instructing them: "Do not go in the way of the Gentiles, and do not enter any city of the Samaritans; but rather go to the lost sheep of the house of Israel." (Matt. 10:5-6).

> "He who receives you receives Me, and he who receives Me receives Him who sent Me. He who receives a prophet in the name of a prophet shall receive a prophet's reward; and he who receives a righteous man in the name of a righteous man shall receive a righteous man's reward. And whoever in the name of a disciple gives to one of these little ones even a cup of cold water to drink, truly I say to you, he shall not lose his reward" (Matt. 10:40-42).

These statements also help explain the somewhat puzzling outcome of the Parable of the Unrighteous Steward in Luke 16:9, where Jesus offers a reprieve for an unrighteous steward (Israel):

> "And I say to you, make friends for yourselves by means of the wealth of unrighteousness, so that when it fails, they will receive you into the eternal dwellings" (Luke 16:9).

A Connection to Isaiah 22

The parable's unrighteous steward alludes to Isaiah 22:15-25, where Shebna, who has charge of the royal household, is being deposed from his office for enriching himself in the nation's time of crisis. He will be replaced by Eliakim, who will be given the *key of David*. In Revelation 3:7, Jesus describes himself in that very manner–as the one possessing the key of David. Possession of that key represents the governmental authority of the kingdom.

In Luke's Parable of the Steward, Jesus tells his Jewish audience (the stewards) to use their assets to help suffering Christians and to be generous and faithful in their use of resources. They were being apprised of the fact that, like the collapse of the Jewish hopes in the Isaiah narrative, the Jewish state, their economy, and infrastructure were about to be entirely destroyed in the coming war. *Mammon, their economy, was about to fail.* When this occurs, the church would receive *the generous Jews* and welcome them into their *eternal* dwellings. This meant that the charitable Jews would not lose their reward in Christ's kingdom due to their faithfulness and generosity.

> *God's grace is so abundant that simply by receiving and doing good to his saints, they were acknowledging the truth of Christ as the Messiah and would be rewarded as one of his own. They had blessed those who came in the name of the Lord (Matt. 23:39).*

Again, we read:

"And whoever in the name of a disciple gives to one of these little ones even a cup of cold water to drink, truly I say to you, he shall not lose his reward" (Matt. 10:40-42).

All of which Jesus spoke in the judgment scene described to his twelve disciples in Matthew 25:31-46 was to take place as outcomes in the first century when:

". . . the Son of Man *comes in His glory*, and all the angels with Him, then *He will sit on His glorious throne*" (Matt. 25:31).

This statement echoes his description earlier in the discourse, relating to 70 AD:

". . . the Son of Man coming on the clouds of the sky *with power and great glory* (Matt 24:30).

Are we to assume that these are events separated by twenty centuries or more?

Matthew's Objectives

I have presented this third part of the Olivet Discourse in a first-century Jewish context because it seems consistent with Matthew's theological objectives: (1) The entire context of Matthew 23–25 is strongly Jewish in character, and (2) very little of the three narratives in Matthew 25 is found in the other gospel accounts. Through the entire discourse, Jesus is showing the disciples how and by what measure the nation would be judged at the approaching end of the age. Again, this does not excuse Christians of all ages from being good stewards of God's provisions and doing works of mercy among those in need. However, these perspectives must be considered legitimate possibilities and an alternative to the proposed transition between Matthew 24 and 25 to a future, final judgment. We must attempt to navigate through potential explanations for these texts. There does not appear to be any discernible transition in the subject matter between these two parts of the discourse. Therefore, we should ask ourselves how this part of the discourse can be understood compatibly with the first two parts, rather than as a shift to events two or more thousand years into the disciples' future. Finally, as in our study of the abomination of desolation in Matthew 24, we again find in the Gospel of Luke a *cohesive perspective on the entire discourse.*

Luke to the Rescue (Again)

In Chapter 17 of Luke, he brings key prophetic statements from Matthew 24–25 into a single series. Luke gives us one set of conditions relating to what Jesus called the *days of the Son of Man*. References to the lightning, the days of Noah, the housetops, mill-grinding, and the corpse *all occur in the same time frame in his account*. How, then, can 2000 years *plus* separate them in Matthew? The break or alleged transition in Matthew 24–25 simply does not exist, regardless of where one might attempt to launch it. Luke clarifies this for us in his gospel.

The following table illustrates how the events in Matthew, alleged to be separated by over two millennia, are united into a single time frame in Luke 17:20-37:

The Olivet Discourse:
Mattthew 24 and Luke 17

Matthew 24–25	Luke 17
Five Statements Three of Five in 70 AD:	**Five Statements** All Five in 70 AD:
v. 17-18 "the housetop" v. 26-27 "just as lightning" v. 28 "where the corpse is"	v. 31 the housetop" v. 23-24 "just as lightning" v. 37 "where the body is" v. 26-27 "days of Noah" v. 35-36 "two women grinding"
Matthew is alleged to shift to a future return with a transition 2000 years or more into the future.	Luke affirms with an unbroken discourse that all events occur in the same period.
Two events occur in the future (?)	Nothing specific to a future second coming
v. 37 "days of Noah" v. 40-41 "shall be two men"	---

Table 12.1
Adapted from Various Sources

Excursus:
A Perspective on Exile

Of the 17 prophetic books of the Old Testament, the majority were written from approximately the eighth through the sixth centuries before Christ. Their foremost emphases were the sins of Israel and Judah, the coming destruction of the northern and southern kingdoms, the fall of Samaria, and the razing of Jerusalem and the temple. God sent the pre-exilic prophets during the entire course of the kingdom era to warn the disobedient nation. The decimation of their land, city, and temple was inevitable. These crises would result in the deportation of God's people from their inheritance, but there was also a promise of re-establishment and restoration.

This enormous volume of prophetic literature relating to the sixth-century BC fall of Jerusalem pointed to an exile of the Jews that lasted only two generations. However, that crisis pales in comparison to the theological significance of the catastrophe of 70 AD. The Roman invasion resulted in the Jewish dispersion and their assimilation into the nations, which has lasted to this day. Their progress in re-establishing nationhood and repossessing Palestine during the last century does not change the fact that the temple, the sacrificial system, and the priesthood are all conspicuously absent from their national economy.

As previously affirmed, this is not a value judgment about Jews. It is an assessment of their circumstances since the Roman invasion two thousand years ago that substantiates the fact that it was the most dramatic transition (other than the cross) in the Bible's redemptive history. The historical people of God were disinherited, and their testimonial city and temple were destroyed. How then could we believe that this would hold only a scant, almost incidental forecast or reference by the New Testament writers? Would this not be a focus in their writings for their contemporary Jewish audiences? To think otherwise, we would have to assume (and many do) that they were looking entirely beyond their immediate audiences to future end-time events. However, Jesus taught no such world-ending scenario in the Gospels. He made clear warnings to his historical people concerning the fate of the nation.

Key Observations from Part II

Our observations do not effect a fundamental change in our core Christian faith. However, they should impact our perception of our time and location in history. We are not, as some suppose, looking ahead to a great apocalyptic calamity but looking back at the great consummation that was accomplished in the past.

1. In the Olivet Discourse, Jesus promised his return in judgment within the generation then living. The entire literary context of Matthew 23:1–26:1 and the synoptic parallels in Mark 13 and Luke 21 describe this. Luke 17:23-37 offers an additional and important perspective on that same context. There is no transition in the prophecy that fundamentally changes its substance from the end of the age to the end of the world.

2. Jesus' return (*parousia*) resulted in the conclusion of the mosaic era. Therefore, the biblical end of the age has already passed into history. We are now living in the biblical age to come while on earth and yet experiencing heavenly realities.

3. The signs of the end, including the great tribulation and the return of Jesus, were fulfilled in the forty-year period after his ascension. The Olivet prophecy highlights the conditions leading up to the Jewish-Roman War that concluded with the fall of Jerusalem and the temple in 70 AD.

4. The so-called *parousia delay*, a theological idea suggesting that the return of Jesus was promised to and anticipated by that first generation but delayed, lacks merit. The delay mentioned in the parables must not be interpreted arbitrarily. It must consider the expectations of that first audience, who, at the time they first heard it, were anticipating a messianic return *in the flesh* after a brief departure of 45–90 days. This was consistent with the rabbinical theology of the day.

5. The apostles' expectation of Jesus' imminent return, as seen in their New Testament letters, was not misguided. It was fulfilled in their generation. Jesus came in the clouds, as promised. Their earlier misconceptions were corrected with the arrival of the Holy Spirit at Pentecost, who brought enlightenment to them regarding the times, just as Jesus promised. He came in the same manner described by the prophets, who spoke of God's presence in judgment upon nations. The linguistic style of the prophecy echoes that of the ancient prophets, in whom dwelt the Spirit of Christ.

6. The ingathering of Israel's *last days remnant* is not in our future but occurred in the first century as part of the conclusion of the previous age. This would suggest that the Jews are no longer hardened to the gospel, but that the door of faith is open to all who would enter. Romans 11:25 informs us that the partial hardening was only to last until the full Gentile complement was added to the first-century remnant.

PART III

CONCERNING FINAL DESTINY

"You surely will not die!" (Genesis 3:4)
-The Serpent

CHAPTER 13

DO WE REALLY BELIEVE IT?
A REALITY CHECK

We have seen the significance of understanding the historical context of the New Testament as it relates to the return or *parousia* of Jesus. However, that same first-century context (the Jewish nation on the threshold of exile) also affects our interpretation of eternal destiny. Apart from that background, this book would merely be an opinion regarding two unrelated Christian doctrines. However, they *are* very much related. If we understand the outcomes of the *parousia*, then we will be able to grasp the meaning of the language of fiery destruction of which the Bible speaks. Therefore, we will now examine how the observations we have made play an important role in what the Bible says about the destiny of the lost.

But first, a reality check.

Shhh! Just Talk about the Good Stuff

It's a doctrine most Christians claim to believe but rarely talk about. I have often questioned whether, in the deepest recesses of our hearts, we actually believe it to be true. Frankly, if we really believed that non-Christians will suffer conscious torment in a fiery chamber called *hell* (or any form of agony) for all eternity, we would probably not be able to sleep at night. Or, we would have to look at ourselves in the mirror and admit that we who know Christ may be the most unloving human beings on the planet. To believe this traditional view and yet continue to lead normal lives borders on absurdity. It would be like relaxing comfortably on the patio as we watch our neighbors' homes burn down with the occupants trapped inside. Could we sit there and not lift a finger to help? Yet, that same indifference toward the alleged horrible destiny of nonbelievers speaks volumes about the absence of genuine conviction in our professed acceptance of the doctrine of hell.

Maybe we don't want to intrude on our neighbor's privacy, or we're afraid of what they might think of us. Worst of all, perhaps we're just too busy with the demands of our own lives. In the simple neighborhood example just described, would any of us think or behave that way? I don't think so. Yet, according to traditional theology, without faith in Jesus, those very neighbors are doomed to an eternity of unimaginable, fiery torment. We, however, remain content to live uncaringly, as a horrifying destiny awaits many of those around us.

I find it amazing that eternal conscious torment is rarely discussed. Over the decades, I have scarcely heard it mentioned, let alone taught. Maybe we feel it is just another one of those peripheral doctrines–that we should focus on faith, discipleship, and other more critical issues, which, of course, include *love*. However, if eternal conscious torment is true, it is certainly not a peripheral issue. What could be more important to humanity? Should we not shout it from our pulpits and our housetops day after day without ceasing? Wouldn't it be understood as the core purpose of the crucifixion of Jesus to provide humanity–our friends, neighbors, family members, and co-workers– with an escape from such a fate? How does this measure up with our last Bible study on love? Are we so shallow, or possibly so self-absorbed, that we need constant reassurance of God's love only for ourselves?

If the traditional doctrine is true, nothing in life could matter more than the single fact that millions upon millions of human beings, created in the image of God, are destined to spend all eternity mercilessly tormented in an abyss of burning fire. If we believed it to be true, wouldn't our Bible studies on love teach us to forget about everything else, go out into the streets, malls, and places of business, *and, out of love,* beg people to believe the gospel? Our burden for humanity's fate would cause us to risk our very lives to pull people out of the blazing inferno that awaits them.

Think about it. Personal blessings, a new church building, Sunday school programs, vacations, baseball games, new cars, and haircuts are all so utterly meaningless. As the people of God who know the fates of the saved and the lost, our brief stay on earth should be entirely devoted to getting out into the streets and saving the lost from a destiny of pain and agony beyond belief. Nothing we can fathom surpasses the gravity and urgency of the unimaginable horror allegedly awaiting those who do not know Christ. Knowing that and doing so little about it should prohibit us from looking in the mirror and calling ourselves *Christians.* So, if I suggest we lack a driving conviction concerning the doctrine, maybe there's an explanation:

Could it be possible that such a portrayal of the destiny of the lost is simply not true?

General Overview

Let me begin with my own conclusion: I do not believe that eternal conscious torment is a biblically accurate doctrine. I say *biblically* so that you understand that this is not a conviction that arose out of an emotional distaste for it or mere philosophical appeals, but as a result of research into the biblical texts. To be frank, I don't like the idea of eternal torment, but personal preferences should never be the foundation for theological conclusions. Like a growing number of Christians, my rejection of this doctrine is based solely on the fact that I do not believe it is taught in the Bible. I would add here that I am not theologically liberal or part of a "questionably Christian" group. Some sects hold similar views. However, having a comparable view regarding a doctrine does not in and of itself create an alliance with or suggest an endorsement of a particular sect.

Given the gravity of the topic, I find it odd that there is a lack of urgency that it would deserve. This lack exists not only among *us* but also in the Bible itself. Consider the fact that, beginning with Adam and Eve and through the first century AD, God dealt with fallen humanity for:

- 100 generations, or
- approximately 4000 years, and
- through 65 books of the Bible.

Through the entirety of that redemptive history, God warned us about unbelief and disobedience. *Yet, astonishingly, he never once mentioned the lake of fire.* This place of final torment is finally introduced to us in the latter half of the last book of the Bible: a highly symbolic prophecy called the Book of Revelation.

Uh . . . did I mention 4000 years?

Give or take a century–that's the generally accepted passage of time between the story of Adam and Eve and the writing of the Book of Revelation. Many people died during those four millennia without having the slightest notion of their eternal fate. Hell and eternal torment are not even hinted at in the Law of Moses, the Historical Writings, or the Prophets. In all of God's warnings about disobedience in ancient history, the lake of fire is never mentioned once. The closest thing mentioned is described by the prophets as *unquenchable fire*. However, as we have seen and will pursue further in our study, that image referred to something drastically different from our traditional view of hell. Yet concerning the lake of fire:

> *God never once mentioned it to Adam, Eve, Noah, Abraham, Moses, or Joshua. David never knew about it or warned us of it. In all of Scripture, not a single prophet referred to it until the apostle John, in the latter part of the last book of the Bible.*

Moses, who brought the Law of God into the world, warned that breaking that Law could bring penalties up to and including death. He never warned about being tortured in eternal agony in the lake of fire. God had countless opportunities throughout biblical history to warn his creation about the fate that (supposedly) awaited the disobedient. How could he be so thoughtless, neglecting to warn millions of people of a destiny they didn't even know awaited them? It would seem to me to be a cruel omission, to say the least (pardon my foolishness).

Death's Conqueror

In contrast, what *is* made clear in the Bible is the promise of life to the faithful and obedient. Conversely, death (not hell) is also made clear as the sobering consequence of unbelief. Death is affirmed as having permanence for those who do not serve God. The termination of life was the fate of all (as we will see in Genesis). It was therefore necessary for God to provide a solution to the dominance and utter permanence of death for those who believe. He accomplished this through the gospel:

> . . . our Savior Christ Jesus, who abolished death and brought life and immortality to light through the gospel (2 Tim. 1:10).

Ultimately, the cross and the resurrection of Christ brought freedom from death's power that came through sin. The gospel offers the promise of eternal life, which is the indestructible life of Christ imparted by the Holy Spirit. The outcomes today are as they have always been: receive life or succumb to the power of death's ultimate end, which is the cessation of existence, or extinction. Physical death is certain for all, both righteous and unrighteous, and will be followed by the inevitability of judgment before God (Heb. 9:27). What, then, would be the point of the following texts unless the outcomes they mentioned (life and death) were permanent? There is no mention of an afterlife of eternal torture.

> I call heaven and earth to witness against you today, that I have set before you *life and death*, the blessing and the curse. So choose life in order that you may live, you and your descendants (Deu. 30:19; *no mention of eternal torment here*).

> "You shall also say to this people, 'Thus says the LORD, Behold, I set before you the way of life and the way of death'" (Jer. 21:8; again, "death" not a lake of fire).

> For the wages of sin is death, but the free gift of God is eternal life in Christ Jesus our Lord (Rom. 6:23; this great, enlightened apostle mentions only "death").

Of course, all of this poses a serious question. The teaching of eternal conscious torment stands firmly on the proposition that humans possess *inherent* (or innate) immortality. This is the belief that we were created with immortality within ourselves. However, the common notion that fallen, unregenerate humans will live forever actually has no strong biblical basis. It is a well-established fact that this concept, called *the immortality of the soul,* is rooted in ancient pagan cultures and found its way into Greek mythology and philosophy. It appears to have been integrated first into Hellenistic Judaism in the centuries before the birth of Jesus. It ultimately found its way into Christian theology through early church fathers who were influenced by Greek philosophers, especially Plato.

Does Everyone Live Forever?
A Look at Conditionalism

In direct contrast to inherent immortality, the teaching of conditional immortality (or conditionalism) holds that human beings, in and of ourselves, *are not immortal.* Immortality is *conditional* upon faith in Christ. Conditionalism is not a recent development. In the history of the church, there has always been a diversity of views regarding mortality and torment. This is affirmed by Schaff:

> During the first five centuries of Christianity, there were six theological schools, of which four (Alexandria, Antioch, Caesarea, and Edessa, or Nisibis) were Universalist; one (Ephesus) accepted conditional mortality; one (Carthage or Rome) taught endless punishment of the wicked.[57]

Like any school of theological thought, there are differing views regarding certain details, but briefly, conditionalism teaches that according to God's Word:

1. We do not possess immortality (an immortal soul) within ourselves. *The wages of sin is death* (Rom. 6:23). The soul's immortality is not taught in the Bible. It can be found in Egyptian and Babylonian mythology and eventually became a teaching of Plato. From there, it was carried into the church's theology.

2. Immortality is the gift of God only to those who are redeemed through faith in Christ Jesus. This is emphasized repeatedly in the New Testament. The only source of that life is the *Spirit of Life in Christ Jesus* (Rom. 8:2), given to us who believe.

3. Because the fallen individual is not inherently immortal, the final state of the unredeemed following the judgment is extinction (or annihilation)–the whole being consumed by death. It is the likely meaning of John's *second death*, the consuming lake of fire in the Book of Revelation (2:11, 20:6, 14, 21:8). This will be discussed further in Part IV.

The Lone Possessor of Immortality

To whatever degree we might understand the non-physical aspect of our being and its temporary consciousness beyond the grave, it can only remain permanently conscious if infused with the Spirit and power of God, because he alone possesses immortality. Concerning this, we are informed in 1 Tim. 6:15-16:

> He who is the blessed and only Sovereign, the King of kings and Lord of lords, *who alone possesses immortality* and dwells in unapproachable light.

Even for those who believe, the Holy Spirit is the one and only source of sustained life after death. He is the life of God, joined together with the believer:

> But the one who joins himself to the Lord is one spirit *with Him* (1 Cor. 6:17, "with him" added for clarity by the translators).

Observe again how Paul emphasizes that the Holy Spirit is the sole source of eternal life in the believer, both now and in resurrection:

> However, you are not in the flesh but in the Spirit, if indeed the Spirit of God dwells in you. But if anyone does not have the Spirit of Christ,

he does not belong to Him. If Christ is in you, though the body is dead because of sin, yet the spirit is alive because of righteousness. But if the Spirit of Him who raised Jesus from the dead dwells in you, He who raised Christ Jesus from the dead will also give life to your mortal bodies through His Spirit who dwells in you (Rom. 8:9-11).

The uniqueness of that resurrection life is *indestructibility*:

[Jesus' permanent priesthood is] . . . according to the power of an indestructible life (Heb. 7:15-16).

Given that the Holy Spirit alone is life (Rom. 8:9-11), it begs the question: Is there another source of indestructible life for unbelievers who do not possess the Holy Spirit, concerning which God has not told us? If he has not told us, then how can we develop afterlife theologies concerning another source of eternal life from what is not written in the Scriptures?

There is much to be understood and ample debate about our condition immediately following death, which is the post-mortem, intermediate state. However, it is evident that God will sustain post-mortem consciousness only for the purpose of facing him in judgment:

And inasmuch as it is appointed for men to die once and after this comes judgment (Heb. 9:27).

If eternal torment is true, then after judgment, God will *allegedly* sustain permanently alive countless numbers of unbelieving people by an undisclosed means, only to torture them mercilessly and endlessly with no possibility of escape. The Holy Spirit, who, according to Romans 8:9-11, is the only source of eternal (permanent) life, is withheld from them. Rather than letting them mercifully go into extinction, these wretched, lifeless zombies will *presumably* be sustained by a sovereign act of God, who will inflict unrelenting and unimaginable torture upon them. This would allegedly be their fate, as opposed to mercifully allowing their mortality to consume them in death. This is affirmed in Article 37 of the honored *Belgic Confession*, an orthodox statement of faith of the Christian Reformed Church in America. It states (in part) that the wicked will be made immortal and will be tormented in the eternal fire:

> The evil ones will be convicted
> by the witness of their own consciences, and shall be made immortal —
> but only to be tormented
> in "the eternal fire prepared for the devil and his angels."[58]

With respect to my Reformed brothers and sisters and those Christian confessions that hold a similar or identical belief, we will shortly see that there is no evidence in the Bible that supports the notion that the unredeemed "shall be made immortal–but only to be tormented." Although his judgments are severe at times, the biblical God has reconciled himself to his creation by giving his Son for it:

> Now all *these* things are from God, who reconciled us to Himself through Christ and gave us the ministry of reconciliation, namely, that God was in Christ reconciling the world to Himself, not counting their trespasses against them, and He has committed to us the word of reconciliation Therefore, we are ambassadors for Christ, as though God were making an appeal through us; we beg you on behalf of Christ, be reconciled to God (2 Cor. 5:18-20).

His *attitude* toward the world is redemptive because of what Christ has done. This is not *universal salvation*, as some believe, but a passionate plea from God to accept his offer of reconciliation. Eternal life comes only through the Holy Spirit, who, because of Christ, has been "*poured out upon all flesh*" (Acts 2:28) to offer and convict, making new birth possible. The options are to receive that life or succumb to the power of death. He commands his church, his ambassadors, to extend mercy and love to all in this life. He knows that without Christ, fallen humans are but rational beasts whose end is the grave:

For the fate of the sons of men and the fate of beasts is the same. As one dies so dies the other; indeed, they all have the same breath and there is no advantage for man over beast, for all is vanity (Ecc. 3:19).

Final and irreversible death, or the termination of existence, is a merciful end from a merciful God. *There is no other source of permanently sustained life after death except the Holy Spirit dwelling within.* The entire notion that God will resurrect unbelievers only to judge them, punish them, and then sovereignly and mercilessly sustain them (apart from the life of the Holy Spirit) in an eternal torture chamber is entirely inconsistent with his revealed nature. It is also contrary to his revelation concerning the Spirit as the only true source of immortality.

The unredeemed have only this temporal, mortal life. Once judged, and possibly experiencing some measure of punishment, death and only death awaits them. Contrarily, those who have been reckoned as righteous because of the Spirit of Life through faith in Christ Jesus will experience an eternal life that shall never be extinguished. Neither can it be extinguished because it is God's divine life and his alone with which we have been endowed. Whether redeemed or unredeemed, human beings in and of themselves do not inherently possess immortality. It is an attribute of God alone and is imparted to us when we are joined to him.

Sins Against an Eternal God

There is a common argument that states that sins against an eternal God must be punished for eternity to be consistent with God's justice. This is not a novel argument. It was one offered by the scholastic theologian Anselm of Canterbury (1033–1108 AD), who was apparently influenced by the concept of justice existing in feudal society in medieval Europe. In feudalism, the severity of an offense was more dependent on the social status of the one offended than the severity of the offense itself. However, I would suggest that just punishments must not be based on man's perception of justice but must be consistent with how they are described and defined in the Law of Moses, which reflects God's own justice. Israel's execution of the Law's judgments was to be suitable and proportional to the crime committed (e.g., Lev. 24:17- 20, *an eye for an eye,* etc.), and not affected by the social status of either party.

This means that under the Mosaic Law, one could not be subjected to torture for stealing a loaf of bread or more harshly punished based on the stature of the one offended. The text of Leviticus 24:17ff, referred to as the *lex talionis* (Latin: *the law of retaliation*), affirms the equality of all human beings:

> If a man takes the life of any human being, he shall surely be put to death. The one who takes the life of an animal shall make it good, life for life. If a man injures his neighbor, just as he has done, so it shall be done to him: fracture for fracture, eye for eye, tooth for tooth . . . (Lev. 24:17-20).

Biblical justice requires that the *crime*, not the status of the person harmed, determines the punishment, even if the one harmed is God. The following are examples of capital sins (*those punishable by death*) in the Law of God. Notice that those against man and those against God were both equally punishable by death. The punishments were inarguably severe; however, there was no provision for excessive torture for sins against God:

Against Man: homicide, striking one's parents, adultery, and kidnapping

Against God: witchcraft, divination, worshiping other gods, violating the Sabbath, and blasphemy

Regardless of whether the capital sin was committed against man or God, the penalty was the same: *death*. The teaching that God's eternal nature requires eternal punishment (because of his deity) seems to fall far short of the *biblical* concept of justice. Once again, the Bible's plain statement about the *ultimate penalty* for sin seems quite clear:

> *The soul who sins will die* (Eze. 18:4, 20; the Hebrew "nephesh," translated "soul," is a living being or creature; the person; the whole as human or animal).

> The wages of sin is *death*, but the free gift of God is eternal life in Christ Jesus our Lord (Rom. 6:23).

> For if you live according to the flesh, you will die . . . (Rom. 8:12)

> *According to the Bible, immortality is a glorious gift from God. It is never described as a horrible, irreversible sentence of unending and unimaginable torture.*

"Conscious" Torment?

A 2012 article published by *Answers in Genesis* dealt with the subject of hell. With due respect to the author and the organization, I was taken aback by the arguments presented in the article. Of particular interest was the defense of the *conscious* aspect of eternal torment. The author used Jesus as the example by considering his personal suffering. He states that because Jesus suffered consciously for our sin, *the unredeemed must consciously suffer* (after death) to bear the judgment for their own sin.[59] I think the author sought to extrapolate quite an extravagant point from Jesus' sufferings.

First, Jesus suffered while alive, not after his death. There is no evidence that his suffering continued after his death. *Second,* he suffered *death* for our sins. His payment of the penalty for sin was accomplished not only by his suffering but also by his death. His suffering ended with his death. In fact, his suffering is often spoken of as *synonymous* with his death:

"And He [Jesus] said to them, "Thus it is written, that the *Christ would suffer and rise again from the dead* the third day" (Luke 24:46).

. . . explaining and giving evidence *that the Christ had to suffer and rise again from the dead* . . . (Acts 17:3).

We cannot separate the redemptive purpose of the two (suffering and death). Together, they constitute his substitutionary judgment for sin and its ultimate consequence, *which is death*:

. . . because of the *suffering of death* crowned with glory and honor, so that by the grace of God He (Jesus) might taste death for everyone (Heb. 2:9).

For while we were still helpless, at the right time Christ *died* for the ungodly (Rom. 5:6).

There is a legitimate possibility that the lost, based on the severity of their sins, *may* experience some suffering in the process of the second death spoken of in Revelation 2:6; 20:6; 20:14; and 21:8. However, Jesus' suffering for sin *while alive* cannot be wrestled into an example of *permanent* conscious suffering of unbelievers *after death*. The entire argument is based on a faulty premise. He was stricken at the cross to absorb the wrath of God as punishment for our sins. However, he did not taste an afterlife of eternal conscious torment. He tasted death for us, which is the wages of sin.

And he decisively conquered it.

CHAPTER 14

IN THE BEGINNING

Bible scholars refer to the widely held *first mention principle* as an important rule or principle of biblical interpretation. This principle establishes that the most basic understanding of a biblical word or concept can be seen in its first appearance in the Bible. Consistent with this principle, conditional immortality is affirmed in the opening chapters of the Book of Genesis. It is apparent from the Bible's seminal narratives that Adam and Eve's ultimate threat for disobedience against God was not hell. God clearly stated that the consequence of their disobedience would be death. When they sinned, God responded to their actions by barring them from the tree of life, which was their source of immortality.

You Shall Surely Die? Or Be Forever Tormented.

The Bible teaches us that Adam and Eve were created in the image of God from the dust of the earth. They were to be his representatives over the creation (Gen. 1:27). Adam's lifeless, created form, shaped from the dust of the ground, became animated by the Spirit-breath of God. As a result, Adam became a living being. Then the Lord God created Eve from Adam. They were placed in the garden and given only one recorded restriction, which was to refrain from eating fruit from the tree of the knowledge of good and evil. The couple was privileged to tend the garden as the habitation of God, populate the earth with children, and eat the fruit of the trees and the produce of the garden. Best of all, they would enjoy immortality by virtue of eating from the tree of life.

There is no evidence in these earliest narratives that *any* aspect of their being (as living souls) was inherently immortal. The text states that when God breathed his (Spirit) breath of life into Adam, he *became* a living soul (Gen. 2:7), not that he *possessed* a soul as a part of his being. Many Bible versions now translate Genesis 2:7 not as *a living soul but* as *a living creature* or *a living being* (see: ESV, ISV, LSV, NAS95, NRSV, YLT). Adam's being appears to have been the combination of two elements: the dust of the ground and the breath of God.

The same Hebrew word for soul (*nephesh*) is used in biblical texts to describe both creatures and humans. The use of the phrase *my soul* in the biblical texts is better understood to mean *my being, I,* or *me.* This certainly presents the possibility that our Christian understanding of *the soul* may be influenced more by Greek philosophy than its original meaning in the Hebrew Scriptures. However, I wish to point out that precisely how human beings are constituted remains for me an open question, and the concepts being set forth are unaffected by one's view of the physiology of human beings. The only exception is that *no aspect* of our being is inherently immortal.

The Image of God

Although Adam and Eve were created in God's image, we cannot assume that likeness included inherent immortality any more than it meant the possession of omnipotence, omniscience, or omnipresence. Those attributes, like immortality, belong to God alone. Therefore, if we are to enjoy it, it must be conferred upon us by God. In the garden, that conferral came by means of the tree of life and *only* from that external source. This tree must have, in some measure, reflected the partaking of God's life-giving Spirit. It is apparent in Genesis that the tree was not an absolute necessity for fellowship with God in the sense of interaction and communication, because in the Genesis account Adam, Eve, and others spoke freely with God even after they sinned. The fruit of the tree was their source of his eternal life, and therefore:

If Adam and Eve were created inherently immortal, they would not need the tree of life to sustain their imperishability. Their immortal, sinless state would have allowed them to maintain a perpetual existence without it.

However, in contrast to this, because of their disobedience to God, they were forbidden access to that sole source of perpetual existence:

. . . and now, he might stretch out his hand, and take also from the tree of life, and eat, and live forever"– therefore the LORD God sent him out from the garden of Eden . . . (Gen. 3:22-23).

God's commandment included the straightforward injunction:

". . . in the day you eat of it you shall surely die" (Gen. 2:17).

Scholars tell us that the Hebrew text reads more literally, *dying, you shall die.* Because of the transgression of our ancient parents, the power of death entered humanity. Although our fallen mortal life continues for a season, God decreed with divine certainty that the power of death at work in us would inevitably conquer. Our existence would cease. We would inevitably return to the dust from where we were formed:

> "By the sweat of your face
> You will eat bread,
> Till you return to the ground,
> Because from it you were taken;
> For you are dust,
> And to dust you shall return"
> (Gen. 3:19).

Though God exhaled his divine (S)spirit-breath into Adam to animate him, it (he) would not continue with him after death. This we learn later in Scripture that at death, the (S)spirit-breath of life returns to God:

> . . . then the dust will return to the earth as it was, and the spirit [or breath] will return to God who gave it (Ecc. 12:7).

The final mortality of the entire human being in the Genesis record, (Gen. 3:19, 22-24) must be reckoned with:

> "Because from it [the ground] you were taken;
> For you are dust,
> And to dust you shall return."
> Then the LORD God said, "Behold, the man has become like one of Us, knowing good and evil; and now, he might stretch out his hand, and take also from the tree of life, and eat, and live forever"– therefore the LORD God sent him out from the garden of Eden, to cultivate the ground from which he was taken. So He drove the man out; and at the east of the garden of Eden He stationed the cherubim and the flaming sword which turned every direction to guard the way to the tree of life.

The text states that God wholly eliminated the possibility of Adam and Eve living forever through the tree of life while in their fallen state. This far-reaching loss is further explained in the following insight from

Adam Clarke (a noted 18th–19th century commentator). Clarke states that Genesis 3:22 should be translated *"The man 'was' as one of Us."*

> This text [Gen. 3:22-24] is allowed to be difficult, and the difficulty is increased by our translation, which is opposed to the original Hebrew and the most authentic versions. The Hebrew has . . . hayah, which is the third person preterite [past] tense, and signifies was, not is . . . there is an ellipsis [omission in the text] of some words which must be supplied in order to make the sense complete.[60]

The highly respected Young's Literal Translation agrees with Clarke's rendering of the Hebrew tense of Gen. 3:22:

> And Jehovah God saith, "Lo, the man was as one of Us."

According to Clarke's comments and Young's translation, the sense of the text is that they would toil in their natural lives until the power of death overtook them and they return to the dust. The Lord declared that these who had borne his image were now fallen, having abandoned his divine splendor. They had chosen the knowledge of good and evil over the experience of heavenly, immortal life. In his great mercy, God would not allow them to continue to eat from the tree of life and, by that means, live forever in their wretched, fallen state. Therefore, he sent them from the garden and removed the possibility of their reentry, guarding its entrance with the flaming sword and the two cherubim.

Whether we approve or disapprove of Clarke's translation or the precision of the explanation, one thing remains: God removed the possibility of humans living forever in our fallen state. That is clear from the text of Genesis 3. Yet, in what seems to be in direct contradiction to this, the church's doctrine of eternal conscious torment teaches the exact opposite of what the Scriptures say by insisting that fallen humans live forever in their resurrected bodies and in the fires of hell.

In Wrath, Remember Mercy (Hab. 3:2)

Both Habakkuk 3:2 and Genesis 8:20-22 remind us of how God's awareness of our pitiful condition provokes him to merciful responses, even in his judgments. When the Eden story is seen through this lens, we understand the merciful character of God's response to the circumstances in the garden. Yes, there would be consequences because of sin. Women would know pain in childbirth, and men would toil for their food by the sweat of their brows. However, God provided a covering for Adam and Eve's shame through sacrificial animal blood and coats from the animals' skins for the couple's nakedness. We see the same merciful response to humanity's condition in the post-flood account in Genesis:

> . . . and the LORD said to Himself, "I will never again curse the ground on account of man, for the intent of man's heart is evil from his youth; and I will never again destroy every living thing, as I have done.
> While the earth remains,
> Seedtime and harvest,
> And cold and heat,
> And summer and winter,
> And day and night
> Shall not cease" (Gen. 8:20-22).

Adam and Eve's helpless, pathetic condition provoked our maker to show pity on them in their weakness. As an ultimate act of grace, the Lord God removed the possibility of them living forever in their fallen, humiliated state. He did not suddenly shift from his act of mercifully covering their sin and the shame of their nakedness, only to usher them abruptly from the garden in blistering anger. The image of the massive finger of an enraged, vengeful God pointing Adam and Eve to the exit is, in my opinion, an unfortunate mischaracterization. I suggest that the scene be better understood as *"I'm sorry, children. I can't allow you to live here anymore."* He had already looked past Eve's shame and provided assurance, even in judgment, that through her he would bring forth a seed to destroy the serpent (Gen. 3:16). His compassion would remain with them all their days until death overtook them and they mercifully returned to dust.

There is not even a hint in this narrative that fallen humankind's fate is an immortal existence in agonizing flames. The final cessation of existence is the ultimate act of divine mercy upon fallen humanity. Apart from Christ, we are but dust, and to that we return (Gen. 3:19). The inner being (spirit) of man, as we have observed, returns to God, who gave it (Ecc. 12:7).

To summarize, the following is my proposed takeaway from this vital Genesis narrative:

1. Adam was created from the dust of the earth and then animated when the (S)spirit-breath of God entered him. This merging of man and the divine Spirit resulted in man becoming a living being, or soul. In this context, the soul appears to be our entire living person.

2. The Hebrew term *nephesh* (translated soul) is used to describe both human and animal life in the Old Testament. Adam's designation as a *living soul* (being) in and of itself does not set humans apart as unique.

3. Adam and Eve were given *the capacity* and *opportunity* for immortality from the tree of life, and only by that means. It remained their privilege if they abstained from eating from the tree of the knowledge of good and evil. It was their test of exclusive devotion to the Lord God.

4. The consequence of their choice to disobey God was *only the loss of the opportunity* for immortality when they were expelled from the garden. They were barred from the tree of life because their *capacity for immortality remained.* According to Genesis 3:22-23,

humanity could still have had immortality *after* the fall had we been allowed to continue eating from the tree, and only by that means. We would continue to live, but forever in a pathetically fallen state. Genesis teaches that God decisively prevented that possibility by prohibiting access to it.

5. Despite the statements in Genesis to the contrary, the doctrine of eternal conscious torment teaches that fallen humanity, though severed from the life of God, will continue to live forever in that fallen state, in resurrected flesh, and in the tormenting fires of hell.

6. Access to the tree of life and immortality through the indwelling Holy Spirit is God's gift to the community of faith. The Holy Spirit is the only source of life. Our capacity to live forever is not within ourselves but conditional upon receiving the Holy Spirit from God under his defined condition. Otherwise, from what we have just observed in the Genesis account, our fate is death, the termination of our existence. The condition upon which immortality is conferred is faith in the Lord Jesus Christ, as it is told to us in Scripture:

    "To him who overcomes, *I will grant* to eat of the tree of life which is in the Paradise of God" (Rev. 2:7).

    "Blessed are those who wash their robes, so that they *may have the right* to the tree of life" (Rev. 22:14).

    So Jesus said to them, "Truly, truly, I say to you, unless you eat the flesh of the Son of Man and drink His blood, *you have no life in yourselves*" (John 6:53).

CHAPTER 15

JESUS & HELL

Now that it has been asserted that the soul is not immortal, the biblical texts that appear to state that the unredeemed live forever and are consigned to an eternal conscious existence of punishment in hell must be addressed. We cannot pretend such texts don't exist but must endeavor to understand them without reading our own presuppositions into them. So, where to begin? I have elected to start with the words of the Lord Jesus, who, as it is claimed, spoke concerning hell.

Our common assumption is that when Jesus spoke of hell, he was speaking about a place or state of unending torment of the lost. However, careful examination of the biblical and historical background of these statements reveals something quite different. Most significantly, our theme, *The Threshold of Exile*, plays an important role in interpreting the actual meaning of Jesus' words. Before unpacking this vital perspective, it can be safely assumed that we are all well aware of the perceptions of an underworld of shadowy, disembodied souls and that eternal conscious torment is typically and inextricably tied to hell. Although it is beyond our scope to delve into the development of this perception in its extensive detail, I will offer the reader a few observations as to how hell and the underworld became part of our Bible and Christian eschatology.

As we have seen, non-biblical views concerning a lower world, post-mortem existence, and torment were integrated into Second Temple Judaism, apparently as a consequence of their interaction with pagan cultural influences. Subsequently, and despite its value, the Septuagint contributed to these pagan ideas by employing certain Greek terms as equivalents to key Hebrew concepts (e.g., hades as sheol and psuche as nephesh, respectively). This left the door open for Greek readers to interpret immortality and the state of the dead based on prevalent philosophical and mythological constructs that were *not* consistent with the Hebrew Scriptures. We have also noted (non-critically) how early Christian fathers coming out of Greek philosophy advanced non-biblical ideas about the afterlife, torment, and the immortality of the soul, transporting them into Christian theology.

By the late fourth century AD, Latin words such as *inferno*, in their various forms, were introduced into the biblical text. They also described pre-Christian mythological descriptions of the underworld and were incorporated by St. Jerome into his c. 405 AD Latin translation, called the Vulgate. This, we understand, was to support the Roman church's existing doctrines of the afterlife. Thus, the dogmas of the underworld, immortality, and eternal torment became well established in the early centuries of the church, although, as we previously observed, eternal conscious torment was not the exclusive view concerning the destiny of the lost.

In later centuries, our word hell (as Old English helle) was already in use in the English-speaking world. It appears in the earliest English translations, having likely come into existence from similar-sounding foreign words carrying the ideas of concealment, cover, cavern, underworld, or hell. Some suggest that it was derived from hel, which meant hidden, concealed, or covered (as in English, helmet), found in Old Norse mythology. Hel was not only the abode of the dead but was also the name of the goddess of death in the underworld.

It is evident that these misconceptions developed over the course of two millennia, having begun at least as early as exilic and post-exilic Judaism and continuing through the first English Bible translations from the sixteenth century AD onward. The mythological terms, concepts, and beliefs concerning the immortality of the soul and underworld torment became fully integrated into the interpretations of the Greek, Latin, and English Bibles and continue to influence Christian eschatology. However, the reality is:

> There is no word or phrase in any Hebrew, Greek, or Aramaic manuscript of the Bible that is required to be translated as "hell." Nowhere in the Scriptures are we told of the place by name or that unredeemed sinners will be consciously tortured there forever.

Neither Jesus nor any biblical apostle, prophet, or writer of the sacred texts ever mentioned hell. Its insertion into the text is entirely based upon the preceding theological assumptions and, unfortunately, biased interpretation. The actual Hebrew word in the Old Testament is sheol, which was poorly translated as hell or hades, and will be examined later. The Greek word employed in the texts of the New Testament and translated as hell is gehenna, which we will now consider.

What Did Jesus Mean by "Hell?"

As we examine the words of Jesus in the Gospels, I must admit that I am troubled by the translation of the biblical Greek term, gehenna, as hell. It has been corrected in many modern translations but is still translated incorrectly in others. Many expositors see no justifiable reason for it. We have also seen that gehenna is the name of a location and should not be translated. It does not differ from Bethlehem or the Mount of Olives. In our English versions, these names stand in their original Hebrew or Greek form, with no attempt to imply or support an assumed theological concept. Understandably, some have sought to justify the translation based on the beliefs of Second Temple Judaism. This is because gehenna was believed to be a place of judgment for the dead, although they were not aware of the term hell, which was a later Christian development. To re-emphasize important observations in earlier chapters, I would contend that the theological views of Jesus' contemporaries are not a justifiable reason to translate any Greek or Hebrew term. Besides gehenna, other Hebrew and Greek words in the original texts of the Bible were also incorrectly translated as hell in earlier English versions. This is true of the Old Testament Hebrew word *sheol* and the Greek words *hades and tartaros*. As mentioned, later translators recognized this error and, in some measure, corrected it.

Other than the Lord Jesus and a single mention by James, no New Testament character or writer makes use of gehenna, the term mistranslated as hell.

The following are all the references to hell in the New Testament (leaving the word gehenna untranslated):

- "the one who says, 'You fool,' is deserving of the gehenna of fire" (Matt. 5:22).
- "better that one part be destroyed and not your whole body be thrown into gehenna" (Matt. 5:29; 30; 18:9).
- "rather the fear the one who is able to destroy both soul and body in gehenna" (Matt. 10:28; Luke 12:5).
- "make him a son of gehenna twice as much as you" (Matt. 23:15).
- "how will you flee from the judgment of gehenna?" (Matt. 23:33).
- "having two [hands, feet, eyes] to go into gehenna, into the unquenchable fire" (Mark 9:43-47).
- "the tongue . . . is set on fire by gehenna" (James 3:6).

Since we have no examples of gehenna in the didactic texts (instructional epistles, etc.) of the New Testament, we must look solely to the biblical, historical, and traditional backgrounds of Jesus' statements. We will gain a better insight into his use of the term by understanding the Old Testament sources from which he drew along with the Jewish traditions with which he was familiar.

We have observed that gehenna is a valley outside of Jerusalem called the Valley of the Sons of Hinnom (in Hebrew: *ge ben-Hinnom*). *Topheth,* which is also mentioned in the Old Testament, is a representative and adjoining segment of the valley. Biblically, gehenna does not refer to a place of never-ending punishment for sinners after death. We have noted how, in the Book of Jeremiah, it relates to the divine judgment of Jerusalem through the agency of the armies of Babylon in 586 BC. It was specifically the place for the disposal of the bodies of Jews who died in the invasion (Jer. 7:32; 19:12). Not only is this description found in Jeremiah, but also in Isaiah.

Isaiah, who prophesied at an earlier time than Jeremiah, mentions it as the place of disposal of the bodies of the Assyrian army (185,000 soldiers) whom God destroyed in defense of Jerusalem (Isa. 30:31-33; 37:33-36). The crux of the issue is this:

Jesus' references to gehenna were to remind the Jews of the consequences of their unbelief through the lens of their prophetic heritage, especially Jeremiah, but also Isaiah and Ezekiel. To the Jews of Jesus' day, their lack of repentance and unwillingness to embrace Jesus would inevitably lead to the same consequences that came about in the times of their disobedient ancestors, specifically the consequences of 586 BC.

The Biblical Perspective

Topheth was a segment of the Valley of Hinnom (gehenna), southeast of Jerusalem. There, the Israelites offered their children to be burned on the idol of the pagan god, Molech. The accounts of this practice are found in Second Chronicles and Second Kings:

Moreover, he (King Ahaz) burned incense in the valley of ben-Hinnom [gehenna] and burned his sons in fire, according to the abominations of the nations whom the LORD had driven out before the sons of Israel (2 Chr. 28:3).

He made his sons pass through the fire in the valley of ben-Hinnom [gehenna]; and he practiced witchcraft, used divination, practiced sorcery, and dealt with mediums and spiritists. He did much evil in the sight of the LORD, provoking Him to anger (2 Chr. 33:6).

He [King Josiah] also defiled [destroyed; made unfit for worship] Topheth, which is in the valley of the sons of Hinnom [gehenna], that no man might make his son or his daughter pass through the fire for Molech (2 Kings 23:10).

Ge-Hinnom/Gehenna in Jeremiah

The prophet Jeremiah later referred to Ahaz's abominable practices in several prophecies. His indictments were not random references to *bad sins*. They provide highly purposeful and descriptive images. The prophet described the coming Babylonian invasion, prophesying that the fall of Jerusalem at the hands of Babylon (586 BC) would resemble those horrific offerings to Molech. The burning of Jerusalem and the fires of Hinnom Valley would keep burning to consume them in the same way the fires of Molech had consumed their children. This was because there would be no way to bury the thousands of dead after the invasion by the powerful and brutal armies of Nebuchadnezzar. The following texts are part of Jeremiah's proclamations of judgment upon Jerusalem. As you read, remember: *Topheth* and *Hinnom* are the Old Testament equivalents of gehenna (hell) in Jesus' warnings to his contemporaries (cf. 2 Kings 23:10).

"So the days are coming when it will no more be called Topheth, or the Valley of the Son of Hinnom, but the Valley of Slaughter; for they will bury in Topheth, because there is no room elsewhere" (Jer. 7:32).

". . . and will cause their people to fall by the sword before their enemies . . . And I will make this city [Jerusalem] a horror . . . in the siege and in the distress . . . This is how I will treat this place and its inhabitants, declares the LORD, so as to make this city like Topheth. The houses of Jerusalem and the houses of the kings of Judah will be defiled like the place Topheth, because of all the houses on whose rooftops they burned sacrifices to all the heavenly host and poured out drink offerings to other gods" (Jer. 19:7-9, 12).

". . . then I will kindle a fire in its gates and it will devour the palaces of Jerusalem *and not be quenched*" (Jer. 17:27).

Because of Israel's disobedience, the fire of God's judgment would not be *quenched* (stopped or turned back). God's irreversible judgment would burn unceasingly until it was finished. It is fundamentally important to our understanding that we again state that the *unquenchable* fire in Jerusalem has clearly not continued to burn since the time of Jeremiah. Yet it is referred to as unquenchable. We cannot define unquenchable (or any biblical term or phrase) in a manner that is suitable to our own purposes. It must mean what Scripture and only

Scripture tells us it means. When the eternal fire of his judgment-presence is manifested in a perceptible manner, it ultimately *consumes* the material object of his judgment:

> . . . for our God is a consuming fire. (Heb 12:29).

Jesus Defines Hell

To end all doubt, in Mark 9:43-47, *Jesus explains the meaning of gehenna* using the imagery in the same way Isaiah and Jeremiah employed it. Here, we are told that *gehenna, the unquenchable fire, and Isaiah's worms and fire* describe the same fate:

> "It is better for you to enter life crippled, than, having your two hands, to *go into hell [gehenna], into the unquenchable fire*, [where their worm does not die, and the fire is not quenched.] . . . It is better for you to enter life lame, than, having your two feet, to be *cast into hell [gehenna], [where their worm does not die, and the fire is not quenched.]* . . . "It is better for you to enter the kingdom of God with one eye, than, having two eyes, to be *cast into hell [gehenna], where their worm does not die, and the fire is not quenched*" (Mark 9:43-47).

> And they shall go out and look
> On the dead bodies of the men
> Who have rebelled against me.
> For their worm shall not die,
> Their fire shall not be quenched,
> And they shall be an abhorrence to all flesh"
> (Isa. 66:22-24).

Here, Jesus tells us that gehenna is the place of unquenchable fire. However, it is not descriptive of post-mortem torment, but has a clear connection to the words of Jeremiah. It was the fire by which Jerusalem was historically destroyed and was about to be destroyed again. Jesus also connects this image to that of a temporal scene of worms and fire described in Isaiah 66:24, which, as we shall see in Chapter 16, does not describe eternal torment.

Ge-Hinnom/Gehenna in Isaiah

Prior to Jeremiah's time, Isaiah's account of gehenna described it as a funeral pyre. It is not depicted as a place of torment but as a place where the Israelites would most likely have disposed of Assyrian corpses. After overpowering and scattering the ten northern tribes of Israel, Assyrian King Sennacherib and his army set their sights on Jerusalem and the southern kingdom. When King Hezekiah of Judah prayed to the Lord, God assured him he was about to obliterate the Assyrians—and he did, all 185,000 of them. In the biblical account, King Sennacherib stood as a proxy for his nation and his army. He personally did not die in this judgment:

> "For at the voice of the LORD Assyria will be terrified,
> When He strikes with the rod . . .
> He will fight them.
> For Topheth has long been ready,
> Indeed, it has been prepared for the king [Sennacherib].
> He has made it deep and large,
> A pyre of fire with plenty of wood;
> The breath of the LORD, like a torrent of brimstone, sets it afire"
> (Isa. 30:31-33).

> Then the angel of the LORD went out and struck 185,000 in the camp of the Assyrians; and when men arose early in the morning, behold, all of these were dead. So Sennacherib King of Assyria departed and returned home and lived at Nineveh (Isa. 37:36-37; cf. 2 Kings 19:35).

Again, a preconceived notion of Topheth as hell would have to be imposed on the texts to interpret them as having something to do with eternal conscious torment. The Jews honored their own dead with burials. For a Jew, as in many ancient cultures, to remain unburied was the epitome of humiliation and disgrace. Topheth was the location of cremation fires for the shameful and dishonorable. Here, it was *made ready* as the place for the disposal of the bodies of the Assyrian army.

As we saw, it would also be for the Jews in their own massive loss of lives in the coming days of their own tragic misfortune. The text of Isaiah informs us that the Assyrian army was camped just outside Jerusalem at Nob (see Isa. 10:5, 32). Therefore, aside from the possibility that Isaiah's speech was purely metaphorical, it is feasible that the dead could have literally been disposed of in gehenna. In either case, he is not speaking of eternal torment in our conceived version of permanent torment in hell.

Ge-Hinnom/Gehenna in Ezekiel

This same imagery of unquenchable fire we saw in Jeremiah is also conveyed by his contemporary, the prophet Ezekiel, in advance of Babylon's destructive campaign:

> "Son of man, set your face toward Teman, and speak out against the south and prophesy against the forest land of the Negev, and say to the forest of the Negev, 'Hear the word of the LORD: thus says the Lord GOD, Behold, I am about to kindle a fire in you, and it will consume every green tree in you, as well as every dry tree; *the blazing flame will not be quenched* and *the whole surface* from south to north will be burned by it. All flesh will see that *I, the LORD, have kindled it; it shall not be quenched.*'" (Eze. 20:46-48).

Here, Ezekiel looks toward the south (Judea) from his vantage point in the northern regions of Babylon (see Eze. 1:1). The exiled prophet sees the invading Babylonian armies bringing a scorching, unquenchable fire sent by God to destroy the land of Israel, Jerusalem—its capitol city—and the temple of God, in judgment. Again, we observe that the use of *unquenchable fire* terminology has nothing to do with eternal conscious torment but follows the meaning of the imagery of Jeremiah. It has a specific reference to the calamity of 586 BC, describing a national judgment that although eternal, is not a never-ending torment of individuals.

Ge-Hinnom/Gehenna in the Roman Siege: 70 AD

As to the certainty of Jesus' warnings, Josephus penned the following concerning the siege of Jerusalem:

> So all hope of escaping was now cut off from the Jews, together with their liberty of going out of the city. Then did the famine widen its progress, and devoured the people by whole houses and families; the upper rooms were full of women and children that were dying by famine, and the lanes of the city were full of the dead bodies of the aged; the children also and the young men wandered about the market-places like shadows, all swelled with the famine, and fell down dead, wheresoever their misery seized them . . . Now the seditious [Zealots] at first gave orders that the dead should be buried out of the public treasury, as not enduring the stench of their dead bodies. But afterwards . . . *had them cast down from the walls into the valleys beneath* . . . (4) However, when Titus, in going his rounds along those valleys, saw them full of dead bodies, and the thick putrefaction running about them, he gave a groan . . . [61]

> While the holy house was on fire . . . a sad clamour of the seditious, who were now surrounded with fire and sword . . . many of those that were worn away by the famine, and their mouths almost closed when they saw the fire of the holy house, they exerted their utmost strength, and brake out into groans and outcries again: Perea did also return the echo, as well as the mountains round about [the city], and augmented the force of the entire noise. Yet was the misery itself more terrible than this disorder; for one would have thought that the hill itself, on which the temple stood, was seething-hot, as full of fire on every part of it, that the blood was larger in quantity than the fire, and those that were slain more in number that those that slew them; for the ground did nowhere appear visible.[62]

The horrible scenes that Josephus describes are precisely what Jesus warned of when he spoke to the Jews about gehenna. It was not a warning of eternal torment but an image of the valleys (of which gehenna represents the whole) where the bodies of their slain were thrown unburied, in utter shame, and left to be burned. Just as

Jeremiah's prophecies warned that Jerusalem herself would be like gehenna in the Babylonian invasion, it was witnessed and vividly recorded as it occurred during the Roman invasion.

Jewish Post-Exile Tradition:
Ge-Hinnom/Gehenna in Second Temple Judaism

Historically, gehenna was a place that was associated with all that was accursed and filthy. It was a place where nameless and evil people and, as some disputedly claim, garbage, were entirely consumed by fire and maggots. Gehenna also appears to refer to common post-exilic Jewish beliefs concerning the afterlife. However, those beliefs were rooted in rabbinical traditions. Some traditions associated gehenna with the post-mortem torment of the ungodly. It was similar to, but not precisely, what is commonly understood about hell today. A major difference was that for most Jews, gehenna was purgative. Nonetheless, it was an abysmal underworld whose basic construct was not entirely unlike ancient pagan mythology that influenced their religion.

This *Second Temple view*, which arose out of intertestamental writings, is not consistent with the use of gehenna in the Old Testament. Its use in the prophets is abundantly clear and must take precedence over rabbinical traditions that were developed during the sixth-century exile and post-exilic periods.

> *It is well attested to that much rabbinical theology was developed and grew out of the nation's interaction with Babylonian and Greek cultures. Accordingly, both Jesus and Paul warned of the influence of Jewish traditions (Mark 7:1-13; Titus 1:14).*

The development of Jewish ideas of life after death in Jesus' time arose in the period following the destruction of Solomon's temple in Jerusalem and the Jews' exile from their land. The Israelite prophets had previously forecast a bright post-exile future for their people. The nation looked ahead to their return to the land and the rebuilding of Jerusalem and the temple. These prophecies, however, were not fully understood because the prophets envisioned something beyond the nation's mere political status. The true release from exile would come through the life, death, resurrection, and universal reign of Jesus, not the exaltation of the kingdom of Israel.

Repeated military defeats and subjugation to pagan powers followed the Jews in the centuries after the exile. Before the time of Jesus, Jewish thinkers, having arrived at the wrong notions concerning the prophets, lost hope in any immediate change. With mistaken hopes unfulfilled, non-biblical writings emerged, mystically describing the better future as *life beyond the grave*. The two generations of the sixth-century Babylonian exile and the subsequent influence of Persian and Greek cultures left the nation with a faith that was heavily influenced by those cultures.

As mentioned, the idea of gehenna (in Jewish tradition) came to represent afterlife punishment, and it appears that souls would be condemned to punishment there. The punishment for some was limited, resembling purgatory. For others, it resulted in annihilation. This is seen in the Babylonian Talmud, which was still in the form of oral tradition at the time of Jesus. Davidson's translation reads:

> The rebellious Jews who have sinned with their bodies and also the rebellious people of the nations of the world who have sinned with their bodies descend to Gehenna and are judged there for twelve months. After twelve months, their bodies are consumed, their souls are burned, and a wind scatters them under the soles of the feet of the righteous, as it is stated: "And you shall tread down the wicked; for they shall be ashes under the soles of your feet" (Mal. 3:21) . . . But the heretics; and the informers; and the apostates [apikorsim]; and those who denied the Torah; and those who denied the resurrection of the dead; and those who separated from the ways of the Jewish community and refused to share the suffering; and those who cast

their fear over the land of the living; and those who sinned and caused the masses to sin, for example, Jeroboam, son of Nebat, and his company; all of these people descend to Gehenna and are judged there for generations and generations, as it is stated: "And they shall go forth, and look upon the carcasses of the men that have rebelled against Me; for their worm shall not die; neither shall their fire be quenched; and they shall be an abhorrence to all flesh" (Isa. 66:24).[63]

Critical Questions

In examining these gospel accounts, we must ask some important questions. How we answer those questions significantly affects our view of the afterlife. Was Jesus just using, or was he validating, Jewish non-biblical traditions with his use of gehenna? Conversely, was he actually referencing the prophets to warn the Jews of what was coming upon their nation by telling them to go back and search the Scriptures for the interpretation of his words?

I submit that the foundational principle of interpretation must be upheld. *Scripture, not Jewish traditions, must interpret Scripture.* The notable J. I. Packer, who held the traditional view of hell, offered the following from the *Chicago Statement on Hermeneutics*, Article XX, which affirms the priority of Scripture over extrabiblical views:

> We further affirm that in some cases extrabiblical data have value for clarifying what Scripture teaches, and for prompting correction of faulty interpretations. *We deny that extrabiblical views ever disprove the teaching of Scripture or hold priority over it.*[64]

Understanding the contemporary thinking of the time can and does aid in biblical interpretation. Jesus, the prophets, and the apostles clearly used common extrabiblical views to illustrate principles to their hearers, yet without endorsing them as God's truth (cf. Isa. 14:9-10; Eze. 32:21; Acts 17:28; 1 Cor. 15:29). As a case in point, nowhere in the New Testament is this use of contemporary Jewish thought better illustrated than in the story of the Rich Man and Lazarus.

The Rich Man and Lazarus

. . . the Pharisees, who were lovers of money, were listening to all these things . . . And He said to them, "You are those who justify yourselves in the sight of men, but God knows your hearts; for that which is highly esteemed among men is detestable in the sight of God. . . there was a rich man, and he habitually dressed in purple and fine linen, joyously living in splendor every day. And a poor man named Lazarus was laid at his gate, covered with sores, and longing to be fed with the *crumbs* which were falling from the rich man's table; besides, even the dogs were coming and licking his sores. Now the poor man died and was carried away by the angels to Abraham's bosom; and the rich man also died and was buried. In Hades he lifted up his eyes, being in torment, and *saw Abraham far away and Lazarus in his bosom. And he cried out and said, 'Father Abraham, have mercy on me, and send Lazarus so that he may dip the tip of his finger in water and cool off my tongue, for I am in agony in this flame.' But Abraham said, 'Child, remember that during your life you received your good things, and likewise Lazarus bad things; but now he is being comforted here, and you are in agony. And besides all this, between us and you there is a great chasm fixed, so that those who wish to come over from here to you will not be able, and *that* none may cross over from there to us.' And he said, 'Then I beg you, father, that you send him to my father's house–for I have five brothers—in order that he may warn them, so that they will not also come to this place of torment.' But Abraham *said, 'They have Moses and the Prophets; let them hear them.' But he said, 'No, father Abraham, but if someone goes to them from the dead, they will repent!' But he said to him, 'If they do not listen to Moses and the Prophets, they will not be persuaded even if someone rises from the dead'" (Luke 16:14-15; 19-31).

So, What About Hades?

Many believe that the account of the Rich Man and Lazarus describes the afterlife, specifically the interim state for those awaiting the final judgment. I wholeheartedly disagree. However, before proceeding, I would advise the reader that there are many insightful books and online resources that offer a variety of perspectives on why

Jesus' illustration *should not* be interpreted as the true state of life after death. I will not engage the narrative and its many details in their entirety. Suffice it to say, the account contains many particulars *that are inconsistent* with other relevant biblical truths and worthy of examination. That is a critical aspect of interpreting Jesus' illustration. I will simply observe a few vital facts about how Jesus used this story and examine why the narrative should not be viewed as an accurate picture of post-mortem existence.

First, in this illustration, Jesus is speaking to the Pharisees and merely using their own traditional beliefs regarding wealth and poverty to portray the eschatological reversal between rich and poor in his kingdom. The context of the illustration is such that it is couched in several remarks about the Pharisees' perceptions of God's favor. Jesus is destroying their assumptions that wealth implies blessedness in the kingdom and poverty implies cursedness. The reverse is also worth noting. There is no teaching in the Bible that suggests that all the "haves" go to hell, even if they're a bit selfish, and all the "have-nots" go to heaven regardless of their spiritual condition.

Second, if Jesus described an accurate picture of post-mortem reality, then we would have to assume that Greek mythology and philosophy provided insights into the afterlife that were not available in the Hebrew Scriptures. The Old Testament Hebrew word *sheol* describes the single destination of both the righteous and the unrighteous dead. *Sheol is pre-Christian* and synonymous with the state of death and sometimes the grave. We are told in the Old Testament *that the dead know nothing and are silent*. Rich, poor, righteous, and unrighteous are all said to lie there without consciousness, knowledge, or personal interaction with anyone. As in the following two prophetic texts, the only observed afterlife activities are clearly satirical descriptions by the prophets as they mock pagan kings and point to the certainty of their destiny in sheol:

"Sheol . . . arouses for you the spirits of the dead . . .
It raises all the kings of the nations from their thrones.
They will all respond and say to you,
'Even you have been made weak as we,
You have become like us'"
(Isa. 14:9-10).

"*The strong among the mighty ones shall speak of him (Pharaoh) and*
his helpers from the midst of Sheol,
'They have gone down, they lie still,
The uncircumcised, slain by the sword'"
(Eze. 32:21).

Neither of these mocking, cartoon-like animations of the dead suggest anything like the states of suffering, bliss, or compartmentalization seen in the Rich Man and Lazarus. The pagan kings and subjects in our texts hardly appear to be in torment or flames and crying out for water.

Third, sheol, not hades, describes the biblical meaning of the state of the afterlife.

Hades was inserted by the Septuagint translators as its equivalent,
but the meaning of sheol did not change or evolve to accommodate
the Greek meaning of hades derived from philosophy and pagan
myth. The state of persons in sheol is biblically described in quite
a different manner than that of hades.

The tables on the following pages show that there is no evidence of a division in sheol between the righteous and the unrighteous. Neither do they depict conscious torment or bliss. In the tables, note that whenever the Hebrew word *sheol* appears in the ancient text, *hades* is given as its Greek counterpart in the Septuagint. However, in context, *only the term is different. The Hebrew meaning does not and should not change*. The change in meaning came from Greek interpreters, who erroneously assumed that the two words were synonymous.

Sheol and Hades in the Old Testament

Text	Explanation
Genesis 37:35 . . . And he [Jacob] said, "Surely I will go down to Sheol in mourning for my son." So his father wept for him.	sheol / hades: the destiny of the righteous in death
Numbers 16:33 So they and all that belonged to them went down alive to Sheol; and the earth closed over them, and they perished . . .	sheol / hades: the destiny of the unrighteous in death
2 Samuel 22:6 The cords of Sheol surrounded me; The snares of death confronted me	Hebrew parallelism: sheol / hades mean death
Job 17:13 If I look for Sheol as my home, I make my bed in the darkness;	Hebrew parallelism: sheol / hades mean the grave; darkness
Job 17:13 Naked is Sheol before Him, And Abaddon has no covering.	Hebrew parallelism: sheol / hades mean destruction (Heb: abaddon)
Psalms 6:5 For there is no mention of You in death; In Sheol who will give You thanks	Hebrew parallelism: sheol / hades as death; no consciousness of God
Psalms 16:10 (LITV) For You will not leave My soul in Sheol; You will not give Your Holy One to see corruption.	Hebrew parallelism: sheol / hades as corruption of the body
Psalms 18:5 The cords of Sheol surrounded me; The snares of death confronted me	Hebrew parallelism: sheol / hades as death
Psalms 31:17 Let me not be put to shame, O LORD, for I call upon You; Let the wicked be put to shame, let them be silent in Sheol.	the wicked silenced in sheol / hades

Table 15.1a (continued on next page)

Sheol and Hades in the Old Testament (cont'd)

Text	Explanation
Psalms 49:14 As sheep they are appointed for Sheol; Death shall be their shepherd; And the upright shall rule over them in the morning, And their form shall be for Sheol to consume So that they have no habitation.	Hebrew parallelism: sheol / hades consumes; meaning death feeds on them (consume: Heb. bahlah: decay)
Psalms 116:3 The cords of death encompassed me And the terrors of Sheol came upon me; I found distress and sorrow. (death was near)	Hebrew parallelism: sheol / hades and death
Proverbs 5:5 Her feet go down to death, Her steps take hold of Sheol.	Hebrew parallelism: sheol / hades and death
Ecclesiastes 9:10 there is no activity or planning or knowledge or wisdom in Sheol where you are going.	No work, device, knowledge, or wisdom in sheol / hades
Isaiah 38:18 For Sheol cannot thank You, Death cannot praise You; Those who go down to the pit cannot hope for Your faithfulness.	Hebrew parallelism: sheol / hades and death / the grave
Hosea 13:14 Shall I ransom them from the power of Sheol? Shall I redeem them from death? O Death, where are your thorns? O Sheol, where is your sting?	Hebrew parallelism: sheol / hades and death
Amos 9:2 Though they dig into Sheol, From there will My hand take them; And though they ascend to heaven, From there will I bring them down.	Rhetorical – sheol / hades can be "dug into" – (the grave?) contrast with heaven
Habakkuk 2:5 [The haughty man] . . .enlarges his appetite like Sheol, And he is like death, never satisfied. . .	Hebrew parallelism: (Personification: sheol / hades has appetite)

Table 15.1b

As you can see from the examples, hades, of Greek origin, was supplied by the translators of the Septuagint in place of sheol. However, the descriptions of activity that are seen in the account of the Rich Man and Lazarus are nowhere to be found in the Old Testament. Other than the two rhetorical observations in Isaiah and Ezekiel, none of the 66 occurrences of sheol in the Old Testament mention it as having separate compartments or describe a conscious state of either bliss or torment.

> As a description of the afterlife, hades cannot exceed or contradict what has already been revealed in the Old Testament. Hades can only represent the state of death, just as sheol does in the Old Testament. Any use of hades that conflicts with its Old Testament meaning would violate the fundamental principle to which we have sought to be faithful: that Scripture must interpret Scripture. Hades must describe conditions as those of the Hebrew sheol, not those arising from Greek mythology.

Relevant Background of the Septuagint

The Septuagint was an important translation. It served as a bridge between the Hebrew and Greek languages, introducing the Hebrew Bible to the Greek-speaking world. It was also the Bible of the first-century church. However, like the English translation of gehenna as hell, the appearance of hades as the Greek substitute for sheol *was an unfortunate development in the translation.* Sheol would have been better left untranslated to preserve its Old Testament Hebrew meaning. The insertion of hades did not result in any alteration of the texts in which it appears, as seen in the preceding tables. However, it reflected the rising influence of Greek mythology and philosophy in Judaism. This is because the LXX was completed and in circulation by the second century BC, *in the historical context of Hellenistic (Greek-influenced) Judaism.*

Hades was not the only insertion into the Hebrew text that engendered a Greek-influenced Old Testament. While hades affected the perception of the *post-mortem location* of deceased persons, the Greek idea of *psuche, the immortal soul,* was employed as the translation of the Hebrew word *nephesh*, which denotes a *living being.* So just as the hades is not the equivalent of the Hebrew term sheol, the psuche does not have the same meaning as the Hebrew term nephesh. To the Greeks, psuche was the alleged immaterial aspect of man that was considered immortal. The Hebrew concept of nephesh implies no such thing. Both Hellenistic concepts, arising from *hades* and *psuche*, are embedded in the narrative of the Rich Man and Lazarus. They influence our view of this narrative and other texts that allegedly support the so-called immortality of the soul and the doctrines of underworld consciousness and torment. Whether we *are* a soul or *have* a soul as part of our being does not affect the essential biblical reality: *we are not immortal.*

Wojciech Szczerba, the Rector of the Evangelical College of Theology in Wroclaw, Poland, offered a well-written article concerning this unfortunate consequence of the LXX translation resulting in the Greek meanings being *read into* the Hebrew Bible.

First, he recognizes the Septuagint as a valuable translation for the Hellenized world. Its primary beneficiary was the extensive, Greek-speaking Jewish community in Alexandria, Egypt:

> The Septuagint was created to give the teaching of the Old Testament to the Greek-speaking community in Alexandria . . . to transfer the thought of [the] Hebrew Bible into the ground of the Greek world (p. 68).

Continuing, the Rector notes a consequential development:

> . . . the Septuagint became not only a translation of the Hebrew Bible into Greek language but at the same time a translation of Greek ideas into [the] language of the Old Testament (p. 75).

Regarding the concept of the *soul*, he adds:

In the case of psuche, this term substitutes in most instances [for the] Hebrew term nephesh. The problem, however, is that in Greek mentality, psuche somehow automatically was understood as the immaterial and most often immortal part of human being . . . [texts] translated with the usage of the noun psuche . . . suggest . . . that [the] soul exists after physical death of a person. In this way application of Greek substitute gives a new shadow to the word (p. 81).

Finally, he summarizes:

Hellenistic [Greek] thought, hidden in concepts, attitudes, values, unconscious presuppositions of both translators and readers, penetrated and modified teaching of the Hebrew Bible (p. 84).[65]

The sum of the matter is that hades, as it is employed in the New Testament, should be understood through the lens of the Hebrew word sheol, which reflects a static state of death and the grave. It must not be permitted to bear any resemblance to the demon-managed domain described in Greek mythology, where there is an abundance of activity, pain, and dialogue.

Characterizations of the afterlife that are inconsistent with sheol must be rejected as myths born out of interaction with Greek and other pagan ideas. When varying from the revealed character of sheol, Jesus must be understood as employing beliefs of the time, not portraying actual afterlife conditions.

Tenney explains the compartmentalized view of the afterlife and its intertestamental development:

The literature of the intertestamental period reflects the growth of the idea of the division of Hades into separate compartments . . . This aspect of eschatology was a popular subject in the . . . literature that flourished in this period. Notable is the pseudepigraphal Enoch (written C. 200 BC) which includes the description of a tour supposedly taken by Enoch into the center of the earth. In another passage in Enoch, he sees at the center of the earth two places-paradise, the place of bliss, in the Valley of Gehinnom, the place of punishment. The above illustrates that there was a general notion in the compartments in Hades that developed in the intertestamental period.[66]

In the same way, psuche, the Greek word translated *soul*, should not possess meanings in the Bible that differ from the Hebrew word *nephesh*. Nephesh is the entire mortal living being, not an immortal aspect of human physiology.

A Brief Summary

If, in the account of the Rich Man and Lazarus, we can find no other biblical evidence of the conditions described, then we can safely assume that Jesus is *using, but not endorsing,* the Second Temple beliefs of his audience to illustrate a point. This is clear from the context. Jesus addressed the *greed* of the Pharisees using a mythical view of the afterlife with which they were familiar. To repeat, Jesus illustrated that wealth does not imply blessedness, and poverty is not a reflection of divine disfavor.

Returning to the Subject of Hell:
Gehenna in the New Testament

The occurrences of gehenna in the New Testament are prime examples of how the Bible interprets itself. A most notable aspect is that, in each case, the text addresses Jews. Gehenna is never mentioned specifically to a Gentile audience. Whether it was the Pharisees, his disciples, or the stated audience of James' epistle, in context, each reference is addressed to a Jewish audience. Gehenna had relevant meaning to *them,* having been spoken of through their own prophets. Most Gentiles, ignorant of those prophecies of old, would not likely have shared the same sentiments about Jesus' words.

There are four historical audiences to whom gehenna is addressed in the New Testament:

1. The Sermon on the Mount (Matt. 5-7):

This was articulated mainly for his disciples (Matt. 5:2). There is every indication it was spoken to people familiar with the Law and the Prophets, which is confirmed in Luke 6:20-49. However, this does not suggest the absence of a larger audience. It is evident that his listening audience included Gentiles from throughout the region.

2. The Twelve (Matt. 10, Matt. 18, and Mark 9):

Matt. 10	Jesus sends out the twelve
Matt. 18	Jesus teaches the twelve
Mark 9	Jesus sits with the twelve (v.35)
Luke 12	Jesus' warns the twelve regarding hypocrisy

3. The Pharisees (Matt. 23):

Jesus confronts the Pharisees for hypocrisy (Matt. 23:15, 33).

4. The Twelve Tribes (James 3):

James writes to the twelve tribes scattered abroad (Jas. 1:1)

Identifying the Jewish audiences stresses how gehenna, drawn from their own prophets, would produce images of their historical tragedy. Jesus told them that their end would be like that of a common criminal. In the coming siege, their lifeless bodies would be thrown over the city walls to be maggot-eaten and burned. They would have been entirely scandalized by the suggestion of such a fate. In each of the gehenna texts, the term could be expanded and reasonably interpreted as *"the consuming fires in Jerusalem and the smoldering, repugnant valleys in the coming siege as described by your prophets."*

Although the interpretation may seem excessively descriptive, remember that there is no single word in the original texts of the Bible that should be translated as hell. Terms and phrases in other languages do not always neatly translate into a single word in English. The Greek, Hebrew, and Aramaic languages of the Bible convey ideas and metaphors germane *to their own time and* culture. This cultural environment also encompasses words in *every* language. Jesus' use of gehenna was intended to convey a striking image from the nation's past. I would also suggest that even if his hearers *perceived* that he was speaking of the afterlife consistent with rabbinical tradition, the fact is, he was not. His use of the Old Testament makes it clear that he was speaking concerning the coming siege, employing the horrible, historic image of 586 BC.

Given that, I invite the reader to consider the following renderings of the hell texts to see if our perception of them changes. The following explanations are what I believe Jesus intended his audience to understand, *but they are not proposed translations*:

The one who says, 'You fool,' is deserving of the consuming fires in Jerusalem and the smoldering, repugnant valleys in the coming siege as described by your prophets (Matt. 5:22).

Better that one part be destroyed and not your whole body be thrown into the consuming fires in Jerusalem and the smoldering, repugnant valleys in the coming siege as described by your prophets (Matt. 5:29-30; 18:9).

Rather, fear the one who is able to destroy both soul and body in the consuming fires in Jerusalem and the smoldering, repugnant valleys in the coming siege as described by your prophets (Matt. 10:28).

. . . having two [hands, feet, eyes] to go into the consuming fires in Jerusalem and the smoldering, repugnant valleys in the coming siege as described by your prophets, into the unquenchable fire where worm does not die, and the fire is not quenched (Mark 9:43-47; cf. Jer. 7:20).

Fear the One who, after He has killed, has authority to cast into the consuming fires in Jerusalem and the smoldering, repugnant valleys in the coming siege as described by your prophets; yes, I tell you, fear Him! (Luke 12:5).

. . . make him a son of the consuming fires in the smoldering, repugnant valleys of Jerusalem (*a shameful and hypocritical person*) twice as much as you [Pharisees] (Matt. 23:15).

How will you flee from the judgment of the consuming fires in Jerusalem and the smoldering, repugnant valleys in the coming siege as described by your prophets? (Matt. 23:33).

I have slightly modified James to make better sense, but it carries the same meaning. I admit it's a bit awkward and will concede that James may be accommodating the Second Temple traditions about gehenna, or possibly the smoldering death residing in the hearts of fallen humanity (cf. Matt 12:34-37):

The tongue . . . is set on fire by the smoldering valleys filled with defiled persons and refuse, as described by your prophets (Jas. 3:6).

Let's Summarize

1. Jesus never mentioned hell, as we understand it today. The actual word in the New Testament's original Greek language is gehenna.

2. Gehenna is the Greek translation of and references the imagery of the Hebrew ge (ben) Hinnom, the Valley of (the sons of) Hinnom in the Old Testament. Jesus used images of gehenna seen in Isaiah, Jeremiah, and Ezekiel as a warning to the Jews of his own time.

3. In each use of gehenna, the historical contexts and literary correspondences indicate that the audiences were primarily Jewish. They, in contrast to Gentiles, would understand its prophetic meaning and references to their own historical writings.

4. Within four decades, the Jews were facing a massacre by the Romans and subjection to the consuming cremation fires of gehenna, both within and outside Jerusalem.

5. Josephus described how, during the Roman siege, the Jews were compelled to throw their dead over the walls of the city into the surrounding valleys for lack of space to bury them. Just as Jesus warned and as Jeremiah prophesied to their ancestors, the city and the valley became a *gehenna filled with the unquenchable fire of judgment,* as they had been in the Babylonian invasion centuries before.

6. It is a reasonable and sound conclusion that Jesus used the texts of the prophets to make the same point to his own Jewish audiences. Jesus' teachings and warnings did not emerge out of a historical vacuum but from familiar Old Testament texts. If we allow *Scripture to interpret Scripture*, we understand gehenna as a symbol of the same temporal fate as it was centuries before in the prophets. It should not be construed as having any connection to post-mortem judgment, especially eternal conscious torment.

7. Although it is an important translation, the use of the Septuagint had unfortunate theological consequences. Key Hebrew terms related to the afterlife were translated and interpreted through the lens of Hellenistic mythology and philosophy rather than remaining true to their Hebrew meaning.

CHAPTER 16

PROOF TEXTS & CONTEXTS

We have observed that 1) immortality is not inherent in any of us, regardless of our redemption status; 2) the term hell is not in the Bible and should not be used to describe the final destiny of the lost; and 3) it is apparent that death (extinction) is the fate of those who are not in Christ. We will now examine several commonly cited texts of Scripture and their contexts to determine whether there is a justifiable reason to accept the doctrine of eternal conscious torment. Is it truly biblical doctrine or a long-standing belief in search of proof texts?

Commonly Cited Proof Texts

There are commonly selected texts that appear in almost every effort to support the doctrine of eternal conscious torment. These are found in the works of most advocates of ECT (aka the traditional view). The texts are cited despite the fact that both the Genesis narrative and Jesus' use of gehenna from the prophets would seem sufficient to dispel the doctrine of ECT. Given that, we will now look at the contexts of several of these various *proof texts* to determine if they, in fact, say what they are alleged to say. Most of these passages will be addressed in this chapter, but we will reserve those cited from the Book of Revelation for our study in Part IV.

The reader is to be aware that I may differ from many proponents of conditionalism in the perspective I offer on some of the so-called eternal torment proof texts. Although I agree that the texts do not speak of eternal conscious torment, I'm not convinced that many of the alleged references refer to a final judgment at the end of the world, as even some conditionalists propose. As has been indicated in my previous remarks, many of these texts seem to describe the consequences of the razing of Jerusalem in 70 AD. This would mean that they describe temporal rather than eternal scenes. Furthermore, despite the helpful insights into key Greek and Hebrew words that I have learned from various biblical language experts, I find that the contexts and intertextual relationships in which many of these "final destiny" texts appear to speak for themselves. That is to say, the context of the so-called proof text often speaks louder than the shades of meaning of a particular Greek or Hebrew word.

That said, my interpretations will be offered on a case-by-case basis and should be understood as my personal views, not those sanctioned by any conditionalist organization. However, I remain deeply appreciative of those who have pioneered the resurgence of conditionalism and contributed so much to my understanding.

#1. Isaiah: Worms and Fire

"For as the new heavens and the new earth
That I make shall remain before me, says the LORD,
So shall your offspring and your name remain.
From new moon to new moon,
And from Sabbath to Sabbath,
All flesh shall come to worship before me, declares the LORD.
And they shall go out and look
On the dead bodies of the men
Who have rebelled against me.
For their worm shall not die,
Their fire shall not be quenched,
And they shall be an abhorrence to all flesh"
(Isa. 66:22-24).

A Future, Final Judgment?

If we are to believe that Isaiah's prophetic description is not a temporal one but concerns the final state of things, then we must accept, *with no supportive context*, that Isaiah 66:24 teaches that *the redeemed will watch those tortured in hell for all eternity*. These conditions are alleged to be consistent with a *literal* new heavens and new earth described by the prophet in Chapter 65. I find this characterization of eternity to be, at the very least, appalling. However, we cannot allow feelings to be the arbiter of truth. Therefore, let's look at Isaiah's immediate narrative setting and then at the larger context in relation to the nation of Israel.

New Moons and Sabbaths

It is believed from Isaiah's text that these dead bodies, purported to be resurrected damned ones, are observed by the righteous *during festival seasons and sabbaths*:

"From new moon to new moon and from Sabbath to Sabbath . . . they will go forth and look . . ." (Isa. 66:23-24).

If Isaiah's prophecy literally reflects a future state of heavenly bliss, then how are the cycles of new moons and sabbaths still being recognized? These were the sacred time cycles that governed the Old Covenant economy in the pre-Christian world. They functioned to provide a countdown to the time of Jesus, the Messiah. Once Jesus came and completed his mission, these former sacred time parameters were no longer necessary in the New Covenant age. They are absent in the afterlife, which is a realm of spiritual reality not governed by the boundaries of space and time (lunar and solar cycles). Why would Isaiah refer to an eternal state governed by the time parameters of new moons and sabbaths? In his letter to the Galatians, the apostle Paul denounces the observance of these Old Covenant norms as futile, even for believers in this life:

> But now that you have come to know God, or rather to be known by God, how is it that you turn back again to the weak and worthless elemental things, to which you desire to be enslaved all over again? You observe days and months and seasons and years. I fear for you, that perhaps I have labored over you in vain. (Gal. 4:9-10).

We are also shown in Revelation that in John's vision of the new Jerusalem, there are no longer any day-night cycles. These examples appear to contradict any consideration of Isaiah's prophecy having reference to a future heavenly or millennial state:

> And he carried me away in the Spirit to a great and high mountain, and showed me the holy city, Jerusalem, coming down out of heaven from God, I saw no temple in it, for the Lord God the Almighty and the Lamb are its temple. And *the city has no need of the sun or of the moon* to shine on it, for the glory of God has illumined it, and its lamp is the Lamb (Rev. 21:10, 22-23).

Furthermore, the legitimacy of the suggestion that the corpses being observed in Isaiah's prophecy refer to *post-mortem human beings* should be questioned as unsupported by the Hebrew meaning:

According to authorities Brown-Driver-Briggs, the Theological Wordbook of the Old Testament, and Strong's Concordance, in Hebrew, "peger" refers to a dead body, corpse, or carcass (see Brown, et al.,[67] Harris, et al.,[68] and Strong[69]).

Isaiah's imagery is consistent with what we have reviewed previously in Isaiah, Jeremiah, Ezekiel, and the Gospels regarding the judgment of gehenna. Although the prophet does not explicitly mention gehenna, we have seen how, in Mark 9, Jesus' warnings about gehenna were drawn directly from the Isaiah 66:24 prophecy. Both the Lord Jesus and the prophet describe a *temporal* judgment scene, as the righteous are seeing the *corpses* of those strewn about the valleys surrounding Jerusalem who perished in the day of the Lord upon Israel (Isa. 66:15-16) When seen in its entire context, this isolated, so-called proof text is not a reference to afterlife torment, but the scene in 70 AD following the destruction of Jerusalem by the Romans. The unquenchable fire in Mark 9 is also drawn from Isaiah 66:24, as the Lord uses the image to describe gehenna. It is evident, therefore, that the Isaiah text depicts the same things as gehenna in Jesus' statements. Isaiah 66:24 marks the end of the context from Isaiah 63–66, which is seen in the tables on the following pages. The heart of Isaiah's prophecy in these chapters depicts God bemoaning the fallen state of his disobedient heritage (Isa. 65ff; cf. Rom. 10:21):

I said, 'Here am I, here am I,'
To a nation which did not call on My name.
"I have spread out My hands all day long to a rebellious people . . .
A people who continually provoke Me to My face . . .

Now, before we examine the larger context, I recommend the reader set aside this book, pick up a Bible, and read Isaiah 63–66 in its entirety. The following tables will demonstrate *how important it is to see the entire context in which a so-called proof text is situated.*

Isaiah 63-66 in Context

Ref	Isaiah's Text	Explanation
63:10	But they rebelled And grieved His Holy Spirit; Therefore, He turned Himself to become their enemy, He fought against them.	Israel's rebellion after being saved out of Egypt – they have become God's enemies (see Luke 19:27)
64:11	Our holy and beautiful house ..., Has been burned by fire...	Isaiah bemoans the nation's loss
65:2	I have spread out My hands ...to a rebellious people (cf. Rom. 10:21)	Israel continuously resisted God's call to repentance
65:3-4	Offering sacrifices in gardens and burning incense on bricks; Who sit among graves and spend the night in secret places; Who eat swine's flesh, And the broth of unclean meat is in their pots . . .	(66:15-17) "Those who sanctify and purify themselves to go to the gardens . . .Who eat swine's flesh, detestable things and mice, Will come to an end altogether," declares the LORD.
65:8-16	. . . I will act on behalf of My servants In order not to destroy all of them. And an heir of My mountains from Judah; Even My chosen ones shall inherit it	Yet a remnant will be protected; they will inherit the promise (see Rom. 11:5-7). The "heir" is the Lord Jesus, and God's true servants will be joint heirs (Gal. 4:7; Rom. 8:16-17)
	. . . My servants will eat, but you will be hungry. Behold, My servants will drink, but you will be thirsty ". . . My servants will be called by another name. ...	The preserved remnant of Israel shall enjoy the blessings of the New Covenant – and be called by another name (Christian)
65:17-25	"For behold, I create new heavens and a new earth; . . .behold, I create Jerusalem for rejoicing And her people for gladness. "	Describes the nature of the New Covenantal arrangements as "new heavens and new earth- in a new Jerusalem
66:5-6	Hear the word of the LORD, you who tremble at His word: "Your brothers who hate you, . . . will be put to shame.	An interlude where God assures his suffering, outcast remnant that he will execute vengeance on their behalf.
	"A voice of uproar from the city, a voice from the temple, The voice of the LORD who is rendering recompense to His enemies.	The war cries from the city and temple. The judgment is there.

Table 16.1a (continued on next page)

Isaiah 63-66 in Context

Ref	Isaiah's Text (cont'd)	Explanation (cont'd)
66:7-8	"Before she travailed, *she brought forth;* Before her pain came, she gave birth to a boy.	The birth (the resurrection) of Jesus as the "firstborn of many brethren" (*before the great tribulation*).
	As soon as Zion travailed, she also brought forth her sons. ". . . nurse and be satisfied with her"	This is the true Zion – the heavenly Jerusalem. This new Jerusalem: "is our mother" (Gal.4:26)
66:15-16	For behold, the LORD will come in fire. . . For the LORD will execute judgment by fire And by His sword on all flesh, And those slain by the LORD will be many.	This is Jesus' *parousia* – the Day of the Lord in fire upon Israel as seen in the Olivet Discourse (the Jewish-Roman War)
66:18-19	. . . the time is coming to gather all nations and tongues . . ."I will set a sign among them and will send survivors from them to the nations: . . . to the distant coastlands that have neither heard My fame nor seen My glory. And they will declare My glory among the nations.	The nations (Gentiles) flow to the latter-day house of the Lord (Isa. 2:2-4) - entering the New Covenant with the Jewish remnant. The apostles of the first-century remnant will be sent out. They could be the "sign" (Isa. 8:18). Possibly a reference to the resurrection of Jesus (Matt. 12:38-40).
66:22-23	"For just as the new heavens and the new earth Which I make will endure before Me,". . . new moon And from sabbath to sabbath, All mankind will come to bow down before Me," says the LORD.	The new covenantal arrangements are permanent, and world-wide. God will be routinely worshiped in every nation under heaven.
66:24	"Then they will go forth and look On the corpses of the men Who have transgressed against Me. For their worm will not die And their fire will not be quenched; And they will be an abhorrence to all mankind	The aftermath of the War of 66-70 AD– more bodies than could possibly be buried. This kept the worms fed and the fires of burning in gehenna valley. Worshipers would see the aftermath of unburied dead throughout the land; the shame and disgrace for those Jews who did not receive a proper burial. This, because they did not receive their Messiah or the apostles bearing the message of the gospel.

Table 16.1b

This horrific last scene in Isaiah 66:24 describes a vast number of unburied dead. Although we have examined the description of the unquenchable fire, there is more. *There are no supernatural worms in the gehenna of either Isaiah's prophecy or Jesus' warning.* What is portrayed is the gruesome image of the many corpses thrown into the valleys around Jerusalem and lying throughout the land, unburied, and fed upon by maggots that ate the vegetation on the sides and ledges of the valleys. The point made by both Isaiah and Jesus is that no one would escape this most dreadful and disgraceful end. *Context matters.* The entire scope of Isaiah 63–66 (which I trust the reader has examined) reflects a continuous narrative leading up to and including first-century history. These texts do not depict a final state of heaven or hell. However, they *do* depict:

- the failure of Israel and the salvation of their remnant

- the opening of the door of faith to the Gentiles

- the apostles being sent out to the nations

- the apostles as gatherers of the elect remnant of Israel

- the day of the Lord: Christ's *parousia* is approaching

- the day comes with the destruction of Jerusalem (70 AD)

Then . . . Isaiah's Concluding Portrait

The conclusion of Isaiah 66 depicts the aftermath of the Roman invasion. Israel's dead lie burning in gehenna like criminals or were left scattered throughout their devastated land. This was the scene observed by passersby for weeks and months to follow. Josephus estimates a loss of over 1 million people just in Jerusalem. Another 97,000 went into exile as Jesus' warnings became a horrible reality for a people who refused to acknowledge the visitation of their Messiah.

#2. Daniel: Shame and Everlasting Contempt

"Now at that time Michael, the great prince who stands *guard* over the sons of your people, will arise. And there will be a time of distress such as never occurred since there was a nation until that time; and at that time your people, everyone who is found written in the book, will be rescued. Many of those who sleep in the dust of the ground will awake, these to everlasting life, but the others to disgrace *and* everlasting contempt" (Dan. 12:1-2).

We have already established in Part II of this book that the first century was an unparalleled period for the Jews. We can confidently say that here, in the Book of Daniel, the angel refers to the same events occurring at the time of the great tribulation in the first century AD. It is the tribulation concerning which Jesus prophesied in the Olivet Discourse. The language of the texts requires it. Although there are interesting possibilities concerning both resurrection and judgment in the prophecy of Daniel 12, we will limit our observations primarily to the relevant context of eternal conscious torment.

Our *time text* is the opening reference, *"at that time,"* when an unparalleled *time of distress* occurs for the nation. Prior to Daniel 12, the previous chapter, Daniel 11, begins with the Persian period and progresses to the first century AD. Daniel 12 is historically continuous with that previous narrative. We are brought to the first century AD and ultimately to the time of the same great tribulation that Jesus heralded in the Olivet Discourse. Observe the texts side-by-side:

Daniel 12:1: The Angel	Matthew 24:21: Jesus
And there will be a time of distress [LXX: *thlipsis*] such as never occurred since there was a nation until that time.	there will be a great tribulation [*thlipsis*], such as has not occurred since the beginning of the world until now, nor ever will.

Table 16.2

In Daniel 12:2, the often-cited phrase *shame and everlasting contempt* is alleged to be the equivalent of post-mortem torment of the lost. I would suggest otherwise. The phrase has numerous references in prophetic literature to the contrary. The future shame and everlasting contempt concerning which the angel spoke can readily be understood from other texts that describe the horrific, humiliating, and disgraceful end experienced by the Jews, as just observed in our examination of Isaiah 63–66. As we have seen, in their own culture, there could be no greater or more permanent shame than the outcomes of the war with Rome.

To the angel's point concerning the righteous arising to life in Daniel 12:1, we know that those Jews who kept the faith of Jesus, along with Gentile believers, were preserved and would experience the life of the age to come:

> "Truly, truly, I say to you, whoever is hearing my word and is believing him who sent me has life in the age *to come*, and does not come into condemnation [or judgment], but has crossed over from death into life" (John 5:24 REB).

> We know that we have passed out of death into life, because we love the brethren. He who does not love abides in death (1 John 3:14).

For those who rejected Christ, there would be a different outcome. They would suffer death, exile, humiliation, and reproach in a manner described in other prophetic texts. The following passages do not speak of everlasting, post-mortem conditions but convey the true meaning of their shame, humiliation, and reproach related to destruction and exile. They describe the consequences of the loss of their city and their exalted status. Each text includes the Hebrew word *cherpah,* translated *reproach*, the same word found in our text of Daniel 12:2. Most of them are from Jeremiah and relate to Israel's exile, not eternal torment. Therefore, I would suggest the following:

Daniel, who was familiar with Jeremiah's prophecy (Dan.9:1-3), was being informed by the angel using the same linguistic conventions concerning shame and contempt as those of Jeremiah. It was not unusual for contemporary prophets to speak in similar terms or see similar visions when inspired by the same Holy Spirit (cf. Isa. 2:2-4; Mic. 4:1-4).

However, unlike Jeremiah, Daniel isn't being told of the outcome of 586 BC but of the final shattering of *the power of the holy people* in 70 AD (See Dan. 12:7). Daniel would understand this to be the Jews. The outcome is delivered to him in the same manner as Jeremiah. At the end of the age, some would experience life in God through Christ. Others would experience the destruction, exile, and humiliation described by the prophets. This would occur in the season of time during which the great tribulation occurred (Dan. 12:1; Matt. 24:21), which was the apostolic era. Let us now examine the prophetic references to shame and disgrace in Jeremiah, as well as in Ezekiel and Nehemiah, that are similar to Daniel:

> "I will make them a terror and an evil for all the kingdoms of the earth, as a *reproach* and a proverb, a taunt and a curse in all places where I will scatter them" (Jer. 24:9).

> '. . . I will make them a terror to all the kingdoms of the earth, to be a curse and a horror and a hissing, and a *reproach* among all the nations where I have driven them" (Jer. 29:18).

> We are ashamed because we have heard *reproach*;
> Disgrace has covered our faces,
> For aliens have entered
> The holy places of the LORD'S house
> (Jer. 51:51).

> Remember, O LORD, what has befallen us;
> Look, and see our *reproach*
> (Lam. 5:1).

Jeremiah also declares that those Judeans who sought refuge in Egypt (from where Israel was once delivered) would also not escape:

"... 'As My anger and wrath have been poured out on the inhabitants of Jerusalem, so My wrath will be poured out on you when you enter Egypt. And you will become a curse, an object of horror, an imprecation, and a *reproach*; and you will see this place no more'" (Jer. 42:18).

"... burning sacrifices to other gods in the land of Egypt, where you are entering to reside, so that you might be cut off and become a curse and a *reproach* among all the nations of the earth" (Jer. 44:8).

"And I will take away the remnant of Judah who have set their mind on entering the land of Egypt to reside there, and they will all meet their end in the land of Egypt; they ... will die by the sword and famine; and they will become a curse, an object of horror, an imprecation and a *reproach*" (Jer. 44:12).

Note the similarity of Ezekiel's warning to that of Isaiah 66:24:

"Moreover, I will make you a desolation and a reproach among the nations which surround you, in the sight of all who pass by" (Eze. 5:14).

Also, in the post-exile setting of Nehemiah:

Then I said to them, "You see the bad situation we are in, that Jerusalem is desolate and its gates burned by fire. Come, let us *rebuild the wall of Jerusalem* so that we will no longer be a *reproach*" (Neh. 2:17).

The concept is especially significant when we consider the use of a key Hebrew word. Jeremiah describes the perpetual shame of Israel's *disinheritance using the Hebrew word olam*. As we will see in the following examples, this word does not always refer to something that continues forever, with the sense of eternality. Also note that, as seen above in Ezekiel 5:14, this text also has a striking resemblance to the words of Isaiah (Isa. 66:24) concerning the desolation of their city and the reactions of the "passersby":

". . . And they have stumbled from their ways,
From the ancient paths . . .
To make their land a desolation,
An object of perpetual [olam] *hissing;*
Everyone who passes by it will be astonished
And shake his head"
(Jer. 18:15-16).

"Everlasting" Reproach?

The desolation of their inheritance results in *perpetual hissing* by passersby. The word perpetual (NASB) is the same word found in Daniel 12:2 and translated as *everlasting*, yet both describe the same thing. It is a disgraced people who have rejected their God and lost their inheritance in full view of the nations:

"Therefore behold, I will surely forget you and cast you away from My presence, along with the city which I gave you and your fathers. I will put an everlasting [*olam: perpetual*] *reproach* on you and an everlasting [*olam: perpetual*] humiliation which will not be forgotten" (Jer. 23:39-40).

John Gill comments on Jeremiah 23:39-40:

. . . they who had been honoured so much and so long as the people of God, and their city counted the glory of the earth; yet now both they and that should be the byword of the people, and had in the utmost contempt, and that for ever, or at least a long time, even for a series of ages; . . . for this cannot be restrained to the short captivity of seventy years in Babylon; . . . and a perpetual shame, which shall not be forgotten; the same thing in different words, to heighten their disgrace, and confirm *the perpetuity* of it.[70]

The Hebrew word olam does not only mean *eternal, forever, or everlasting.* Besides its generally understood–and sometimes disputed–sense of eternity, olam very often carries the idea of *temporal perpetuity*. For example, the NASB translates olam as perpetual when referencing priestly statutes:

> "You shall gird them with sashes, Aaron and his sons, and bind caps on them, and they shall have the priesthood by a *perpetual* [olam] statute. So you shall ordain Aaron and his sons" (Exo. 29:9).

Of course, the priesthood was perpetual during *that age and* not intended to last beyond it. It was not eternal in duration, but in quality. It was divine, instituted by God, yet it was superseded by Christ:

> Now if perfection was through the Levitical priesthood (for on the basis of it the people received the Law), what further need *was there* for another priest to arise according to the order of Melchizedek, and not be designated according to the order of Aaron? For when the priesthood is changed, of necessity there takes place a change of law also (Heb. 7:11-12).

Ben Witherington observes:

> 'Olam' has been loosely translated 'forever' but the problem with this translation, according to my esteemed colleague Bill Arnold in his 1 Samuel commentary, is . . . In the phrase *berit olam* (loosely forever covenant or eternal covenant) it becomes clear that *olam* actually means a covenant of a definitely long but with specified duration. In other words, it doesn't exactly seem to be a synonym for our word 'eternal' which means infinitely going on into the future.[71]

Witherington is not alone in his assessment of the meaning of olam. Like all Hebrew and Greek words, olam has a semantic range (range of meanings). Therefore, that offers sufficient reason to believe that Daniel 12:1-2 may not be speaking of post-mortem bliss or torment but rather the future of his people at the end of the Old Covenant age. This would be consistent with the context of the entire flow of Daniel 11 and 12, as well as the implications of the texts of Jeremiah, who was Daniel's contemporary.

Other Considerations in Daniel 12:1-2

1. The final visions of Daniel 11 pertain to his people (the Jews) in the latter days. They describe the flow of the nation's history after the Babylonian exile up to Roman rule in Israel. Chapter 12 foresees the great tribulation, concluding with the Jewish revolt and the shattering of the power of their nation (*the holy people*) in Daniel 12:7. Finally, we see that during this time, a portion of the nation will have eternal life, understanding, and lead many to righteousness. This also corresponds, as we have seen, to Isaiah's vision of the role of the first-century remnant of Israel:

    "I . . . will send survivors from them to the nations: Tarshish, Put, Lud, Meshech, Tubal and Javan, to the distant coastlands that have neither heard My fame nor seen My glory. And they will declare My glory among the nations" (Isa. 66:19).

2. The time to which Daniel's vision (Dan. 12:1-2) refers is demonstrably consistent with Matthew 24, the Olivet Discourse, which we have determined is a first-century prophecy of the destruction of Jerusalem and not the end of the world. In Daniel 12:7, we learn that all these future events will come to their completion in the 3 ½ years during which the power of the holy people (the Jews) is shattered. As we have seen, this was the duration of the first-century Roman invasion (66-70 AD).

3. The resurrection described to Daniel is one uniquely pertaining to the Jews. It very likely refers to the national resurrection in Ezekiel's prophecy in Ezekiel 37. *That prophecy first concerned the return of the Jews to Israel after their 70-year exile in Babylon, and God characterized it as a resurrection:*

    "Therefore prophesy and say to them, Thus says the Lord GOD, 'Behold, I will open your graves and cause you to come up out of your graves, My people; and I will bring you into the land of Israel. Then

you will know that I am the LORD, when I have opened your graves
and caused you to come up out of your graves, My people. *I will put
My Spirit within you and you will come to life* . . . (Eze. 37:12-14).

In the natural realm, the prophet Haggai affirms the presence of
the Spirit among the returned remnant of the Jews and the fulfillment
of God's promised resurrection of the nation, which was a
foreshadowing of Christ:

"As for the promise which I made you when you came out of Egypt,
My Spirit is abiding in your midst; do not fear!" (Hag. 2:5).

The True Return from Exile

The outcomes of the national resurrection in Daniel 12:2 looked to
a future time, governed by the time text in the preceding verse, looking
ahead to how those Jews who received Jesus would partake of new life
in Christ, the life of the coming age of the Holy Spirit. Those who did
not, as Daniel is shown, would see the death, destruction, shame, and
reproach in the day of the Lord upon the nation (Dan. 12:1, 7).

In the Gospel, a clue to the time of this national resurrection may
be apparent in the Lord's Prayer, alluded to in Matthew 6:9 and Luke
11:2, where we, today, typically recite the words, "*Hallowed be your
name.*" I certainly will not find fault with our common recital of the
prayer and the acknowledgment that God's name (his character and
essence) is holy. However, I am also intrigued by the Apostolic Bible's
grammatical construction of that phrase, and the term "hallow" or,
better yet, "sanctify" in Matthew's account.

For those of us who are not grammatically knowledgeable, the
construct in the original text apparently conveys the sense of "*do this.*"
Using that grammatical construction, the prayer is read accordingly, as
follows:

Our father, the one in the heavens, *sanctify your name!*
(Matt. 6:9 ABP)

For Jesus' Jewish hearers and Matthew's later readers, the petition to the Father to *"sanctify your name"* is a direct reference to Ezekiel 36:23, where God says:

> *"I will sanctify my great name,* which was profaned among the heathen and which you [Israel] have profaned in the midst of them . . ."

The prophecy would have reference to the exercise of God's sovereign will to act on behalf of Israel for the sake of his own name (his reputation) by returning them to their land after the Babylonian exile. In doing so, he would demonstrate his power among the nations and show that he was not a feeble god incapable of saving his people. Jesus prayed for the vindication of the Father's name through his own life and ministry, *resulting in the true fulfillment of Ezekiel 37, which was the true resurrection of the dead bones, reviving them with his Spirit, and restoring them to their inheritance* in Christ's messianic kingdom. In Daniel 12:1-2 and the resurrection of the nation, some would inherit life in the olam haba; others would reject God's offer and know only loss and disgrace, *neither of which refer to eternal conscious torment.*

As a final note, Daniel's reference to those *written in the book* (12:1) is mentioned in Revelation 20:10-15, where *those not found in the book of life* were thrown into the lake of fire. It is therefore assumed that both Daniel and Revelation speak of the lost suffering never-ending torment. We'll address this in our study of the Book of Revelation.

#3. Jesus: Eternal Fire/Hell of Fire

> "It is necessary that temptations come, but woe to the one by whom the temptation comes! And if your hand or your foot causes you to sin, cut it off and throw it away. It is better for you to enter life crippled or lame than with two hands or two feet to be thrown into the eternal fire. And if your eye causes you to sin, tear it out and throw it away. It is better for you to enter life with one eye than with two eyes to be thrown into the hell [gehenna] of fire" (Matthew 18:6-9 ESV).

Since we have covered the subject of the unfortunate translation of gehenna as hell in the teachings of Jesus, we will not go over that ground a second time (see Ch. 15: Jesus & Hell). I see no persuasive evidence in this text that would suggest that Jesus was warning of something other than what we have already observed. He describes the eternal fire *as synonymous with gehenna*, which we know to be a physical location and the unfortunate destiny of tens of thousands of Jews after the Roman invasion.

Note how, in Matthew 18, two consecutive statements from the lips of Jesus establish that synonymous relationship between the two:

Matthew 18:8	Matthew 18:9
. . . and be thrown into *the eternal fire*.	. . . to be thrown into *the hell [gehenna] of fire*.

Table 16.3

This section of Matthew also has as its parallel, Mark 9:43-48, where we saw how Jesus quoted from Isaiah 66:24 regarding the worms and fire. We have surveyed the context of Isaiah 63-66 leading up to Isaiah 66:24, the aftermath of the invasion. It has been demonstrated that this does not refer to eternal conscious torment. The other texts provide definitive meaning to Jesus' warnings. Again, we take the opportunity to remind the reader that:

Scripture must interpret Scripture. We cannot arbitrarily assign meanings to texts that are not clarified and explained in other biblical texts. The context of Isaiah 63-66 points to conditions and events leading up to the war and its tragic aftermath in Isaiah 66:24. Therefore, Jesus' use of that text was intended to bring the threat of the imminent destruction–the day of the Lord–to bear on his contemporary audience.

#4. Jesus: Eternal Punishment/Eternal Life
The Sheep and the Goats

"When the Son of Man comes in his glory . . . he will place the sheep on his right, but the goats on the left. Then the King will say to those on his right, 'Come, you who are blessed by my Father, inherit the kingdom prepared for you from the foundation of the world.' . . . Then he will say to those on his left, 'Depart from me, you cursed, into *the eternal fire prepared for the devil and his angels* . . . And these will go away *into eternal punishment,* but the righteous into eternal life" (Matt. 25:31-46).

I consider this an unfortunate example of a so-called proof text without context. In Chapter 12, we saw how Matthew 25 is a continuation of the Olivet Discourse, and I suggested it pertains to the separation of sheep and goats in God's own household. The mixed flock consisted of both believing and unbelieving Jews in the time of the apostles (the transition era). Jesus' disciples were interested in the fate of their own people and not the least bit conscious of a world-wide judgment scene to occur at some point far removed from their time. A great separation was coming, and it was to be based on how their people, the Jews, responded to the messengers of the gospel:

For *it is* time *for judgment to begin with the household of God*; and if *it begins* with us first, what *will be* the outcome for those who do not obey the gospel of God? (1 Pet. 4:17).

We saw that in the disciples' trial mission to the cities of Israel, those who received God's messengers and showed benevolence would not go unrewarded, as in Matthew 25. The entire context also seems to relate to the first-century Jewish response to the gospel:

". . . *go to the lost sheep of the house of Israel* . . . Whoever does not receive you, nor heed your words, as you go out of that house or that city, shake the dust off your feet. Truly I say to you, it will be more tolerable for the land of Sodom and Gomorrah in the day of judgment than for that city . . . He who receives you receives Me, and he who receives Me receives Him who sent me. He who receives a prophet in *the* name of a prophet shall receive a prophet's reward; and he who receives a righteous man in the name of a righteous man shall receive a righteous man's reward. *And whoever in the name of a disciple gives to one of these little ones even a cup of cold water to drink, truly I say to you, he shall not lose his reward"* (Matt. 10:5-42).

Audience Relevance

As we have seen in our study of Matthew 23–25, the disciples were anticipating the olam haba, the age to come. Jesus spoke to that expectation throughout the entire discourse. Now, his concluding statements in the prophecy depict the judgment scene described as a separation between sheep and goats. We must understand the narrative in that same context.

First, the parable must not be interpreted in an overly literal manner. There are obviously no literal sheep or goats. No one is being judged *solely* on the criteria of their participation in prison, hospital, or food distribution ministries. The Jews were facing judgment based on how they treated the messengers of the gospel, as seen above in Matthew 10:40-42 and in Matthew 23:

"You serpents, you brood of vipers, how will you escape the sentence of hell [gehenna]? Therefore, behold, I am sending you prophets and wise men and scribes; some of them you will kill and crucify, and some of them you will scourge in your synagogues, and persecute from city to city" (Matt. 23:33-34).

I have suggested that the sheep and the goats are not people of the Gentile nations of the world. They were the people of God's Old Covenant household *who lived among the nations.* We saw in Chapter 12 how Jesus' description alludes to Ezekiel 34:17 concerning his own flock. This is consistent with the Parable of the Ten Virgins, who were two companies. They are Old Covenant Jews and New Covenant Jews. The judgment falls upon the Jews in God's Old Covenant household. The Old Covenant age is closing as the new is emerging. The judgment occurs when Jesus comes in glory (Matt. 24:30) in the destruction of Jerusalem. Some not only rejected the gospel but also mistreated the people of God, both Jewish and Gentile Christians, failing to show mercy to them when they were in need.

Second, Scripture must interpret Scripture. Here lies what I believe to be a fundamental error in interpreting Jesus' remarks concerning eternal torment. It is assumed that because both life and punishment are described as *eternal*, they must be of the same *duration*. If the sheep live forever, then the goats allegedly must also be punished forever. However, this interpretation fails to look outside the text to see how other texts interpret these outcomes. It also assumes that the word *eternal* must refer to the *duration* of the punishment, when in fact, its description may imply its *quality* (as divine). Our study will not delve into this in depth, but this *qualitative aspect* of the Greek *aion/aionios* in the text is consistent with the widely researched range of meanings of the word.

Eternal Punishment and Eternal Life

Conditionalists have observed that Jesus does not condemn the goats to eternal or continual punishing, but to eternal punishment. It is final and irreversible. The nature of that is the *consuming* fire that Jude describes for us. It is like the complete annihilation of Sodom and Gomorrah, which was a spatial example of annihilation:

> Just as Sodom and Gomorrah and the cities around them, since they in the same way as these indulged in gross immorality and went after strange flesh, are *exhibited as an example in undergoing the punishment of eternal fire* (Jude 1:7).

If we choose to interpret *eternal* punishment based only on a single text (Matt. 25:46), we could easily make the same comparison from John 3:16, where the promise of eternal life is set *opposite of perishing*, not eternal torment:

> For God so loved the world, that He gave His only begotten Son, that whoever believes in Him *shall not perish*, but have eternal life. (John 3:16; cf. John 10:28).

Also, in Romans 6:23, eternal life is placed opposite of *death*, not eternal torment:

> For the wages of sin is *death*, but the free gift of God is eternal life in Christ Jesus our Lord (Rom. 6:23).

Other texts give us unfettered confidence that eternal life–or the life pertaining to the age to come–is synonymous with immortality. They convey that *immortality* is from God and has been gifted to us:

> . . . and *I give eternal life to them, and they will never perish*; and no one will snatch them out of My hand (John 10:28).

> To those who by perseverance in doing good *seek for glory and honor and immortality, eternal life* . . . (Rom. 2:7).

In contrast, in the following *didactic* texts (that do not use symbolism to convey their meaning), there is nothing to suggest that the fate of the lost is an endless *process of torment*:

> For *the wages of sin is death*, but the free gift of God is eternal life in Christ Jesus our Lord (Rom. 6:23).

> . . . turning the cities of Sodom and Gomorrah to ashes he condemned them to extinction, making them an example of what is going to happen to the ungodly (2 Pet. 2:6 ESV).

> . . . those who live according to the sinful nature *will die* (Rom. 8:13).

> . . . the gospel is foolishness to those who are *perishing* (1 Cor. 1:18).

> . . . those who please the sinful nature from that nature will reap *destruction* (Gal. 6:8).

> . . . their destiny is *destruction* (Phil. 3:19).

> . . . *they perish* because they refused to love the truth (2 Thess. 2:10).

The eternal punishment of which Jesus spoke is final, permanent, irreversible, and multi-dimensional. Its temporal manifestation is consuming fire that destroys corrupt persons and godless civilizations. Its spiritual manifestation results in extinction–the cessation of existence for the lost who are perishable. However, it brings perpetual torment for the devil and his angels, who are immaterial beings.

Final Observations Concerning Sheep and Goats

1. *Eternal punishment* in Matthew 25:46 is synonymous with *eternal fire* in Matthew 25:41. They describe the same fate in the narrative.

2. In our preceding observation (#3), in Matthew 18:18-19, Jesus defined that same *eternal fire* as synonymous with *gehenna*.

3. Chapter 15 (Jesus & Hell) shows that *gehenna* is not hell but a prophetic description of the fate of the Jews in 70 AD. They were consumed in the burning of Jerusalem and in the valleys below.

4. Based on these synonymous relationships, we can confidently say that eternal punishment is eternal fire; eternal fire is gehenna, which is not hell but the consuming fires of Jerusalem in 70 AD.

5. The Sheep and the Goats is a description of the fates of believing and unbelieving Jews in the first century AD as a consequence of their treatment of the gospel messengers. Yet, it contains relevant lessons for Christians and the importance of charitable works.

6. Other texts compare the fates of the righteous and the wicked. Whether or not this judgment is upon first-century Jerusalem, as I have proposed, it remains that *the nature of the judgment* is not eternal conscious torment. This is irrespective of whether the text has all unbelievers or a first-century civilization in view.

#5. Paul: Everlasting Destruction

This is evidence of the righteous judgment of God, that you may be considered worthy of the kingdom of God, for which you are also suffering—since indeed God considers it just to repay with affliction those who afflict you, and to grant relief to you who are afflicted as well as to us, when the Lord Jesus is revealed from heaven with his mighty angels in flaming fire, inflicting vengeance on those who do not know God and on those who do not obey the gospel of our Lord Jesus. They will suffer the punishment of eternal destruction, away from the presence of the Lord and from the glory of his might, when he comes on that day to be glorified in his saints, and to be marveled at among all who have believed, because our testimony to you was believed (2 Thess. 1:5-10).

The apostle Paul wrote to a first-century church that, at that very time, had suffered persecution and affliction apparently from Jews in their own community (cf. 2 Thes. 2:14). McReynolds literally translates 1 Thessalonians 2:14 as:

. . . that the same you suffered also you by the own *co-tribesmen* just as also themselves by the Judeans.[82]

The likelihood is that the Thessalonian Jews (their co- tribesmen) were the persecutors of the recipients of Paul's letter, just as Judean locals had plagued the believers in that region. Paul's description of their judgment is descriptive of how, as history has informed us, Jews from throughout the empire would flock to Jerusalem for the Passover in 70 AD. It was there, at the *parousia* of Christ, that God would enter into judgment with them. The context is that *relief was coming and would arrive as the revelation of Jesus in flaming fire* to inflict vengeance upon the persecutors. Nothing in this text suggests he is expecting something that is far removed from his audience. The imminent *parousia* of Jesus in the first century would bring immediate relief to their sufferings as their enemies would be drawn to Jerusalem, God's furnace (Matt. 13:36-41), and there be vanquished.

Paul was not expecting his readers in Thessalonica to look forward to relief from this persecution some 2000 years later or beyond. He promised a very real and soon-coming arrival of Jesus in judgment to deliver his people from their current situation. Paul describes the end of their persecutors as:

> . . . eternal destruction away from the presence of the Lord and from the glory of his might . . . (2 Thes. 1:9, which was to occur on the day he would be revealed in flaming fire).

As for the prospect that this text speaks of *post-mortem eternal conscious torment away from* the presence of the Lord, there is an apparent contradiction with another so-called eternal torment proof text in Revelation 14:10. We will examine that passage in more detail in Part IV:

> If anyone worships the beast and its image and receives a mark on his forehead or on his hand, he also will drink the wine of God's wrath, poured full strength into the cup of his anger, *and he will be tormented with fire and sulfur in the presence of the holy angels and in the presence of the Lamb.*

For our present analysis, is eternal torment *in* the presence (Revelation 14:10) or *away from* the presence (2 Thess. 1:9) of the Lord? Two texts supposedly describing the same outcomes of the Lord's alleged final judgment seem to have contradictory descriptions, as observed in *Hell Under Fire* (see Morgan et al. 2004), a defense of the traditional view. The contributors appear to lack agreement concerning this contradiction:

On page 12, according to Morgan and Peterson:

> . . . they will suffer everlasting conscious punishment away from the *joyous* presence of God.

The editors apparently inserted the word *joyous* into their quote from 2 Thessalonians 1:9. I can't speak for them, nor do I suggest that the authors intentionally manipulated the text, but it appears to be an attempt to provide an implied idea that helps to explain away the contradiction.

On Page 103, "Paul on Hell," Moo states:

They will be punished with everlasting destruction and *shut out from the presence of the Lord* and from the glory of his might.

But on page 114, "The Revelation on Hell," citing Revelation 14, Beale observes:

. . . the torment takes place not only *in the presence* of the Lamb but also of the holy angels . . . The point is that those who have denied the Lamb will be forced to acknowledge him as *they're being punished before him*[72]

On his "Desiring God" website, the respected John Piper suggests the following:

These are not contradictory descriptions.

The first text describes the presence and power of the Lord as glorious in the sense of being thrilling to the souls of the saints. As the next verse says, "He comes on that day to be glorified in his saints, and to be marveled at among all who have believed" (2 Thessalonians 1:10). Unbelievers will be excluded from this experience. Christ will not be beautiful or marvelous to them.

The second text simply says the angels and the Lamb will be attending this punishment.[73]

With all due respect to these highly regarded men of God, I find the arguments to be less than satisfactory. The destruction that is described in 2 Thessalonians 1 occurs *away from the presence* of the Lord in the same way that the torment occurs *in his presence* in Revelation 14. I fail to see how these explanations reconcile the two texts. Most importantly, I suggest that 2 Thessalonians 1:5-10 does not speak of future unending torment but of the loss of privilege and the experience of destruction as the Lord came in judgment upon first-century Israel. Jesus specifically told them that their rejection of the gospel and their persecution of the church would result in this:

> "Truly I say to you, all these things will come upon this generation. "Jerusalem, Jerusalem, who kills the prophets and stones those who are sent to her! How often I wanted to gather your children together, the way a hen gathers her chicks under her wings, and you were unwilling. "Behold, your house is being left to you desolate! (Matt. 23:33-38).

Their consignment to a future *away from the presence of the Lord* must be understood in light of their historical privilege and how that loss is seen in the prophets. *First,* we see a description of the presence of the Lord among Israel as they went forth to possess the land:

> For by their own sword they did not possess the land,
> And their own arm did not save them,
> *But Your right hand and Your arm and the light of Your presence*
> For You favored them
> (Psa. 44:3).

Second, observe how they would be cut off and cast away from that presence because of their disobedience:

> "If only you had paid attention to My commandments!
> Then your well-being would have been like a river,
> And your righteousness like the waves of the sea.
> Your descendants would have been like the sand,
> And your offspring like its grains;
> Their name would never be cut off or destroyed *from My presence*"
> (Isa. 48:18-19).

Third, we have seen in Isaiah 66 and Daniel 12 that the nature of the casting away of Israel from his presence involved exile, the destruction of their city, and a future of perpetual humiliation and reproach.

"Therefore behold, I will surely forget you and *cast you away from My presence*, along with the city which I gave you and your fathers. I will put an everlasting [perpetual]* *reproach* on you and an everlasting [perpetual] humiliation which will not be forgotten" (Jer. 23:39-40)

[*The Hebrew word olam is better translated here as "perpetual," as we have previously seen in the Daniel 12:1-2 analysis].

For through the anger of the LORD *this [Nebuchadnezzar's siege of Jerusalem, and exile of the Jews]* came about in Jerusalem and Judah until *He cast them out from His presence.* And Zedekiah rebelled against the king of Babylon (2 Kings 24:20).

As repeatedly emphasized, the apostles (as well as the prophets) drew from a common linguistic well in describing the consequences of Israel's rejection and loss of privilege. The texts of Second Thessalonians must be carefully examined in the context of their intertextual relationship to the Old Testament if we are to understand them correctly.

Finally, relief was expected for the Thessalonians, *along with Paul and his companions, in their own day*:

. . . and *to give* relief to you who are afflicted and to us as well when the Lord Jesus will be revealed from heaven with His mighty angels in flaming fire, (2 Thes. 1:7).

The revelation of the Lord Jesus was going to bring relief for Paul and the Thessalonians from their present persecutions. I would suggest that nothing in the context or grammar of Paul's stated expectation concerning the appearance of Jesus from heaven suggests that this refers to something 2000 years or more into their future–an end of the world event. This great, inspired apostle's entire context resonates with a first-century expectation of the soon-approaching parousia of Christ in their day, and with it, relief and deliverance from the first-century forces of persecution who were arrayed against the people of God.

#6. Jude: The Punishment of Eternal Fire

Just as Sodom and Gomorrah and the surrounding cities, which likewise indulged in sexual immorality and pursued unnatural desire, serve as an example by undergoing a punishment of eternal fire. (Jude 1:7).

The reader may have quickly noticed that we have frequently referred to this text. I find it very odd that it is commonly cited *to support* eternal conscious torment. As we have seen, it portrays the opposite. Jude offers a most striking and authoritative biblical illustration of how unending torment is a misconception and that God's eternal judgment is by *consuming* fire. We have already seen the importance of this text in relation to the annihilation of the wicked, so I will add just a few more comments.

Jude, Lamentations, Sodom, and Gomorrah

There is another reference to Sodom and Gomorrah in the Old Testament that also looks at the nature of their judgment. We know that they were entirely consumed *in a single day* by the fire of God's wrath (Gen. 19:24-27). Jude 1:7 informed us that this judgment serves as a visual *example* (Greek: *deigma*: a thing shown, an exhibit, or specimen) that provides the meaning of *the punishment of eternal fire*. It is God's unquenchable, consuming fire. Similar to Jeremiah 17:27, this fire, *whose source was the eternal God,* was not extinguished until its intended purpose was accomplished. The people of Sodom and Gomorrah are not still burning today, and Jude tells us it is set forth as an illustration of God's judgment of the wicked.

These things we have observed, but there is an additional and important perspective provided for us in the Book of Lamentations, where Jeremiah compares the siege and burning of Jerusalem by Nebuchadnezzar in 586 BC to the fiery destruction of Sodom and Gomorrah. There are some differences in the various translations of the text of Lamentations 4:6; however, several time-tested commentators agree on its meaning. It is important for our study to carefully consider what is indicated by their near-identical interpretations. Our text reflects Jeremiah's deep and heart-wrenching lament over the fate of Jerusalem in the sixth century BC:

> For the punishment of the iniquity of the daughter of my people *is greater than the punishment of the sin of Sodom*, that was overthrown as in a moment, and no hands stayed on her (Lam. 4:6 KJV).

The following remarks by commentators are incredibly telling. Please read them carefully and consider what is being described:

Keil and Delitzsch:

> Jerusalem, in comparison with that judgment of God [on Sodom], suffers a *greater punishment* for her greater sins: *for her destruction by the hand of man brings her more enduring torments*.[74]

Jamieson, Faussett, and Brown:

> Jeremiah thus shows *the greater severity of Jerusalem's punishment than that of Sodom*.[75]

Expositor's Bible Commentary:

> .. . . the poet does not mean to compare the guilt of Jerusalem with that of Sodom, but rather the fate of the two cities. The punishment of Israel is greater than that of Sodom . . . now in the race for a first place in the history of doom, Jerusalem has broken the record . . . the doom of Sodom was sudden . . . but Jerusalem fell into the hands of man . . . and *she had to endure a long, lingering agony*.[76]

John Gill:

> . . . a shower of fire from heaven, *which consumed it at once*; whereas the destruction of Jerusalem was *a lingering one, through a long and tedious siege*; the inhabitants were gradually wasted and consumed by famine, pestilence, and sword, and *so their punishment greater than Sodom's*.[77]

Beloved, carefully ponder those observations. Jude 1:7 informs us that the fire that consumed Sodom and Gomorrah is a vivid spatial example of *God's punishment of the wicked in eternal fire*. However, according to Lamentations 4:6, the judgment upon those two cities was more merciful than what was experienced by the inhabitants of Jerusalem at the hands of Babylon in 586 BC.

The prophet bemoans the fact that Sodom and Gomorrah's (eternal, fiery) punishment was swift and consuming, whereas Jerusalem's fate was an agonizing, protracted experience of misery, starvation, pain, and death. Isn't it utterly ironic that Jerusalem's extended experience of torment in 586 BC was more excruciating than the so-called eternal torment of hell, exemplified by Sodom and Gomorrah (Jude 1:7), which was swift and decisive?

What Does it Mean?

It further clarifies that God's *eternal* punishment is expeditious and all-consuming. Eternal fire does not burn its victims for eternity. Eternal fire means that the source of the fire of judgment is not human or circumstantial but God himself, the Eternal One. The description is *qualitative*. His eternal fire burns because *he* is eternal, and it is also *quantitative* because it continuously burns, consuming until it has reduced its subject to ashes. This is also seen in 2 Peter 2:6, which echoes Jude 1:7, speaking of God's judgment on the ungodly:

. . . if by turning the cities of Sodom and Gomorrah to ashes he condemned them to extinction, making them an example of what is going to happen to the ungodly (2 Pet 2:6 ESV).

The apostle also uses a similar Greek word as Jude (*hupodeigma*) to stress that Sodom and Gomorrah's destruction is in fact a model, pattern, and example of God's eternal fire of judgment, which is, as in the case of the two ancient cities, swift and consuming.

#7. Jude: Utter Darkness

[These people are] wild waves of the sea, casting up the foam of their own shame; wandering stars, for whom the gloom of utter darkness has been reserved forever (Jude 1:13).

Since we are told that Jude's example of Sodom and Gomorrah illustrates eternal fire, it is not likely that this text speaks of eternal conscious torment. If it is not a synonym for hell, what might Jude be describing when he speaks of the *gloom of utter darkness* that awaits these individuals who have troubled the infant church? Let's examine a few possibilities:

It could be the darkness of death and the grave, which would be consistent with our proposition that death awaits the ungodly. Job likens the grave to a bed in the darkness:

If I look for Sheol (the grave) as my home,
I make my bed in the *darkness*
(Job 17:13).

It might also refer to the darkness of *alienation* from the light of God, which the lost will never possess because of unbelief, as in the words of Jesus to Nicodemus:

"*This is the judgment*, that the Light has come into the world, and men loved the darkness rather than the Light . . ." (John 3:19).

Another possibility is, as the local idiom (expression) in Jesus' day suggests, *exclusion* like that of the Jews who remained in unbelief. It is as those removed from a feast by its host—sent out of the banquet hall into the darkness of the night, causing weeping and anger at their rejection from the feast:

". . . but the sons of the kingdom will be cast out into the outer darkness; in that place there will be weeping and gnashing of teeth" (Matt. 8:12).

The phrase *weeping and gnashing of teeth* in Matthew 8:12 has no connection to post-mortem torment. The image is one depicting how the former sons of the kingdom exhibited anger, agony, and disappointment as they experienced the agonizing effects of months of famine and plague during the siege of their beloved city.

Summary

Although far from exhaustive, the preceding has hopefully provided the reader with suitable alternate explanations of many so-called *eternal conscious torment* proof texts. When read in their contexts and compared with other Scriptures, these alleged proofs appear to say nothing concerning a destiny of perpetual torture by fire for the lost. In many cases, the imagery clearly alludes to other biblical sources that explain the meanings of such things as shame and disgrace, unquenchable fire, and the judgment of Sodom and Gomorrah. Even Matthew 25:46, which is commonly used to compare eternal life as having an equal *duration* to eternal punishment, misses the point. The judgment is in God's own household, The fire of judgment refers to the events of 70 AD, and the final, irreversible, and tragic disinheritance of Israel in the first century.

These and similar texts require that we take a fresh look at biblical terms like eternal punishment, eternal fire, and unquenchable fire. They tell us that the judgments are final and irreversible. They inform us that the fire will burn while there is substance to consume, but no longer. It is unquenchable because no human being can put it out until it has finished its course. Even though physical fires set by Babylon (586 BC) and Rome (AD 70) destroyed Jerusalem centuries apart, their true quality is not of this earthly domain but divine and eternal because it is from God himself. Its function does not differ from the supernatural fire that consumes the lost, resulting in their final extinction, not eternal conscious torment.

PART IV

THE BOOK OF REVELATION

*Though St. John the Evangelist saw many strange
monsters in his vision, he saw no creatures
so wild as one of his own commentators.*
-G. K. Chesterton

CHAPTER 17

THE BOOK OF REVELATION
THE TIME IS NEAR: REVELATION 1–5
AND INTRODUCTORY NOTES

The Revelation of Jesus Christ, which God gave Him to show to His bond-servants, the things which must soon take place . . . the time is near (Rev. 1:1-3).

Anyone who has researched the Book of Revelation recognizes that there are a wide range of perspectives regarding its content. This section will not introduce or analyze various viewpoints but will give special attention to those indicators in the prophecy that provide evidence of its concrete historical orientation (see "Time Texts" in Part II; Chapter 10). Without these interpretive controls, we are left to speculate on the 22 chapters of John's extraordinary visions.

Revelation 1–3:
This Generation Shall Not Pass . . .

. . . is what Jesus told them so many years ago, but it has now almost passed. It had been a long time, just as the Lord cautioned, since those eventful days when the apostles witnessed his great discourse on the Mount of Olives, where he taught them concerning the end of the age. Soon afterward, they saw firsthand his horrifying crucifixion, glorious resurrection, and spectacular ascension into heaven. Then, in the wake of Pentecost, they discovered within and among themselves a previously unknown source of courage and power endowed upon them through the promised Holy Spirit.

In the decades that followed, they boldly passed on his warnings, promises, and directives to the churches that were birthed during that season. The gospel had been preached throughout the world and had taken root in all the nations, just as Jesus told them. Now, worse than ever before, the churches were wrought with tribulation, ridicule, and difficulty on every side. Most, if not all of John's closest companions, that small band of original disciples who were the first recipients of Jesus' great teachings, had now been martyred by the Romans, some at the urging of the Jewish leaders.

One might imagine this apostle sitting pensively at the seashore, alone, resting upon a large rock, and gazing out at the horizon. He may be remembering how he and those companions were told of the things to come in their generation. He had heard from the lips of the one who was the Word of Life–God in the flesh–how the olam hazeh, their current age, would finally see its end. He assured them that the olam haba, their long-anticipated age to come, was getting ready to dawn in their generation. Until now, everything Jesus had said would occur had come to pass. There had been wars and skirmishes throughout the Roman Empire. John may have reflected on the various earthquakes and famines that were witnessed in the Mediterranean region.

There were frequent appearances of false prophets who attempted to insert themselves into Jewish and Christian sacred hopes, some boldly claiming to be the Messiah. Roman and Jewish persecutors forced confessions out of many Christians, who feared torture and death. Some of these even betrayed their Christian brothers and sisters, and even family, in order to save their own lives, just as Jesus had affirmed. Now, John, one of the last, or possibly even the last remaining apostle, had been banished by Nero Caesar to the Island of Patmos, a prison colony in the Aegean Sea, off the coast of Asia Minor.

And he sat, wondering, waiting . . . and perhaps even doubting.

Abruptly, without warning, this great apostle *becomes in spirit* as heaven and earth strangely merge. He finds himself exposed to a dimension outside the realm of space and time. Then he hears a resounding, trumpet-like voice coming from behind him, announcing a directive:

"Write in a book what you see, and send it to the seven churches" (Rev. 1:10-11).

As he turns, he is overcome by an image of what appears to be a man of incomprehensible glory. The figure, shining with the brilliant radiance of the sun, is standing in the middle of seven golden lampstands. Dumbfounded by the sight, John can do nothing but fall face down as lifeless in his presence. The magnificent appearance is none other than that of the glorified Jesus, reaching out to touch John and assuring his servant as to his identity, telling him not to fear. His glorious Lord declares that he is alive and in full control of the churches and their destinies. John is told that he is going to see important things and they will be communicated through symbols and images. Importantly, they are *about to take place.* He is to write down all that he is shown and send it to the churches in Asia Minor.

The revelation pertained to Christ's coming in the clouds of glory, just as he promised nearly a generation ago. There is a sense of urgency now because the events surrounding the Lord's arrival will commence shortly. The churches were at the threshold of the long-awaited *parousia,* and there were vital communications prepared for all of them. In John's greeting, the apostle reflects with unbridled joy and anticipation. He cannot restrain himself and exclaims:

> Behold, He comes with the clouds, and every eye will see Him, even those who pierced Him, and all the tribes of the land will wail because of Him. Yes! Amen! (Rev. 1:7 LSV)

In the letters to the churches (Revelation 2 and 3), the Holy Spirit emphasized not only the need for perseverance but also repentance:

> ". . . repent and do the deeds you did at first; or else I am coming to you" (Rev. 2:5).

> ". . . repent; or else I am coming to you quickly" (Rev. 2:16). ". . . what you have, hold fast until I come" (Rev. 2:24-25).

> ". . . if you do not wake up, I will come like a thief, and you will not know at what hour I will come to you" (Rev. 3:3).

> ". . . I also will keep you from the hour of testing . . . which is about to come upon the whole world [empire] . . . I am coming quickly; hold fast what you have" (Rev. 3:10-11).

Most of the churches were commended for their good works and steadfastness in the faith. However, the Spirit exposed the need to overcome the hindrances that were prevalent among them. The great tribulation was about to begin, and the Lord's coming was imminent in their time. These hindrances were intolerable compromises from which they needed to separate themselves. If not, they would be stumbling blocks in the coming days. They were being called to overcome and, in doing so, gain their full reward.

Revelation 1–3:
Audience Relevance

An incredible amount of effort has been expended on speculative, futuristic interpretations of John's great Revelation. We have already seen this in the Olivet Discourse (Part II), where Jesus plainly stated that his prophecy would entirely come to pass before the end of that generation. Likewise, the opening and closing words of the Book of Revelation (and numerous texts between) are more than adequate to provide us with its context as well as John's target audience. Like a massive pair of book ends, its first and last chapters form an inclusio within which the contents, timing, and relevant audience reside:

> The Revelation of Jesus Christ, which God gave Him to show to His bond-servants, the *things which must soon take place* . . . Blessed is the one who reads aloud. . . and those who hear, and who keep what is written in it, for *the time is near* . . . *John to the seven churches that are in Asia* (Rev. 1:1-4).

> . . . the God of the spirits of the prophets, sent His angel to show to His bond-servants the things *which must soon take place* . . . "Behold I am coming quickly . . . And he said to me, 'Do not seal up the words of the prophecy of this book, for the time is near'" (Rev. 22:6-10).

Who's Perspective of Time?

As we previously observed (Chapter I), some teach that these time references in Revelation don't necessarily indicate *literal* nearness in time. They should be understood as having been spoken from God's perspective and not ours, referring again to the "one day is as a thousand years" argument from 2 Peter 3:8. However, if Peter's statement, which is so often taken out of context, is the standard for all biblical prophecy, we must ask ourselves:

How exactly would God communicate nearness in time if it were necessary to do so?

Let's consider the following examples:

First, how would the Jerusalem prophets who were visiting Antioch have signaled the famine that was *about to* take place?

> And in those days there came from Jerusalem prophets to Antioch, and one of them, by name Agabus, having stood up, signified through the Spirit a great scarcity *is about to be* throughout all the world— *which also came to pass in the time of Claudius Caesar* . . . according as anyone was prospering, determined each of them to send for ministry to the brothers dwelling in Judea (Acts 11:27-29 LSV).

Imagine the men in attendance, reflectively stroking their beards, discussing among themselves and with the leading women how this is probably God's timing and not man's. Their subsequent inaction would have had disastrous consequences for the impoverished Jerusalem church that had been ransacked by persecution (cf. Acts 8:1-3). Also consider the tragic loss of the opportunity to create a bond of fellowship between the Gentile church in Antioch and the Jewish church in Jerusalem through the financial support they provided, which was prompted by the prophecy.

Second, consider the angel prodding Peter in Acts 12 (while he was sleeping), providing the apostle with an escape opportunity after Herod imprisoned him:

> And behold, an angel of the Lord suddenly stood near Peter, and a light shone in the cell; and he struck Peter's side and woke him, saying, "*Get up quickly.*" And his chains fell off his hands (Acts 12:7).

The word *quickly* is the same Greek word (*takhos*) that appears in Revelation 1:1. Some interpret the meaning as not so much the *timing* of the events but *how rapidly* they will occur, *whenever* they occur. Should we then translate Acts 12:7 as follows?

> "It doesn't matter when you get up, Peter, but when you do, do it quickly!" (Which, of course, is absurd).

Third, the following warnings in Ezekiel, like those in Revelation, were spoken as a prelude to Jerusalem's prior invasion and destruction in 586 BC:

"Thus says the Lord GOD, 'A disaster, unique disaster, behold it is coming! 'An end is coming; the end has come! . . . behold, it has come! . . . The time has come, the day is near . . . Now I will *shortly* pour out My wrath on you'" (Eze. 7:5-8).

One wonders if such methods of interpretation would have been of any help to Judah in the sixth century BC. Does Ezekiel seem to be the least bit concerned about elastic time? Or that "a thousand years is like a day, and a day like a thousand years?" Was he suggesting that this coming destruction at the hands of Nebuchadnezzar was not necessarily soon, but in *God's indecipherable time?*

Interestingly, there were some in Israel at that time who refused to believe the urgency of Ezekiel's words. God had something to say through the prophet about their imprudent mindset:

"Son of man, behold, the house of Israel is saying, *'The vision that he sees is for many years from now,* and he prophesies of times far off.' Therefore, say to them, 'Thus says the Lord GOD, None of My words will be delayed any longer.'" (Eze. 12:26-28; compare Rev. 10:6 - "there will be delay no longer").

Finally, consider the use of the phrase "about to" in other texts in Revelation, especially in letters to the churches:

". . . you are *about to* suffer. Behold, the devil is *about to* cast some of you into prison" (Rev. 2:10).

". . . the hour of testing . . . which is *about to* come upon the whole world [*oikoumene*: empire]" (Rev. 3:10).

Were these urgent warnings? Or, were they merely references to things that may or may not occur, depending on God's own indeterminable timing? Yes, they were urgent. This earnestness did not only pertain to the letters. John was also told to write concerning things that *were about to occur after* these initial correspondences:

> Write what things you saw, and what things are, and what things are *about to occur* after these things (Rev. 1:19 LITV).

Serious consideration must be given to the proposition that John's vision, in its entirety, concerned things that were about to take place soon and quickly. If this is not the case, ask yourself again:

> *How else would God communicate nearness in time if it were necessary to do so? How would his audience know for certain that a season of crisis was approaching in their time? Why the urgency if the visions didn't pertain to their time and circumstances?*

Location, Location, Location

As we journey through Revelation, *our theme, Israel's historical location as being on the threshold of exile,* remains a focal point of John's visions as the warnings of the New Testament are reaching their fulfillment. Hopefully, the reader will see how that theme is apparent. As Revelation unfolds, the nation of Israel is now entering the period of their final judgments. These judgments were to encompass not only Jerusalem but their entire land, as well as the Mediterranean Region. Considering this, let us again be reminded concerning the New Testament's use of ge (the land) and oikoumene (the empire) in John's visions (see Chapter 1).

As opposed to the entire planet, the first-century *land* of Israel and the Roman *empire* are focal points of much of the vision, which is consistent with the book's historical context. My comments on Revelation will consider these alternatives as appropriate, seeking to be faithful to the text in every respect and relying on reputable original language resources and the context in which they are used.

A Word About Repetition

In our examination of the Book of Revelation, the reader may notice a degree of repetition not only in the visions themselves but also in my commentary on the text. For example, such repetition in the visions includes how each series of judgments in Revelation brings similar great concluding disturbances, for example:

- **Seals (8:5):** peals of thunder, sounds and flashes of lightning, and an earthquake

- **Trumpets (11:19):** flashes of lightning, sounds and peals of thunder, an earthquake, and a great hailstorm

- **Bowls (16:18, 21):** flashes of lightning, sounds and peals of thunder, a great earthquake, and huge hailstones

Also, compare the *trumpet* and *bowl* judgments:

Activity	Trumpets	Bowls
Prelude: Jewish Remnant Preserved	7:1	14:1
Each 2nd affects the sea	8:7	16:2
Each 3rd affects the rivers	8:10	16:4
Each 4th affects the heavens	8:12	16:8
Each 5th affects people	9:1	16:10
Each 6th affects the Euphrates	9:14	16:12
Each 7th describes the end	11:15	16:17

Table 17.1

This repetition of certain aspects of John's visions is divinely ordained and has noteworthy biblical precedents found in two Old Testament stories: one concerning Joseph, the other, Daniel.

Joseph Interprets Pharaoh's Dreams

Our first example (or precedent) is found in the story of Joseph. In Genesis 41, Pharaoh of Egypt has a dream of famine in the land that *he personally sees twice*. As Joseph interprets the dreams for him, he points out that the duplication of the dream means it is from God–specifically because the same individual saw the dream twice. Note Joseph's instruction to Pharoah:

> And the doubling of Pharaoh's dream means that the thing is fixed by God, and *God will shortly bring it about* (Gen. 41:32 ESV).

Pharoah is told that not only is the matter from God but also that its replication to the same individual was a sign that it would come to pass shortly. The implications for the book of Revelation must be considered. Many of John's visions have redundancies (or parallels) that are seen from slightly different vantage points, but they were given to the same person: John. If we take Joseph's explanation as a precedent, those repetitions of John's visions, with their different perspectives, would indicate that the events were going to come to pass very soon.

Daniel and Nebuchadnezzar

A second highly relevant precedent is found in the book of Daniel. In the second chapter, King Nebuchadnezzar of Babylon has a dream of a magnificent statue consisting of several metals in descending order from a head of gold. Daniel is called upon to interpret the king's dream for him. He informs Nebuchadnezzar that he, the king, is the head of gold. The remaining portions of that statue represent empires and their kings that will follow successively after him over several centuries. Then, in Daniel 7, the prophet himself dreams concerning the same historical sequence. However, in contrast to what Nebuchadnezzar saw, which was *a glorified man,* Daniel sees the same succession of empires for what they really are. These empires (Babylon, Persia, Greece, and Rome) are nothing more than *ravenous beasts.* Later, the angel of the vision tells Daniel that the concluding aspects of these visions were to be sealed because *they would occur long after his time:*

> The vision of the evenings and mornings
> Which has been told is true,
> But keep the vision secret,
> For it pertains to many days in the future
> (Dan. 8:26)
> But you, Daniel, shut up the words and seal the book, until the time of the end (Dan. 12:4 ESV).

In Daniel's case, the two visionary experiences were given to different individuals. This may indicate that the timing of the fulfillment of these things, *unlike that of Joseph's experiences,* would be farther off in the future. However, there is more. In Chapter 7, Daniel was shown the spiritual principalities behind the empires in Nebuchadnezzar's dream. This is evident from the fact that Daniel sees a vision of a goat and a ram in Chapter 8, which pertains to the historical conflict between Persia and Greece.

In Chapter 10, the heavenly messenger informs the prophet that he (the angel) is engaged in spiritual warfare involving the "princes" (principalities) of those two nations. They were two of the beasts in Daniel's vision in Chapter 7. Also, the little horn of Daniel 7:8 is said to have "eyes *like* a man," meaning the true essence of the horn was not human. Daniel's experience of seeing the spiritual powers behind human kingdoms is also an important feature of Revelation, and the reader will see how it is vital to its interpretation.

Other Considerations

First, Revelation is a series of visions that were communicated to John through symbols. These symbols must be interpreted through the lens of the Bible's own system of symbols. The metaphorical elements of languages in secular culture change with technology, the shape of the world, and varying worldviews. The words employed in any language reflect the images of its culture at any given time. However, biblical symbolism is fixed within the context of the Bible itself. It was consistent throughout its 1500 years of unfolding revelation. Because of this, we should not be looking for skyscrapers, helicopters, or bomber planes in Revelation. Its symbols allude to the places, events, and structures within its own history, how they are described there, and their implied meaning.

Second, the reader should become acquainted with time sequence in Revelation. The words "Then I saw" should not be assumed to mean "Then this happened." John saw many similar events from different perspectives, so we should not assume there is a chapter-by-chapter time sequence to its entire 22 chapters or to a specific section when that may not be the case. However, there is an apparent general sequence that moves toward the conclusion of the visions.

Third, you will see Revelation as predominantly fulfilled history. The challenge is to determine not only biblical evidence of its fulfillment but also, to the extent possible, historical evidence. As we saw in the Olivet Discourse, the most important evidence is a narrative's own self-witness as to its timing and fulfillment. In many cases, historical evidence is available, but at times, there is an absence of known details. Therefore, we must resign ourselves to the fact that, in some instances, *you just had to be there.* Popular speculative interpretations are also difficult to prove because John's visions are viewed as future events. Specifically in Revelation 10, John hears seven great thunders, the meaning of which he is not permitted to disclose:

I heard a voice from heaven saying, "Seal up the things which the seven peals of thunder have spoken and do not write them." (Rev. 10:4)

Paul writes to the church in Thessalonica about the man of sin, but the data remains a private communication between Paul and that first-century church concerning things he taught while he was among them. We are not privy to the exact nature of all the details:

Do you not remember that while I was still with you, I was telling you these things? *And you know what restrains him now*, so that in his time he will be revealed (2 Thes. 2:5-6).

As for Revelation, we must evaluate the evidence in the book itself that indicates the time and nature of its characters and events. Having established that, although we may not fully grasp each detail, we can be confident that it must have occurred within the stated parameters given to John by the Holy Spirit.

External data (from early Christian writings, etc.) may be of value, but the internal content of Revelation, its allusions, and its references must be given priority. Scripture must interpret Scripture. This is especially relevant as we "hear" the echoes of the prophets of old, who prophesied the first destruction of Jerusalem in 586 BC. The Book of Revelation contains many images and allusions to prophetic warnings and descriptions related to that event.

For example, Ezekiel, a pre-exilic prophet, contains much of the same language and imagery found in Revelation. Many expositors have made this observation. These include episodes such as a vision of the four creatures before the throne, the nearness of the time, eating the book, the sealing of saints, the vine of the land, and the river of life. Ezekiel's prophecy warns of what was soon to occur, which was the destruction of Jerusalem in the sixth century BC. The following are but a few examples:

Ezekiel and Revelation

Events Will Occur Shortly	Rev. 1:1, 3	Eze. 7:1-12
Sealing the Righteous	Rev. 7:3	Eze. 9:1-4
No More Delay	Rev. 10:1-7	Eze. 12: 25-28
Eating the Book	Rev. 10:8 -11	Eze. 40-43
Jerusalem compared to Sodom	Rev. 11:8	Eze. 16:49
Gathering the Jewish Remnant	Rev. 14:1-5	Eze. 34
The Vine of the Land (Isa. 5:1-7)	Rev. 14:18-20	Eze. 15
The Great Harlot	Rev. 17-18	Eze. 16, 23
The River of Life	Rev. 22:1-2	Eze. 47:1-12

Table 17.2

Revelation 4–5:
The Stage is Set

After these things I looked, and behold, a door *standing* open in heaven, and the first voice which I had heard, like *the sound* of a trumpet speaking with me, said, "Come up here, and I will show you what must take place after these things" (Rev. 4:1).

In Revelation 4, we pass from the initial vision and letters to the churches. Upon seeing a doorway in heaven, the apostle is bidden by a voice to "*come up here.*" John enters and is immediately in the Spirit a second time (4:2). The opened door reveals the throne room of heaven, where God's glory radiates with unfathomable brilliance. The Enthroned One is encircled by a great rainbow. Great angelic creatures and heavenly elders fill the room. Amidst the beauty and glory of the chamber, in its very center is the Crucified One, seen as a slaughtered lamb, the perpetual reminder of how access to this divine glory came to be. He is there in the center of the chamber, along with the candlestick-like presence of the Holy Spirit, while multitudes of the redeemed worship unceasingly.

In Revelation 5, there is great joy because the Lamb is deemed worthy to open the seals of the scroll of judgments about to be released upon the land. An age characterized by law, the physical accoutrements of the temple with its outward ritual observances, and a favored city is about to come to an end. The cross had demonstrably put an end to the benefit they provided, but now they must be entirely removed. A new age is about to be birthed, but not without great pain, judgment, and tribulation. The sealed book is about to be opened. Fearful judgments are about to commence. *Worthy is the Lamb! It is the day of the Lord!*

CHAPTER 18

THE BOOK OF REVELATION
THE END HAS COME: REVELATION 6–11

At the time of John's Revelation, the nation of Israel had been on a *threshold* for nearly two generations. A little over 70 years prior, their Messiah had been born, lived, and conducted his ministry to the nation until his crucifixion in c. 30 AD. We have seen that, like their ancient ancestors in the wilderness, the Jews were given a probationary period of forty years to repent and turn to God. We also observed that, during this time, an elect remnant was preserved as the rest of the nation refused God's offer of salvation in Christ. Some allied themselves with the Roman Empire and even persecuted the messengers of Christ who offered that hope. That season of opportunity had now ended. The nation was about to pass through a portal from which there would be no return.

Revelation 6:
"What Will Be the Sign of Your Coming?"

Behold, a white horse, and he who sat on it had a bow; and a crown
was given to him, and he went out conquering and to conquer.
(Rev. 6:2).

Revelation 6 provides a look at the overall conditions leading up
to the Jewish-Roman War. This chapter links Revelation to its parallels
in the Olivet Discourse (Matthew 24 and the Synoptics). John did not
record the discourse in his Gospel; however, in the vision of the *Seven
Seals*, he *sees* all that the disciples were *told* would occur before the end
of their generation.

Seven Seals	Olivet Discourse		
Revelation 6	Matt. 24	Mark 13	Luke 21
Wars 6:1-2	24:6	13:77	21:10
International Strife 6:3-4	24:7	13:8	21:10
Famine 6:5-6	24:7	13:8	21:11
Pestilence 6:7-8	–	–	21:11
Persecution 6:9-11	24:9-13	13: 9-13	21:12-19
Earthquakes 6:12-17	24: 7	13:8	21:11
Cosmic Collapse 6:12-17	24:15-31	13:14-27	21:20-27

Table 18.1

Four riders carry all that is symbolic of the conditions brought
about by divine judgment upon a nation. Jesus is portrayed as the
conqueror on the white horse, leading the charge against his enemies.
David Chilton suggested that Jesus removed the war bow from above

the great throne to conduct the advance (cf. Rev. 4:3; Hab. 3:9-11; Luke 19:27).[78] The land of Israel is rupturing under the weight of war, famine, and pestilence. Meanwhile, the souls of historical martyrs under the altar in heaven are anxiously petitioning God for their vindication and glorification. The martyrs are given white robes and told to be patient a little longer. The days of God's vengeance concerning which they cry allude to Luke's version of the Olivet Discourse, in which we are again reminded concerning his coming:

". . . because these are *days of vengeance*, so that all things which are written will be fulfilled" (Luke 21:22).

The image of these martyrs is not an easy one to explain. There may be a clue in Hebrews 9:8-9 (written just before the outbreak of the war). The writer sees that the deceased saints were not yet glorified. They were not given full entry to the throne room of heaven until the Old Covenant system was entirely eradicated and the full complement of martyrs was fulfilled:

The Holy Spirit *is* signifying this, that the way into the holy place has not yet been disclosed while the outer tabernacle is still standing, which *is* a symbol for the present time (Heb. 9:8-9).

The writer of Hebrews tells us that the God-ordained temple was still standing. The semantic range of (Greek) *echousēs stasin allows that it had standing or place*, or possibly, in opposition. The context seems to suggest it had standing that God originally sanctioned. This is captured in the Literal Standard Version of the text:

By this the Holy Spirit was making evident that the way of the holy [*places*] has not yet been revealed, the first dwelling place yet having a standing (Heb. 9:8 LSV).

It appears that the souls (persons) could not be released into the heavenly sanctuary until its earthly replica was moved out of the way.

Of course, the writings of the apostles teach that the saints were able to access the throne of grace representatively through prayer and repentance while still in their earthly bodies. However, the postmortem martyrs are still waiting for the fall of the temple and their actual release into the heavenly sanctuary. In Revelation 11:19, we hear the seventh trumpet, and we are told *that the temple in heaven was opened,* as if to say that the time of the consummation had arrived, and they could now enter and receive their reward:

> And the nations were enraged, and Your wrath came, and the time came for the dead to be judged, *and the time to reward Your bond-servants* the prophets and the saints and those who fear Your name, the small and the great, and to destroy those who destroy the earth [land]. And the temple of God which is in heaven was opened; and the ark of His covenant appeared in His temple, and there were flashes of lightning and sounds and peals of thunder and an earthquake and a great hailstorm (Rev. 11:18-19).

Chapter 6 closes with an echo of the words of Jesus to some women of Jerusalem on his way to the cross. We must consider these references as relevant to our interpretation of the timing of Revelation as they relate to an imminent invasion of Israel by a foreign army. Even in the throes of great suffering, Jesus calls on the text of Scripture to exhort the women concerning what was soon to come upon their nation:

> ". . . stop weeping for Me, but weep for yourselves and for your children. For behold, the days are coming when . . . they will begin TO SAY TO THE MOUNTAINS, 'FALL ON US,' AND TO THE HILLS, 'COVER US'" (Luke 23:28-30).

John is given the same text in this vision of Revelation 6:

> . . . and they said to the mountains and to the rocks, "Fall on us and hide us from the presence of Him who sits on the throne, and from the wrath of the Lamb" (Rev. 6:16).

The words are a vivid example of metalepsis (explained in Part I) that recall the words of the prophet Hosea. The context of the quote is needed to fully understand the meaning behind it. Here, Jesus quotes a text from Hosea that was prophesied in the generation just prior to the historical fall of the northern kingdom of Israel in 722 BC. The accounts in Luke and Revelation invite us to re-examine the conditions under which the words were first spoken. That historical situation provides the basis for understanding their use in a newer context. Hosea's words provide warning of an imminent invasion by a foreign army sent to judge God's disobedient nation:

> Also the high places of Aven, the sin of Israel, will be destroyed;
> Thorn and thistle will grow on their altars;
> Then they will say to the mountains,
> "Cover us!" And to the hills, "Fall on us!"
> (Hos. 10:8).

Revelation 7:
The Preservation of Israel's Remnant

As **Revelation 7** opens, another remarkable scene unfolds as the Jewish remnant is seen:

> After this I saw four angels standing at the four corners of the earth [land], holding back the four winds of the earth [land], so that no wind would blow on the earth [land] or on the sea [i.e., nations] or on any tree. And I saw another angel ascending from the rising of the sun, having the seal of the living God; and he cried out with a loud voice to the four angels to whom it was granted to harm the earth [land] and the sea [nations], And I heard the number of those who were sealed, one hundred and forty-four thousand sealed from every tribe of the sons of Israel (Rev. 7:1-4).

As God seals his beloved remnant with the promised Holy Spirit (cf. Eph. 1:13), an astonishing image of four great angels who carry out his judgments appears. They open their enormous wings to restrain the winds of calamity, as this sealing is being accomplished during the apostolic mission to the land and the nations. John sees these enormous creatures perched upon the four corners of the *land* until the sealing of the remnant is completed. It is seen as accomplished because they are already God's elect. I suggest the translation should use *land* (Greek: *ge*) rather than *earth* because the land of Israel is viewed as having four corners in Ezekiel 7:2, which is another similarity between the two books, as previously mentioned:

> "And you, son of man, thus says the Lord GOD to the land of Israel, 'An end! The end is coming on the four corners of the *land* [Heb: eretz; in context, the land of Israel]" (Eze 7:2).

The angels prevent the destructive forces from converging upon the land. They hold back the unseen principalities behind the human forces from launching the invasion until the full complement of the *promised* remnant has been preserved. Peter, *writing to dispersed Jews*, provides this same assurance to them. The day of the Lord, the revelation of a man of sin, and the dissolution of the heavens and the land (the land, temple, and its services) will not begin until the sealing of all is accomplished, as Peter wrote:

> . . . with the Lord one day is like a thousand years, and a thousand years like one day. The Lord is not slow about *His promise*, as some count slowness, but is *patient toward you [or: us]*, not wishing for any to perish but for all to come to repentance. But the day of the Lord will come like a thief, in which the heavens will pass away with a roar and the elements will be destroyed with intense heat, and the earth [land] and its works will be burned up (2 Pet. 3:8- 10).

Although it is not commonly considered, I'm offering an alternative explanation of Peter's often quoted words, considering the first-century context and Jewish recipients of the letter. Although this text has a wider application, the "*you*" to whom Peter writes is the remnant of the Jewish dispersion (1 Pet. 1:1; 2 Pet. 3:1). We have seen that, according to Romans 11:5, this remnant was being gathered in the first century. They were to be comforted knowing that God, in his perfect patience, would ensure that every one of his elect remnant was gathered in before the judgments of the day of the Lord began.

Speculatively, the restraining angels of Revelation 7 could also be the force(s) holding back the appearance of the *man of sin* and the commencement of widespread calamity on the land, to which Paul refers in 2 Thessalonians 2:6:

> And you know what restrains him now, so that in his time he [the man of sin] will be revealed (2 Thes. 2:6).

Returning to the Throne Room

The scene shifts again to the throne room, where John sees an innumerable number of Gentiles who have come out of the great tribulation–quite likely Nero's persecution–and are now standing in adoration before the Lord. The palm branches have symbolic meaning to both Jews today and their ancestors. They are a symbol of the Feast of Booths (*Sukkot,* or Tabernacles). According to the prophets:

> It will come about that all of the survivors [i.e., those who remain] of the nations who came against Jerusalem will come there from year to year to worship the King, the LORD of the Heavenly Armies, and to observe the Feast of Tents [Booths] (Zec. 14:16 ISV).

Again, Chilton observes this as a forward-looking, prophetic scene intended to bring assurance to suffering churches of their ultimate victory through the great tribulation. The saints reading and hearing this prophecy were given to see that they were not broken and defeated but destined for a glorious, unimaginable future:

> The point, for the first-century Christians reading it, was that the Tribulation they were about to suffer would not destroy them . . . God saw them, . . . not scattered, isolated groups of poor and persecuted

individuals accused as criminals by a merciless, demonic power-State; they were, rather, a vast throng of conquerors, who had washed their robes and made them white in the blood of the Lamb, standing before God's throne and robed in the righteousness of Jesus Christ.[79]

Revelation 8–9:
The March of Rome

"*I have come to cast fire upon the earth [land]; and how I wish it were already kindled!*" (Luke 12:49).

When the Lamb broke the seventh seal, there was silence in heaven for about half an hour . . . *Then the angel took the censer and filled it with the fire of the altar, and threw it to the earth [land]*; and there followed peals of thunder and sounds and flashes of lightning and an earthquake (Rev. 8:1-5).

Revelation 8 opens with an eerie silence in heaven. Then, an angel fills a censer from the altar and casts it to the land, followed by trumpeting angels. These angels cast fire and destruction upon a third of the land and a third of the sea. A third of the sun, moon, and stars are darkened (we will see the historical and geographical significance of the fractional reckoning momentarily). The implication, based on Chapter 7, is that the people of God have now been removed to safety. Historically, the chronological sequence of the Jewish-Roman War is seen vividly in this chapter. We are given both an earthly view of these historical events as well as a glimpse into the realm of the unseen forces at work. The character and actions of those forces will also be seen in Chapter 9. Here, in Chapter 8, the star *Wormwood* (Rev. 8:11) falls from heaven. Wormwood is described in the Old Testament as a deceptive narrative (false prophecy):

"Because they have forsaken My law which I set before them, and have not obeyed My voice nor walked according to it . . . Behold, I will feed them, this people, with wormwood and give them poisoned water to drink" (Jer. 9:13-15).

"Therefore, thus says the LORD of hosts concerning the prophets,
'Behold, I am going to feed them wormwood
And make them drink poisonous water,
For from the prophets of Jerusalem
Pollution has gone forth into all the land"
(Jer. 23:15).

For the first-century Jews, this *wormwood* was the misleading hope engendered by the false prophets who prophesied deliverance and victory over the Romans. Josephus offers an example:

Now there was then a great number of false prophets suborned by the tyrants Zealots] to impose on the people, who denounced this to them, that they should wait for deliverance from God; and this was in order to keep them from deserting . . . Now a man that is in adversity does easily comply with such promises; for when such a seducer makes him believe that he shall be delivered from those miseries which oppress him, then it is that the patient is full of hopes of such his deliverance.[80]

Not only were futile promises of deliverance proclaimed, but there were also those among the Jewish elite who endorsed *allegiance* to Rome, as in Revelation 13, where the land beast serves Rome's interests by promoting worship of the sea beast. In other words, neither the pro-Rome nor the anti-Rome factions in Israel reflected the truth of God but were deceptions:

. . . they did not receive the love of the truth so as to be saved. For this reason God will send upon them a deluding influence so that they will believe what is false (2 Thes. 2:7-11).

Destruction in Galilee

Now that the remnant has been sealed, the march of Roman General Vespasian's troops begins with his northern (Galilean) campaign. This is the northern *one-third* of the holy land and is illustrated in the following graphic of first-century Israel:

A Third of the Land

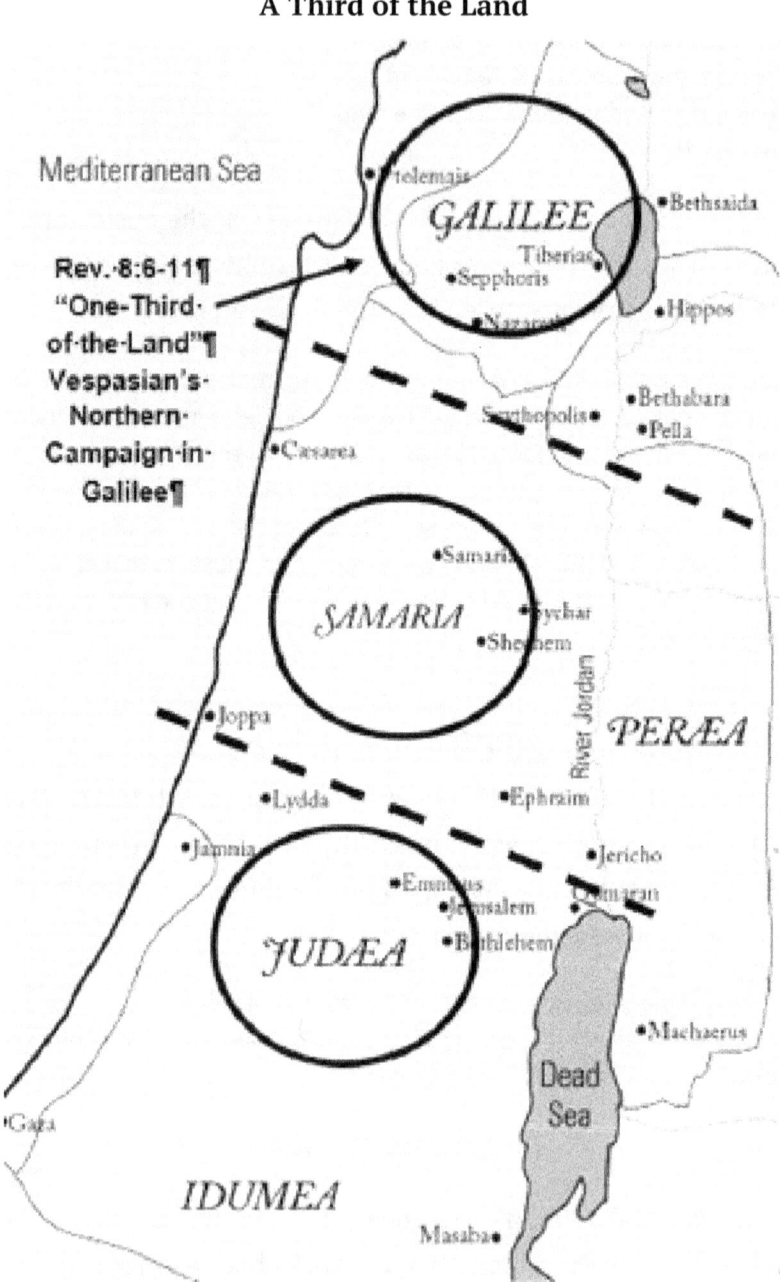

Vespasian's Galilean Campaign Map By Wikipedia User: Andrew c, CC BY 3.0
https://commons.wikimedia.org/w/index.php?curid=743768, Edited to Suit

From May to November of 67 AD, Vespasian's legions marched through Galilee, bringing death and destruction. They burned the cities and ravaged the countryside, killing thousands on the Sea of Galilee and as far south as the Israelite seaport of Joppa on the Mediterranean coast.

Revelation 9 presents an important set of complex dynamics involving the activities of the *visible* powers, who are driven by the forces of the unseen world. John observes the demonic "star" from Chapter 8, who is now releasing hordes of *locust-like* creatures who bring indescribable misery to the people of the land. In order for us to understand the dynamics depicted in Revelation 8 and 9, it is important to revisit what we saw earlier in our study of the Olivet Discourse.

We previously saw the major historical developments in the Roman invasion concerning Nero's suicide and the suspension of the war. That history precedes Revelation 9. We'll recall how, upon hearing news of Nero's death, Vespasian suspended the war. He focused his attention on the chaos that erupted in Rome. After the violent deaths of three would-be emperors, Vespasian himself was declared emperor. The value of this history cannot be underestimated because the new Emperor Vespasian appointed his son, General Titus, to resume the war effort against Israel. Titus was the one who put down the rebellion in Israel and destroyed the city, empowered by the *Apollyon* spirit. This is the *destroyer* who comes into view in Revelation 9:11.

King of the Locusts

> They have as king over them, the angel of the abyss; his name in Hebrew is Abaddon, and in the Greek, he has the name Apollyon (Rev. 9:11).

Titus led the 15th legion, *Apollinaris*, toward Jerusalem. After a five-month siege, he completed his mission, utterly destroying the city and the temple. The name Apollyon (Greek: *destroyer*) bears resemblance to the 15th Roman legion, *Apollinaris,* which Titus led into Jerusalem in 70 AD. It was named after the Greek god Apollo. Additional forces, also led by Titus, took part in the final assault on the city, as shown in the second half of Revelation 9. Again, we note that Revelation 9:11 focuses not so much on the man, Titus, but on the *demonic power* at work behind him. We will see the importance of this in later chapters of Revelation.

Revelation 9:14-19 describes the Roman legions under Titus' command. The generals of these legions may be the *angels* bound at the Euphrates. They were kept there, having been prepared by God for this hour in history. The number four, symbolizing universality, may represent that the legions encompassed the whole Roman empire (*the oikoumene*) that were unified to go to war against Jerusalem. As they marched toward the city, they brought destructive fire and devastation everywhere in their path. As with Titus, there were demonic forces (*angels*) behind the leaders of these legions of human soldiers. Upon being summoned from the Euphrates in the north, they travel through the northern regions of the land before arriving at Jerusalem.

This invading force is not to be understood as a literal army of 200 million "mounted soldiers." The task of obtaining daily food and water to supply such a vast army of horses and their riders is inconceivable. John is most likely describing the *innumerable hordes of demonic spirits* that have been summoned to destroy Jerusalem. Their number in relation to the number of human horsemen is incidental. The Gadarene demoniac whom Jesus cured in Mark 5:1-20 was *possessed by a legion of demons*, which by most estimates numbered 5,000–6,000 Roman soldiers. Both Revelation and the Gospel account most likely refer to an extremely large number:

> And He was asking him, "What is your name?" And he *said to Him, "My name is Legion; for we are many" (Mark 5:9).

Most importantly, Jerusalem is not the only foe in view. Unholy forces came from the entire empire (Rome's client kingdoms) to join Titus (Apollyon: The Destroyer) in waging war on the Lamb, assuming that the stamping out of the Jewish nation would also result in the end of the church (cf. Rev. 17:14). As mentioned previously, the church was still viewed as a sect of Judaism.

Revelation 10:
The Mystery Accomplished

. . . and he had in his hand a little book . . . He placed his right foot on the sea and his left on the land; and he cried out with a loud voice, as when a lion roars . . . Then the angel whom I saw standing on the sea and on the land lifted up his right hand to heaven, and swore by Him who lives forever and ever, . . . that there will be delay no longer . . . But in the days of the voice of the seventh angel, when he is about to sound, then the mystery of God is finished, as He preached to His servants the prophets (Rev. 10:1-7).

Chapter 10 turns our gaze to a radiantly attired, holy angel breaking through the heavenly realm. The angel's positioning conveys that God's rule has been established over both Gentiles (the sea) and Jews (the land). He has the characteristics of, and is most likely, the Lord Jesus Christ, whose feet are planted firmly on the sea and the land. As promised by the prophet Isaiah, in the last days, which was the season leading up to the end of the age, the Gentiles would join with the Jews, flowing to the mountain of the house of the LORD (the kingdom of God). This was to begin during the last days of Jewish national privilege:

Now it will come about that In the last days
The mountain of the house of the LORD
Will be established as the chief of the mountains,
And will be raised above the hills;
And all the nations will stream to it
(Isa. 2:2 ff).

The prophets often saw Gentile inclusion in the new age. However, according to Ephesians 3, they apparently did not fully grasp the complete picture. The Gentiles would be made co-heirs of the promises *as full covenant members* with Jewish believers. This was a mystery that was concealed from even them:

> . . . that by revelation there was made known to me . . . the mystery of Christ, *which in other generations was not made known to the sons of men*, as it has now been revealed to His holy apostles and prophets in the Spirit; *to be specific,* that the Gentiles are fellow heirs and fellow members of the body, and fellow partakers of the promise in Christ Jesus through the gospel (Eph. 3:3-6).

Here, in Revelation 10:7, we are shown that the mystery has not only been revealed but is now also accomplished. The word *finished* is the Greek term *etelesthe (from teleo)*. *Teleo* has a range of meanings, which include *complete, finish, execute, accomplish, initiate,* etc. I think *accomplished* best suits the context. That which would continue in the age to come was accomplished in the transition from the Old Covenant. The vision of Isaiah was being fulfilled in the latter days of the olam hazeh (their current age) exactly as promised.

The integration of Jew and Gentile into one body in Christ was not going to wait until the new age dawned. The core of the all-inclusive church was now established under Christ's headship. That this body continued to grow throughout Christian history until today does not violate the constraints set forth in Revelation's time statements–that it would be fulfilled shortly (in the first century AD). In the same way, on the Day of Pentecost, Peter quoted the prophet Joel concerning the reception of the Holy Spirit by people from all nations in *those same last days*:

> . . . *this is* what was spoken of through the prophet Joel: 'and it shall be *in the last days*,' God says, 'that I will pour forth of my spirit *on all mankind* . . . (Acts 2:16-17).

That outpouring has not ceased simply because Joel's prophecy was "fulfilled" at Pentecost. The outpouring of the Spirit continues, as does his work throughout the duration of the church age. Then, in Revelation 10:6, we are told that there will be no further delay in demolishing the old system. It is time for olam haba, the age to come, to emerge. Seven peals of thunder make announcements that John hears but is not permitted to write down. As noted in the previous chapter, we will not speculate here as to why.

As the episode concludes, John is given a book to consume. It is most likely the prophetic message for his ministry after his release from Patmos. It is sweet to his taste, suggesting that the long-anticipated future of one new man—Jews and Gentiles together in Christ—is a desirable one. However, the implications for his fellow Jews are bitter as he digests the dreadful realities of what is unfolding before his eyes. All that had once defined his culture and worldview was on the brink of destruction at the hands of the formidable Roman forces. One might also get the sense that John, as was typical of the prophetic tradition, was tasting God's own grief at what was about to come upon his ancient people.

Revelation 11:
The Consummation—A First Look

In Chapter 11, John is shown the temple and told to measure it. He is given a rod and instructed to measure the inner temple but to ignore the outer precincts that are given over to the Gentiles.

> Then there was given me a measuring rod like a staff; and someone said, "Get up and measure the temple of God and the altar, and those who worship in it. Leave out the courtyard which is outside the temple and do not measure it, because it has been given to the nations; and they will trample the holy city for forty- two months. And I will grant *authority* to my two witnesses, and they will prophesy for 1,260 days, clothed in sackcloth" (Rev. 11:1- 3).

Admittedly, there are elements of this chapter that are difficult to interpret as historical. *However, they are difficult to interpret from any perspective*. Despite that difficulty, there may be no clearer evidence of the pre-70 AD date of Revelation than this vision. John is told to measure *the temple*. It was still standing at the time of John's visions. The common interpretation that this is a future, rebuilt temple cannot be substantiated. The temple in Revelation 11 is the existing physical structure that *John* was told to personally measure (or assess). Let's consider the following reasons why this was Herod's first-century temple before its destruction in 70 AD.

First, in Ezekiel 40:1-5ff, the prophet is shown a visionary structure that is about to be measured. He is allowed to observe but not take part in the measuring process. An object existing outside the material world could only be measured by a being, such as an angel, who existed outside the material world.

In contrast, John could measure the temple that was materially present and standing in the world at that time. We cannot presume to understand precisely how this was accomplished, but it was not a visionary future temple. Let's compare the two accounts. John is told to measure *the temple*, whereas Ezekiel sees a vision of a structure *like a city*:

> Then there was given me a measuring rod like a staff; and someone said, "*Get up and measure the temple* of God and *the altar*, and those who worship in it" (Rev. 11:1).

> In the visions of God, He brought me into the land of Israel and set me on a very high mountain, and on it to the south *there was a structure like a city* . . . there was a man whose appearance was like the appearance of bronze, with a line of flax and a measuring rod in his hand . . . *So, he measured* . . . (Eze. 40:1-5).

Similarly, in Revelation 21, John sees *a vision* of the new Jerusalem. Like Ezekiel, an angel, *not John*, prepares to measure it:

The one who spoke with me had a gold measuring rod to measure the city, and its gates and its wall . . . and *he measured* (Rev. 21:15-16).

It appears to be a reliable pattern. Both Ezekiel's and John's visionary structures had to be measured by an angel. However, in Revelation 11, John was instructed to measure a structure that was standing physically at the time he saw it. Therefore, he could conduct the assessment.

That structure ceased to exist as of August 70 AD, so John must have seen it before that time.

Second, Ken Gentry has pointed out in *The Great Tribulation–Past or Future?* how the assumption that Revelation 11 describes a future visionary temple is a *suppressed premise.*[81] This means that, contextually, there is nothing in the text to support such a conclusion. The interpretation is based on futurist theological precommitments.

Third, the entire city was to be trampled over by the Gentiles for 3½ years (42 months):

[The outer court] is given unto the Gentiles: and the holy city shall they *tread underfoot forty* and two months (Rev. 11:2).

This same trampling of first-century Jerusalem is paralleled in Luke 21:20-24, part of the Olivet Discourse:

"But when you see Jerusalem surrounded by armies, then recognize that her desolation is near . . . and they will fall by the edge of the sword, and will be led captive into all the nations; Jerusalem will be trampled underfoot by the Gentiles until the times of the Gentiles be fulfilled" (Luke 21:20-24).

The Bible attests to the fact that no sacred text stands on its own as a singular witness:

. . . every fact is to be confirmed by the testimony of two or three witnesses (2 Cor. 13:1; cf. 2 Pet. 1:20).

Therefore, it is apparent that the texts of Luke and Revelation provide mutual scriptural witnesses to the events. We have previously established (in Part II) that this period of 3½ years in Revelation 11:2 was a reference to the Roman advance on Jerusalem in 66–70 AD. Luke's Gospel and John's vision mutually confirm these events.

This is further strengthened in Second Kings, where we are shown that the measuring rod was also an instrument for demolition. In the following text, spoken through unnamed prophets, the measurement symbolizes the approaching destruction of Jerusalem by Nebuchadnezzar in 586 BC:

> ". . . therefore, thus says the LORD, the God of Israel, 'Behold, I am bringing such calamity on Jerusalem and Judah, that whoever hears of it, both his ears will tingle. 'I will stretch over Jerusalem the line [LXX: "measure"] of Samaria and the plummet of the house of Ahab, and I will wipe Jerusalem as one wipes a dish, wiping it and turning it upside down. I will abandon the remnant of My inheritance and deliver them into the hand of their enemies, and they will become as plunder and spoil to all their enemies; because they have done evil in My sight, and have been provoking Me to anger since the day their fathers came from Egypt, even to this day'" (2 Kings 21:12-15)

The *line or measure of Samaria* in verse 13 means that the destruction of the Northern Kingdom of Israel and its capital by Assyria will be the "metric" by which Judah (the Southern Kingdom, the City of Jerusalem, and the temple) will also be demolished. The apostle John was to mark out the structure and territory for their overthrow by the Roman armies.

The Two Witnesses

The two witnesses of Revelation 11 remain an enigma. There are many plausible explanations as to their identity, ministry, death, and ascension. Here again, my personal uncertainty about our available interpretations *is offset by the sense of certainty concerning its timing.*

Since the temple in this context is a first-century structure, the account of the two witnesses must also be history. If they were prophesying judgment, as the fire from their mouths suggests, the city's inhabitants and visitors (Jews: *those who dwell on the land*, v. 10) would have rejoiced to see their demise. Their deaths are attributed to the Roman beast (11:7), who has yet to be formally introduced but is most likely Titus (or Rome as an entity). Titus led the siege and destruction of Jerusalem. The witnesses could have died during the siege as the Roman legions pummeled Jerusalem by catapulting large stones into the city, some weighing over 70 pounds and killing many.

Resurrection and Judgment

The concluding images of this chapter are equally challenging. They depict the consummation of the age, which arrives with the judgment of the old system under the Satan-led Roman forces. The enraged armies of Rome's client kingdoms under Titus' leadership converge on the Jews, who themselves had become the enemies of God. We will soon be given a glimpse of the unseen, diabolical forces that empowered the Roman armies and the venomous hatred that inspired them. Here, we see it was given to them to judge Israel. It was given to them to *destroy those who destroy the land* (Rev. 11:18 YLT). The prophets previously spoke of Israel's defilement of the land that God gave them:

> "I brought you into the fruitful land
> To eat its fruit and its good things
> But you came and defiled My land,
> And My inheritance you made an abomination"
> (Jer. 2:7).

> "Son of man, when the house of Israel was living in their own land, they defiled it by their ways and their deeds . . . Therefore, I poured out My wrath on them for the blood which they had shed on the land, because they had defiled it with their idols" (Eze. 36:17-18).

They also spoke of brutal enemies being used to bring about judgment upon historical Israel:

> 'I will pour out My indignation on you; I will blow on you with the fire of My wrath, and I will give you into the hand of brutal men, skilled in destruction" (Eze. 21:31).

Why Not a Resurrection?

A startling aspect of this chapter is that a resurrection and judgment occur, which would have most likely included both those who died under the Old Covenant and those in the apostolic transition period. As shocking as it may appear to some, the suggestion that a resurrection and judgment may have occurred in the first century has merit for several reasons:

First, there were many dead who were raised when Jesus came forth from the grave:

> And Jesus cried out again with a loud voice, and yielded up His spirit. And behold, the veil of the temple was torn in two from top to bottom; and the earth shook and the rocks were split. The tombs were opened, and many bodies of the saints who had fallen asleep were raised; and coming out of the tombs after His resurrection they entered the holy city and appeared to many (Matt. 27:50-53).

Second, in the final chapter of Revelation, John and his first-century audience are told:

> "Behold, I am coming quickly, and My reward is with Me, *to render to every man according to what he has done*" (Rev. 22:12).

In this context, the phrase *every man* most likely refers to those who lived and died during the Old Covenant age (including the transition period that we have been examining). It is not outside the realm of possibilities that this could have been part of God's wrapping up of the Old Covenant order– the *first resurrection* spoken of in Revelation 20:5.

Third, in 1 Corinthians 15, Paul speaks of the resurrection occurring at Christ's coming (*parousia*). However, there appears to be only one *parousia* anticipated in the New Testament, as we observed in our study of the Olivet Discourse. That *parousia* was his coming in the first century to judge Jerusalem. This favors a full preterist position on the resurrection (an observation, not an endorsement).

> But now Christ has been raised from the dead, the first fruits of those who are asleep . . . For as in Adam all die, so also in Christ all will be made alive. But each in his own order: Christ the first fruits, after that those who are Christ's at His coming [*parousia*] (1 Cor. 15:20-23).

Fourth, we must also consider Paul's words before Governor Felix in Acts 24 and also those to Timothy:

> . . . having hope toward God, which they themselves [the Jews] also wait for, [that] *there is about to be a resurrection of the dead,* both of righteous and unrighteous (Acts 24:15 LSV)

> . . . and he reasoning concerning righteousness, and self-control, and *the judgment that is about to be,* Felix, having become afraid, answered, "For the present be going, and having time, I will call for you" (Acts 24:25 LSV).

> I fully testify, then, before God, and the Lord Jesus Christ, *who is about to judge* [the] living and dead at His appearing and His Kingdom (2 Tim. 4:1 LSV)

Paul's words rattled Felix. He fearfully and immediately dismissed Paul. Luke, the author of Acts, employs the Greek word *mello* (about to) in both of these texts in Acts, as does Paul in Second Timothy. McReynolds' *Word Study Greek-English New Testament* translates it as *about to* in all of its 109 occurrences.[82] Could Paul have anticipated the same imminent resurrection and judgment seen in Revelation 20:5? It certainly allows for the possibility that this resurrection was among the concluding acts concerning all things Old Testament.

... he who hears My word, and believes Him who sent Me, has eternal life, and does not come into judgment, but has passed out of death into life. Truly, truly, I say to you, an hour is coming *and now is*, when the dead will hear the voice of the Son of God, and those who hear will live. . . .Do not marvel at this; for an hour is coming, in which all who are in the tombs will hear His voice, and will come forth; those who did the good deeds to a resurrection of life, those who committed the evil deeds to a resurrection of judgment" (John 5:24-29).

The text speaks of believers being *passed out of death into life* and could suggest that New Covenant believers (now victorious over death) will no longer enter a *sleep* at death but go directly into the presence of God. The resurrection of the Old Covenant saints, who slept under the power of death, has passed. Now that Jesus abolished death, it no longer has any holding power over the New Covenant Christian:

... our Savior Christ Jesus, who abolished death and brought life and immortality to light through the gospel (2 Tim. 1:10).

These observations are not meant to be the writer's hard-and-fast doctrinal positions. They are concepts developed from other New Testament texts, recognized by some, and worthy of consideration.

The last verse of Revelation 11 depicts the conclusion of the first set of visions. Great convulsions are evocative of a *covenantal inauguration* like that of the Old Covenant in Exodus 20:

For you did not come near to the mountain touched and scorched with fire, and to blackness, and darkness, and storm, and a sound of a trumpet . . . (Heb. 12:18-19; cf. Exo. 20:18 LSV).

The meaning behind this vision is that John is seeing a covenantal inauguration, *not a covenantal conclusion,* as would be suggested if we employed a futurist interpretation of Revelation. The New Covenant and the reign of God have been fully inaugurated. The heavenly visions appear to be complete. However, there remain eleven chapters filled with visions yet to be explained.

CHAPTER 19

THE BOOK OF REVELATION
A NEW VANTAGE POINT: REVELATION 12–14

Revelation 12–14 serve as a prelude to the second half of Revelation in a similar way that Chapter 6 opened the first half. The main distinction is that the earlier Chapter 6 staging of the visions mirrors the Olivet Discourse. It focuses on the judgments coming upon *Israel* as the old order is coming to an end. The staging of the visions in Chapter 12 brings the *church* into view as it struggles to remain faithful in the face of severe trial and persecution. Therefore, this interlude depicts *the historical and theological context for the first century covenantal transition, which occurs in the face of great tribulation and spiritual conflict.* Revelation's main earthly players and the spiritual forces behind them are symbolically described in these chapters.

Revelation 12:
The Woman, Her Offspring, and the Dragon

In Revelation 12, the woman represents the collective body of the faithful of Israel. She depicts those of the nation who have recognized Jesus as the Messiah, and she is initially seen in her heavenly appearance. Clothed with Christ (the sun), she has overcome the Law, represented by the moon on which she stands. The moon is the lesser luminary (Gen. 1:16) that governed the night of the Old Covenant. Having overcome the curse of the Law, she is also crowned (Greek: *stephanos,* a victor's crown) with twelve stars, as having come out from the twelve tribes of natural Israel who remained under the Law's power and its curse. This is an image of victory:

> For the law of the Spirit of life in Christ Jesus has set you free from the law of sin and of death. For what the Law could not do, weak as it was through the flesh, God did: sending His own Son in the likeness of sinful flesh and as an offering for sin, He condemned sin in the flesh, so that the requirement of the Law might be fulfilled in us, who do not walk according to the flesh but according to the Spirit (Rom. 8:2-4).

Her giving birth suggests that she is the new, heavenly Jerusalem, described by the apostle Paul as the church's mother:

> Now this Hagar is Mount Sinai in Arabia and corresponds to the present Jerusalem, for she is in slavery with her children. But the Jerusalem above is free; *she is our mother* (Gal. 4:25-26).

She is giving birth to Jesus, *the firstborn from the dead.* However, the death of Jesus is not mentioned. This one, who is born in Revelation 12, is not Christ after the flesh. That birth was the *last Adam* (1 Cor. 15:45-49). The new Jerusalem is the mother of a new community of the resurrection, of whom Christ is the *firstborn son:*

> He is also head of the body, the church; and *He is the beginning, the firstborn from the dead,* so that He Himself will come to have first place in everything (Col. 1:18; cf. Rev. 1:5).

As we saw, the woman is presented as a heavenly entity, but she also has an earthly expression in a people. This is the believing Jewish remnant, saved out of the tribulation. They heeded Jesus' warning (Luke 21:20) to flee the city before its destruction. This is evidenced by her flight from Jerusalem to safety in the wilderness in Revelation 12:6. The image also alludes to the flight of the Israelites from Egypt to the wilderness as the waters of the Red Sea drowned the Egyptian army (Exo. 14:27; 15:22). Jerusalem had just been characterized spiritually as Sodom and *Egypt* in Revelation 11:8, therefore, this escape from Jerusalem can be seen as her escape from spiritual Egypt. Jerusalem, like the Egyptians in the Exodus story, was about to be drowned by the flood of the invading Roman armies (we have previously surveyed the flood metaphor; cf. Dan. 9:26; Matt. 24:28-39).

The dragon who is waiting to devour her child is Satan. He is the real antagonist behind the hostile local powers of Rome and Israel. The dragon's heads are the seven Caesars who ruled historically during Rome's occupation of Israel. The ten horns could represent the ten provinces of the empire or possibly the ten actual Imperial Roman Caesars who ruled from 27 BC to 70 AD. This would be consistent with available Caesar lists found in ancient records. Among the ten, three of them–Galba, Otho, and Vitellius–were omitted from the principal seven heads because their reigns were temporary. We have observed how each of them unsuccessfully contended for supreme power after Nero's death. Since the war was temporarily suspended, none of them engaged in oppression of either Jews or the church.

The dragon's tail swept away a third of the stars and cast them down to the *land* (cf. Lam. 2:1). The dragon's tail represents the false prophets who led many astray, just as Jesus warned in the Olivet Discourse (Matt. 24:11). These imposters were unwittingly in the dragon's service. Some offered false hopes of deliverance, while influential Jewish authorities promoted allegiance to the emperors.

Neither represented the truth of God. Isaiah provides insight into this interpretation, as we note that beasts and dragons are portrayed as having tails:

> The head is the elder and honorable man,
> And the *prophet who teaches falsehood is the tail*
> (Isa. 9:15).

Israel's leaders had become the tail of the dragon (who was in power over foreign nations), like Moses had forewarned them:

> He shall lend to you, but you will not lend to him; he shall be the head, and you will be the tail (Deu. 28:44).

After giving birth, the woman flees to the wilderness, which, as noted previously, is her flight from Jerusalem to Pella. There she is cared for by God for 3½ years, or 1260 days, based on the Jewish 360-day year. This was the duration of the Roman campaign against Israel, leading to its eventual destruction. Her *eagle-borne* escape continues the allusion to their historical departure from Egypt:

> "You yourselves have seen what I did to the Egyptians, and how I bore you on eagles' wings, and brought you to Myself" (Exo. 19:4).

The war in heaven (v. 7) resulted from Christ's redemptive work of cleansing the heavenly sanctuary with his own blood. Satan (the dragon) wanted the Old Covenant to remain in force because the power of the Law, although holy, was his tool. As a prosecutor, he used it as a condemning force over the saints as he stood before God's judgment seat. This is alluded to in Revelation 12:11. However, he and his angels are overcome by the hosts of heaven and thrown down to the earth [the land]. I would suggest that this war began at Jesus' ascension. The accuser could no longer enter the throne room and accuse God's people once Jesus, our Great High Priest, thoroughly cleansed the heavenly tabernacle with His own blood:

[Moses] . . . took the blood of the calves and the goats, with water and scarlet wool and hyssop, and sprinkled both the book itself and all the people, saying, "this is the blood of the covenant which God commanded you." And in the same way he sprinkled both the tabernacle and all the vessels of the ministry with the blood. And according to the Law, one may almost say, all things are cleansed with blood, and without shedding of blood there is no forgiveness. *Therefore, it was necessary for the copies of the things in the heavens to be cleansed with these, but the heavenly things themselves with better sacrifices than these.* For Christ did not enter a holy place made with hands, a mere copy of the true one, but into heaven itself, now to appear in the presence of God for us; nor was it that He would offer Himself often, as the high priest enters the holy place year by year with blood that is not his own. Otherwise, He would have needed to suffer often since the foundation of the world; but now once at the consummation of the ages He has been manifested to put away sin by the sacrifice of Himself (Heb. 9:19-26).

The heavenly war's duration was the transition era preceding the final conflict of 66-70 AD. The blood of Christ removed the serpent's filth and the pervasive stains of sin. Now the accuser was being cast out of the heavens entirely. When this occurred, he had only a short time left (3½ years) to destroy God's holy seed, the church, before his approaching imprisonment. However, they overcame him (possibly alluding to the great persecution under Nero's reign of terror):

. . . by the blood of the lamb, the word of their testimony, and they did not love their lives even unto death (Rev. 12:11).

Having been thrown down, the dragon now takes up residence in the oppressing forces of the Roman army. He pursues the church as she flees Jerusalem, but *the land swallows the flood*. As we have seen, the flood depicts the advance of the army.

This incredible feature of the vision reflects how the land of Israel is personified as a friend of the church. The land, as the theater of the Jewish-Roman conflict, absorbed the dragon's wrath, which was his attempt to annihilate the fleeing believers. The war on the land hindered his ability to pursue, and because of this deterrence by the war's engagements, the believers could flee to safety.

Enraged, the dragon then purposes to destroy God's people in other parts of the empire (i.e., *the rest of her children*). Remember, he was initially thrown down to the land (of Israel). Whatever purposes of God were to be fulfilled in Jerusalem's destruction; the dragon had other plans. His war was, as it always has been, with the Lamb and the church, which is Christ's earthly expression. This will be seen in Revelation 17:13-14.

Revelation 13:
Two Beasts

In Chapter 13, we see that the dragon has empowered the sea beast, who is given the support of the land beast. As noted, the first century time frame of Revelation would likely mean that the seven-headed sea beast is Rome, who has taken on the express image of the dragon from Chapter 12. The details of the beast are developed more thoroughly in Revelation 17.

This seven-headed beast has integrated all the power and characteristics of the oppressive empires that have gone before (Greece, Persia, and Babylon). Their descriptions are taken from the seventh chapter of Daniel, but in reverse order. Daniel was utterly mesmerized by the fourth beast and wanted to understand its meaning. This beast was the most terrifying. He was extremely strong and different from the rest. This is because the previous beasts in Daniel's vision were subordinate principalities under Satan.

In Daniel 10, we see the angel of the Lord informing Daniel that he was engaged in conflict with the *Prince* of Persia, who was trying to hold on to power while the *Prince* of Greece was aggressively trying to seize dominance in the civilized world. The angel specifically referred to them as *princes*. They were principalities subservient to the dragon and were the beasts behind two of the empires in the vision described in Daniel 7.

However, because the time was so critical for the dragon, he turned and absorbed the powers of these lesser principalities (and Babylon) into himself. John's presentation of these beasts in reverse chronological order might suggest that the dragon begins with the most recent and continues to the most ancient. Then, the full power of the dragon, the enemy of God, was concentrated in one empire: Rome.

The imagery of the dragon being greater than the principalities of the three prior empires and causing Rome to integrate their strengths (Rev. 13:4) was not unusual. According to Corbett, the assimilation of the power of lesser gods by a greater god was common in Mesopotamian mythology:

> The image of a god or goddess might develop as local gods were assimilated to the gods of invaders, for example when Babylonians absorbed the older Sumerian gods. The Babylonian god Marduk was considered to be the ruler of the whole world as he assimilated the powers of lesser gods in the second part of the second millennium BCE . . .[83]

The Mortal Head-Wound

There are a variety of historical possibilities concerning the mortal head wound of the sea beast. The most common observation is the suicide of Nero in 68 AD, which resulted in the near collapse of the empire. Upon his appointment as Caesar in 69 AD, Vespasian brought stability back to the empire.

The emperors were deified and worshiped in temples of the imperial cult. There are inscriptions in Ephesus labeling Nero Caesar *Almighty God* and *Savior,* and another inscription found in Salamis gave him the title *God and Savior.* The worship of Caesar was inadvertently the worship of the dragon—Satan himself. Kraybill offers insight into the pressures being imposed by political and religious structures to engage in tokens of allegiance to the Caesars and the empire:

> The book of Revelation provides a constellation of images and narratives that help us understand how ideologies shape the world. Revelation makes abundant use of symbols, and John understands how these forge political and spiritual identity. In particular, Revelation highlights the way worship, with its reliance on symbol, expresses and shapes allegiance. The last book of the Bible is not a catalog of predictions about events that would take place two thousand years later . . . The central political reality in the author's day — the late first century — was the indomitable Roman Empire and its "divine" emperors. The pressing issue for John's readers was how Christians, who gave their highest loyalty to Jesus, should conduct themselves in a world where economic and political structures assumed that everyone would worship the emperor.[84]

This blasphemous arrogance of the empire is noted in the vision, as is the power given to the sea beast to persecute the saints for 42 months, which is seen in Revelation 13:5-7. The arrogance of the beast is also seen in Daniel 7, concerning a specific horn of the beast, who is likely Titus:

> . . . had eyes and a mouth uttering great *boasts* . . . (Dan. 7:20)

The description of the first beast concludes with the admonition to Christians that they remain patient in suffering. The Holy Spirit admonishes the suffering believers that they were not to align with either the Jewish resistance or the Romans, who prosecuted the war against Israel. They were not to take up arms and engage in the conflict from either side. The Christian's warfare is spiritual, and our allegiance is to Christ and to him alone. They were being plainly warned that any attempt to either defeat or align with Rome or the Zealots would only result in great loss and, ultimately, death or captivity. God's sovereign plan was playing out, and there were destinies being fulfilled. This is the meaning of the closing words:

If anyone has an ear, let him hear. If anyone is destined for captivity, to captivity he goes; if anyone kills with the sword, with the sword he must be killed. Here is the perseverance and the faith of the saints (Rev. 13:9-10).

This admonition is given to the churches to persevere and resist the temptation to take up arms, especially while under persecution. This reminds us of Paul's earlier admonition to the churches:

For our struggle is not against flesh and blood, but against the rulers, against the powers, against the world forces of this darkness, against the spiritual forces of wickedness in the heavenly places (Eph. 6:12).

For though we walk in the flesh, we do not war according to the flesh, for the weapons of our warfare are not of the flesh, but divinely powerful for the destruction of fortresses (2 Cor. 10:3-4).

The captivity mentioned in Revelation 13 echoes Jesus' declaration in the Olivet Discourse, where the outcome of the conflict is affirmed:

. . . and they will fall by the edge of the sword, and will be led captive into all the nations; and Jerusalem will be trampled underfoot by the Gentiles until the times of the Gentiles are fulfilled" (Luke 21:24; cf. Jer. 15:1-6).

The land beast arises out of the land of Israel, promoting allegiance to Rome. The Roman authorities in Israel and the Sadducees are worthy of consideration, as they were strongly pro-Roman and encouraged demonstrations of allegiance to the empire throughout the first century. The composite civil and religious imagery is a beast that appears as a two-horned lamb that spoke like a dragon. Like the sea beast, this beast is also a composite figure because of its *two* horns.[85] Here, we recall Daniel Chapter 8, where a two-horned beast represents two nations forming a singular beastly power with one purpose:

The ram which you saw with the two horns represents the kings of Media and Persia (Dan 8:20).

The *civic horn* was most likely the Roman-appointed officials in Israel who served the interests of the empire. They oversaw their appointed jurisdictions in *the land* and maintained lucrative relationships with the Jewish aristocracy. It is likely that the Sadducees were the *religious horn*. Many of them were among the chief priests inciting the people, and who themselves were calling for Jesus to be crucified, as recorded in John's Gospel:

> So they cried out, "Away with Him, away with Him, crucify Him!" Pilate *said to them, "Shall I crucify your King?" *The chief priests answered,* "We have no king but Caesar" (John 19:15).

They had the appearance of a lamb–harmless, gentle, and holy–but in their mouths were the words and the breath of the dragon, which was Rome, to whom they gave their true allegiance. Power and influence drove these so-called religious leaders. The unholy collaboration between these two governmental bodies is outlined by Goldwurm (cited in McKenzie 2012, 220-221):

> The Roman rulers followed Herod's example of bestowing the sacred office [high priest] upon the highest bidder. As the Sadducees had no lack of money, they offered huge personal bribes to the procurators, and a candidate of their choice became high priest. The Roman officials soon realized that the office of high priest was an infallible source of income. at frequent intervals they would dismiss the current [high priest] and auction off the position to the highest bidder. In the beginning of the era of the Roman procurators to the destruction of the temple . . . nearly 60 years, this exalted office had 30 occupants.[86]

Also, Richard Horsley observes:

> The Jewish aristocracy . . . appear to have pursued their own political-economic interest as collaborators with the Roman government . . . The Jewish high priests performed faithfully in the interests of the Roman government upon who their position as provincial aristocracy depended . . . analysis of the decades leading up to the great revolt, indicates that the aristocracy remained consistently pro-Roman [87]

We have already observed the occurrence of strange and "miraculous" signs that were performed in the first century by deceptive means. Rodney Thomas has shown how they were common in the empire and employed by pro-Roman elites to influence the masses through deception and wonders (see Thomas 2010).[45] These displays were designed to promote exclusive loyalty to the empire by inciting fear of any form of rebellion, especially among the poor, impressionable masses.

The Mark of the Beast

Commentators have noted how those who refused to worship or acknowledge Caesar as "Lord" could not buy or sell in the trade guilds throughout the empire. The mark on the right hand or forehead is most often viewed by interpreters like those in Ezekiel 9:4-6 or Ephesians 1:13 (the Holy Spirit). These are non-visible markings or seals. Until recently, I also held that view.

However, Phillip Kayser notes that the *kharagma* of the beast refers to a coin, the engraving of an image, or a mark left by branding.[88] This is a different word than the marking by the Spirit in Ephesians, which is *sfragidzo,* a seal. The beast's mark on the forehead or right hand would be something *visible.* Revelation 13:17 informs us that no one could buy or sell without the mark. A merchant had to distinguish between those who had the mark and those who did not. There had to be something visible that would allow them access to the trade guilds that affirmed, "*Yes, my allegiance is to Caesar.*"

Remarkable Historical Evidence

Several hundred years before, in the intertestamental period, after Alexander the Great's death in 337 BC, his Greek kingdom was parceled out to his four generals. Of the four kingdoms, the Ptolemies (Egypt, the king of the south in Daniel 11:5) were the first to take control of

Israel and Jerusalem. Kayser's observations continue, describing that an edict given by Philopator, the ruler of the Ptolemies, is contained in III Maccabees 2:29, where it reads:

> . . . those [Jews] who are registered are also to be branded on their bodies by fire with the ivy-leaf symbol of Dionysus.

Under Roman rule, the practice of branding in this manner continued to be common practice. Runaway slaves were branded with the letters FUG, which stood for *fugitive* in Latin. All slaves were called *stigmas*, which is like the related word *mark*, because the slaves were branded with a stigma. Sometimes they were routinely branded with the name of their master. Caesar's own soldiers voluntarily branded themselves with the name or his symbol as a mark of loyalty and submission. Kayser mentions that there is evidence of soldiers being branded with the name of their general. These marks were called *stigmata*. The soldiers bore the *stigmata* on their hands.

Emperor Vespasian's name was *Titus Flavius Vespasianus*. Nero's name was *Nero Claudius Caesar Augustus Germanicus*. It would be quite a task to brand their full names, or even parts of them, on someone's body–especially their hand. However, the *number* of their name, which was a common means of identifying someone, could easily fit on a coin in a box (placed in the phylactery worn by the Jews). It would be a coin or branding on their arm with Caesar's number. John's message in Revelation 13 is a warning to the churches: *"Don't take that mark, whatever it may cost you. Don't take it!"* In contrast, we might envision the aristocratic, pro-Roman forces in Israel saying:

> *"Take the number of the beast. You're showing that we're loyal and don't want war with Rome. It's okay to serve two masters. You don't need to be exclusive. You can go to synagogue, you can have your religion, and you can study your Scriptures, as long as you acknowledge that Caesar is supreme Lord."*

Finally, *the number of his (the beast's) name,* 666, has been observed to be an accurate calculation of Nero Caesar (Heb: Neron Kaisar) employing Hebrew gematria (the use of letters as numbers). There are manuscript variants of Revelation 13 that have 616 in place of 666. This is likely because when Nero appears in Latin transliteration, it calculates out to 616. The charts below illustrate how names are calculated using gematria.

Other possibilities, such as *Vespasian* and *Titus,* can also be calculated from the details on their coins (English is substituted for Hebrew and Greek in the tables):

The Example of Roman Caesars

The Hebrew Version: NRWN QSR (*Nero Caesar*) yields a numerical value of 666:

N	R	W	N	Q	S	R	Sum
50	200	6	50	100	60	200	666

Table 19.1

The Latin Version: NRW QSR (also *Nero Caesar*) transliterated into Hebrew, yields 616:

N	R	W	[omit]	Q	S	R	Sum
50	200	6	-	100	60	200	616

Table 19.2

Also of interest is that the Greek word lateinos, which denotes *a Latin-speaking man or a Latin man,* also works out to 666 in Greek:

L	A	T	E	I	N	O	S	Sum
30	1	300	5	10	50	70	200	666

Table 19.3

Unfortunately, some have foolishly suggested that this *Latin-speaking man* is a reference to the Pope. However, its true first-century significance is that it would not require a specific Caesar but identify the beast as coming from among the succession of *Roman* leaders. Nero's designation may have only been offered because he was in power at the time of the Revelation. It is the dragon that is the true beast behind these individuals, who themselves are merely human pawns.

Despite modern-day speculation regarding the Pope or various world leaders as the "antichrist," the gematria points to the first-century Roman Empire. This is strongly supported by other internal evidence in Revelation, so it is not merely a random option for 666. I refer the reader to Duncan McKenzie's discussion on the subject. He offers some excellent examples of various possibilities.[89]

Revelation 14:
The Lamb, the 144,000, and the Two Harvests

Revelation 14 opens with the same company of saints as is seen in Revelation 7. The major difference is that in Chapter 7, they were being *gathered*. In Chapter 14, the remnant is *completed, sealed, and standing on Mount Zion with Jesus, the Lamb*. Mount Zion is the new, heavenly Jerusalem, not the old, earthly mountain city. This is noted by the writer of Hebrews, writing to a Jewish audience that they had arrived:

> For you have not come to a mountain that can be touched and to a blazing fire, and to darkness and gloom and whirlwind . . . But *you have come to Mount Zion* and to the City of the living God, the heavenly Jerusalem, and to myriads of angels (Heb. 12:18-22).

This scene is also part of Joel's prophecy, which Peter quotes at Pentecost (Acts 2:17ff). It concerned the last days and the outpouring of the Holy Spirit. In that same context, Joel's prophecy continues with the following, which directly corresponds to John's vision:

"For on Mount Zion and in Jerusalem
There will be those who escape,
As the LORD has said,
Even among the survivors whom the LORD calls"
(Joel 2:32).

Heaven provides the musical accompaniment as the long-anticipated remnant of Israel, those purchased from the earth (or possibly, land), worship before God, and they:

- are chaste (cleansed by Christ's blood)

- follow the Lamb as his disciples

- are the firstfruits of God's harvest being gathered into the church

- speak the truth of the gospel, not the unfortunate distortions learned from their Judaic cultural traditions (cf. Mark 7:8-13)

Five Angels Speak

Now that the remnant is complete, major angelic announcements commence:

The first angel announces the "eternal gospel" (Greek: *ainonian gospel*), probably voiced through the empire-wide ministry of the apostles. The unusual use of the Greek adjective *aionios (pertaining to the age)* in conjunction with the gospel might suggest that the good news being proclaimed is specifically that *the age to come* (olam haba) is commencing. The highly-prized remnant body of Israel had now been gathered from all the nations through the Spirit-empowered missions of the church. The previous age (the old heavens and earth) has passed away. Now, the long-awaited, promised kingdom has arrived:

This *gospel of the kingdom* shall be preached in the whole world as a testimony to all the nations, and then the end will come (Matt. 24:14).

A second messenger follows with the announcement that Babylon *is* fallen. Babylon's destruction is likely being announced proleptically–that is, as certain but not yet historically accomplished. However, she has already fallen from her place in the economy of God because of her behavior among the nations. In Revelation 17 and 18, we will see that this is first-century Jerusalem. The announcement is followed by the chilling, thundering voice of a *third* angel:

> If anyone worships the beast and his image, and receives a mark on his forehead or on his hand, he also will drink of the wine of the wrath of God, which is mixed in full strength in the cup of His anger; and he will be tormented with fire and brimstone in the presence of the holy angels and in the presence of the Lamb. And the smoke of their torment goes up forever and ever; they have no rest day and night, those who worship the beast and his image, and whoever receives the mark of his name (Rev. 14:9-11).

Excursus: Revelation 14:9-11
The Question of Eternal Conscious Torment

This text is commonly quoted to support the doctrine of eternal conscious torment. However, as we have seen in previous texts alleged to describe it, there are reasons to believe it depicts something much different. The angelic announcement has established allusions to Old Testament descriptions of memorial smoke, God's historical presence among the Israelites, their exile, and their forfeiture of God's rest.

Torment and Smoke

The angel announces that those who are judged will suffer torment. However, carefully notice how the announcement asserts that *the smoke* continues in perpetuity, but it does not assert the same for their *torment*. The smoke, not the torment, is perpetual. We will examine the torment further, but first, the smoke is the memorial of judgment by God's consuming fire, as with Edom:

[Edom's] streams will be turned into pitch . . .
Its land will become blazing pitch!
It will not be quenched night and day;
Its smoke will rise forever
(Isa. 34:9-10).

Similarly, Sodom and Gomorrah:

. . . and he looked down toward Sodom and Gomorrah . . . and . . .
the smoke . . . ascended like the smoke of a furnace (Gen. 19:28).

The memorial smoke is also referred to in the Law of Moses as the
offering is consumed:

And the priest shall offer it [the grain offering] up *in smoke as its
memorial portion* on the altar . . . (Lev. 2:2, 9, 16; 5:12; 6:15).

Like the aroma of Noah's sacrifice after the flood, the smoke is a
memorial–a reminder to God that his wrath has been spent:

. . . The LORD *smelled the soothing aroma*; and . . . said to Himself,
"I will never again curse the ground on account of man . . .and I will
never again destroy every living thing, as I have done (Gen. 8:20-21).

Lands, cities, and sacrifices are all consumed by fire in these
examples. Only the memorial smoke rises continually before God. As
the smoke rises from his consuming fire long after it has gone out, it
serves as a reminder that his judgment has been fully accomplished.

In the Presence of the Lamb

In keeping with the theme of Revelation concerning the 70 AD fall
of Jerusalem, the Lamb is spoken of as being *present* during the
judgment of unbelieving Jews–those dwelling upon the land–and who
worshiped the beast:

And bow before it [the image of the beast] shall all who are *dwelling
upon the land* (Rev. 13:8 YLT).

In Luke 19, Jesus told the Parable of the Servants and the Minas to Jewish leaders who were expecting the immediate appearance of the kingdom of God. He was illustrating to them how their expectations rested on faulty assumptions. Their rejection of his ministry and rule would be *judgment in his presence*. They would be *slain*, not tortured forever. He was warning yet again of their looming fate:

> "But his citizens hated him and sent a delegation after him, saying, 'We do not want this man to reign over us' . . . But these enemies of mine, who did not want me to reign over them, bring them here and *slay them in my presence*" (Luke 19:14, 27).

No Rest Day and Night

Revelation 14:11 describes a *temporal* state. As we have seen previously, there are no day and night cycles in the eternal realm (cf. Rev.21:22-25; Isa 66:24). The image of writhing, tortured post-mortem human beings is nowhere to be found in this text. The nation had forsaken the Lord and bowed to Caesar. Although individuals could repent (cf. 14:9), the nation was now subject to the Deuteronomic curses certain to befall them if they forsook their covenant with God:

> "the LORD will scatter you . . . Among those nations *you shall find no rest*, and there will be no resting place for the sole of your foot. . . and *you will be in dread night and day*" (Moses: Deu. 28:63- 66).

Jeremiah laments after the Babylonian invasion of 586 BC:

> Judah has gone into exile under affliction
> And under harsh servitude;
> She dwells among the nations,
> *But she has found no rest* . . .
> (Lam. 1:3)

> Our pursuers are at our necks;
> We are worn out, *there is no rest* for us
> (Lam. 5:5).

Like Sodom and Gomorrah:
Consuming Fire

As we saw in Part III, Peter warned of a Sodom and Gomorrah-like judgment that was *imminent* upon the empire:

> . . . and if He condemned the cities of Sodom and Gomorrah to destruction by reducing them to ashes, having made them an example of what is coming [about to be] for the ungodly (2 Pet. 2:6; A. T. Robertson offers the Greek of "about to be" as mellontōn asebesin, "unto ungodly men of things about to be.")[90]

The focus of Revelation 14:9-11 is not eternal conscious torment, but rather, it echoes previous Old and New Testament descriptions of the final judgment upon the land and the disinheritance of the Jews from their privileged place in God's economy. The people of God had joined the ranks of the pagan nations; therefore, God was holding them accountable for their words on that fateful day when they, with one voice, declared their allegiance to an ungodly empire, one that would soon tun against them and destroy them:

> . . . Pilate made efforts to release Him, but the Jews cried out saying, "If you release this Man, you are no friend of Caesar; everyone who makes himself out to be a king opposes Caesar. . . . And he *said to the Jews, "Behold, your King! So they cried out, "Away with Him, away with Him, crucify Him!" Pilate *said to them, "Shall I crucify your King?" The chief priests answered, "We have no king but Caesar."
> (John 19: 12-15)

Just as Jesus warned, God did not forget that defiant rejection of their long-awaited Messiah and their declaration of allegiance to Rome:

> "But I tell you that every careless word that people speak, they shall give an accounting for it in the day of judgment. For by your words you will be justified, and by your words you will be condemned"
> (Matt. 12:36-37)

As we will see, the Roman beast to whom they professed their loyalty would ultimately turn on them and bring destruction. The promised rest from their enemies would finally be stripped away, and their torment would be immeasurable, as the Romans brought devastation upon their world. In contrast, in Revelation 14:13, we learn that even as Israel rejected God's offer of rest, those faithful ones who persevered under trial and who died in the Lord *will enter their rest*:

> And I heard a voice from heaven, saying, "Write, 'Blessed are the dead who die in the Lord from now on!' Yes, says the Spirit, so that *they may rest* from their labors, for their deeds follow with them (Rev. 14:13).

The Two Harvests of the Land: "Behold! He Comes with Clouds!"

We now come to the two harvests of Revelation 14, the first of which portrays faithless Israel's gathering to Jerusalem and entrapment in the siege. Then, in the second, we see the Roman invasion that brought destruction and bloodshed throughout the whole land. However, the initial scene is that of the Lord Jesus–the Son of Man–being described as coming on the clouds to execute judgment.

The fourth angel announces the first of two harvests. This first harvest is consistent with Jesus' words in the Parable of the Weeds (Tares), which pertains to the *end of the age*. Again, the reader is reminded that this parable is not about the end of the world. He says that first the weeds will be gathered and thrown into a furnace of fire:

> "The field is the world; and as for the good seed, these are the sons of the kingdom; and the tares are the sons of the evil one; and the enemy who sowed them is the devil, and the harvest is the end of the age; and the reapers are angels. So just as the tares are gathered up and burned with fire, so shall it be at the end of the age. The Son of Man will send forth His angels, and they will gather out of His kingdom all stumbling blocks, and those who commit lawlessness, and will

throw them into the furnace of fire; in that place there will be weeping and gnashing of teeth. Then the righteous will shine forth as the sun in the kingdom of their Father. He who has ears, let him hear." (Matt. 13:38-43).

This is a striking image of the Jews being gathered to Jerusalem for the great feast of Passover in 70 AD, unprepared for what was about to befall them. The siege would bring unspeakable pain and anguish (weeping and gnashing of teeth). Notably, historical references to the *furnace* refer to *Jerusalem*:

"His rock will pass away because of panic,
And his princes will be terrified at the standard,
Declares the LORD, whose fire is in Zion and *whose furnace is in Jerusalem*" (Isa. 31:9).

Ezekiel also prophesies regarding 586 BC:

". . . you have become waste metal, therefore, behold, I am going to gather you into the midst of Jerusalem . . . As silver is melted in the furnace, so you will be melted in the midst of it; and you will know that I, the LORD, have poured out My wrath on you" (Eze. 22:19-22).

The following are accounts of this gathering to the furnace. They describe the historical realities as the symbols in Jesus' parable came to life.

Josephus writes:

. . . those that perished during the siege one million one hundred thousand. Of these, the greater part were indeed of the same nation but did not live in the city itself, for they had come up from throughout the country to the Feast of Unleavened Bread and were suddenly shut up [in Jerusalem] by an army.[91]

Kate Lohnes offers a description of how the invading Roman army drove the Zealots to retreat to Jerusalem during Vespasian's northern (Galilean) campaign (cf. Revelation 8:6-12):

Nero sent the general Vespasian to meet the Jewish forces, an endeavour that pushed the majority of the [Jewish] rebels into Jerusalem by the time Vespasian was proclaimed emperor in 69 CE.[92]

The entire scene is one of the Zealot leaders, their forces, and finally a multitude of Jews who later gathered (voluntarily) in Jerusalem for the Passover in 70 AD.

Then **a *fifth*** angel calls for a *second* harvest. As the nation is gathered into the furnace of Jerusalem, we are provided with a vision of the Romans marching throughout the land, bringing death and destruction over its entire length and breadth. This is the reaping of the clusters of the *vine of the land*. As previously seen, this is the nation of Israel from Isaiah's *Song of the Vineyard*:

"For the vineyard of the LORD of hosts is the house of Israel
And the men of Judah His delightful plant.
Thus, He looked for justice, but behold, bloodshed;
For righteousness, but behold, a cry of distress"
(Isa. 5:7).

Then the angel swings his sickle over the land, throwing his harvest into the winepress of God's wrath:

So the angel swung his sickle to the earth [land] and gathered the clusters from the vine of the earth [land], and threw them into the great wine press of the wrath of God. And the wine press was trodden *outside the city*, and blood came out from the wine press, up to the horses' bridles, for a distance of two hundred miles [Greek: 1600 stadia] (Rev. 14:19-20).

The focus of the prophecy has expanded beyond the city to the entire land. The wine press is trampled *outside the city*. This is an image of Rome's forces wreaking devastation upon the cities of the entire land. Bloodshed is everywhere throughout the whole of Israel (to the horses' bridles). The reference is hyperbole and alludes to the death of *Jezebel*, the evil queen who sought to kill Elijah:

He said, "Throw her down." So they threw her down, and *some of her blood was sprinkled on the wall and on the horses,* and he trampled her underfoot (2 Kings 9:33; note again the reference to trampling found in Luke 21:24, regarding Jerusalem's fall).

Like the historical reference in Second Kings, the one who sought to kill the righteous is brought to a humiliating end. Jezebel is also mentioned in Revelation 2 as a Jewish false prophetess who had been given time to repent, but would not. She was now about to be thrown into great tribulation:

"But I have this against you, that you tolerate the woman Jezebel, who calls herself a prophetess . . . I gave her time to repent, and she does not want to repent . . . Behold, I will throw her on a bed of sickness, and those who commit adultery with her into *great tribulation,* unless they repent." (Rev. 2:20-22; cf. Matt. 24:21).

Second Kings employs both images of her being *trampled underfoot* and *her blood on the horses* (Rev. 11:2 and 14:20, respectively; cf. Luke 21:24). Revelation 2 speaks of Jezebel being thrown into great tribulation, which alludes to the Olivet Discourse. These allusions have first-century Israel and Jerusalem in view. The bloodshed extended over 1600 stadia, or about 180–185 miles (200 miles in the NASB). This is the approximate north-to-south distance of Israel's land.

Summary of Revelation 14

This concludes a remarkable chapter in Revelation that is replete with valuable accounts and images that demonstrate:

1. (14:1-5) The gathering of the first-century remnant is completed. These are the Jews who were joined to Christ and inherited the kingdom prior to the fall of Babylon (Jerusalem).

2. (14:6-7) The announcement of the good news that the age to come (olam haba) was about to commence.

3. A contextual analysis of *the smoke of torment*, revealing that it refers to the temporal suffering of torment of the Jews in Jerusalem and the cities throughout their land (14:8-11) in the Roman conflict. It also reflects their exile and *their loss of God's rest as opposed to eternal conscious torment.*

4. The blessedness of the saints who persevere in the face of incredible calamity (14:12-13).

5. The gathering (first harvest) of the Jews to Jerusalem (the furnace), which is consistent with Jesus' Parable of the Weeds (14:14-16; cf. Matt. 13:38-43).

6. The first harvest is followed by a second, bringing bloodshed throughout the land. This is consistent with the history of the Jewish-Roman War (14:17-20).

CHAPTER 20

THE BOOK OF REVELATION
THE END OF THE AGE: REVELATION 15–16

In Revelation 15, we now come to a scene where John sees that seven bowls are about to be poured out, and in them, God's wrath is finished. First, he sees a stunning vision of the saints gathered on a sea of glass mixed with fire. They are playing harps and singing the Song of Moses and the Lamb. It is a song of deliverance, possibly a remembrance of Exodus 15, a type of Christ's deliverance of his people. Some believe it to be the song of witness against the nation that God gave to his servant Moses in Deuteronomy 31:19; 32:1-44).

Like Glass Mixed with Fire

John sees something *like* a sea of glass mixed with fire before God's throne. This is illustrative of God's judgment and grace. The mixture speaks of the covenantal transition of which we have been speaking, now being described in John's visions. Let's see how:

In Daniel 7, the prophet saw a river of fire:

A river of fire was flowing
And coming out from before Him
(Dan. 7:10).

In Exodus 24, Moses and the elders of Israel saw a pavement of sapphire:

. . . and they saw the God of Israel; and under His feet there appeared to be a pavement of sapphire, as clear as the sky itself (Exo. 24:10).

In Revelation 22, John saw the water of life coming from the same throne:

Then he showed me a river of the water of life, clear as crystal, coming from the throne of God and of the Lamb (Rev. 22:1).

These various descriptions speak of God's trial and judgment, his accessibility, and ultimately, his offer of life. Each prophetic vision is a scene that applies to the times that it describes. Daniel 7 describes a season of great *trial and judgment*, which is presented as fire before the throne. He is looking centuries ahead to the time of great judgment and tribulation in the first century.

In Exodus 24, Moses and the seventy elders of Israel saw a pavement of sapphire that reflected God's *accessibility*. They *ate and drank before God—in his presence—and saw him* on the Holy Mountain (Exo. 24:10-11). This great event occurred at the threshold of the design and building of the tabernacle. God came down on the pavement to dwell among them on earth. Finally, in Revelation 22, John saw the Spirit as *life* proceeding from the throne. This is a picture of the ultimate restoration of the life of God, the Holy Spirit, flowing out from heaven as a result of the cross, resurrection, and ascension of our Lord Jesus Christ.

The mixture seen here in Revelation 15 combines the images of a season of great trial and judgment for Israel, while at the same time, great grace and accessibility are being extended to those Jews and Gentiles who have received Christ. It is a vivid illustration of the transition period from law to grace that we have observed throughout this study.

The Song

The song, which was first sung by Moses in Deuteronomy 32, is both a testimony to God's greatness and, at the same time, a testimony against Israel because of their sin and breaking of the covenant. The Lord told Moses that it would be sung in their future:

"Then My anger will be kindled against them in that day, and I will forsake them and hide My face from them, and they will be consumed . . . because of all the evil which they will do, for they will turn to other gods. Now therefore, write this song for yourselves, and teach it to the sons of Israel; put it on their lips, so that this song may be a witness for Me against the sons of Israel" (Deu. 31:17-19).

In this vision, John hears the song of Moses *and* the song of the Lamb. The Greek word *kai,* translated and, is better translated as *even,* or *which is to say.* As we have seen, this is the *explicative* or *epexegetic*al sense of this Greek word that is common in the language. To remind the reader, it means that the second word or phrase explains the first; they are one and the same. The song of Moses *is* the song of the Lamb because what Moses originally prophesied is fulfilled in Christ.

The Stage is Set for the Bowl Judgments

The temple *of the tabernacle of testimony* in heaven opens, and the angels, dressed appropriately in temple-service attire (priestly garments), receive their golden bowls of wrath. This is the inner sanctuary where, as we are told in Exodus 25:10-16, the stone tablets of the testimony (covenant) were stored. The enclosure that stored the witness (the testimony) of their broken covenantal commitments to God is now opened to testify against the unbelieving nation, as Chilton explains:

> The basic treaty document of the Covenant was the Decalogue [Ten Commandments]; this was often called the Testimony, emphasizing its legal character as the record of the Covenant oath . . . The Tabernacle, in which the Testimony was kept, was therefore called the Tabernacle of the Testimony . . . in Revelation the temple (Greek: *naos*) is the Sanctuary, or holy place.[93]

Then, a great glory cloud of smoke fills heaven's inner sanctuary, and no one can enter until the bowl judgments are completed. These plagues resemble those poured out on Egypt at the time of Israel's exodus. Then, the voice of the LORD is heard thundering from the temple:

"Go and pour out on the earth [land] the seven bowls of the wrath of God" (Rev. 16:1).

Revelation 16:
Judgments On the Land Begin

Many of the bowl judgments parallel the trumpet judgments of Revelation 8 and 9, but with one major difference. The trumpets signaled judgments upon one-third of the land. We connected that to the northern (Galilean) campaign of the Romans. Those trumpets of Chapters 8 and 9 heralded a kind of *warning shot* ahead of the bowls to come, bringing devastation to just the northern third of the land. However, the nation has been unwilling to repent (Rev. 16:9). Therefore, there will be no more warnings. The time for the final judgments has arrived (Rev. 15:1). Now John sees the entire land of Israel and the once holy city under the deluge of the invading Roman army as each angel pours out the contents of a bowl that reflects conditions upon the land.

The first bowl brings loathsome and malignant sores:

This was likely due to death, famine, disease, and lack of sanitation. Dead bodies filled the streets of the cities of Israel. Jerusalem was under siege for five months. Those trapped inside had no access to food and water. The Zealots burned the storehouses containing years of food supplies. Josephus describes unbelievable conditions, recording accounts of starvation, putrefying bodies, and cannibalism.

The second bowl is poured on the sea, and it becomes like the blood of a dead man:

Josephus writes of a massacre on the Sea of Galilee where the Romans slaughtered thousands of Jews.[94] In Vespasian's attack on the Jewish seaport of Joppa, the Jewish ships were crushed against the rocks during a storm. The ensuing Roman slaughter left over 4,000 bodies along a blood-saturated coast.

The third bowl is poured out on all the rivers and streams, and they turn to blood:

Again, Josephus writes:

The whole of the country . . . was filled with slaughter, and [the] Jordan [River] could not be passed over, by reason of the dead bodies that were in it, but because [the modern Dead Sea] was also full of dead bodies, that were carried down into it by the river.[95]

The fourth bowl is poured on the sun, and it causes people to be scorched with fire:

The sun typically symbolizes rulers. This bowl likely refers to the Zealot leaders in Jerusalem who exercised *tyrannical oppression* upon the inhabitants of the city. Many unwilling inhabitants had to be forced to fight against Rome, and those who resisted were executed.

The fifth bowl is poured upon the throne of the beast:

It is common to assume that the direction of the judgments now turns toward the Roman *sea* beast. Therefore, the fifth bowl would symbolically reflect the political turmoil that we observed previously, which arose after the suicide of Nero in 68 AD. However, I would suggest that because this judgment is coming upon the *land*, the darkness being poured out is on the throne of the *land* beast. In Revelation 13, we saw that this was the elite class in Jerusalem (the Sadducees, wealthy citizens, and the high priesthood) who were in league with the Roman rulers who governed the land. Their throne was in Jerusalem. The darkness is vanishing leadership, as the Zealots murdered the high priest and slaughtered many priests on the altar of God. King Herod Agrippa II had already been expelled from Jerusalem by the Zealots in 66 AD, before its destruction. All this happened while the city's inhabitants suffered immeasurable agony. There was now no leadership, no light of God, as darkness settled over the land.

"Spiritually Called Egypt"

This entire section of Revelation deals with the judgments on the Jews and alludes to those plagues that God sent upon Egypt in the Exodus story. Egypt, as we are told in Revelation 11, is also Jerusalem's spiritual designation (Rev. 11:8). In the oracles concerning Egypt (Ezekiel 29–32), God speaks to Ezekiel about Egypt while

Nebuchadnezzar is destroying Israel and Jerusalem. Like the darkness that the fifth bowl pours over the throne, Ezekiel prophesies in the last of these seven oracles against Egypt:

> "And when I extinguish you,
> I will cover the heavens and darken their stars;
> I will cover the sun with a cloud
> And the moon will not give its light.
> All the shining lights in the heavens
> *I will darken over you*
> And will set darkness on your land"
> (Eze. 32:7-8).

The darkness over the nation also echoes Jesus' words in the Olivet Discourse:

> "But immediately after the tribulation of those days the sun will be darkened, and the moon will not give its light, and the stars will fall from the sky, and the powers of the heavens will be shaken"
> (Matt. 24:29).

As in Ezekiel, first-century Israel would experience the covering of their heavens and the darkening of their stars. This speaks of the removal of God's appointed rulers of the people, both civic and religious, along with the entire national economy under God. Some rulers would flee, and some would be executed, leaving no leadership except for the *scorching,* chaotic, and oppressive Zealot factions.

The sixth bowl dries up the Euphrates River to make a way for the kings of the east:

When General Vespasian was made Emperor in 69 AD, he brought stability back to the empire. This bowl reflects the return of his armies (led by his son, General Titus), who brought reinforcements from the Euphrates, where they were stationed.[96] The scene continues as unclean spirits are released (like frogs) to gather the client states of

Rome to join the conflict. Here, we are seeing what was really behind the human leaders of Rome. They are demonic entities employing human hosts to do their bidding. This will be central to our understanding of Revelation 19. The frog imagery continues the allusions to the plague of frogs upon Egypt.

These *unclean spirits,* like frogs, go forth to influence the kings of the whole *empire.* Some would interpret this as referring to the whole world as the planet. However, the word in Revelation 16:14 is *oikoumene,* which, in this text, is *better translated empire, not the world.* These client kings are being gathered for the war of *the great day of God, the Almighty.* These are human kings and the principalities that are controlling them. The dragon, as the lead summoner, has the power to gather the principalities that are under his authority. They are the forces behind Rome, as the empire summons support from their (human) client kingdoms. These demonic hordes do not realize that the battle is the Lord's. The armies are being brought together to fulfill God's purposes, not their own. They give their resources and authority to Rome for this *one hour* in history (Rev. 17:13-14).

> As we have previously seen, their objective was to destroy Jerusalem, but in doing so, they assumed that they would destroy the church, which was presumed to be a sect of Judaism.

Then comes a parenthesis. The Lord is *coming like a thief.* It's a way of saying, "*The time is now; this is the day of the Lord:*"

> But the day of the Lord will come like a thief, in which the heavens will pass away with a roar and the elements will be destroyed with intense heat, and the earth [land] and its works will be burned up (2 Pet. 3:10).

Again, Peter's prophecy speaks of Jerusalem, the temple, its elements of service, and the land, not the sky and the planet. It's now coming to a fiery end, but no one expects what's about to happen next.

The seventh bowl is poured upon the air, and once again the voice of God thunders:

It is done!

The great city, Jerusalem, is split into three parts as the contents of the bowl bring great lightning and thunder, followed by an earthquake. Josephus offers a historical record, as Jerusalem was on the brink of its fall to the Romans. The city was actually divided into three Zealot factions, each holding a portion of it.[97] As for the great hailstones, the Roman ballistas catapulted white boulders weighing a talent (75–85 pounds) over Jerusalem's walls (Jewish law required the adulteress wife to be stoned; cf. John 8:4-5). The Zealot lookouts who were stationed on the walls warned the city as they were being launched, which reduced their effectiveness. The Romans then blackened them, making them harder to see, which caused many more Jews to be injured or killed.[98]

Finally, we read that *"Babylon the Great"* is remembered before God for her sins. This is more than the intellectual activity of recalling things in the mind. God never *forgot* the Babylon of Revelation. The Hebraic notion of remembrance is not merely a mental activity but action-based. God is now acting to bring to account (punish) the sins of the city and the nation. From what we have seen in Revelation, it appears this reference is to first-century Jerusalem. She has passed the point of no return. Now her judgment is final:

> Babylon the great was remembered before God, to give her the cup of the wine of His fierce wrath (Rev. 16:17-19).

As the Bowl Judgments reach their conclusion, we now turn to John's visions concerning the harlot Babylon and the beast who carries her. The following chapter will provide some clarity as to how the connection between Babylon and God's once-holy city came to be.

CHAPTER 21

THE BOOK OF REVELATION
THE HARLOT AND THE BEAST: REVELATION 17–19

In Revelation 17–18, we find more detailed descriptions of two central figures that were introduced earlier in Revelation: Babylon and the sea beast. The great harlot is portrayed as having adulterous relationships with the kings of the land and the scarlet-colored Roman beast upon which she is riding. These relationships are described as ultimately leading to her fall and judgment. We will now examine why this harlot is first-century Jerusalem.

Ancient Jerusalem as the Harlot

The mystery woman is the great harlot, having people in many nations and in her own land who have fallen under her adulterous influence (Rev. 17:1-2). The prophets frequently used the imagery of the harlot to describe Jerusalem's (Israel's) unfaithfulness. The great prophet Isaiah cried from the depths of his soul concerning Jerusalem:

> How the faithful city has become a harlot,
> She who was once full of justice!
> Righteousness once lodged in her,
> But now murderers.
> (Isa. 1:21)

This is often a specific reference to the nation's unfaithfulness to her *marriage* covenant with God, seen in light of her idolatry, unjust social and commercial practices, and dependence upon foreign nations. In Revelation, as is the case in other prophetic literature, the principal city or the nation's ruler is used interchangeably with the nation itself (e.g., Jerusalem as Israel; Pharaoh as Egypt; Nebuchadnezzar as Babylon, etc.). David Keppel describes the relationship between the harlot and the beast:

> The relation of Jerusalem to Rome is very aptly symbolized by the figure of the woman – Jerusalem – seated upon the beast – Rome. Up to a few years before its destruction Jerusalem was strongly pro-Roman. People and rulers united in the cry, "We have no king but Caesar." On the other hand the Harlot-city used the power of Rome, as a rider uses the power of his horse, in persecuting the church. She was drunken with blood shed by the Roman sword.[99]

David Chilton also provides valuable insights:

> Tyre and Nineveh are the only two cities outside of Israel that are accused of harlotry—had both been in covenant with God. The kingdom of Tyre in David and Solomon's time was converted and her king entered a covenant with Solomon and assisted in the building of

the temple (1 Kings 5:1-12; 9:13; Amos 1:9); Nineveh was converted under the ministry of Jonah (Jon. 3:5-10). The later apostasy of these two cities could rightly be considered harlotry.[100]

Although they are viewed as harlots, neither Nineveh nor Tyre have any contextual affiliation with the Book of Revelation. That leaves Jerusalem as the only other city ever mentioned in the Bible as a harlot. The suggestion that Rome is the harlot city has no corroborating scriptural witness that would designate the city or the empire to be such. There is no evidence that, in its history, Imperial Rome was ever in a covenantal relationship with God. The harlotry designation belongs only to those who have broken their covenant with God. In contrast, the repeated accusations by the prophets concerning Israel bear witness to her appearance as the Great Harlot in this vision.

A Harlot's Forehead and a Cup of Blood

In Revelation 17:5, her forehead is described. She has no shame. As in Jeremiah, she is open for business and advertising it:

"Therefore, the showers have been withheld,
And there has been no spring rain.
Yet you had a harlot's forehead;
You refused to be ashamed"
(Jer. 3:3).

In Revelation 17:6, she is drunk with the blood of the prophets and saints. In Revelation 18:24, we learn that in her:

. . . was found the blood of prophets and of saints and of all who have been slain on the earth [land].

Compare Luke 13:33-34:

. . . it cannot be that a prophet would perish outside of Jerusalem. "O Jerusalem, Jerusalem, the city that kills the prophets and stones those sent to her!

Although Jesus and the first century Christian martyrs fell at the hands of the Romans, Paul held the Jews of *that generation* (not all generations) who colluded with Rome to be responsible for their deaths:

> For you, brethren, became imitators of the churches of God in Christ Jesus that are in Judea, for you also endured the same sufferings at the hands of your own countrymen, even as they did from the Jews, who both killed the Lord Jesus and the prophets, and drove us out. They are not pleasing to God, but hostile to all men, hindering us from speaking to the Gentiles so that they may be saved; with the result that they always fill up the measure of their sins. But wrath has come upon them to the utmost (1 Thes. 2:14-16).

Jesus previously declared:

> ". . . you will scourge in your synagogues, and persecute from city to city, *so that upon you may fall the guilt of all the righteous blood shed on earth [land]*, from the blood of righteous Abel to the blood of Zechariah, the son of Berechiah, whom you murdered between the temple and the altar. "Truly I say to you, all these things will come upon this generation" (Matt. 23:34-36).

The Great City

Jerusalem is called the great city in Revelation 11:8. This is obvious because the text states it is *where the Lord Jesus was crucified*. The harlot is referred to in Revelation 16:9, 18:10, and 18:19 as the *great city*. Revelation's own self-witness supports the prospect that first-century Jerusalem is being described in those references as well. Note Jeremiah's description of Jerusalem, *the great city*, as having forsaken the Lord and worshiping other gods:

> And many nations will pass by this city, and every man will say to his neighbor, "Why has the Lord dealt thus with *this great city*?" And they will answer, "Because they have forsaken the covenant of the Lord their God and worshiped other gods and served them" (Jer. 22:8-9).

The following table shows the occurrences of the phrase *the great city* in the Bible. Outside of Jerusalem, only Nineveh and Gibeon are designated as such, but neither has a place in Revelation. Babylon is not mentioned as *a great city* until the Book of Revelation.

"The Great City"

Book	No. of Verses	City
Genesis	1 verse	Nineveh
Joshua	1 verse	Gibeon
Jeremiah	1 verse	Jerusalem
Jonah	4 verses	Nineveh
Revelation	8 verses	Jerusalem / Babylon

Table 21.1
Source NASEC 1998, e-sword version[101]

The Babylon-Jerusalem Connection

In attempting to associate Jerusalem with Babylon, there seems to be no explicit biblical reference to Israel or Jerusalem as that city. We have previously introduced how the Bible makes clear statements, types, and representations regarding Jerusalem as Sodom and Egypt (Rev. 11:8). Her judgments are likened to those that fell upon Sodom (Isa. 1:9). In another example, the apostle Paul draws a sharp distinction between Abraham's two sons, Ishmael, and Isaac, as told in Genesis 21:8-12. We are told in Galatians how Ishmael was born of the [Abraham's] flesh. Isaac was born of the Spirit (as God's gift).

> For it is written that Abraham had two sons, one by the bondwoman and one by the free woman. But the son by the bondwoman was born according to the flesh, and the son by the free woman through the

promise. This is allegorically speaking, for these women are two covenants: one proceeding from Mount Sinai bearing children who are to be slaves; she is Hagar. Now this Hagar is Mount Sinai in Arabia and corresponds to the present Jerusalem, for she is in slavery with her children . . . And you brethren, like Isaac, are children of promise. (Gal 4:22-28).

In Paul's allegory, he likens Israel according to the flesh to Hagar's son *Ishmael*, the son who was cast out of the inheritance (4:30). The church is likened to Isaac, the son of promise, who receives the inheritance. However, concerning the Jerusalem-Babylon connection, we find no clearly stated association. How, then, do we make the case?

First, we must go back to Israel's ancestral foundations. God called Abram (Abraham) out of Ur of the Chaldeans, which was a city in the Babylonian Empire. Although his heritage was Hebrew, he was culturally Babylonian:

And He said to him [Abram], "I am the LORD who brought you out of Ur of the Chaldeans, to give you this land to possess it" (Gen. 15:7).

By the sixth century BC, the Jews had been an established, though divided nation under their kings for several hundred years. However, their continued idolatry and disobedience resulted in God's appointment of the Babylonians to invade the land and destroy their city and the temple. Many Jews were exiled to Babylon, which had been their country of origin centuries earlier. When they were released from captivity after seventy years in Babylon, many chose to remain, having established a new lifestyle. They were two generations removed from Jewish life centered around Jerusalem and the temple. Many had no connection to that previous life. Babylon was the place of their birth and livelihood, and they were accustomed to the culture, so they had no desire to return to the city or land of their ancestors, especially considering that it was in ruins. Like Abraham, their ancestral heritage did not alter the fact that they were cultural Babylonians.

Even among those who left, a whole new generation of Jews knew only Babylon as their normative culture and Aramaic (the language of Babylon) as their normative language.

Rabbi Berel Wein, an American Orthodox Rabbi, offers helpful insight:

The Jews who were exiled to Babylon after the destruction of Judea established a Jewish community that lasted continuously until modern times, a period of more than 2,500 years . . . Babylon came to feel like home in many ways, the Talmud points out (Pesachim 87b-88a). *After all, Abraham had come from there.* Furthermore, the Babylonian language, Aramaic, was close to the language of the Jewish people.[102]

The Beast:
The Empire, its Rulers, and Unseen Influences

In Revelation 17:8, the angel gives John a somewhat puzzling description of the beast upon whom the harlot is riding. This description is most certainly the subject of much scholarly debate. It is necessarily difficult because the events it describes are themselves historically complex. As many expositors have observed, I would also assume that the realities behind these characterizations were being veiled by the Holy Spirit from the watching eyes of the Roman authorities. They would have undoubtedly viewed it as treasonous literature, creating even more fuel for fires of persecution.

The vision is a portrayal of what has been described in earlier chapters. It illustrates Rome's descent into civil war after the death of Nero, and the resulting chaos. The subsequent historical events come into view: the fall of three subsequent emperors and the re-establishment of the empire under Vespasian. These are all alluded to in this account. As observed, this was the infamous *Year of the Four Emperors*. These complex political developments affect our understanding of Revelation's portrayal of the beast. The turmoil and civic upheaval are captured in the riddled descriptions provided by the angel to John. They are hidden, yet discernable with some help from our comprehension of John's historical situation and Daniel's visions.

Let us now see if we can unpack the angel's description considering the history of the period:

> The beast that you saw was, and is not, and is about to come up out of the abyss and go to destruction. And those who dwell on the earth [land], whose name has not been written in the book of life from the foundation of the world, will wonder when they see the beast, that he was and is not and will come. "Here is the mind which has wisdom. The seven heads are seven mountains on which the woman sits, and they are seven kings; five have fallen, one is, the other has not yet come; and when he comes, he must remain a little while. "The beast which was and is not, is himself also an eighth and is [one] of the seven, and he goes to destruction (Rev. 17:8-11).

"The beast was, and is not, and is about to come out of the abyss"

Titus appears to be the human host of the beast, who was *about to come out of the abyss* at the time of Revelation. It is important that we understand that there is a demonic entity, *the Destroyer,* operating through Titus. We observed this in our review of Revelation 9, where John saw that this spirit would be *let out of the abyss.* It would empower Titus to siege Jerusalem for five months, ending with its destruction. The angel again informs John that this entity *is about to* come out of the abyss. Here, John is also told that *the entity "was and is not," meaning it had been previously active.* This suggests that it had, at one time, been operating through a previous adversary of the people of God. Ladd, Beale, and McKenzie support this interpretation.[103]

The precise identity of this previous (human) adversary is not conclusive, but at the same time, it is not required to support our interpretation. This beast, who is about to arise in Titus, had previously worked through a now deceased antagonist. This is not entirely out of the question. Remember that John the Baptist came in the "spirit and power" of Elijah (a godly rather than an ungodly example). Of course, John was not the same man as Elijah, but the Gospel informs us that the same measure of the Spirit that was upon Elijah was with John:

"Behold, *I am going to send you Elijah the prophet* before the coming of the great and terrible day of the Lord" (Mal. 4:5)

It is he [John the Baptist] who will go as a forerunner before Him *in the spirit and power of Elijah* (Luke1:17).

"But I say to you that *Elijah has indeed come*, and they did to him whatever they wished, just as it is written of him" (Mark 9:13).

Interestingly, there was a myth circulating in the first century referred to as *Nero Redivivus*. In Latin, it meant Nero was going to be revived, that is, come back to life. Of course, it was just a myth, but could this revival of the tyrant not have been the man but the deceased Nero's demon spirit returning from the abyss to manifest in Titus? The counterfeit is remarkable. Just as John heralded the kingdom of God, the host of Nero's spirit in Titus boasted the supremacy of Rome.

We know from the Gospels that the abyss from which this spirit returned is the habitation of "homeless" demonic entities:

And Jesus asked him, "What is your name?" And he said, "Legion"; for many demons had entered him. They were imploring Him not to command them to go away into *the abyss* (Luke 8:30-31).

Titus, like Nero, hated both the Jews and the Christians. He wanted to destroy Jerusalem, as previously noted, not only to get rid of Judaism, but he held the common understanding of the times that Christianity was a sect of Judaism. It also needed to be stamped out. Even in his own words, by destroying the Jews, he would also demolish the Christian sect. This was affirmed by an ancient historian:

Titus is said, after calling a council, to have first deliberated whether he should destroy the temple, a structure of such extraordinary work. For it seemed good to some that a sacred edifice, distinguished above all human achievements, ought not to be destroyed, inasmuch as, if preserved, it would furnish an evidence of Roman moderation, but, if destroyed, would serve for a perpetual proof of Roman cruelty. But on the opposite side, others and Titus himself thought that the temple ought specially to be overthrown, in order that the religion of the Jews and of the Christians might more thoroughly be subverted; for that these religions, although contrary to each other, had nevertheless proceeded from the same authors; that the Christians had sprung up from among the Jews; and that, if the root were extirpated, the offshoot would speedily perish.[104]

The destiny of this beast was *to go to destruction*. This is not the destruction of the Roman Empire or a human leader of Rome. Some who suggest that Revelation cannot be a first-century account make this mistake based on the historical fact that neither Rome nor an emperor were *destroyed* during or following the razing of Jerusalem. This creature, who arose from the abyss, is not a human or political entity that goes to destruction. It is the unholy, demonic destroyer behind them that will be destroyed at Jesus' parousia. This will become evident as we examine Revelation 19.

. . . and those who dwell on the land will wonder

The most common preterist opinion is that this refers to the revival of the empire under Vespasian after Rome's civil war, the cessation of the Jewish conflict, and the Year of the Four Emperors. We might consider how Rome's remarkable rebound from near collapse would have undoubtedly caused great wonder among the nations, especially those *who dwell on the land*: the Jews. The nation would have had a false sense of *peace and safety* with the suspension of the war. We have observed how multitudes of Jews went up to Jerusalem to celebrate the Passover in 70 AD. Little did they know that *sudden destruction* was awaiting them, as they would be inescapably trapped within the city walls by the recommissioned Roman army led by Titus:

> While they are saying, "Peace and safety!" then destruction will come upon them suddenly like labor pains upon a woman with child, and they will not escape (1 Thess. 5:3).

The seven hills are seven kings . . . five have fallen, one is

The description of Rome as the *city on seven hills* is of lesser importance than its political infrastructure; *they (the hills) are seven kings*. This corresponds to Daniel 7, where the fourth empire is Rome:

> The fourth beast will be a fourth kingdom on the earth . . . As for the ten horns, out of this kingdom ten kings will arise; and another will arise after them, and he will be different from the previous ones and will subdue three kings (Dan. 7:23-24).

Daniel's fourth beast, who was in power at the time of Jesus, had eleven horns. There were ten emperors who governed Imperial Rome until Jerusalem's destruction. Titus was Daniel's eleventh (the small horn), who uprooted three and also destroyed Jerusalem:

1.	Julius	49–44 BC	
2.	Augustus	31 BC–14 AD	
3.	Tiberius	14–37 AD	
4.	Gaius (Caligula)	37–41 AD	
5.	Claudius	41–54 AD	
6.	Nero	54–68 AD	
	Galba*	*68–69 AD*	⎤
	Otho*	*69 AD*	⎬ Three uprooted before Titus
	Vitellius*	*69 AD*	⎦
7.	(10) Vespasian	69–79 AD	
8.	(11) Titus	79–81 AD	

In Revelation, the angel explains to John that the seven hills are *seven kings, among whom five have fallen.* The five previously deceased emperors were:

1. Julius
2. Augustus
3. Tiberius
4. Gaius (Caligula)
5. Claudius

The *one who is* would be the sixth in succession:

6. Nero

The ruler of Rome at the time of the Revelation was Nero, the sixth in succession. The Revelation was seen toward the latter part of his reign (c. 64–68 AD), during which he engaged in cruel and cold-hearted persecution of the church. Following Nero's death, the three succeeding emperors strove to consolidate their power but did not engage in hostilities with or persecute Jews or Christians. They also failed to establish legitimate power throughout the empire. Since the Bible is *redemptive* history, it typically distinguishes only leaders or empires that directly affect God's people as *beasts*. Daniel 7 offers an excellent example. Therefore, the three interim emperors are omitted from John's list. Vespasian, who initially engaged in the war with the Jews, becomes the real seventh king as a result of the angel in Revelation 17 leaving them out.

The three interim leaders (italicized in the previous list of eleven) are:

- Galba
- Otho
- Vitellius

These three omitted rulers in Revelation are being removed as the eleventh horn in Daniel 7 rises to power. This is observed in Daniel 7:8:

> While I was contemplating the horns, behold, another horn, *a little one [the eleventh]*, came up among them, and three of the first horns were pulled out by the roots before it; and behold, this horn possessed eyes like the eyes of a man and a mouth uttering great boasts (Dan. 7:8; Dan 7:24).

Titus is described in Daniel 7 as a *little horn* because during the uprooting of Galba, Otho, and Vitellius, who all died violent deaths, he was still a general, but Titus was rising to power. He is said to have been influential in the removal of the three. In Brian Jones' *The Emperor Titus,* the author informs us how Titus was a major factor in gaining control of the empire for his father.[105] With that, let's continue unpacking the remainder of the angel's riddle.

. . . the other has not yet come;
and when he comes, he must remain a little while.

The seventh in succession:

7. Vespasian

After being proclaimed Emperor, Vespasian, while attending to the empire's matters in Egypt, left his son Domitian briefly in charge of administering the affairs in Rome. Militarily, it was time to carry out the mission that had been suspended. He sanctioned General Titus to resume the assault on Jerusalem. I believe that this is what is meant by Vespasian's *remaining a little while.* Although he was now emperor of Rome, his beastly role in the invasion was diminished. It was now Titus' war. The Destroyer had come out of the abyss and found its host.

The spiritual entity, the Destroyer, (cf. Rev. 9:11) was now empowering Titus to attack and destroy Jerusalem.

And the beast which was, and is not,
even he is the eighth, and is [one] of the seven

This strange description is ascribed to Titus, *the eighth emperor,* who, after his father's death, reigned from 79–81 AD. The revised list of emperors (with Daniel's three horns omitted) now appears as follows:

1.	Julius	49–44 BC
2.	Augustus	31 BC–14 AD
3.	Tiberius	14–37 AD
4.	Gaius (Caligula)	37–41 AD
5.	Claudius	41–54 AD
6.	Nero	54–68 AD
7.	Vespasian	69–79 AD
8.	Titus	79-81 AD

The word *one* (in the phrase, *one of the seven)* is not in the text, although some translators supply it. The eighth ruler is *of the seven:* Titus. After completing his assignment to destroy Jerusalem, Titus assumed an influential place alongside his father, Vespasian, the seventh ruler. Thus, Titus could be described as "of the seven." As previously noted, the two even bore the same name, *Titus Flavius Vespasianus.* Apparently, he was so influential that he was viewed as a co-emperor during Vespasian's reign. This is evident in Josephus' works, as he often refers to Titus as *Caesar,* while Titus was still a general and his father ruled Rome.

Titus assumed full control of the empire after Vespasian's death in 79 AD. Josephus' work dates to the latter half of Vespasian's reign, while Titus was still a general, yet repeatedly refers to him as "Caesar." Poole affirms the dating of Josephus' history of the war:

Josephus' first work, *Bellum Judaicum (History of the Jewish War)*, was written in seven books between AD 75 and 79, toward the end of Vespasian's reign. . . . Josephus presents a detailed account of the great revolt of AD 66–70.[106]

Then, in Revelation 17:16-17, we are told the beast will hate the harlot and turn on her to burn and devour her. From Rome's standpoint, she was a useless, annoying harlot who needed to be discarded. However, it was God who put his purpose in their hearts to bring about his judgment on her.

Revelation 18 opens with the angelic declaration that Babylon is fallen, having become *the habitation of demons* (Rev. 18:1-3). This echoes Jesus' warning concerning that generation in Israel:

"Now when the unclean spirit goes out of a man, it passes through waterless places seeking rest, and does not find it. Then it says, 'I will return to my house from which I came'; and when it comes, it finds it unoccupied, swept, and put in order. Then it goes and takes along with it seven other spirits more wicked than itself, and they go in and live there; and the last state of that man becomes worse than the first. *That is the way it will also be with this evil generation"* (Matt. 12:43-45).

Revelation 18: The Dirge

Revelation 17 provides an *identification* of the harlot (Jerusalem) and the beast (Rome). Revelation 18 is the *dirge*, as the angel announces that Babylon has fallen. In Revelation 18:4-8, those who are faithful are exhorted to leave the ancient modes of worship and practice and the lure of Judaism. This departure is most likely spiritual because, by this time, the disciples of Jesus had physically fled the city, however:

There was a temporal dimension to the warning. We have seen that during the period when the war was suspended, the Passover was to be celebrated in the spring of 70 AD. Jewish Christians, in particular, might have been tempted to enjoy this cultural celebration with fellow Jews in Jerusalem. John's warning was to remove themselves, both physically and spiritually, from their ties to their previous heritage. If not, they would perish in the siege.

Warnings that God's judgment was about to fall so decisively on the old system should have been sufficient for anyone who still had ties to it. Those ties, held so tightly, would undoubtedly cause them to disregard Jesus' warnings and ultimately lead to their unnecessary demise. Those who might be entertaining the idea that "the old is better" (Luke 5:39) were being given a final warning to wrench themselves fully and finally away from it. They were to depart both physically, spiritually, and emotionally from the lure of the old system and its principal city.

Merchants Lament their Loss

In Revelation 18:9-19, the neighboring cities and nations that profited from her merchandise now lament Jerusalem's fall. Her greed and idolatrous commercial dealings, through which she and others had become rich, will be no more. The many listed aspects of her commercialism and the sounds of a vibrant, prosperous city will no longer be found in her, and the merchants lament.

Note the stark contrast between the merchants' assessment of Jerusalem as a great and prosperous city (verses 9-19) as opposed to God's assessment of her sins and harlotries (verses 20-23). What was once the holy city of God is now seen as a center of great importance to worldly commercial enterprises.

From God's viewpoint, she has become suitable only for his judgment and destruction. Instead of shining the light of Messiah to the world, she became a stumbling block to those looking to her for the knowledge of God. Jerusalem was now only worthy of being cast into the sea among the Gentiles. Revelation 18:21 echoes Jesus' words in Matthew 18:

> Then a strong angel took up a stone like a great millstone and threw it into the sea, saying, "So will Babylon, the great city, be thrown down with violence, and will not be found any longer (Rev. 18:21).

> ". . . but whoever causes one of these little ones who believe in Me to stumble, it would be better for him to have a heavy millstone hung around his neck, and to be drowned in the depth of the sea"
> (Matt. 18:6).

The dirge of Chapter 18 echoes the cries of Jeremiah the prophet as he declared God's judgment over the great harlot. In Revelation 18, we read:

> "And the sound of harpists and musicians and flute-players and trumpeters will not be heard in you any longer; and no craftsman of any craft will be found in you any longer; and the sound of a mill will not be heard in you any longer; and the light of a lamp will not shine in you any longer; and the voice of the bridegroom and bride will not be heard in you any longer; for your merchants were the great men of the earth, because all the nations were deceived by your sorcery."
> (Rev. 18:22-23).

Centuries earlier, Jeremiah had declared the same outcome for *Jerusalem* and the cities of Judah. The following would result from the Babylonian invasion of the sixth century BC:

> "Then I will make to cease from the cities of Judah and from the streets of Jerusalem the voice of joy and the voice of gladness, the voice of the bridegroom and the voice of the bride; for the land will become a ruin" (Jer. 7:34).

> For thus says the LORD of hosts, the God of Israel: "Behold, I am going to eliminate from this place [Jerusalem], before your eyes and in your time, the voice of rejoicing and the voice of gladness, the voice of the groom and the voice of the bride" (Jer. 16:9).

Finally, in Revelation 18:24, the blood of her prophets and saints, along with all who were murdered on the land, was found in her. She is now being brought to account for her bloodshed (cf. Matt. 23:34ff).

And in her was found the blood of prophets and of saints and of all who have been slain on the earth [land] (Rev. 18:24).

"Therefore, behold, I am sending you prophets and wise men and scribes; some of them you will kill and crucify, and some of them you will flog in your synagogues, and persecute from city to city, so that upon you will fall the guilt of all the righteous blood shed on [the] earth [the land] . . ." (Matt. 23:34-35).

Revelation 19:
Burning, Bliss, and Battle

The rejoicing of the saints in the previous chapter spills into **Revelation 19**. God is justified in his judgment of the harlot. It is the exercise of his vengeance because she has polluted the land by shedding the blood of the righteous (cf. Num. 35:33). The smoke of the burning city rises perpetually before God as a memorial of his judgment on her, which again aligns her with her spiritual identity as Sodom (cf. Rev. 11:8; Gen. 19:28). The resounding voice of a great multitude is heard:

HALLELUJAH! For the Lord our God, the Almighty, reigns!

In verses 6–10, the burning harlot city was the Old Covenant wife of God. Her judgment for harlotry makes way for the Lord Jesus to take on a new bride, the church, who will be seen in her glory in Revelation 21. The saints are clothed in fine linen, having been prepared for the wedding feast.

McKenzie makes an important observation concerning the Parable of the Wedding Feast in Matthew 22. It reflects the same sequence as Revelation 18–19. In both the parable and John's vision, the wedding feast follows the destruction of the city.[107] This correspondence between the two texts provides sound evidence that both John's vision and Jesus' parable describe the time of Jerusalem's fall.

> "The kingdom of heaven may be compared to a king who gave a wedding feast for his son. And he sent out his slaves to call those who had been invited to the wedding feast, and they were unwilling to come . . . But they paid no attention and went their way, one to his own farm, another to his business, and the rest seized his slaves and mistreated them and killed them. But the king was enraged, and he *sent his armies and destroyed those murderers and set their city on fire.* Then he said to his slaves, *'The wedding is ready,* but those who were invited were not worthy. Go therefore to the main highways, and as many as you find there, invite to the wedding feast'" (Matt. 22:1-10).

The Parousia of Christ

The *parousia*, as we have learned, is the arrival or second coming of Christ and occurs in verses 11–16. It is concurrent with the fall of Jerusalem. He descends from heaven on a white horse, followed by the army of the saints, clothed in white linen. The fact that the saints accompany him shows they are in heaven. This lends credibility to the proposition that a first-century resurrection involving the previously deceased saints has already occurred. The Lord Jesus, who leads them, is described as the faithful, true, and righteous one. His flaming eyes speak of his capacity to judge with truth, and his many crowns symbolize that he, as king, has conquered many nations.

He has a *hidden name,* one that is known only to him. In the ancient world, to name someone was to confer certain characteristics on them. This would give the one who names a certain degree of power over the one named. The person named could be controlled to some extent because their behavior could be predicted. This is why Jesus demanded the demons declare their names before he cast them out (Mark 5:9; Luke 8:30). The patriarch Jacob (the schemer) wanted to know the name of the angel of the Lord with whom he wrestled at Peniel. He assumed that this would give him insight into the character of God so that he could manipulate him for his own purposes (Gen. 32:29). However, here, in Revelation, we are not given a name by which we can manipulate him. He is the One who cannot be manipulated or controlled because:

HE IS KING OF KINGS AND LORD OF LORDS

He rules by his sword, which is the Word of God, and brings the nations under his authority. As he arrives, an angel calls for the birds of the air to take part in the supper of God. The Roman invasion left multitudes dead in this great arena.

In the unseen realm, the beast and his principalities gather to make war with the Lord Jesus and his army. This was the objective of the powers and principalities behind Rome all along. Armageddon was the rendezvous point for Titus and his invading forces (Rev. 16:13-16). The *battle of Armageddon is already lost*. Upon Jerusalem's destruction, our great king simply seizes the forces of the dragon, who were already defeated at the cross, and casts them into the lake of fire.

Jesus came not to destroy Rome as a national entity but to destroy the principalities and powers behind the empire, as seen in Daniel:

> But the court will sit for judgment, and his [the beast's] dominion will be taken away, *annihilated and destroyed forever.* 'Then the sovereignty, the dominion and the greatness of all the kingdoms under the whole heaven will be given to the people of the saints of the Highest One; His kingdom will be an everlasting kingdom, and all the dominions will serve and obey Him (Dan. 7:26-27).

Daniel 7 appears to read that the beast will be *"annihilated and destroyed forever."* However, Rome, as an empire, wasn't annihilated or destroyed. After 70 AD, Rome continued for several centuries. Even their conflicts with surviving Jewish loyalists and persecutions of the church continued for some time into the near future. To resolve this apparent difficulty, we turn to Keil & Delitzsch's Old Testament Commentary. These great commentators often provide valuable insight into the original Hebrew meanings in the text. They point out, regarding Daniel 7:12 (under the sub-heading of Daniel 7:26), that:

> . . . that which is said (Dan_7:12) about the taking away of its power and its dominion is strengthened by the *inf* . . . (*to destroy*) . . . (*and to consume*) . . .[108]

As opposed to the *destruction* of the beast itself, Daniel's vision, interpreted by the angel, actually informs us that the beast's *power to annihilate and to destroy* the people of God was taken away forever. J.P. Green's Literal Translation follows these commentators in his translation of the text:

> But the judgment shall sit, and they shall take away his rulership,
> *to cut off and to destroy* until the end (Dan. 7:26 LITV).

Excursus:
Concerning the Reign of Christ

The powers behind the Roman invasion, which concluded with the destruction of the city and the temple, fulfilled Daniel's prophecy by shattering the power of the holy people, the Jews (Dan. 12:7). The parousia of Christ at this time would also be *their* own destruction. These powers would never be able to put out the lamp of God's people, the church, in the way they were commissioned to do to Israel. Although Jewish-Roman conflicts continued for several years after 70 AD, the center of Jewish life and their economy were left in ruins. Returning to Daniel 7, the interpreting angel goes on to say:

> . . . then the sovereignty, dominion and the greatness of all the kingdoms under the whole Heaven will be given to the people of the saints of the highest one, in His kingdom will be an everlasting kingdom, and all dominions will serve and obey Him (Dan. 7:27).

The beast (the power working through Titus) and the false prophet (the syncretistic powers behind the Sadducees and their local Roman cohorts) are thrown into the lake of fire. Notably, the Sadducees disappeared from history after the Jewish-Roman War. The remaining principalities, many of which are still active in the world and its systems, no longer have any power to destroy the people of God.

I would suggest here that many of God's people have mistaken ideas concerning the reign of Christ on earth. It is thought to be an era of world peace with the Lord Jesus sitting bodily on a throne in the rebuilt temple, centered in new Jerusalem. From there, it is alleged, he will rule over the nations of the world. I do not believe that image is consistent with how Jesus described his reign to his disciples:

> He presented another parable to them, saying, "The kingdom of heaven is like a mustard seed, which a man took and sowed in his field; and this is smaller than all other seeds, but when it is full grown, it is larger than the garden plants and becomes a tree, so that *the birds of the air come and nest in its branches*" (Matt. 13:31-32).

This imagery of his kingdom rule is taken directly from Daniel 4, where the prophet describes the Babylonian kingdom of Nebuchadnezzar:

> The tree that you saw, which became large and grew strong . . . whose foliage was beautiful and its fruit abundant . . . under which the beasts of the field dwelt and *in whose branches the birds of the sky lodged* — it is you, O king; for you have become great and grown strong, and your majesty has become great and reached to the sky and your dominion to the end of the earth (Dan. 4:20-22).

The beasts of the field and the birds of the air are the Bible's way of describing the seen and unseen powers of the nations of the world. We have seen from Daniel's visions how beasts are characterized as rulers of nations. In the Parable of the Sower, Jesus likens unclean spirits to birds of the air:

"Listen to this! Behold, the sower went out to sow; as he was sowing, some seed fell beside the road, and the birds came and ate it up . . . These are the ones who are beside the road where the word is sown; and when they hear, immediately Satan comes and takes away the word which has been sown in them" (Mark 4:3-4; 14-15).

These unseen powers influence the nations. They have been brought under the dominion of Christ in the same manner as Babylon's sovereignty at the time of Daniel. Jesus' description of his kingdom was that it would resemble that of Nebuchadnezzar. Its nature would be like an ancient Suzerainty (sovereign/vassal) covenant with the nations of the world. Recall that God *reconciled* the world to himself through the cross of Christ. Through Jesus, he entered a covenant of peace, as Paul explains in Second Corinthians:

Now all these things are from God, who reconciled us to Himself through Christ and gave us the ministry of reconciliation, namely, that God was in Christ *reconciling the world to Himself*, not counting their trespasses against them, and He has committed to us the word of reconciliation. Therefore, we are ambassadors for Christ, as though God were making an appeal through us; we beg you on behalf of Christ, be reconciled to God (2 Cor. 5:18-20).

Again, this is not *universal salvation*. Paul uses covenantal language concerning peaceful subordinance. It reflects God's attitude toward the nations because of Christ's sacrifice. Our ambassadorship among them is to bring God's offer of peace. Seen and unseen rulers of the earth may retain a measure of authority, but *Jesus is king over them. He is the King of Kings, as was Nebuchadnezzar as a type in Daniel 2:36.* Like the custom of an ancient Suzerain/Vassal treaty, the nations are granted autonomy, but it is restricted by one major guideline, which does not include moral perfection. We know that righteousness exalts a nation (Prov. 14:34), and God has ways to deal with nations and their sins. However, in Psalm 2, David declares the primary constraint, as God addresses, not average individuals but rulers of the nations:

"But as for Me, I have installed My King
Upon Zion, My holy mountain.
I will surely tell of the decree of the LORD:
He said to Me, 'You are My Son,
Today I have begotten You.
Ask of Me, and I will surely give the nations as Your inheritance,
And the very ends of the earth as Your possession'
You shall break them with a rod of iron,
You shall shatter them like earthenware."
Now therefore, O kings, show discernment;
Take warning, O judges of the earth.
Worship the LORD with reverence
And rejoice with trembling.
Do homage to the Son, that He not become angry, and you perish in
the way,
For His wrath may soon be kindled.
How blessed are all who take refuge in Him!
(Psa. 2:6-12).

The principal constraint is this: they must honor the Son of God.

How do the nations pay homage to the Son of God, as commanded in Psalm 2? They honor him by *allowing the church to flourish.* This is evident in Acts 9, when Paul, the apostle, was yet Saul of Tarsus, a persecutor of the early church, was struck down from his horse by Jesus. In that encounter, the risen Lord spoke these words:

. . . and he [Saul] fell to the ground and heard a voice saying to him, "Saul, Saul, *why are you persecuting Me*?" And he said, "Who are You, Lord?" And He said, "*I am Jesus whom you are persecuting*" (Acts 9:4-5).

Saul's persecution of the church was persecution of Jesus. In this, we are shown that to honor the Son, as in Psalm 2:12, the nations must give place to the church, allowing it to function without interference or persecution. If oppression of the church is prevalent, a nation will come under God's judgment. No one can say how long until, or in what manner, that nation will be judged, but we can be certain it will. God's patience is immeasurable (2 Pet. 3:8), and his ways are past finding out (Rom. 11:33). There are often larger divine purposes involved that factor into God's judgment of a nation and bringing immediate relief to his oppressed people.

When God entered his covenant with Abraham, he told the patriarch that his descendants (the Hebrews) would enter Egypt and remain there until an appointed time because God's purpose had something to do with the Amorites, a principal culture in Canaan:

> God said to Abram, "Know for certain that your descendants will be strangers in a land that is not theirs, where they will be enslaved and oppressed four hundred years . . . Then in the fourth generation they will return here [to Canaan], for the iniquity of the Amorite is not yet complete" (Gen. 15:13-16).

At the time appointed by God, after four centuries in Egypt and the fourth generation of enslavement there, the Hebrews would be freed. In their deliverance, God would judge Egypt for their treatment of his people:

> "But I will also judge the nation whom they will serve, and afterward they will come out with many possessions" (Gen. 15:14).

A generation after their departure from Egypt, the broader scope of God's purpose would become evident. After forty years in the wilderness, God appointed Joshua, the successor of Moses, to lead his people into Canaan to cleanse and occupy the land. Its inhabitants were utterly immersed in the most depraved practices imaginable, but it was to become the place of God's domain, where his people, city, and temple would eventually reside. We don't always know the wide-ranging nature of God's purposes when he appears to delay his judgments on nations that oppress his people, and that doesn't diminish the meaning of Psalm 2 in the least. Psalm 2 and the Parable of the Mustard Seed in Matthew 13:31-32 depict the true nature of Christ's reign in our time. It is depicted as his ancient suzerainty covenantal relationship with the nations of the earth, including its warnings, blessings, and sanctions.

There are particulars in this ancient treaty worth understanding that are beyond the scope of this book, but they will aid in a better comprehension of Jesus' rule in the world today. Hopefully, this will become clearer as we turn our attention to Revelation 20. There is no break in the narrative at the end of Revelation 19. The context continues through Revelation 20:1-3.

CHAPTER 22

THE BOOK OF REVELATION
THE MILLENNIUM: REVELATION 20–22

As Revelation 20 opens, another highly significant event is portrayed. This scene, as we have indicated, is a continuation of the events of Revelation 19. An angel comes down out of heaven, takes hold of the dragon, who is Satan, and binds him in chains (the nature of which we do not necessarily understand). The arch-enemy of God is thrown into an abyss that is sealed for a period called *the thousand years*, or *the millennium*.

The Millennium:
Satan is Bound for a Thousand Years

> . . . so that he would not deceive the nations any longer, until the thousand years were completed; after these things, he must be released for a short time (Rev. 20:3).

This thousand-year period is a figurative expression representing a *long time or a large number*. It is not to be understood as a precise number of years. There appears to be no biblical text that confirms the reign of Messiah as being limited to a thousand or any specific number of years. However, there is evidence that "a thousand" is used figuratively in Scripture to mean "a great many" or something similar:

> May the LORD, the God of your fathers, increase you a thousand-fold more than you are (Deu. 1:11).

> "One of your men puts to flight a thousand, for the LORD your God is He who fights for you, just as He promised you" (Josh. 23:10).

> "For every beast of the forest is Mine,
> The cattle on a thousand hills"
> (Psa. 50:10).

> For a day in Your courts is better than a thousand *outside*
> I would rather stand at the threshold of the house of my God
> Than dwell in the tents of wickedness
> (Psa. 84:10).

> He has remembered His covenant forever,
> The word which He commanded to a thousand generations
> The covenant which he made with Abraham
> (Psa. 105:8-9).

These texts are obviously not to be taken literally. They employ hyperbole, meant to convey a large quantity or an extensive length of time. Take special note of Psalm 105:8-9. If taken literally, the Abrahamic covenant that was fulfilled in Christ will last 1,000 generations, or approximately 40,000 years. This would suggest that, as of this writing, life on earth will go on for about 36,000 additional years, as there are no *generations* of people born in the afterlife. It would also indicate that popular warnings of the approaching end of the world are not very accurate.

Revisiting Revelation's Bookends

The thousand-year millennium is a long and prosperous church age. From the perspective of the New Testament, it is the promised age to come. This era commenced with the destruction of Jerusalem and the subjugation of the spiritual powers under the rule of Christ. It continues unabated for an unspecified period until *the thousand years are completed*. This, of course, projects Revelation beyond its stated bookends: that its contents, in their entirety, were about to come to pass *shortly* (Rev. 1:1-3; 22:6). However, I do not believe this view violates the *spirit* of the text or the urgency of its transmission to the churches. For example, as we previously saw in Revelation 10:

> When he [the seventh angel] is about to sound, then *the mystery of God is finished*, as He preached to His servants the prophets (from Rev. 10:1-7).

In Revelation 10, we observed that the mystery of God was accomplished within the time parameters of the book, as Jesus stood upon the land and the sea (the Jews and the Gentiles). Yet the uniting of Jew and Gentile into one body in Christ continues today, well past that initial accomplishment in the period of 30–70 AD. This precedent allows for a similar view of Revelation 20. The millennial reign of Christ broke into history in 70 AD. It is accomplished, yet that reign continues to increase through the church age. Also, the twenty-four elders in Revelation 11:17 fall on their faces before the throne of God, acknowledging the *commencement* of his reign:

We give You thanks, O Lord God, the Almighty, who are and who were, because *You have taken Your great power and have begun to reign* (Rev. 11:17).

Christ's having "begun to reign" was accomplished in the first century; however, we would hardly think that he is no longer reigning beyond that era.

Millennial Conditions

Jerusalem has been destroyed, and the marriage of the Lamb has occurred and possibly continues through this epoch based on the preceding perspectives. The powers and principalities that were commissioned to destroy Jerusalem have been judged and moved out of the way. The Roman Empire continued, but the demonic powers behind it were either destroyed or subjugated under Christ's kingship. However, we have also seen that:

Satan, as an entity, is bound and out of business until the end of the millennium. He no longer walks about like a roaring lion (1 Pet. 5:8). That time has passed.

At this present time, he is bound. However, we should qualify the binding and absence of Satan during the church age by re-examining an important distinction found in Revelation 12. There, John saw a war in heaven:

. . . and there was war in heaven, and Michael and his angels waging war with the dragon, the dragon and his angels waged war. And they were not strong enough, and there was no longer placed for them in Heaven, and the great dragon was thrown down, the serpent of old, who is called the devil, and *Satan who deceives the whole world was thrown down to Earth and his angels were thrown down with him.*

Both Satan and his hordes were thrown out of heaven in Revelation 12. However, *only Satan*, the devil, is bound for the period of the millennium. Note that the *binding of his angels along with him is conspicuously absent* from the description of the millennium in Revelation 20:

> Then I saw an angel coming down from heaven, holding the key of the abyss and a great chain in his hand. And he laid hold of the dragon, the serpent of old, who is the devil and Satan, *and bound him* [only] for a thousand years (Rev. 20:1-2).

There *is, therefore,* demonic activity in the world today. There are still rulers and authorities in the cosmos that are under the dominion of God and the dominion of the saints, as we saw in Daniel 7:27:

> Then the sovereignty, the dominion and the greatness of all the kingdoms under the whole heaven will be given to the people of the saints of the Highest One; His kingdom will be an everlasting kingdom, *and all the dominions will serve and obey Him.*

Revelation 20 includes details regarding the resurrection and judgment that remain open for discussion, but I will offer a few observations.

I am inclined to agree with the view in Russell's *The Parousia*[109], that the Old Testament and first-century martyrs constituted the *first resurrection* (20:4). However, I currently hold that the millennial reign continues, and they are now reigning with Christ. The rest of the dead (20:5) are those not in Christ who are raised for judgment at the end. Again, I remind the reader that there remain open questions and that these are loosely held perspectives, not hard-and-fast positions.

As the millennium draws to a close, the dragon is released and surrounds the camp of the saints. As of this writing, this appears to be an assault or threat upon the body of Christ before this time-space continuum is finally brought to its (assumed) conclusion. Fire comes down from heaven and destroys (devours) the adversary, however, I'm not convinced that this depicts a "return" of Jesus."

Then Satan is thrown into the lake of fire, where the beast and the false prophet are being tormented:

And the devil who deceived them was thrown into the lake of fire and brimstone, where the beast and the false prophet are also; and they will be tormented day and night forever and ever (Rev. 20:10).

The Lake of Fire

Notably, the three beings thrown into the lake of fire to be consciously and permanently tormented are all *spiritual entities*. They are not *consumed* like human beings because they are constituted differently. In Revelation 20:14, *death* and *hades* were also thrown into the lake of fire, but they are post-mortem, impersonal states that cannot be *tormented*. They are consumed and destroyed. There is an important distinction in John's description of these events:

In the description of the wicked "persons" being thrown into the lake of fire, perpetual torment is conspicuously absent from the text. They are not described as being tormented day and night "forever and ever." Only the demonic entities experience the state of perpetual torment.

We should not assume that all beings, whether spiritual or physical, are affected the same by this judgment. Branches and twigs (metaphors often used to describe the wicked in judgment) consume quickly in fire as compared to rocks, bricks, and other more durable, fire-resistant substances. Furthermore, we have already seen in Jude 1:7 and 2 Peter 2:6 that the wicked are quickly and entirely consumed by "eternal fire" in the same manner as Sodom and Gomorrah. That is the standard by which we define judgment of the ungodly. Since the Scriptures have already described the fate of lost humanity in that way, there is no need for John to elaborate further on their fate. Their extinction by fire has already been disclosed in the Scriptures.

For the lost, the lake of fire is the *second death* (Rev. 20:14; cf. 21:8). That is their fate. There is no process of *perpetual perishing, perpetual destroying, or perpetual ruin.* Just as the first death destroys the body, the second death destroys whatever consciously remains of the individual at the time of resurrection and judgment. The final result is the cessation of existence.

> *There is no permanent life of torture to which human beings are consigned. There is no inherent, immortal soul in man to live beyond this judgment. The fate described is consistent with both the Old and New Testament texts. The end of the lost is death.*

As a final consideration concerning the lake of fire, let us remind ourselves that in Part III of our study, we saw that the texts cited by those who support eternal conscious torment do not contextually support that interpretation. That leaves only the descriptions of the lake of fire as the main support for the doctrine. However, theological doctrine is not to be built upon texts selected from a highly symbolic prophecy such as the Book of Revelation. Our conclusions must be drawn from didactic texts, not from prophetic symbols that have a variety of possible meanings. I am convinced that the traditional doctrine of hell, despite its primacy in church history, does not meet the standards of good biblical exegesis due to its deficient use of narrative context and its dependence on often highly debatable symbolic images. We have also observed a frequent neglect of the use of historical context and the use of Scripture to interpret Scripture. Therefore, I believe the traditional view must be rejected.

> *As for the lake of fire, we again take note that after 4000 years of biblical revelation, here, in the final book of the Bible, the lake of fire is mentioned, and symbolically, for the first time!*

> *Uh . . . did I mention 4000 years?*

Moving on to Revelation 21, John sees the new heaven and the new earth. As we learned previously, this is not a new sky and a new planet.

Then I saw a new heaven and a new earth; for the first heaven and the first earth passed away, and there is no longer *any* sea (Rev. 21:1).

Revelation 21:5 *does not* say: "Behold, I make all new things."

Revelation 21:5 *does* say: "Behold, I make all things new."

I would point out once more that the new heavens and earth [land] describe a new covenantal relationship. The image portrays God with redeemed humanity in the new heaven, now open and no longer closed as it had been for all the centuries since Adam. It has been renewed and cleansed by the blood of Christ, and a place has been prepared for the saints, at our demise, to reside with God in the eternal realm. The old structure of the temple, its services, and its restricted access have passed away. The new *land*, which is the new covenantal domain, is now extended beyond the borders of Israel and encompasses the whole world.

In Romans 4:13, we are told that Abraham was made the *heir of the world*, not just the *land* of Israel:

For the promise to Abraham or to his descendants that he would be *heir of the world* [Greek: *kosmos*] was not through the Law, but through the righteousness of faith (Rom. 4:13).

Now, everywhere, the children of Abraham crop up through the evangelistic efforts of the church. New fires are lit in every country and every nation as the entire world becomes the covenant domain of God.

This New Covenant domain is where God's Spirit is present, renewing and empowering people in every nation. This is further conveyed to us in John's next remark: "there was no more sea."

No More Sea

We have seen how the sea represented the raging Gentile nations, the place from which the dragon and the beasts emerged. As the world now becomes (spiritually) a land mass, there are no more world-dominant Gentile empires to rise out of the *sea* like the four beasts seen by Daniel. God's dominion is global, eternal, and ever-expanding in the world. John sees this new creation in the spiritual realm, and the benefits are described for those who have conquered death and obtained immortality. I believe what John describes in Revelation 21 and 22 is a continuation or expansion of Revelation 20. It is the millennium in greater detail—a heavenly perspective of what we will see from our place in the heavenly Jerusalem. Its description begins in Revelation 21, as the new Jerusalem is coming down out of heaven from God. It is experienced yet unseen by those of us who yet remain in mortal flesh. We experience the heavenly realities as we pass from this life into the eternal realm.

No More Death, Sorrow, or Pain

"If this is the millennium, why is there still death, sorrow, and pain?" is a question I've heard more than once, and it's a reasonable inquiry. However, we must remember that John's visions include things he saw occurring in heaven as well as on the earth. Therefore, his vision of the millennium includes conditions in both realms. The millennium for departed saints is the experience of glorification—the redemption of their physical bodies.

Depending on one's view of the resurrection, these may be solely Old Testament saints. That being acknowledged, I think there is merit in the belief in the immediate passage from death to life and glorification for the New Testament saints. Death has been defeated for us, so there may not be a delay until some future resurrection to receive our full reward, as is possibly what is meant by Jesus words:

Truly, truly, I say to you, he who hears My word, and believes Him who sent Me, has eternal life, and does not come into judgment, but has passed out of death into life (John 5:24).

The diagram shows the change from the previous age to the current one The circle on the right illustrates the millennium in both the heavenly and the earthly reams.

The Ages and the Millennium

Heavens Closed:
(Heb. 9:1-15) Saints
awaiting redemption

OLD COVENANT AGE:
OLAM HAZEH

Saints on Earth: Under
death-awaiting the
promise:
(Heb. 11:13-16)

Rewarded-glorified
saints in Heaven
(No more death,
sorrow, pain: Rev 21:4)

NEW COVENANT - MILLENNIAL AGE:
OLAM HABA

Saints on Earth:
Awaiting glorification
yet experiencing the
Holy City and reigning in
life: (Rom. 5:15)

Transition Period:

The Millennium Commenced with the Destruction of Jerusalem and the Dissolution the Old Order in 70 AD

"The saints on earth experience heavenly realities but are still awaiting glorification. We still intermingle with the unredeemed–those who are "outside" the city. These are seen in John's final chapter:

"Blessed are those who wash their robes, so that they will have the right to the tree of life, and may enter the city by the gates. Outside are the dogs, the sorcerers, the sexually immoral persons, the murderers, the idolaters, and everyone who loves and practices lying. (Rev. 22:14-15).

Then, in Revelation 22, we see that the tree of life and the river of life are there. There is no more curse, meaning that the Adamic liabilities have been forever wiped away from God's people. This is especially true of the power of death:

> . . . *the river of the water of life,* clear as crystal, coming down from the throne of God and from the lamb. In the middle of the street and on either side of the river was the tree of life bearing 12 kinds of fruit, yielding its fruit every month; *and the leaves of the tree are for the healing of the nations* (Rev. 22:1-2).

Here, I will propose a question to the reader regarding the healing of the nations in Revelation 22:2. The devil's power has been broken. He has been thrown into the lake of fire along with the beast and the false prophet. All evil ones have been destroyed, and God's judgments have taken place.

If this is all future, as some claim, why will the nations still need healing?

What nations still need healing? If all of this pertains to an *end-of-the-world scenario,* as some teach, there should be no need for healing anything. However, if John's visions describe the historical events immediately preceding, and those launching, the church age, there is continuity in Revelation, and the 17th through 22nd chapters would follow the resulting sequence:

Revelation 17:

Harlot Babylon (Jerusalem) and the Roman beast that is carrying her are described. The powers at work in the invisible realm are exposed. A spirit of harlotry has taken over Jerusalem. Satan and his principalities have control over Rome and its emperors. They are seen doing the bidding of the harlot, who is using the beast to accomplish her purposes, especially persecution of the church.

Revelation 18:

Babylon is judged. The dirge for the fallen harlot Babylon is seen and heard (in 70 AD). These are the howling cries of her merchant lovers. They do not mourn for the demise of a *holy city* but for their own resultant economic losses. This is seen in contrast to God's view of her as a harlot who is no longer to be trusted with his divine treasures.

Revelation 19:

The marriage of the Lamb and his new bride occurs. The *parousia* of Christ and the seizure of the demonic powers controlling Rome ensue as Jerusalem is destroyed. As he had in the past, God judges the very enemies he allows to carry out judgment on his people. They do not escape. The returning king simply disposes of the enemies he had already defeated at the cross. There does not appear to be a "battle" of Armageddon. The location was merely the rendezvous point for Titus' troops en route to Jerusalem.

Revelation 20:

The reign of Christ in the church age begins in 70 AD, as Jerusalem (Babylon) and the powers fall. Satan alone is bound, but the other principalities and powers are not. They remain for an unspecified season, but under Christ's dominion. After having been previously enthroned, the Lamb now returns to bring his enemies under subjection to his rule.

Revelation 21-22:

The millennium vision is expanded to include the new Jerusalem, the new heavens and earth, the river of life, and the tree of life. The role of the church during the millennium is one of bringing healing to the nations. During this age, there is the concurrent presence of the lost, who are seen *outside the city.* It is a time when temporal cultures continue to exist as the church brings the offer of the gospel to the nations (Rev. 22:15-17).

Healing Leaves

The healing leaves of the tree offer a very interesting image that is being presented in John's vision:

> . . . and the leaves of the tree [of life] are for the healing of the nations (Rev. 22:2).

When a tree takes in all the moisture that it can absorb with its roots, a process called *transpiration* takes place. Its leaves emit any excess moisture that it has absorbed. Revelation's image is of the church as she fills herself with the Spirit of Life, taking in all she can of the fullness of God. When that happens, *spiritual* transpiration occurs in the form of the church's labors in the world, which bring life and healing wherever we (the leaves) go. That includes our own neighborhoods in whatever country we reside in. It's very much like the imagery that the prophet saw in Ezekiel 47:1-12.

The Lord asks the prophet (my slightly embellished version):

"Have you seen this, son of man? You're languishing about being in exile, missing out on your priestly duties in the temple, and brooding over the lost opportunity to enjoy your own little pastorate. The Babylonians have crushed your hopes of playing in the "puddle" of the temple, but here's a challenge."

Then, Ezekiel is told to:

Follow the river. Go out 1500 feet, then 1500 more, then 1500 more. Go to where you can't cross, where you can't touch the bottom, where they are gathering in the fish from the nations.

In Ezekiel 47:12, we read:

"By the river on its bank, on one side and on the other, will grow all kinds of trees for food. Their leaves will not wither and their fruit will not fail. They will bear every month because *their water flows from the sanctuary, and their fruit will be for food and their leaves for healing*" (Eze. 47:12).

This is the reign of Christ. This is the church, whose leaves are the leaves of the tree of life, bringing life to our neighborhoods and to the nations. They are its pastors, teachers, missionaries, cargo ships, trucks, and at-risk community developers. They are healing resources going everywhere in the world, bringing God's loving care and the offer of new life through the gospel. As it goes forth to all nations, they become habitations for the Spirit of God, who is the *Spirit of Life*.

In his final vision, John sees that there are still people outside the city. They are not burning in hell. They are living in the world around us. Although we experience the new Jerusalem in our earthly journey, we cannot yet see it from this side of eternity, but it is here among us. One day, we will be manifestly living in the city (Rev. 3:12). But today, there's still a world going on filled with those who desperately need the hope of the gospel. There is a simultaneous, ongoing existence between the godly and the ungodly that I believe is reflective of the millennium in John's vision. How, if, and when it will end, I'm not sure. Like you, there's so much I still don't understand. However, in this age, I am certain that the church exists among fallen humanity and their fallen societies, for whom we offer the world's only hope–the risen Savior and King, Jesus Christ.

THE THRESHOLD OF EXILE

FINAL THOUGHTS

Upon completion of this book, the reader has undoubtedly amassed a volume of questions regarding the return of Jesus, humanity's alleged immortality, and the fate of the lost. Be encouraged. We should never fear, but rather take full advantage of such occasions to enlarge our understanding. Therefore, I challenge you, the reader, to make the most of this opportunity and to open your heart to the new possibilities that have been presented.

Our Core Premise

There is so much more that could have been written. However, I have endeavored to stay true to a critical premise. Our interpretation of last things must consider how Jesus and his apostles reconnected their audiences to Israel's history, especially the threat of exile and the eventual tragedy that occurred in 586 BC. The way the authors of the New Testament brought this tragedy to bear upon their own generation has enormous implications for our interpretation of New Testament eschatology. Hopefully, your introduction to this proposition has helped you become more acquainted with reading God's Word in context, allowing Scripture to interpret Scripture, and respecting audience relevance. Israel's historical location as once again having been on the threshold of exile in the first century is vital to an accurate understanding of the New Testament's prophetic outlook. When properly understood and integrated into our interpretation of the texts, radical changes can take place in our view of the return (*parousia*) of Jesus, eternal destiny, and the conditions under which immortality is attained.

I am convinced that the perspectives that have been presented here are not peripheral but central to our understanding of God, his character, and his eternal purpose in Christ. They also have a uniquely powerful impact on our presentation of the gospel of Christ to the world. We need to wrench ourselves, our children, and the gospel itself from the popular notions of a coming *superhuman, world-ruling monster* taking up residence in a temple in Jerusalem and a *global tribulation* culminating in a third of the Jewish population being eliminated while all Christians suddenly fly away to heaven. In contrast, John's great visions teach us that we are the leaves of the tree of life, set free from the power of sin and death through the cross of Christ, to bring the healing love of God not only to the farthest reaches of the globe but also to our neighbor next door.

Finally, we must distance ourselves from the theological notion that God loves us and wants to save us, but if we don't accept his offer, he will send us into a blazing inferno to be tortured and in agony forever. This, it is proposed, is the fate of the lost, rather than mercifully allowing them to ultimately succumb to the power of death, the power under which, apart from Christ, they live and die. The gospel found in the Word of God is an offer of the Spirit's permanent, indestructible life, attainable only through faith in God's indescribable Son, the Lord Jesus Christ.

In Christ's Unfailing Love,
Soli Deo Gloria.

BIBLIOGRAPHY

1. John Gill, *John Gill's Exposition of the Bible* (1816), Public Domain, e-sword Version 13.0.0., Copyright © 2000-2021, Rick Meyers, All Rights Reserved Worldwide.

2. Marvin R. Vincent, *Word Studies in the New Testament* (1887), Public Domain, e-sword Version 13.0.0., Copyright © 2000-2021, Rick Meyers, All Rights Reserved Worldwide.

3. Kenneth Gentry, Jr., *Before Jerusalem Fell: Dating the Book of Revelation* (Tyler: Institute for Christian Economics, 2016).

4. James J. O'Donnell, "Pliny, Letters 10.96-97," Accessed October 17, 2022, https://faculty.georgetown.edu/jod/texts/pliny.html.

5. Brian Jones, *The Emperor Domitian* (London/New York: Routledge, 1992), 117.

6. James Stuart Russell, T*he Parousia: A Critical Inquiry Into the New Testament Doctrine of Our Lord's Second Coming* (United Kingdom: Daldy Isbister & Company, 1878), 322-323.

7. Henry Cowles, *The Revelation of John; with notes, critical, explanatory, and practical* (New York: Appleton, 1871), 14, Google Digitized, Accessed July 13, 2019, https://babel.hathitrust.org/cgi/pt?id=hvd.ah3x79&view=1up&seq=1.

8. Philip Mauro, *The Seventy Weeks and the Great Tribulation*, Chapter 12: "The Importance of the Destruction of Jerusalem," 1922, Accessed June 29, 2018, http://www.life.org/Tribulation.html.

9. Robert Eisenberg, *Divided We Fall: The Roots of the Great Jewish Revolt Against Rome*, 2006, Accessed August 12, 2022, https://www.mcgill.ca/classics/files/classics/2006-7-09.pdf, 148-149.

10. Publius Cornelius Tacitus, *The Annals of Tacitus*, c.109, XV, 44, 2-5, Accessed April 15, 2020, http://penelope.uchicago.edu/Thayer/E/Roman/Texts/Tacitus/home.html.

11. Edward Fudge, *The Fire That Consumes: A Biblical and Historical Study of the Doctrine of Final Punishment* (Lincoln: iUniverse.com, Inc., 2001).

12. James Orr, *The International Standard Bible Encyclopedia*, "Death" (Gen. Ed. 1939), e-sword Version 13.0.0., Copyright © 2000-2021, Rick Meyers, All Rights Reserved Worldwide.

13. Kaufmann Kohler, "Immortality of the Soul" (1901-1906), JewishEncyclopedia.com, Accessed March 24, 2019, http://jewishencyclopedia.com /articles/8092-immortality-of-the-soul.

14. George Wisbrock, *Death and the Soul After Life* (Oakbrook: ZOE-Life Books, 1990), Foreword: F. F. Bruce, p. i, Permission granted by F.F. Bruce Copyright International, Bath, England, and Nashville, Tennessee.

15. Louis Berkhof, "Immortality of the Soul," (Excerpted from *Berkhof's Systematic Theology*, 1938, eBook), Monergism by CPR Foundation, Accessed October 15, 2022, https://www.monergism.com/immortality-soul.

16. Richard B. Hays, *Echoes of Scripture in the Letters of Paul* (New Haven/London: Yale University Press, 1993), 14-24.

17. Flavius Josephus, *Wars of the Jews,* e-sword Version 13.0.0., Copyright © 2000-2021, Rick Meyers, All Rights Reserved Worldwide, 7.1.1.

18. Kenneth Gentry, Jr., *Navigating the Book of Revelation* (Kindle Edition) (Chesnee: GoodBirth Ministries, 2016), Loc 328.

19. Philip Schaff, *History of the Christian Church, Vol. I* (Grand Rapids: Eerdmans, 1978), 336-337.

20. Michael Vlach, "Israel and the 'Trans-generational You' with Implications for Matthew 24." Posted 2017, Accessed February 20, 2020, blogspot.com/2017/02/israel-and-trans-generational-you-with.html.

21. Robert Jamieson, Andrew R. Fausset, and David Brown, *A Commentary, Critical and Explanatory, on the Old and New Testaments* (1871), e-sword Version 13.0.0., Copyright © 2000-2021, Rick Meyers, All Rights Reserved Worldwide.

22. Klaus Berger, "Parousia - Exegetical Findings," Sacramentum Mundi Online, General Editor Karl Rahner, SJ., Accessed August 1, 2021, http://dx.doi.org/10.1163/2468-483X_smuo_COM_003081.

23. Dennis Bratcher, "The Gospels and The Synoptic Problem: The Literary Relationship of Matthew, Mark, and Luke," CRI/Voice, Accessed January 19, 2020, http://www.crivoice.org/synoptic.html.

24. Robert H. Charles, *Book of Enoch* (Gresham: Postomorrow Books, Translated 2013), Accessed November 22, 2019, http://www.pseudepigrapha.com/pseudepigrapha/1enoch_all.html. ; (1 Enoch 71:15).

25. Nicholas Thomas Wright, *The New Testament and the People of God* (Minneapolis: Fortress Press, 1992), 333.

26. Nicholas Thomas Wright, *Jesus and the Victory of God* (Minneapolis: Fortress Press, 1996), 345.

27. Alfred Edersheim, *The Life and Times of Jesus the Messiah* (Peabody: Hendrickson, 2000), 775.

28. Kaufmann Kohler, "Eschatology," *Jewish Encyclopedia, Volume 5* (pg. 214, Pesiḥ. R. 15; Pesiḥ. v. 49b, after Hosea v. 15, under "Renewal of The Time of Moses," Published 1901-1906, Accessed January 5, 2021, http://www.jewishencyclopedia.com/ articles/5849-eschatology.

29. Josephus, Wars of the Jews, 20.8.6.

30. Thomas Newton, *Dissertations on the Prophecies* (1825), 2015 Digitized Edition, pg. 333, Accessed October 30, 2021, https://archive.org/details/ThomasNewtonDissertationsOnThePropheciesWhichHaveRemarkablyBeen/page/n191.

31. Tacitus, *The Annals of Tacitus*, (various). See:
    https://penelope.uchicago.edu/Thayer/E/Roman/Texts/Tacitus/home.html

32. "List of Roman civil wars and revolts," Wikipedia, Last edited on May 25, 2022 (Edited to
    include data from 36-70 AD only),
    https://en.wikipedia.org/wiki/List_of_Roman_civil_wars_and_revolts#1st_century.

33. Eusebius of Caesarea, *Eusebius' Ecclesiastical History* (Peabody: Hendrickson Publishers,
    1998), 2.8.1.

34. George P. Holford, *The Destruction of Jerusalem* (Nacogdoches: Covenant Media Press,
    2001), 20-21.

35. Tacitus, *The Annals of Tacitus*, XII:43.

36. Ibid, XV:44.

37. Archibald T. Robertson, *A Harmony of the Gospels for Students of the Life of Christ* (New
    York: George H. Doran Company, 1922).

38. Gill, *John Gill's Exposition of the Bible*, Isaiah 8:8.

39. Josephus, *Wars of the Jews*, 4.3.12-4.4.3.

40. James Jordan, "The Abomination of Desolation, Part 1," Posted May 22, 1991,
    Accessed February 20, 2022, https://theopolisinstitute.com/the-abomination-of- desolation-
    part-1/.

41. Josephus, *Wars of the Jews*, 2.19.6-7.

42. Eusebius of Caesarea, *Eusebius' Ecclesiastical History* (Peabody: Hendrickson
    Publishers,1998), 3.5.3.

43. Josephus, *Wars of the Jews*, 6.9.3.

44. Ibid, 6.9.2.

45. Rodney L. Thomas, *Magical Motifs in the Book of Revelation* (London/New York: T&T
    Clark/Bloomsbury Academic, 2019), 77-78.

46. Josephus, *Wars of the Jews*, 6.5.2-3.

47. George P. Holford, *The Destruction of Jerusalem* (Nacogdoches: Covenant Media Press,
    2001), 18-19.

48. Josephus, *Wars of the Jews*, 4.9.2.

49. Rabbi Jack Abramowitz, "13. Did the Prophets Foretell the End of the World?", Orthodox
    Union, Accessed May 15, 2022, https://outorah.org/p/20785.

50. Carl F. Keil and Franz Delitzsch, *Commentary on the Old Testament* (1866-1891), e- sword
    Version 13.0.0., Copyright © 2000-2021, Rick Meyers, All Rights Reserved Worldwide.

51. Andrew Perriman, Andrew "Did Jesus promise to return within the lifetime of his disciples?", Posted March 20, 2018, Accessed September 12, 2019, http://www.postost.net/2018/03/did-jesus-promise-return-within-lifetime-his-disciples.

52. Bernard Ramm, *Protestant Biblical Interpretation: A Textbook of Hermeneutics, 3rd revised edition* (Grand Rapids: Baker, 1970), 223.

53. John Edwards, "A Question About the 'Double Fulfillment' Hermeneutic," Posted 2008, Accessed July 13, 2018, https://www.christian-faith.com/a-question-about-the- double-fulfillment-hermeneutic.

54. Paul Penley, "When Heaven and Earth Passed Away: Everything Changed." Posted 2015, Accessed July 30, 2018, http://www.reenactingtheway.com/blog/when-heaven-and-earth-passed-away- everything-changed 879420187179853150181.

55. Brooke F. Wescott and Fenton J.A. Hort, *The New Testament in Original Greek.* (New York: Harper and Brothers, 1881), Accessed October 24, 2021, https://biblehub.com/texts/matthew/24-37.htm.

56. Josephus, *Wars of the Jews*, 6.9.3.

57. Philip Schaff and Johann J. Herzog, *The Schaff-Herzog Encyclopaedia of Religious Knowledge* (Grand Rapids: Baker Samuel M. Jackson Ed., 1951), Online Edition, pg. 96, Accessed February 2, 2017, CCEL.org. http://onlinebooks.library.upenn.edu/webbin/book/lookupid?key=olbp27827.

58. *The Belgic Confession,* Article 37, Translation © 2011, Faith Alive Christian Resources/CRCNA, used with permission, Accessed August 28, 2022, https://www.crcna.org/welcome/beliefs/confessions/belgic-confession#toc-article- 37-the-last-judgement.

59. Tim Challies, "Would He Condemn People to Eternal Torment?", Posted June 24, 2012, Accessed on September 15, 2020, https://answersingenesis.org/eternal- torment/.

60. Adam Clarke, *Adam Clarke's Commentary on the Bible* (1810-1826), Public Domain, e-sword Version 13.0.0., Copyright © 2000-2021, Rick Meyers, All Rights Reserved Worldwide.

61. Josephus, *Wars of the Jews*, 5.12.3-4.

62. Ibid, 6.5.1.

63. William Davidson, *The Babylonian Talmud, William Davidson Edition* (Electronic Edition), Accessed June 20, 2020, https://www.sefaria.org/Rosh_Hashanah.17a.4?lang=bi [Talmud translation] from The William Davidson digital edition of the Koren Noé Talmud, with commentary by Rabbi Adin Even-Israel Steinsaltz.

64. James I. Packer, "The Chicago Statement on Biblical Hermeneutics" (Chicago: November 10-13, 1982 - The original 1978 document is located in the Dallas Theological Seminary Archives), Accessed November 22, 2021, www.alliancenet.org/the-chicago-statement-on-biblical-hermeneutics.

65. Wojciech Szczerba, "THE LANGUAGE OF THE SEPTUAGINT AS A WINDOW ON THE PHILOSOPHY OF THE HEBREW BIBLE," Lingua Ac Communitas, Warszawa - Poznan, 1999, Accessed October 9, 2022, https://www.academia.edu/45405036/THE_LANGUAGE_OF_THE_SEPTUAGIN T_AS_A_WINDOW_ON_THE_PHILOSOPHY_OF_THE_HEBREW_BIBLE.

66. Merrill Tenney (ed.), *The Zondervan Pictorial Encyclopedia of the Bible, Vol. 3* (Grand Rapids: Zondervan Publishing House, 1975), 7.

67. Francis Brown, Samuel Driver, and Charles Briggs, *Brown-Driver-Briggs' Hebrew Definitions* (Originally published Boston: Houghton, Mifflin and Company, 1906), Public Domain, e-sword Version 13.0.0., Copyright © 2000-2021, Rick Meyers, All Rights Reserved Worldwide.

68. R. Larid Harris, Gleason Archer, Jr., and Bruce K. Waltke, *Theological Wordbook of the Old Testament 1980* (Chicago: The Moody Bible Institute, 1980).

69. James Strong, S.T.D., LL.D., *Strong's Exhaustive Concordance* (1890), Public Domain. e-sword Version 13.0.0., Copyright © 2000-2021, Rick Meyers, All Rights Reserved Worldwide.

70. Gill, *John Gill's Exposition of the Bible.*

71. Ben Witherington, "Hell? No??", Posted March 16, 2011, Accessed January 17, 2021, https://www.patheos.com/search?q=Hell+No#gsc.tab=0&gsc.q=Hell%20No&gsc. page=1 (Filed under "Hell? No?? | Guest Contributor).

72. Christopher Morgan and Robert A. Peterson (Gen. eds.), *Hell Under Fire* (Grand Rapids: Zondervan, 2004). Contributions Cited: Charles Morgan, Robert Peterson: p12 "Introduction;" Douglas Moo: p103. "Paul on Hell;" Gregory Beale: p114 "The Revelation on Hell.

73. John Piper, "The Presence of the Lamb and the Sufferings of Hell," Posted July 5, 2012, Accessed January 12, 2021, https://www.desiringgod.org/articles/the- presence-of-the-lamb-and-the-sufferings-of-hell.

74. Keil, et al, *Commentary on the Old Testament.*

75. Jamieson, et al, *A Commentary, Critical and Explanatory, on the Old and New Testaments.*

76. *Expositor's Bible Commentary*, Accessed September 2, 2021, https://biblehub.com/commentaries/expositors/lamentations/4.htm (Version Not available).

77. Gill, *John Gill's Exposition of the Bible.*

78. David Chilton, *Days of Vengeance* (Tyler: Dominion Press, 1990), 186-187.

79. Ibid, 220.

80. Josephus, *Wars of the Jews*, 6.5.2.

81. Thomas Ice and Kenneth Gentry, *The Great Tribulation--Past or Future? Two Evangelicals Debate the Question* (Grand Rapids: Kregel, 1999).

82. Paul R. McReynolds, *Word Study Greek – English New Testament.* 3rd Corrected ed. with New Revised Standard Version, New Testament and Word Study Concordance (Wheaton: Tyndale House, 1998).

83. Lionel Corbett, *The God-Image: From Antiquity to Jung* (Asheville: Chiron Publications, 2021), pg. 141, Accessed March 16, 2022, https://play.google.com/books/reader?id=ve5MEAAAQBAJ&pg=GBS.PT144.w.0.1.61_127.

84. J. Nelson Kraybill, *Apocalypse and Allegiance* (Grand Rapids: Baker Publishing Group/Brazos Press, 2010), 15.

85. Lloyd Dale, *Studies in Revelation*, Chapter 2: "The Beasts of Revelation," Accessed August 12, 2022, http://www.lloyddale.com/books.html.

86. Hersch Goldwurm, *History of the Jewish People: The Second Temple Era. The Art Scroll History Series*, ed. Nosson Scherman and Meir Zlotowtz (Brooklyn: Mesorah Publications, 1982), 149, Cited in: Duncan W. McKenzie, *The Antichrist and the Second Coming: A Preterist Examination; Vol. II: The Book of Revelation.* (Maitland: Xulon Press, 2012), 220-221.

87. Richard A. Horsley, "High Priests and the Politics of Roman Palestine: A Contextual Analysis of the Evidence in Josephus." *Journal for the Study of Judaism in the Persian, Hellenistic, and Roman Period*, 17(1), 23–55, Accessed July 5, 2022, http://www.jstor.org/stable/24657973. doi: https://doi.org/10.1163/157006386X00040, (https://brill.com/view/journals/jsj/17/1/article-p23_4.xml?language=en).

88. Phillip Kayser, "The Mark of the Beast," Posted October 1, 2017, Accessed June 5, 2022, https://kaysercommentary.com/Sermons/New%20Testament/Revelation/Revelati on %2013/Revelation%2013-16-18.md.

89. Duncan W. McKenzie, *The Antichrist and the Second Coming: A Preterist Examination; Vol. II: The Book of Revelation* (Maitland: Xulon Press, 2012), 187-194.

90. Archibald T. Robertson, *Word Pictures in the New Testament* (1930-1933), e-sword Version 13.0.0., Copyright © 2000-2021, Rick Meyers, All Rights Reserved Worldwide.

91. Josephus, *Wars of the Jews*, 6.9.3.

92. Kate Lohnes, "Siege of Jerusalem," *Encyclopedia Britannica*, Posted 2018, Accessed April 5, 2022, https://www.britannica.com/event/Siege-of-Jerusalem-70.

93. Chilton, *Days of Vengeance,* 388-389.

94. Josephus, *Wars of the Jews*, 3.10.9.

95. Ibid, 4.7.6.

96. Ibid, 5.1.6.

97. Ibid, 5.1.1.

98. Ibid, 5.6.3.

99. David Keppel, *The Book of Revelation Not a Mystery* (Digital Version), 1918, pg. 47, Accessed August 13, 2018, https://play.google.com/books/reader?id=rp9AAAAAYAAJ&pg=GBS.PA20.

100. Chilton, *Days of Vengeance*, 424 footnote 2.

101. NASEC 1998, *New American Standard Exhaustive Concordance*, Updated Edition, The Lockman Foundation (Chart from NASB 95 search: "great city"), e-sword Version 13.0.0., Copyright © 2000-2021, Rick Meyers, All Rights Reserved Worldwide.

102. Rabbi Berel Wein, "Babylon and Beyond," Jewish History.org, website produced by the Destiny Foundation, Accessed March 3, 2022, https://www.jewishhistory.org/babylon-and-beyond/.

103. McKenzie, *The Antichrist and the Second Coming: Vol. II*, 232-233

104. Sulpitius Severus, Chronica. From: Philip Schaff (Editor), "The Sacred History of Sulpitius Severus," NPNF-211. Sulpitius Severus, Vincent of Lerins, John Cassian by Philip Schaff (Grand Rapids: Christian Classics Ethereal library), 402- 404, Downloaded from http://www.ccel.org/ccel/schaff/npnf211.html, Accessed November 4, 2022; Also cited in Duncan W. McKenzie, The Antichrist and the Second Coming: A Preterist Examination: Vol. I Daniel and 2 Thessalonians (Maitland: Xulon Press, 2009), 120.

105. Brian W. Jones, The Emperor Titus (New York: St. Martin's Press, 1984), 44-45, Cited in Ducan W. McKenzie, The Antichrist and the Second Coming: A Preterist Examination: Vol. I Daniel and 2 Thessalonians (Maitland: Xulon Press, 2009), 115.

106. G. William Poole, "Flavius Josephus: Jewish priest, scholar, and historian," Encyclopedia Britannica, Accessed August 12, 2022, https://www.britannica.com/biography/ Flavius-Josephus.

107. McKenzie, The Antichrist and the Second Coming: Vol. II, 288-289.

108. Keil, et al, Commentary on the Old Testament.

109. James Stuart Russell, The Parousia: A Critical Inquiry Into the New Testament Doctrine of Our Lord's Second Coming (United Kingdom: Daldy Isbister & Company, 1878), 519-522.

www.ingramcontent.com/pod-product-compliance
Lightning Source LLC
Chambersburg PA
CBHW061548120626
46550CB00004B/1409